T0122755

Police Department, 1904– Seated (L-R): Police Chief Ryan, Sergeant Ramsey, Corporal Hastening. Standing (L-R): Lee Monham, Thomas Flippo, Louis Atkins, Johnny Robinson, Bill Spencer, Willie Done, Archie Relford, Willie Paine, Doct Wadley, Henry Gilmore, Roland Haley, Dolly Brunsfield, Archie Jestere, Fred Dish, John Steve.

St. Joseph Drum Corp, ca. 1940 (L-R):Sallie Junkan Ballard, Mary Sanguinetti Whitam, Helen Korndoffer Howe, Mary Magdeline Middleton, Gloria Simmons Vasser, Sister Mary Junkin, Sara Blewett McGehee, Ann Burns Garrity.

1938–St. Joseph Catholic High School Pep Squad in front of the school, corner of Commerce and State Sts.

Unidentified policeman and H. P. Darsey

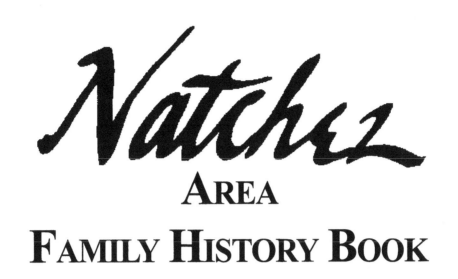

Natchez AREA FAMILY HISTORY BOOK

TURNER PUBLISHING COMPANY

Turner
PUBLISHING COMPANY

TURNER PUBLISHING COMPANY
Publishers of America's History

Book Commitee Chairman: Rosey Dow
Publishing Consultant: Keith Steele
Book Designer: Elizabeth Sikes

Copyright © MMIV Natchez Historical Society
All rights reserved.
Publishing Rights: Turner Publishing Company

Library of Congress Catalog No.: 2004101996

ISBN: 978-1-68162-525-6

Limited Edition, First Printing 2004 A.D.
Additional copies may be purchased from the Natchez Historical
Society.

Contents

Parade the day the bridge opened, 1940

The Mississippi at Natchez

This River is in us–
its gravid emptiness, its motion–,
and we dream ourselves in it–
drop of spring rain catching light's array...

Close beside it,
we are stirred, we are calmed,
in its moving eternity, in its silent answer
to nature's convulsions...

Peter Buttross, Jr.
Natchez Poet

Acknowledgements

Special thanks to Joseph V. Frank, Mimi Miller, Walter Tipton, and the office of Mayor Hank Smith for their cooperation and support during this project. Many thanks also to the various businesses, churches, schools and organizations in Natchez for their hard work in putting together their histories to make this volume more complete. And very much special thanks to the hundreds of family members who dug through old photos, chased down forgotten facts and put together these fascinating family histories for future generations. Without community effort this work would never have happened.

FAMILY HISTORY BOOK COMMITTEE

Beverly Aldridge
Shirley Booth
Candace Bundgard
Carolyn Cole
Rosey Dow, chairman
Betty McGehee
Barbara Haigh
Joan McLemore
Helen Rayne
Polly Scott
Ella Young

City of Natchez Flag

The City of Natchez flag was adopted in 1994. It has a length that is one-half times its width. The field is divided diagonally, red over blue, and is separated by a white convex wave. It is surrounded by a yellow border. In the canton of the red field, a yellow sun-disc proudly displays "Natchez" in stylistic cursive script.

The colors of the flag recall the French, Spanish, English, United States of America and Confederate States of occupation. The convex wave represents the river that has played such a major part in Natchez history and prosperity. The sun-disc symbolizes the Native Americans that inhabited the area and gave their name to the city. The colors are representative of the golden wealth of the city, the red blood of her people who make Natchez such a vibrant place, and the blue representing the spirit of unity in her people, making a brighter future through civic pride.

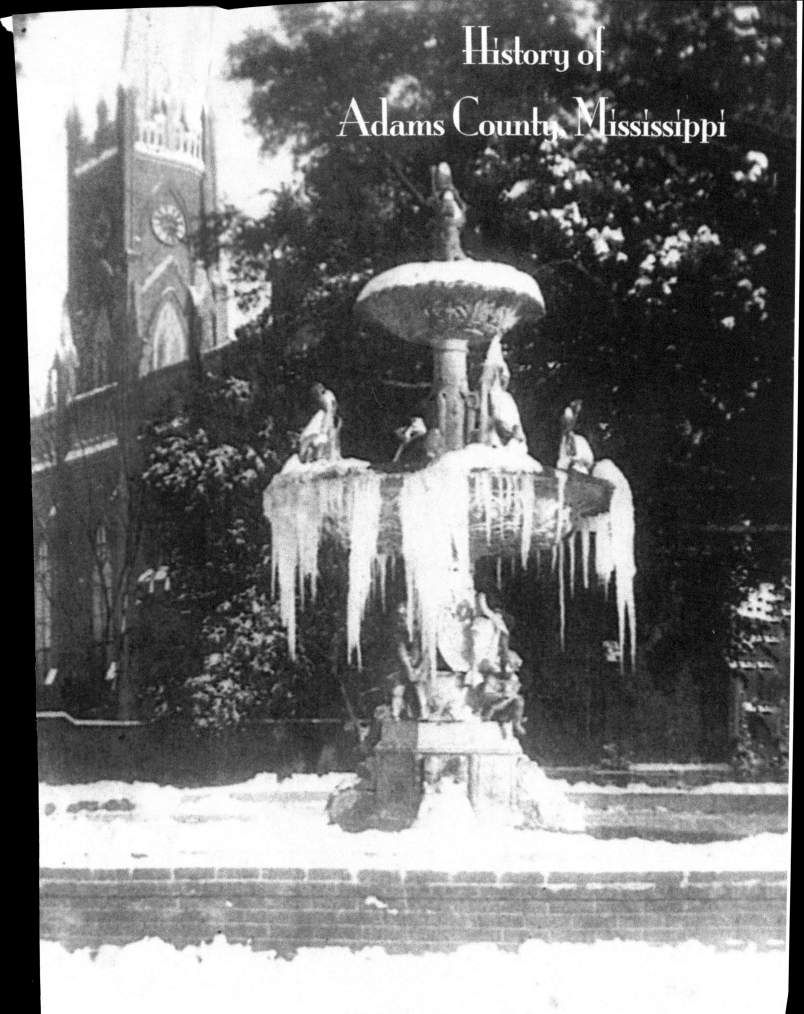

History of
Adams County, Mississippi

Overview of Natchez History

Native Americans

The city of Natchez was named for the Natchez Indians who were living in scattered villages when Europeans first explored the area. Many scholars believe the Natchez Indians to have been the last surviving vestige of an earlier and more advanced group called the Mississippian Culture that began about A.D. 1000 and reached its zenith not long before the onset of European exploration in North America. The Mississippian Culture flourished along the banks of the Mississippi River, and contact with the Indian cultures of Mexico may have sparked their cultural achievements. The people worshipped the sun and built large ceremonial mounds. The two largest surviving mounds of the Mississippian Culture are Monk's Mound in Cahokia, Illinois, and Emerald Mound near Natchez.

Hernando de Soto probably met the Natchez Indians when he explored the Mississippi River in the early 1540s. The Natchez Indians were a matrilineal society with distinct social classes. The monarch was the "Great Sun" and a member of the Sun class, or royal family. The sister of the Great Sun was more important than his wife, and the first nephew born to a sister of the Great Sun was heir to the throne. The classes beneath the Sun class were the "Nobles" and the "Honored People." Commoners were called "Stinkards." Each class married the class below, with the Stinkards marrying into the Sun class. Only sons of women born into the Sun class, however, could become the Great Sun. Although peaceful people, the Natchez practiced ritualistic human sacrifice.

The Natchez depended on agriculture. During the prehistoric period, their territory extended from the vicinity of Vicksburg, Mississippi to the Homochitto River south of Natchez. By the time of European exploration the majority of the Natchez Indians lived in and around the present city of Natchez. Population decline due to European diseases was probably the reason for the shrinking of their territory. Historical documents reveal that the Natchez Indians were living in nine village areas near the present town of Natchez, but archeologists have identified and studied only seven of these. The main village at this time was the Grand Village, located within the city limits of Natchez. National Historic Landmark sites in the Natchez area associated with the Natchez Indians and their ancestors include the Grand Village, Emerald Mound, and the Anna Site.

Three Indian cultures, the Natchez, Chickasaw, and Choctaw, were dominant at the time of European settlement in what is today the state of Mississippi. Linking these Indian nations was a footpath that extended through Chickasaw and Choctaw territory to the territory of the Natchez. This footpath became known as the Natchez Trace.

European Exploration

European exploration of Mississippi began with Hernando de Soto who entered northeast Mississippi in late 1540, crossed the Mississippi River in 1541, and returned to the Mississippi River somewhere north of Natchez where he died in 1542. In 1682 Rene Robert Cavalier, Sieur de la Salle, conducted an expedition that brought the French to the Lower Mississippi Valley where they encountered the Natchez Indians.

In 1700, Pierre Le Moyne, Sieur d'Iberville, visited the Natchez Indians. About the same time, Jesuit priests established a mission in the country of the Natchez. In 1714, Antoine de la Mothe, Sieur de Cadillac, governor of Louisiana, established a trading post on the Mississippi River not far from the villages of the Natchez.

French Colonial Period

The opening of a trading post at Natchez probably spurred the construction of a fort in 1716. Jean Baptiste Le Moyne, Sieur d'Bienville, brother of Iberville, built Fort Rosalie and named it in honor of the wife of the Minister of Marine, le Comte de Pontchartrain. The establishment of the fort in 1716 marked the beginning of permanent European settlement in Natchez and the town's official birth. The fort stood just south of the future site of historic home Rosalie. For defense, the French located the fort on top of a hill near the edge of a high bluff overlooking the Mississippi River. For farming, it was on the edge of an elevated strip of extremely rich soil, well watered, and blessed with a mild climate. The Natchez tribes had already cleared much of the land, and they taught the French their farming techniques.

Fort Rosalie stood on a high bluff, but the support structures, which included a church and rectory, houses and warehouses, were on a terrace between the bluff and the Mississippi River which is now known as Natchez-under-the Hill. As the population grew, the French divided the province into nine districts. One of these was the Natchez District with Fort Rosalie as its center of government. During the early French period, settlers produced tobacco and wheat, and small quantities of indigo, silk, rice, cotton, pitch, tar, and dressed timber. Fur trading was also an important part of the Natchez District economy.

As the population of the Natchez region grew, so did the hostility between the French and the Natchez Indians. In 1729, the Natchez Indians revolted. In 1731, the French destroyed the Natchez Indians as a nation. The French sold the conquered Natchez Indians as slaves, but some Natchez escaped and found refuge among other Indian nations, including the Chickasaw

and the Cherokee. Natchez Indians were among the Cherokees who marched on the "Trail of Tears" in the 1830s. The Natchez still maintain their identity in parts of Oklahoma and the Carolinas.

After the massacre at Fort Rosalie the economy became depressed, and the French soon lost interest in the Natchez settlement. Nonetheless, they established a provisional fort southwest of the original Fort Rosalie and built a new fort on the site of the original one. For 30 years a garrison of approximately 50 men at the fort made up the French occupation.

English Colonial Period

In 1763, England defeated France in the French and Indian War. The Treaty of Paris ceded to Great Britain all French territory east of the Mississippi except New Orleans, so the Natchez District joined the British Empire as part of British West Florida. Fort Rosalie became Fort Panmure and remained the English government headquarters. The population expanded under British rule, with large land grants given to British military officers to reward them for their service in the war. When the American Revolution broke out in April 1775, many American loyalists and neutralists sought refuge in the area. Ten log houses and two frame houses located under the bluff made up the first town settlement at Natchez.

In February 1778, James Willing brought the Revolutionary War to Natchez when he arrived with a party of raiders and hoisted the American flag over Fort Panmure. By exaggerating the size of his force, Willing persuaded the citizens of Natchez to sign a pledge of neutrality. In 1779, Spain seized control of the Natchez District shortly after declaring war against England.

Although the English were in control of the Natchez District for less than 20 years, the large numbers of Anglo-Americans living there became the dominant influence on the culture of Natchez. The English also established the first real semblance of a town along the waterfront that was later known as Natchez Under-the-Hill.

Spanish Colonial Period

Natchez prospered under the Spanish government. The Spaniards confirmed the standing English land grants and offered liberal land grants to new settlers. Unlike the French, the Spanish had no restrictions against Jewish immigration, and the first Jewish settlers arrived during this period. Almost 40 years after the departure of the Spanish, the older residents still spoke of the Spanish time as the golden age. As late as 1797, at the close of the Spanish period, the citizens were mostly English and Americans. Few Spanish inhabitants actually settled there. For most of the 18th century, Natchez was a colonial outpost and frontier settlement, yet its people had developed a reputation for sophistication.

The agricultural economy of Natchez underwent rapid change during the Spanish period. When tobacco, the money crop under both the french and English, collapsed about 1790 indigo took first place until about 1795 when insects destroyed the crop. In 1796, David Greenleaf built the first public cotton gin at Selsertown, a nonextant settlement located between Adams and Jefferson counties. By the end of the Spanish era, cotton was firmly established as the money crop of the Natchez region. Cotton did not rot or spoil after being picked. It could easily be stored until enough was gathered to justify a trip to a gin; after ginning and pressing into a bale, its value per volume was high; and its imperishability made transportation easy. Cotton could be grown profitably on any scale, from the subsistence farm to the largest plantation. With the growth of the cotton economy during the later years of the Spanish period came greater dependence upon slave labor.

From 1779 until 1789, the commandant of Fort Panmure was the governing authority of the territory. In 1789, Manuel Gayoso de Lemos became the first civilian governor. The town on top of the Natchez bluff came into being because of civilian rule. In 1791, Gayoso engaged John Girault to survey the city. Girault submitted a town plan to Gayoso, who, in June 1791, commissioned Girault to lay out the city, leaving the area between what is now Canal Street and the Bluff for a parade ground. The plan was a grid that included six streets running north and south, with the first street east of the bluff being designated First Street (now Canal) and the sixth street designated as Sixth Street (now Rankin). Seven streets ran east and west, with the center street designated as Main Street. The streets north of Main were designated as First North (now Franklin), Second North (now Jefferson), and Third North (now High). The streets south of Main were First South (now State), Second South (now Washington) and Third South (now Orleans). Each square in the town plan was further divided into four lots. The southwestern quarter of each square was designated lot 1, the northwestern quarter, lot 2, the southeastern quarter, lot 3, and the northeast quarter, lot 4.

Two maps of the original town plan, one undated by Thomas Freeman and the other by William Dunbar in 1794, are located in the Adams County Courthouse. The town grid quickly expanded eastward by the addition of Seventh Street (Pine Street/Martin Luther King). In the 1830s, a new street, Broadway, was laid out between First Street (Canal) and the edge of the Bluff.

The Spanish also established Silver Street, leading from the town on top of the bluff to a new river landing below. Historic maps document that the original landing established by the French was below the plateau of French settlement (box factory site/Lady-Luck Casino parking lot).

The signing of the Treaty of San Lorenzo (also called Pinckney's Treaty) on October 27, 1795, began the transition of power in the Natchez District from Spain to the US to establish the Mississippi Territory. This treaty was one of the most successful ever negotiated by the US. In addition to promising Americans the right of free navigation on the Mississippi River and the free use of New Orleans' port, the act established the right of the United States to the land on the east bank of the Mississippi River above the 31st parallel, an area whose seat of government was located at Natchez. The 31st parallel extended across the Mississippi Territory at the present boundary between Mississippi and southeastern Louisiana.

The shift from Spanish to American control of the Natchez District dragged on for almost two and one-half years as officials argued over the exact boundary. The United States appointed Andrew Ellicott to work with the Spanish commissioner, Natchez planter William Dunbar, to determine the 31st parallel. One of Ellicott's instructions was to persuade the Spanish to leave the area.

Andrew Ellicott arrived in Natchez in 1797 and encamped on the southern end on a ridge that is the present site of the House on Ellicott Hill. Ellicott raised the American Flag at his encampment in defiance of the Spanish flag that flew at nearby Fort Rosalie, less than a mile away. For over a year, Ellicott told the Spanish to leave. On March 30, 1798 the Spanish evacuated Fort Rosalie. At this time, Natchez contained about 90 houses with massive yards around most of them.

Restored Mount Locust on the Natchez Trace is a textbook example of an early planter's cottage constructed during the Spanish period. The architectural character of Mount Locust is similar to King's Tavern in downtown Natchez, which probably dates to shortly after 1794. The house was occupied by Mrs. Postlethwaite on Jefferson Street, between Union and Rankin. It once was a tavern owned by a man named King, a place to stop for refreshment on the long overland journey north from New Orleans for river men who had finished selling their goods. Like Mount Locust, King's Tavern features chamfered posts, wide beaded siding, wood-shingle roofing, rose-headed nails, board-and-batten doors, and interior walls finished in boards rather than plaster.

The only extant house in Natchez constructed for a Spaniard is Texada Tavern, built for Manuel Texada, ca. 1798, the year that Natchez became part of the Mississippi Territory. Other extant buildings dating to the Spanish period include the Governor Holmes House, the Griffith-McComas House, Richmond (center section), Airlie, and Hope Farm, home of Carlos de Grand Pre. All have been extensively enlarged and remodeled, and only Airlie exhibits many of the architectural details that are typical of Natchez buildings constructed during the period. The grandest house built at this time was Concord, the home of Spanish Governor Gayoso. Built in the early 1790s, Concord most resembled the House on Ellicott Hill (ca. 1800). Unfortunately, Concord burned in 1901.

Spain's greatest influence on the physical character of Natchez was the laying out of the town plan and the development of Silver Street. Modern attempts to attribute the forms of early Natchez architecture to French or Spanish origins have usually proved fruitless. No buildings survive from the French period. Buildings dating to the Spanish period were almost all built by Anglo-Americans for Anglo-Americans. Any Natchez architectural ties to the architecture of France or Spain relate more to connections between Natchez and the West Indies than to the colonial history of Mississippi. Natchez and the West Indies shared a similar mixture of national influences, trade interests, some settlers, and a warm climate, and therefore developed similar building traditions.

Mississippi Territorial Period

On April 7, 1798, a little more than a week after the Spanish departed from the fort, the US Congress created the Mississippi Territory with Natchez as the capital. The original boundaries of the territory were the Chattahoochee River to the east, the Mississippi River to the west, Spanish Florida to the south and on the north, a line drawn east from 32 degrees 28 minutes, a point near the mouth of the Yazoo River. By 1813, the Mississippi Territory included all the land within the present boundaries of Alabama and Mississippi.

Congress patterned the government of the Mississippi Territory after the Northwest Territory with one major difference: slavery was illegal in the Northwest Territory but permitted in the Mississippi Territory. Winthrop Sargent of Massachusetts, secretary of the Northwest Territory, became governor of the Mississippi Territory. During the territorial period, the seat of government moved from the fort to the town. Natchez developed a growing reputation as a town with a split personality. The town on top of the bluff gained all the trappings of genteel society. The town below the bluff, known as "Natchez Under-the-Hill," quickly gained a reputation as one of the roughest and rowdiest ports on the Mississippi River. Here docked the keelboats and the flatboats and, beginning in 1811, the steamboats. Taverns, gambling halls, and brothels lined the principal street. Transient river travelers like boatmen, gamblers, trappers, and fishermen were largely responsible for the dissipation observed by travelers during the territorial period.

In 1798, most of the Mississippi Territory was Indian country, with the only significant White settlement, St. Stephens, located on the Tombigbee River in what became Alabama. In 1799, the territorial legislature created Mississippi's first two counties, Adams and Pickering, later renamed Jefferson. Natchez became the county seat of Adams County.

Winthrop Sargent, a New England Federalist, experienced difficulties in governing the new territory. He showed a preference for appointing members of the Natchez upper class who had been closely associated with the Spanish authorities. An association of planters espousing the principles of Jeffersonian Republicanism opposed this and pushed to remove him. A year after Thomas Jefferson became President, Sargent was replaced by William Charles Cole Claiborne from Tennessee. Gloucester, the house that Sargent acquired and enlarged in

1807, is one of the most architecturally significant Natchez buildings from the territorial period.

In 1801 the territorial capital was moved from Natchez to Washington, a village six miles north. In the same year, the territorial legislature established Jefferson College in Washington, Mississippi's first government-chartered institution of higher learning. Today, Washington is only a crossroads, and Natchez is the only incorporated town in Adams County.

Robert Williams succeeded Claiborne. In 1809, Williams was replaced by David Holmes, who served as governor throughout the remainder of the territorial period and became the first governor of the state of Mississippi. From 1798 to 1803, the year of the Louisiana Purchase, Natchez was the most southwesterly outpost of the United States. To improve communication the federal government designated the Natchez Trace as a post road in 1800 and relocated it to pass through Washington rather than the Pine Ridge settlement. Despite the improvements to the Natchez Trace, most settlers continued to arrive in Natchez by water. The Trace remained important as a trade route for boatmen from points north who floated goods down the river and returned home by land. The Trace began to diminish in importance by 1815 when steamboats made it possible to travel up the Mississippi River. Eventually; the Trace fell to ruin except in sections used for local traffic.

With territorial status, improvements in cotton production, and the ability to ship cotton on steamboats, the era of "King Cotton" began, and Natchez economy boomed. The proprietors of the public cotton gins gave planters receipts specifying the amount of cotton delivered, and these receipts, by usage at first and afterward by law, became the paper currency of the territory. In 1810, John Henderson offered his house, The Elms, for sale for either cash or cotton. In 1800, Dunbar and Bernard Lintot erected "a large and commodious warehouse" at the Natchez landing for the reception of cotton. Storage charges were twelve and one-half cents per bale per month.

As Natchez soil wore out, planters expanded their cotton plantations across the Mississippi River to the fertile flat land of Louisiana. By 1817, Concordia Parish had become a planting province of Natchez. Although slave labor had been an important part of overall agricultural production in Natchez since 1716, its tremendous growth after 1800 was due to the rapid expansion of the region's cotton economy. Natchez probably had the only permanent slave market in Mississippi during the territorial period, although other markets were later established in towns like Vicksburg. During the colonial and early territorial periods, slave sales were held at the landing and throughout the town, but, by the early 1790s, more slave transactions began to take place at the Forks-of-the-Road slave market on the eastern edge of town. According to historian D. Clayton James, the slave markets at Natchez (Forks-of-the-Road) and New Orleans (located across the river in Algiers) eventually became the two busiest slave markets in the entire South.

A significant population of free African-Americans began to emerge in Mississippi during the territorial period, and most of these lived in Natchez. Many of the prominent free African-Americans were mulattos who got their start in life through inheritances from the white owners who fathered them and later freed them. Will and probate records in Adams County indicate that stable relationships between white males and black women, slave and free, were more common and more openly acknowledged during the colonial and territorial period than after statehood. These relationships may have been more readily accepted when men outnumbered women during the frontier period of the city's history.

During the territorial period, many settlers came as the town developed a reputation as a place to get rich in a short time. Growing sophistication in Natchez architecture reflected the increasing affluence of territorial settlers. Natchez builders began to use academic embellishments to dress up building forms that had developed locally. At Texada these embellishments include carved wood cornices and Federal-style interior millwork. Between 1798 and 1801, on the site of Andrew Ellicott's encampment, local merchant James Moore built the House on Ellicott Hill. A National Historic Landmark, this structure is a sophisticated and grand example of early vernacular architecture of the Lower Mississippi Valley.

Other important Natchez area examples of early territorial architecture is Gloucester which features the gouge-carved millwork that is typical of finer Natchez houses built during the territorial period. The first Natchez building to combine both the details and the form of academic architecture was Auburn, a National Historic Landmark designed and built in 1812 by Levi Weeks for Lyman Harding, both natives of Massachusetts. The importance of the classical portico at Auburn reached far beyond Natchez. It was one of the first Southern houses to have the two-story white columns that came to epitomize what is colloquially known as "Southern Colonial" architecture.

In 1815, a second influential house was built on The Forest Plantation for Dinah Dunbar, widow of planter William Dunbar. A drawing by the governess at The Forest depicts a large, two-story house with peripteral, or encircling, colonnade. The Forest was probably the first house in America to have one. Dunleith, built in 1856, is the only surviving house in Mississippi with a peripteral colonnade.

Statehood and Prosperity

By 1815, the population of the Mississippi Territory had grown so large that Natchez area leaders began to push for division of the territory. They feared loss of influence as the population grew in the eastern portion of the territory. The boundary was established from north to south to give each of the two new territories access to the Gulf. President Madison signed the act dividing the territory in 1817 and authorized a state constitutional convention for the western portion that became the state of Mississippi. The eastern portion became the state of Alabama in 1819.

The state constitutional convention convened in August 1817 in Washington, Mississippi. The delegates designated Natchez as the first state capital. Texada became its legislative hall. Natchez remained the capital only until 1821, when the legislature voted to relocate, first to Columbia, then to Monticello, and finally, in 1822, to Jackson.

During the antebellum period, planters focused their attention on the fertile flatlands of the Mississippi Delta stretching from Vicksburg to Memphis, bordered by the Mississippi River on the west and the Yazoo River on the east. During the 1830s, a new Mexican strain of cotton increased production. In 1833, Rush Nutt introduced Petit Gulf cotton to Natchez. Nutt developed the seed on his Laurel Hill Plantation, located near Petit Gulf, later known as Rodney, in Jefferson County. The Petit Gulf seed produced a long staple cotton that was easily picked, had a greater yield and would not rot. Nutt improved the cotton gin beyond its former capabilities and attached a steam engine to it as well. Rush Nutt's Laurel Hill Plantation burned in the 1980s, but his son Haller Nutt's octagonal residence, Longwood, survives.

After the Panic of 1837 some Natchez families found themselves bankrupt. However, many who were ruined by the Panic recouped their wealth by the time of the Civil War. Cotton merchant and planter Frederick Stanton was bankrupt by 1840, but rebounded to build the city's most palatial townhouse, Stanton Hall, in 1857.

In the aftermath of the Panic of 1837, a tornado struck Natchez in 1840. One of the most devastating tornadoes in American history, it killed about 300 people, many of whom were passengers on steamboats docked at Natchez Under-the-Hill. Natchez spent the decade of the 1840s rebuilding and repairing the damage.

Natchez failed in the 1830s to establish railroad connections. John Quitman tried to initiate a railroad line to the town but succeeded in building only about 25 miles of track before the project went bankrupt in 1840. Natchez remained without railroad connections until after the Civil War. By 1860, this failure had allowed nearby Vicksburg, which was both a river port and railroad center, to surpass Natchez in commercial importance.

In 1831, a group of Natchez planters organized the Mississippi Colonization Society. The group was affiliated with the American Colonization Society, which sponsored the formation of the country of Liberia on the west coast of Africa. Stephen Duncan, John Ker, and James Railey of Adams County also served as officers of the national organization. Although the charters of both the national organization and the Mississippi chapter expressed as their purpose the resettlement of free African-Americans in Africa, the Natchez organizers of the Mississippi Colonization Society were focused on using Liberia as a vehicle to free slaves. Before its demise in the early 1840s, the Mississippi Colonization Society had relocated 571 Mississippi African-Americans, almost all of whom were previously slaves, to Liberia. The Mississippi Colonization Society ceased to exist after the Mississippi legislature enacted a law in 1842, forbidding the manumission of slaves by will.

Natchez would have withered had the planters moved their families away from Natchez to the sites of their planting activities, but they generally preferred the convenience of life near town to life on the plantation. The planters also believed that lowland areas were prone to yellow fever and other diseases. Consequently, most of the more prosperous planters established their families in grand townhouses like Stanton Hall and Choctaw, or in suburban villa estates like Melrose and Longwood on the outskirts of Natchez. These villas combined the convenience of a townhouse location with the beauty and serenity of a country estate. Residing on a suburban villa estate enabled planting families to enjoy the benefits of town life in a pastoral setting, free from the isolation of plantation life and the dirt and noise of city life, and far from the cotton fields that supported them.

About 1821, Samuel Postlethwaite built Clifton, a mansion sited on a rise at the northern end of the public common. Based on the image in Audubon's landscape, Clifton was a two-story mansion with giant-order columns that formed a colonnade across the front very similar to Rosalie. It had beautiful gardens around it as well as summer houses. The Union army demolished the mansion to construct an earthwork fortification known as Fort McPherson.

In 1823, the giant-order, or two-story-tall, porticoes of Auburn and Arlington were echoed at Rosalie, a National Historic Landmark. The Rosalie portico combined with other architectural features to produce the first complete form of the "grand mansion" common to Natchez and, to a lesser extent, other areas of the South. As introduced at Rosalie, this form is based on a nearly cubical brick block crowned by a hipped roof with balustrade encircling the apex of the roof. Of the five openings on the front, the center three are sheltered by a portico supported by giant-order columns. The columns are repeated at the rear, where they form a colonnade that extends the full width of the rear elevation.

In addition to Melrose, the other extant Natchez houses that exhibit the form of the grand Natchez mansion established at Rosalie include Choctaw, Belmont, and Magnolia Hall. Two Natchez houses completed in 1858, Stanton Hall and nonextant Homewood, exhibit a variation of the form. At both Stanton Hall and Homewood, the rear colonnade is replaced by a double tier of columns.

The Greek Revival style became popular until after the Civil War. Local landmarks of the style include Ravenna (1835) and The Burn (1836), the two earliest residential buildings in that style, as well as D'Evereux (1836), the Commercial Bank and Banker's House (1838), the front section of Richmond (ca. 1838), Melrose (1847), Dunleith (1856), Stanton Hall (1858), Homewood (1858, no longer standing), and Magnolia Hall (1858). The Commercial Bank and Banker's House, Melrose, Dunleith, and Stanton Hall are National Historic Landmarks.

Greek Revival buildings built after 1855 tended to be embellished with details reflecting the newly popular Italianate style. Significant examples of the style are The Wigwam and The Towers, both ca. 1859 remodelings of earlier cottage-form houses into Italianate mansions. Longwood, National Historic Landmark, features an onion dome evocative of Moorish architecture, but the house's architectural detailing is Italianate.

The earliest documented example of Gothic Revival architecture in Natchez and the state is St. Mary's Chapel (dedicated 1839) at Laurel Hill Plantation (established in the 1770s). The state's grandest example of Gothic Revival is St. Mary's Cathedral, built in 1842. This style was never very popular in Natchez, with residential examples limited to Glenfield on Providence Road, the Pintard House on North Union, and the Angelety House on St. Catherine Street, all three dating from the 1850s.

Secessionist Politics and the Eve of the Civil War

Throughout the 1850s, sectional differences centering on the institution of slavery and its expansion into the western territories grew. In 1860, disunion fever began to sweep the South. Unlike their counterparts in Charleston, the majority of the Natchez planters supported the Union and were opposed to secession. Stephen Duncan (probably the richest nabob of them all in the 1850s, from Carlisle, Pennsylvania) of Auburn strongly expressed his loyalty in the *Natchez Courier* in 1860. The diary of scholar and planter B.L.C. Wailes (born in Georgia) agreed with Duncan. John McMurran (Melrose) supported Millard Fillmore in the 1856 election because McMurran felt he was the only candidate who could save the Union. Planter James Surget later remarked to a Union general and his wife: "I know it is contrary to the general impression, but the large slaveholder was against secession."[1]

Some Natchez nabobs, however, supported secession. Prominent among these were Douglas Walworth (born in Natchez) and George Malin Davis (born in Pennsylvania), who became the second owner of Melrose in 1865. Davis chaired the December 1860 county meeting where delegates were chosen for the state secession convention in Jackson. Despite Davis's leadership, the secessionists were defeated by the unionists, and Natchez sent pro-Union delegates to the state secession convention.

When the state secession convention convened in Jackson in January 1861, the Adams delegates could not hold back the surging tide of rebellion. John Quitman (native of Rhinebeck, NY) of Monmouth had died earlier in 1858, without experiencing the disunion he had abetted. A Mexican War hero, governor, and congressman, Quitman, perhaps more than any other Mississippi politician, promoted the idea of an independent nation or confederacy of Southern states.

Before and during the Civil War, Natchez was a town divided. Even the town's two newspapers took opposing views during the secession crisis.

---

[1]Matilda Gresham, *Life of Walter Quintin*

Gresham (Chicago: Rand McNally & Co., 1919), 234.

The Civil War

Once the Civil War began most of the planter class gave belated support to the cause of Southern independence. Vicksburg had already surpassed Natchez in commercial importance, and the Confederate army chose to fortify Vicksburg instead of Natchez since it had railroad connections. Natchez was left defenseless during the Civil War except for a home guard of men too old or infirm to serve in the army.

When Union warships came upriver to Natchez in May 1862, the Mayor of Natchez surrendered to the commander of the U.S. *Iroquois.* The following September, Natchez witnessed its only military conflict when the Union gunboat *The Essex* docked at Natchez for supplies. The "Silver Greys," the Natchez home guard, became excited and fired on the boat, killing one sailor and wounding several others. In retaliation the gunboat shelled the city. Seven-year-old Rosalie Beekman was the only victim of the bombardment.

On July 4, 1863, Vicksburg surrendered to General Grant. Shortly afterward, Union forces took control of Natchez without resistance. Many of the city's mansions became officers' quarters and hospitals. The homes of people known to be strong Confederates were especially targeted.

Some members of the Natchez planter elite remained loyal to the Union throughout the Civil War and received reparations for losses sustained during the war. Among the Unionists were the Levin R. Marshall family at Richmond, the Haller Nutt family at Longwood, the Sargent family at Gloucester, the Merrill family at Elms Court, the Winchester family, and members of the Surget family. Most were natives of Natchez.

Shortly after arriving in Natchez, the Union army began construction of a large earthworks fortification in the northern suburbs of the city. Named Fort McPherson, it encompassed several of the suburban villa estates, including The Burn, The Towers, Cottage Gardens, Melmont, The Wigwam, Airlie, and Riverview.

Unlike Vicksburg, Natchez was not strategically important to the Confederate army. However, the city was very useful to the occupying Union forces as a stopping point between Memphis and New Orleans. The city also served as a supply base and provided hospital facilities for Union wounded. Of the 5,000 Union soldiers stationed in Natchez during the summer of 1864, more than 3,000 were black. One former Natchez slave, Wilson Brown, won the Congressional Medal of Honor for his valor at the Battle of Mobile Bay in 1864. Union soldiers, white as well as black, occasionally played havoc with the property of the planting class and the planters themselves. George Washington Sargent, son of territorial governor Winthrop Sargent, was murdered at Gloucester, the family residence, by Union soldiers who came to rob him. John McMurran of Melrose was wounded in December 1864 when fired upon by a black Union soldier stationed at the picket line near Melrose.

Reconstruction and Race Relations

The Civil War and two successive crop failures in 1866 and 1867 caused the economic collapse of the Natchez planter class. Much of the cotton grown before and after the war was burned by the Confederate army to keep it from falling into the hands of Union troops. Approximately $80 million worth of cotton was destroyed in New Orleans alone. Much of this cotton belonged to Natchez planters who had placed it in the hands of cotton commission merchants. As a result, the credit system that fueled the cotton expansion now became its undoing.

Few were immediately able to resume planting at the end of the war. Some died, and others had been wounded. Their work animals and other equipment had been confiscated by both the Union and Confederate armies. Soldiers also damaged or destroyed plantation fences and buildings. Their lands were also overgrown, eroded, or flooded due to destruction of the levees.

Some of the richest Natchez nabobs, including Stephen Duncan and Levin R. Marshall, left Natchez and relocated to the North. Even Confederate general, Charles Dahlgren, relocated to Brooklyn, New York after the Civil War. John and Mary Louisa McMurran also considered moving to the North and might possibly have relocated had McMurran not died unexpectedly in a steamboat accident.

According to 1860 and 1870 census records, less than 25% of Adams County's antebellum planter families survived as holders of plantation estates in 1870. The planting class of the South was replaced by a new ruling elite of merchants, bankers, and manufacturers. Former slave owners who started out in law or medicine now opened offices to earn a living. Wives and daughters became teachers. Men and women who had once lived like kings now existed through strict economy. Some of the owners of suburban villa estates began to operate mini-farms to sell butter, milk and eggs.

A small number of the Natchez planting elite survived the Civil War and continued to prosper after the Civil War. Among these were James Surget and other relatives of the Surget family like Katherine Surget Minor. The continued prosperity of the Surget family is probably because they were the largest landowners in Adams County. Other survivors appear to have invested heavily in the North's railroads, stocks, and securities. Selling investments in the North enabled Mary Louisa McMurran to satisfy the estate debts of her husband. Another survivor among the Natchez planting elite was attorney George Malin Davis, second owner of Melrose, who increased his property holdings after the Civil War. During the antebellum period, Davis lived at Choctaw in downtown Natchez. After the Civil War, he expanded his property to include the townhouse mansion, Cherokee, and the two suburban estates, Concord and Melrose.

Although diminished in fortune, the old planter class and their descendants continued to remain in the upper tier of Natchez society. In the decades immediately after the Civil War, many of these families, like the Nutts, struggled to maintain appearances, to take occasional trips, and to educate their sons and daughters in Northern schools. Contrary to what might be assumed, Lincoln's assassination shortly after Lee's surrender at Appomattox in April 1865 distressed the Natchez community and caused unease about the future of the conquered Confederacy. Most Southerners had thought that Lincoln would treat the conquered South with compassion. Many Natchez people may have regarded Lincoln with the sentiments later expressed on page 36 of *Reminiscences of a Mississippian in Peace and War*, the memoirs of Confederate veteran Frank Montgomery of Natchez:

I believe Mr. Lincoln to have been a good man, and I think the course of events proved him to be a great man, and I am sure if there had been no secession that there would have been no interference by him, or with his consent with the rights of the southern states. I do not think Mr. Lincoln ought to be blamed in the south for the course he took, for he could not do otherwise, and as for the south, no other course with honor was left than to secede and leave the result to the God of battles, if war should come, which most doubted and few wanted.

Accepting the reality of defeat and the need to rebuild the economy, Natchez newspapers advised their readers to work to build a new South. An 1865 contract between planter James Gillespie and his former field hands on Hollywood Plantation outlined the changing status forged between former masters and slaves. The contract provided that the former slaves could occupy without rent, the cabins that they had previously occupied as slaves. The owner of the Hermitage Plantation leased his entire plantation to 26 freedmen for five years at a rent of eighteen bales of cotton per year.

Established on March 2, 1865, the Freedmen's Bureau helped newly freed African-Americans adjust to freedom. This was one of the last pieces of legislation approved by Abraham Lincoln. As guardians of the freedmen, the bureau had the power to make their contracts, settle their disputes with employers, and provide general care. The Freedmen's Bureau was instrumental in establishing and staffing schools to educate African-Americans. In 1865, Natchez had 11 schools for blacks with 20 teachers and more than 1,000 students of all ages. The Natchez branch of the Freedman's Savings and Trust Company, located at the corner of Main and Commerce Streets, was later Britton and Koontz Bank.

In 1867, Congress passed the Reconstruction Act. The major effect of the act was to take all legal authority from the state governments of the 10 states of the Confederacy and to impose military rule. The 10 states were divided into five military districts under commanding officers who reported to General Grant as Secretary of War. In July 1868 Governor and Mrs. Benjamin Humphreys were forcibly ejected from the Governor's Mansion in Jackson, and General Adelbert Ames soon took charge as military governor of Mississippi. In 1869, Mississippi elected as governor a Delta planter and former Confederate officer, James L. Alcorn, who advised people to accept reconstruction and urged inclusion of African-Americans in state and local government. Alcorn assumed office in 1870, and Adelbert Ames moved to Natchez soon afterwards. In late 1873, Adelbert Ames was elected governor of Mississippi, and, in early 1874, the Ames family returned to Jackson.

The family of William Johnson, the free black diarist of antebellum Natchez, continued to live in the downtown house built by Johnson in 1841. Johnson's widow, Ann, died in 1866, and his son Byron became head of the household. The Johnson family and other black freedmen had to confront changing social circumstances. They were no longer part of a small elite caste that was legally separated from the great masses of African-Americans who had been slaves. Like the Natchez planting class, the Johnson family experienced economic hardship. To ease the family's financial problems, the Johnson children rented a portion of the William Johnson House to boarders, and the Johnson daughters taught school in newly created schools for African-American students.

Some former slaves refused to become sharecroppers and tenant farmers. Instead they became postbellum planters. Notable among these were the Mazique family, who acquired China Grove Plantation in 1870, and the Rounds family, who bought Glen Aubin Plantation in 1874. Both the Mazique and Rounds families were assisted in acquiring their plantations by Wilmer Shields, white plantation manager and heir of William Newton Mercer. Shields was acquainted with both the Mazique and Rounds families. In 1891, Alexander Mazique, son of August and Sarah Mazique, acquired Oakland Plantation where he was born a slave, from the widow of Wilmer Shields. Members of the Mazique and Shields families enjoyed a close relationship well into the 20th century.

Opportunities for higher education were made available to blacks during Reconstruction. In 1871, Mississippi established Alcorn College. Hiram Revels became president of Alcorn College after he finished his term of office as US senator. In 1877, the Baptist Missionary Convention established the Natchez Seminary which later moved to Jackson and became Jackson State University. In 1885, the Baptist Church established Natchez College which continued operation until the early 1990s.

Natchez African-Americans did not wait long after the Civil War to become involved in local politics. In 1869, former slave John R. Lynch was appointed Justice of the Peace for Adams County and became the first African-American to hold political office in Mississippi. Lynch was a former slave of Alfred Vidal Davis at Taconey Plantation, and later became a house servant at Dunleith. In 1870, Lynch was elected to the Mississippi House of Representatives and was named Speaker of the House at the age of 24. In 1872, he was elected to the US Congress and served until the 1880s.

Minister Hiram R. Revels, one of the most famous black politicians of post-Civil War Natchez, arrived in the city immediately after the Civil War and assumed the pastorate of Zion Chapel African Methodist Episcopal Church. In 1870 Revels was elected to the US Senate by the Mississippi Legislature and became the first black man to sit in either house of the US Congress. When Revels returned to Mississippi to serve as the first president of Alcorn College, he became a landowner and planter, as did fellow politician John Lynch.

Reconstruction ended during the Hayes administration. Federal troops departed from Mississippi in 1877. Once federal troops left the state, black participation in politics declined sharply. In 1890, Mississippi enacted a new state constitution which discouraged participation of the poor and uneducated in political affairs. In 1868, Mississippi had 87,000 black registered voters; in 1892, the number had dropped to 9,000. In Natchez, the poll taxes and literacy tests, and perhaps fear of violence, caused a corresponding decline.

The courthouse precinct in Natchez had 1,200 registered black voters in 1870 and only 15 in 1902.

Rise of the Merchant Class

After the Civil War, the planter class lost its economic influence and affluence to a newly prosperous merchant class, many of whom were European Jews who arrived in Natchez during the 1840s. After the Civil War, these immigrants assumed positions of importance in the community. Two prominent men were Henry Frank and Isaac Lowenburg who came to Natchez as merchants attached to the Union army. In the 1880s, Isaac Lowenburg became the first Jewish Mayor of Natchez. Frank and Lowenburg were two of the wealthiest men in Natchez during the postbellum period.

Few grand buildings were erected during the first two decades after the Civil War. Only the merchant class could afford to build grand homes. Mansions like Dunleith, owned by planter A.V. Davis, became home to newly prosperous merchants like Hiram Baldwin. New commercial buildings and residences appeared all over the city between 1880 and 1908. Natchez diversified from cotton production to cotton manufacturing, and entrepreneurs built two cotton mills and a cotton seed oil plant. In 1882, the Natchez-to-Jackson railroad was opened, and, for the first time, the city was linked by rail to the rest of the country.

Subdivisions of antebellum suburban villa estates created late-19th-century suburban neighborhoods. Entrepreneurs Henry Frank and Isaac Lowenburg subdivided the grounds of Clifton. The Clifton Heights neighborhood became the most fashionable in Natchez, and the majority of the houses were built for newly affluent Jewish families. The descendants of Natchez nabob S.S. Boyd of Arlington, in reduced circumstances, sold a portion of Arlington, which was subdivided to create Arlington Heights. Similarly, suburban estates in the northern part of town were subdivided into building lots, including The Burn, The Wigwam, Cottage Gardens, Airlie, Shields Town House, and Melmont.

Tourism and Historic Preservation

Although the city did not yet view its great mansions as tourist attractions in the late 19th century, it did use them as illustrations in literature promoting Natchez as a beautiful community with a climate conducive to good health and good business. In the early 1900s, one of the city's grandest mansions, the Harper House on Broadway Street, was demolished for construction of a factory. No public outcry arose.

In 1907, the boll weevil invaded Natchez. This was a final disaster from which the small farmer could not recover. Twenty years later, the cotton belt was filled with unpainted shacks, washed-out fields, rattle-trap cars, dirt, poverty, and disease.

Increased manufacturing in the North and the agricultural shake-up caused by the boll weevil together provided the major impetus for the migration of many African-Americans to northern cities. In these northern cities, African-Americans often formed social clubs and retained some of their regional ties. African-Americans formerly of Natchez organized the Natchez Club of Chicago, an organization that sponsored the erection of the Rhythm Club marker in the Natchez bluff park in honor of 209 African-Americans who died in a fire at the Rhythm Club on April 23, 1940. The Natchez Club of Chicago recently sponsored the erection of a state historic marker in front of Holy Family Catholic Church on St. Catherine Street.

The historic architecture of Natchez testifies to the final decline of the area's cotton-based economy. No grand houses rivaling those in Clifton Heights were built after 1908. On the eve of the Great Depression during the mid to late 1920s, Natchez experienced an economic surge that is reflected in civic construction projects that included two new high schools, a new hospital, and a new city hall.

New industrialization came to Natchez in the 1920s when a box factory opened on the plateau below the site of Fort Rosalie, the area of the original French settlement. The box factory was an important source of employment for the white members of the community and provided new opportunity for Natchez African-Americans, who, for the first time, were given jobs on the assembly line. The smoke stack of the box factory still stands on the plateau below the fort site.

The bluff near Rosalie, looking south, 1941. The smoke stack is National Box Co.

Inspired by the garden clubs of Virginia, the women of Natchez formed the Natchez Garden Club in 1929. In 1931, the club hosted a state convention and members were amazed at the interest in the old houses. As a result, they decided to host a tour of houses in spring 1932 to boost the local economy; they called it the Natchez Pilgrimage. City officials and the local business community scoffed at the women's plans, but the Natchez Pilgrimage was an enormous success the very first year. Using proceeds from the Pilgrimage, the Garden Club bought and restored the House on Ellicott Hill. The Pilgrimage sparked the rehabilitation of many historic houses in the Natchez area by providing money to finance the work. Private preservation efforts were further boosted as owning an old house became a symbol of status in Natchez.

In the mid-1930s, legislation was enacted to establish two national parkways, the Blue Ridge Parkway and the Natchez Trace Parkway, and the federal government became involved in preservation in the Natchez area. In 1937, the National Park Service acquired Mount Locust in conjunction with the development of the Natchez Trace Parkway. At the same time, The National Park Service also acquired the Native American site, Emerald Mound.

In the late 1930s, Armstrong Tire and Rubber opened a plant in Natchez. It was soon followed in the 1940s by International Paper Company and Johns Manville. Also, in the 1940s, oil and gas were discovered in Adams County. Workers from rural Adams County and surrounding counties poured into Natchez to take factory jobs or work in the growing oil industry, and their needs for housing spurred the further subdivision of some of the suburban villa estates. The Burn, Linden, Montebello, and Roselawn were all subdivided into small lots for the construction of small houses for the city's growing number of factory and oil field workers.

The first bridge spanning the Mississippi River at Natchez opened in 1940 and was initially a toll road. The colonnade, now at the Canal Street entrance to the Natchez Visitor Reception Center, originally flanked the toll booth. With the coming of the bridge came the demise of the ferry and Natchez Under-the-Hill became a ghost town. Under-the-Hill's rebirth began in the early 1970s with the opening of the Silver Street Saloon. In 1990, 50 years after the opening of the first bridge, a second span was constructed to handle the increased traffic between Mississippi and Louisiana.

The oil and gas industry became the major industry in Natchez after the mid-1940s and reached its peak in the 1970s and early 1980s. John Callon, president of Callon Petroleum, bought Melrose in 1976. Following a two-year renovation, the Callon family opened Melrose daily for the first time in its history and hosted some of the city's most important social gatherings between 1978 and the sale of the house in 1990 to the National Park Service.

Although the Natchez Pilgrimage helped assure the preservation of the city's mansion houses, the growing number of automobiles and the prosperity that followed new manufacturing jobs, the discovery of oil, and World War II began to erode the city's historic commercial

Cold Day: Ferries at Vidalia prepare to cross an icy Mississippi River on a cold winter's day in January 1940, one of the best-remembered storms of that era.

Guards on Natchez side of bridge, ca. 1942. Regular Army personnel were placed on the bridge beginning Dec. 7, 1941 until the end of WWII.

The official opening of the Toll House Bridge, 1940

Parade the day the bridge opened, 1940

district. Aerial views of Natchez record a city that had changed little since 1880.

Alarmed by the growing destruction of buildings following World War II, the city of Natchez, in 1954, enacted the first historic preservation ordinance in Mississippi. The ordinance was relatively weak and protected only pre-Civil War buildings, but it set the stage for the stronger ordinances that followed in 1980 and 1991. Earlier in 1952, Natchez became one of the first cities in Mississippi to embrace land-use planning, which helped preserve the city's historic residential and commercial neighborhoods.

The Civil Rights Movement came to Natchez during the 1960s. The number of black elected and appointed officials grew rapidly. By 1995, Mississippi had the highest percentage of black elected officials in the United States. Today, approximately 51% of the city's population is black.

In the 1970s, the state of Mississippi, through the Mississippi Department of Archives and History, became involved in historic preservation in the Natchez area. The Department of Archives and History acquired the endangered Grand Village of the Natchez Indians and established a small museum and interpretive center. It also acquired Jefferson College, where it undertook Mississippi's first academic restoration.

In 1974, the private, nonprofit Historic Natchez Foundation was organized. The foundation opened an office with full-time staff in 1979 and has become one of the most active preservation organizations in the nation. Beginning in the 1980s, the African-American community began to demonstrate increased interest in promoting and preserving its heritage. This interest is manifested in the formation of the Natchez Association for the Preservation of Afro-American Culture (NAPAC), an organization which opened a museum and interpretive center in the Old Natchez Post Office, located on the site of William Johnson's barber shop.

In the mid-1980s, the local oil economy of Natchez collapsed. For the first time, the city of Natchez and the business community began to view the historic resources of the city as resources to rebuild a depressed economy. With the support of public and private entities, the city of Natchez began to seek involvement from the National Park Service in the preservation of its historic resources. In 1988 Congress authorized the establishment of the Natchez National Historical Park, which included acquisition of the site of historic Fort Rosalie and the great mansion Melrose. The legislation also created a preservation district to aid in preserving the city's historic resources. In 1990, the legislation was amended to allow for the acquisition by donation of the William Johnson House.

Development of the Natchez National Historical Park was thwarted in 1990 with Mississippi's legalization of dockside gambling. The most desirable gambling development areas were within and adjacent to the boundaries of the proposed national park. In 1999, large areas of the Fort Rosalie site remain in private ownership due to dockside gambling and its effect on property values.

In the 1990s, the city of Natchez also began to take an active role in promoting the city's historic resources. Heritage tourism began to be recognized as big business, and the city of Natchez opened a large visitor's center in 1998, jointly operated and funded by the National Park Service. The 1990s also marked greater involvement by African-Americans in heritage tourism. The Holy Family Catholic Church Gospel Choir began performing three nights a week during Spring Pilgrimage. Titled the "Southern Road to Freedom," this program represents a musical history of the African-American experience in Natchez. During Fall Pilgrimage, the Voice of Hope entertains with gospel music in a dinner theater format.

Natchez City Hall

Located at 124 South Pearl Street, Natchez City Hall was designed by architect A.N. Austin of Jackson, Mississippi and constructed in 1924. An expression of Colonial Revival style, the two-story, symmetrical brick building rests on a partially raised basement and features the yellow color popular for brick buildings in the 1920s.

The construction of Natchez City Hall was controversial because its site was the location of an earlier city hall and market built in 1837. Natchez preservationists waged the city's first major preservation battle in their failed attempt to save existing historic structures. The 1924 construction of Natchez City Hall launched the historic preservation movement in Natchez.

In 1994 the city of Natchez moved its Council Chambers across the street to the Old Natchez First Federal building and converted the old chamber into office space for the Engineering Department and Planning Department. The Mayor and Board of Aldermen meetings take place in the Council Chambers. Natchez City Hall houses the Mayor's office and other department offices. Official minutes of the meetings, ordinances and financial records for the city of Natchez are maintained at City Hall.

The Mayor is the Chief Executive Officer of the city of Natchez and has executive control, direction and supervision over department heads, except Judiciary and the Board of Aldermen. These 16 departments include the city attorney, city clerk, municipal judge, building inspector, engineering, fire, housing, planning and zoning, police, public works, recreation, traffic, tourism, senior center, water works and community development.

The regular Mayor and Board of Aldermen meetings are held on the second and fourth Tuesdays of each month. The Mayor has the deciding vote on all questions in which the board members are equally divided. Issues pertaining to laws, construction, elections, public health, economic development, and other governmental functions are discussed at these meetings. Upon request, citizens can speak about matters in which they would like to inform the public as well as appeal decisions previously imposed by certain city boards and commissions.

The six member Board of Aldermen are elected officials and serve as the legislative representatives of the city, representing the resi-

Natchez City Hall, 1924

15

dents in their respective wards. They also chair committees such as Health, Utilities, Street, Fire, Recreation, Police, Public Properties and Education. Reports and updates on these committees are passed on to the public at the regular board meetings.

Natchez City Hall is historically significant as the center of government for the city of Natchez. On September 11, 2002, the Mississippi Department of Archives and History designated Natchez City Hall as a Mississippi Landmark.

City Of Natchez Mayors

1803-1809	Mayor Samuel Brooks
1810-	President John Shaw
1812-1813	President A. Campbell
1814-	President Samuel Brooks
1815-1817	President Edward Turner
1818-	President Samuel Brooks
1819-1820	President Edward Turner
1821-	Presidents Edward Turner and W.W. Walker
1822-	President W.W. Walker
1823-	President J.H. McComas
1824-	Presidents J.H. McComas and Wm. Burns
1825-	Presidents Wm. Burns and John I. Guion
1826-	Presidents John I. Guion and W.R. Richards
1827-	Presidents Howell Moss and S. Postlethwaite
1828-1831	President S. Postlethwaite
1832-1835	President Eli Montgomery
1836-	President C. Rawlings
1837-	Presidents C. Rawlings and Henry Tooley
1838-	President Henry Tooley
1839-	President J.A. Lyle
1840-1842	President Samuel Cotton
1843-	Presidents John M. Duffield and John R. Stockman
1844-1846	President J.R. Stockman
1847-1950	Mayor J.R. Stockman
1851-	Mayor Benedam Pendleton
1852-	Mayor George J. Dicks
1853-	Mayor B. Pendleton
1854-1858	Mayor Robert W. Wood
1859-	Mayor John Hunter
1860-	Record not accessible
1861-1863	Mayor John Hunter
1864-1867	Mayor William Dix
1868-	Same officers continued in office, until removed by Military Governor in 1869
1869-	Mayor John H. Weldon
1870-1872	Mayor Robert W. Wood
1873-1882	Mayor Henry C. Griffin
1883-1886	Mayor Isaac Lowenburg
1887-1888	Mayor Wm. H. Mallery
1889-1922	Mayor W.G. Benbrook
1923-1927	Mayor Luther A. Whittington
1928-1936	Mayor S.B. Laub
1937-1946	Mayor W.J. Byrne Sr.
1947-1948	Mayor L.C. Gwin Sr.
1949-1951	Mayor Audley B. Conner
1952-1956	Mayor Walter Abbott
1956-1961	Mayor Troy B. Watkins
1962-1967	Mayor John J. Nosser
1968-1988	Mayor Tony Byrne
1988-1992	Mayor David Armstrong
1992-2000	Mayor Larry L. "Butch" Brown
2000-	Mayor F.L. "Hank" Smith III

Melrose

The acreage at the end of the dirt lane that later became Melrose Avenue was only a used-up cotton field in 1841 when John T. McMurran purchased it from his wife Mary Louisa Turner's cousins to begin construction of their Melrose estate. Until that time, the McMurrans lived at Holly Hedges on the corner of Washington and Wall Streets in downtown Natchez with their son, John T. McMurran Jr., and daughter, Mary Eliza. Jacob Byers, a native of Hagerstown, Maryland, designed the Greek Revival mansion and oversaw its construction. The records at Andrew Brown's sawmill indicate that Byers was picking up cypress timbers and flooring for the house in 1847. The earliest letter written by Mrs. McMurran indicating her residence at Melrose is dated January 1849.

The 16,000-square-foot Melrose mansion has a full basement, two floors of living space, and a full attic above with a roof monitor situated on top. Clerestory windows around the base of the monitor could be opened to allow warm air to rise up the stairway and out the top of the house. The runoff rainwater from this portion of the roof led to an attic cistern that fed a system of running water in the house. The National Historic Landmark mansion features some of the finest brickwork in America. The stuccoed walls and columns under the front portico and rear gallery were originally scored and marbleized in pale rose, tan, and cream colors. The mansion's appearance from the front is easily differentiated from other Natchez houses because of the pairing of columns in either side of the portico with an extended space in between. The use of *faux* finishes continued inside the mansion, where cypress doors were grained to resemble oak or maple, and cypress baseboards

to look like burled walnut or white marble. Purple Vermont slate covered the mansion roof, though wood shingles were used on the estate's outbuildings.

The original furnishings of the home included either wall-to-wall carpets or oilcloths throughout, and expensive hand-blocked wallpapers or a pale rose striated glaze on all the plaster walls. The house retains a very high percentage of original furnishings today, including heavy mahogany paw-footed pieces in the Classical Revival style, pieces with thick curving elements in the Empire style, and a much more delicately carved parlor set in the Rococo Revival style. The carving on the back of the chairs in this set provided the inspiration for Gorham silver's "Melrose" pattern in 1948. Much of the Melrose furniture came from Philadelphia, but the massive library bookcases, the solid mahogany dining room punkah (or "shoofly"), and a pair of walnut armoires were fabricated in Natchez. A marble-top center table by Joseph Meeks in New York toured the country in 1993-94 with an exhibit entitled "Classical Taste in America." Melrose furnishings that would have been imported from Europe include the English dining china, the gilded French mirrors, and the green-and-gold silk brocatelle fabric for the drawing room draperies and upholstery. Artwork that originally hung in the house included three portraits of political figures admired by Mr. McMurran: John C. Calhoun, Zachary Taylor, and Chief Justice John Marshall.

A pair of two-story Greek Revival dependencies flank the rear of the mansion. One held the kitchen downstairs and three rooms for slaves to occupy upstairs. The other had a downstairs room with concrete troughs that might have been used to hold water for laundry or to cool dairy products, with two rooms for slaves above. From these buildings the slaves could hear the service bells that rang on the back gallery of the mansion, operated by bell cranks or pulls in various rooms of the house. Two more bells rang in the mansion basement, where two rooms were originally finished out with con-

Melrose mansion west facade, kitchen building visible behind

crete floors and fireplaces. One may have been a winter kitchen, and the other a slave dwelling.

An underground cistern topped by a pump sits between the mansion and the kitchen building, fed by the rainwater running off the main roof of the house. Underground cisterns also sat just to the east of the kitchen and dairy buildings, their pumps covered by lattice topped with a tin roof. A pair of small square brick structures just beyond these two cisterns completes the courtyard behind the main house. One holds two privy chambers, and the other served as a place to store smoked meat. Other outbuildings on the estate were constructed of white clapboards, including a barn, carriage house, and two slave cabins.

Melrose southwest bedroom

Melrose carriage house

During the antebellum period approximately 20 slaves lived at Melrose at any one time. The McMurrans' personal and domestic servants most likely lived in the spaces nearest the mansion, with groundskeepers, horse grooms, or carriage drivers living in the more distant cabins. Some of their names are known, such as Billy Taylor, John Jr.'s valet who went with him into service with the Confederate Army in 1861. Rachel the cook had a way of making stewed chicken that particularly impressed John Jr.'s wife Alie in 1857. William the carriage driver continued to work for the McMurran family after the Civil War, when they had sold Melrose and moved across the bayou to Woodlands, home of Mrs. McMurran's mother, Eliza Turner.

Elizabeth and George Malin Davis came to live at Melrose at the beginning of 1866. Probably because Mr. Davis was known as a strong supporter of secession, Union forces occupied their downtown home, "Choctaw." Though they later returned to Choctaw, their daughter Julia Davis Kelly lived at Melrose with her husband Dr. Stephen Kelly and their son George. When Julia died of tuberculosis in 1883, her husband returned to his New York home with George, and the Melrose mansion was closed for the remainder of the 19th century. However, the families of former Davis slaves, Jane Johnson and Alice Sims, lived on the estate as tenant farmers and caretakers. In 1901 George Malin Davis Kelly returned to Natchez with his new bride Ethel to survey his inheritance that included the Natchez mansions Choctaw, Cherokee, Concord, and Melrose, as well as plantations in Louisiana. With the birth of their daughter Marian in 1909, they decided to leave New York behind and make Natchez their permanent home with Melrose as their primary residence. The Kellys' restoration at Melrose in the early years of the 20th century are credited as the first acts of historic preservation in the state of Mississippi, and an annual preservation award is presented by the Historic Natchez Foundation in their honor.

Mrs. Kelly belonged to the Natchez Garden Club, and Melrose was included on Spring Pilgrimage tours from the very beginning in 1932. Mrs. Kelly also augmented the furnishings collection at Melrose by adding select pieces from their other Natchez homes. George M.D. Kelly lived at Melrose until 1946, as did Jane Johnson who had probably been his childhood nursemaid and continued to work for the family as a cook in the 20th century. She was said to be 103 at the time of her death. Mrs. Kelly lived until 1975, assisted by employees such as Fred Page who still works at Melrose today. After Mrs. Kelly's death the Melrose estate was sold to John and Betty Callon who subsequently carried out a major restoration of the property. In 1990 the 80 acres remaining of the original estate were purchased by the National Park Service to become the first site associated with Natchez National Historical Park. The magnificent architecture, the acreage, the original outbuildings, and fine original furnishings all contribute to an ideal venue for interpreting the Natchez planter aristocracy and slavery.

The William Johnson House

The tornado that struck Natchez in 1840, killing 300 people and destroying property throughout downtown, also provided an opportunity for rebuilding, and William Johnson extensively mined the ruins of the Parker Hotel on State Street for bricks and other materials used in constructing his new 2-1/2 story home in 1841. The property was owned by his mother-in-law, Harriet Battles, who had lived in an earlier wood frame house on the same site that had burned along with most of the block in 1839. The series of diaries and account books that William Johnson kept from just before his marriage to Ann Battles in 1835 until his death in 1851 provide a wealth of information about the construction of his house as well as overall life in Natchez. These papers were purchased from Johnson's descendants in the 1930s by Louisiana State University, and first published in 1952.

The house faces north at 210 State Street, constructed with a cellar for storing coal, wine, and other foodstuffs below the western one-half of the house. The first floor was an open commercial space that Mr. Johnson rented out. Upstairs, Johnson and his wife lived with their 10 children and probably Amy Johnson and/or Harriet Battles. The second floor of the house, accessed by stairs on the back gallery, held three bedrooms and a parlor, and the boys slept in the attic of the house. A separate kitchen building with an attached dining room stood behind the house, and Johnson also installed lattice on the first-floor rear gallery for use as an outdoor dining room. The kitchen building that currently stands behind the house replaced the original kitchen in the 1890s.

In addition to using salvaged materials in the house's construction, Mr. Johnson also used his bartering skills to obtain furnishings for the house - including three grained doors for the parlor that he won on a horse-racing bet. He provided a very comfortable home for his family, with wallpaper used in some rooms and cal-

Melrose slave cabins

cimine paint in others, carpets on the floors, and framed pictures on the walls. Johnson's diaries and ledgers also provide considerable insight into his furnishings purchases. Framed artwork that he purchased included a map of Texas, a print of The Last Supper, and a print of Martin Van Buren. High-quality original furniture that survives include tester beds, a marble-top washstand, bureau, leather-covered lounge, small sideboard, and gilded mantle mirror. His family tradition maintains that the massive mahogany armoire is a piece that Johnson bought second-hand out of the Natchez mansion "Arlington."

William Johnson's family continued to reside in the home after his murder in 1851. The children continued to live there after their mother's death in 1866, and the three Johnson daughters who did not marry lived there on into the 20th century. At some point in the late 19th century, the family changed their surname spelling to "Johnston." Dr. William Johnston, William Johnson's grandson through his youngest child, Clarence, studied medicine at Howard University in Washington, DC. He and his wife Sallie lived in the home during the 20th century, and she was a well-respected seamstress in the community. In the 1920s they carved up the first floor for their residence, while other family members and boarders continued to live upstairs. Mrs. Johnston's niece, Mary Louise, came to live with the family about that time and continued to reside there until Sallie Johnston passed away in 1975.

At that time the house was purchased by the Preservation Society of Ellicott Hill. Their intent was to restore the home for interpreting William Johnson's life, but they were unable to complete the project. The city of Natchez purchased the site from them, and in 1992 it and the next-door structure that shares a common wall were added to Natchez National Historical Park by an act of Congress. The site should be open to the public in 2004, with modern exhibits interpreting William Johnson's Natchez on the first floor and restored furnished rooms upstairs.

The William Johnson House

Parade the day the Bridge opened, 1940

Back row, L-R: unknown, Mrs. Hulda Fowler, Mrs. Margaret Pitchford. Seated: Nora Grady Burns

A sister watching the students play at the old Cathedral School at the corner of Main and Union Sts., ca. 1930's

Two fireman, L-R: Bob Garrity, unknown

Letty Craig, Shields Family nurse, ca. 1940's

Old Emma, wash woman at Lansdowne, ca. 1940's

Old Mary, maid at Hope Farm, ca. 1940's

A refugee camp set up in Natchez during the flood of 1922

Businesses, Organizations and Churches

1942 Mainstreet between Commerce and Pearl. (Picture courtesy of Marie A. Kossum)

GILLIARD HUNTING CLUB

Left: Above is a picture of the famous Gilliard Hunting Club which was organized in Natchez and this area in the 1880s and which was one of the oldest hunting clubs of the country. The club had hunting trips and enjoyed trap-shooting. The above picture was taken in 1916. All who are in the picture are not identified, but those who have been indentified are: Standing, left to right, unknown, Tom Wickliffe, unknown, Dunbar Merrill, unknown, J. Balfour Miller, Dr. Stuart Handy, Miss Katherine Grafton who is now Mrs. J. B. Miller, Tom Green, Dr. E. H. Buie, unknown, unknown, unknown, William McLain, unknown, Lamar Lambert, unknown, C. C. Eyrich, unknown, Capt. Joe Stone, unknown. (Photo courtsey J. Balfour Miller.)
Right: Other members of the Gilliard Hunting Club included Dr. R. D. Sessions (shown above, sitting, far left) and sons, Ferd and Proby

ROSECRAFT CLUB

A group of ladies met, shared comradeship, lively discussions of current events, played cards and enjoyed light refreshments. This occurred as frequently as convenient, perhaps monthly in the 1920s.

Then, one Sunday on the steps in front of Jefferson Street Methodist Church, Mrs. G.R. Hightower suggested to Mrs. S.J. Greer that they ought to organize a garden club whereby they could exchange seeds and plants and learn from each other. So, Rosecraft Club was organized April 29, 1929. An organizational meeting and covered dish luncheon was held at the home of Mrs. Reed Walser. Mrs. Hightower was elected as first President and Mrs. Greer as Secretary. A Constitution and By-Laws was drawn up providing for a monthly meeting to be held on the second Friday of the month, a total membership not to exceed 24 members (a hostess and co-hostess each meeting in private homes), dues of $1.00 each per year payable in December, a provision for dropping any member absent for six consecutive meetings without valid reason and the commitment to be non-federated. Char-

ter members, in addition to Mrs. Hightower and Mrs. Greer were Mrs. J.C. Stowers, Mrs. R.D. Walser, Miss Annie Bailey, Miss Bessie Bailey, Mrs. Libby Carrol, Mrs. J.L. Cooley Jr., Mrs. H.J. Chapman, Mrs. Janie D. Cooper, Mrs. A.B. Dille, Miss Claribel Drake, Mrs. W.P. Henderson, Mrs. Frank Junkin, Mrs. S.H. Lambdin, Mrs. W.T. Mallory, Mrs. B.W. Prospere, Miss Ada Reddy, Mrs. J.D. Shields, Mrs. Wm. K. Stowers, Mrs. John Stowers and Mrs. Ella S. Bliss as honorary member.

Meetings have always begun with a devotional, roll call answer with what is happening in that person's garden and a program provided by a member or invited guest on timely garden subjects and climaxed with delightful refreshments.

Rosecraft Club continues the tradition today.

Right: Mrs. W. J. Mallory (Joyce), Mrs. S. J. Greer (Annie Ruth), Mrs. Frank Junkin (Josephine), and Mrs. John Stowers (Effie).

THE PROGRESSIVE STUDY CLUB (1890–)

This year (2003) is, at least, the 113th anniversary of Natchez's earliest known literary club called The Progressive Study Club. Each of the 12 members takes responsibility for the meeting place and program in turn. Things are much simpler these days with the study theme being AS YOU LIKE IT enabling each to delve into what ever study suits her fancy. The group meets once a month September to June (with the exception of March).

Originally, there were 20 to 25 members. They met twice a month in members' homes, with two people allotted 20 minutes for each program. The meetings started with Quotations, which could be a sage or familiar saying, a poem, bible verse or such. After the business meeting, the program, using the theme of the year, was given, followed by discussion. The first recorded year book lists as its theme "Songs and Legends of France." Several research authorities were studied in preparation for the program. Later themes were a study of France from Charlemagne to Napoleon; Spain: Her Art, Literature, Legends and Architecture; Holland and the Netherlands; Great Britain and Her Colonies and A Study of Shakespeare, which lasted four years and covered all Shakespearean plays. In later years they studied "The Chateaus of France," "A Year of Modern Thought," "Modern Drama." In 1913-1914 they were apparently concerned with social issues, studying "Leo Tolstoy," "The Ob-jective Value of Social Work," "Spirits of Youth and the City Streets," "Nietzche and the New Morality," "Philanthropy: It's Success and Failure," "The Principles and Chief Dangers of the Administration of Charity," Modern Christianity," "The Genteel Tradition in American Philosophy." Later themes were "Modern Drama," "The 18th Century," "Great Rivers of the World," and studies of Mexico, Canada and Mississippi Authors.

Club colors were white, blue and gold; its motto: "Ad Astra per Aspera." It has operated under three names, Woman's Progressive Club, Woman's Progressive Literary Club and the Progressive Study Club.

EARLY MEMBERS

Mrs. John Ayers
Mrs. Andrew G. Campbell
Mrs. Richard Ellis Conner
Mrs. J.H. Davis
Mrs. Rosalie Quitman Duncan
Mrs. A. Morell Feltus
Miss Corrine Henderson
Miss Mary Beltzhoover Jenkins
Mrs. George Gillson Klapp
Miss Eva Chadbourne Lovell
Miss Alice Quitman Lovell
Miss Sarah Walworth McPheeters
Miss Frances Augusta Means
Mrs. Martha Welles Means
Mrs. Robert Bruce Montieth
Mrs. William Benneville Rhodes
Mrs. Wilson Rumble
Miss Jane Stockman
Mrs. Hibernia Inge Trabue
Miss Clara Walworth
Miss Sarah Ernestine Walworth
Mrs. John Pereander Walworth
Mrs. Thomas Claiborne West
Mrs. J. Cadwallader Williams
Mrs. Clarence W. Wilson

2003 MEMBERS

Betty Barnes
Candace Bundgard
Rosey Dow
Mary Emily Martin
Helen Rayne
Susanne Tomlinson
Eulalie Bull
Alma Carpenter
Claudia Hobdy
Paige Parker
Betty Rogillio
Margaret Wesley
Carol Hubert
Barbara Haigh

GOVERNOR GEORGE HARLAN COLONIAL DAMES XVII CENTURY

The Governor George Harlan Chapter of Natchez, MS, was organized at the Judge George Armstrong Library, Natchez, on April 15, 1983, with Mrs. Clement C. Lumsden Jr. serving as Organizing Chapter President. The charter meeting was held in the Carriage House Restaurant, Natchez, on August 6, 1983 with 49 charter members. The chapter was named for Governor George Harlan, colonial ancestor of organizing president Lumsden, as well as members Mrs. James D. Erven, Mrs. C. Bernard Gibson, Mrs. William B. Sheffield III and Mrs. Douglas M. Wesenburg. Harlan was Governor of the "Three Lower Provinces," now known as the state of Delaware.

Mrs. Lumsden presided as chapter president, and Mrs. Harmon A. Gardner of Vicksburg, Mississippi, and the President General of the National Society Colonial Dames XVII Century and Honorary President of the Mississippi State Society of the National Society Colonial Dames XVII Century, presented the Charter to the chapter. Other distinguished guests were Mrs. John P. Harkins, Recording Secretary General; Mrs. Fountain D. Dawson, Grand Marshall; Honorary State Presidents: Mrs. J.E. Martin, Mrs. Stewart Montgomery, Mrs. Bruce Nicholson, Mrs. C.G. Meadow III, the Mississippi State Society President Mrs. W.B. Stewart, as well as 36 members and guests from other chapters in Mississippi. Each charter member was introduced as she signed the charter.

The Objects of the Society are as follows: To aid in the preservation of the records and of the historic sites of our country; to foster interest in historical colonial research; to aid in the education of the youth of the country; to commemorate the noble and heroic deeds of our ancestors, the founders of our great Republic; to maintain zealously those principles of virtue, courage and patriotism which led to the independence of the colonies and the foundation and establishment of the United States of America; to maintain a Library of Heraldry and preserve the lineage and Coats-of-Arms of our Armorial ancestors; to develop a library specializing in the 17th century American colonial data.

Since its organization, chapter presidents have been:

Mrs. Clement C. Lumsden Jr., Mrs. Volney L. Barker, Mrs. A. Boyd Sojourner, Mrs. Robert F. Costa, Mrs. Earl D. Rogers, Mrs. Walter C. Thornhill, Mrs. Calvin C. Young Jr. and Mrs. Victor P. Vegas. Chapter member Mrs. Walter C. Thornhill served as the President of the Mississippi State Society from 1999-2001.

As of July, 2002, the chapter had inducted 81 members.

By Mrs. Porter Crowell, Chapter Historian

Gov. George Harlan Colonial Dames XVII Century Organizing Officers 1983-85

Natchez Scottish Heritage Society

The Natchez Scottish Heritage Society was organized September 26, 1995 at Hilltop Ramada Inn, Natchez, Mississippi, by a group led by Bobby and Polly Scott of Natchez. The objects of the Society are to promote the study of and the preservation of the Celtic Heritage and culture among the members of the society and the community. Membership is open to anyone who claims Celtic ancestry and/or is interested in Celtic culture. This Society is the only one of its kind in Southwest Mississippi.

The elective officers of the Society are the President, the Vice-President, the Secretary, and the Treasurer. The term of office is for two years. Regular monthly meetings, held at the gymnasium of the First Presbyterian Church, Natchez, are on the fourth Friday nights of each month unless otherwise announced. Reminders of meetings are posted in the "Tracings" of the Natchez *Democrat*.

The Natchez Scottish Heritage Society cooperates with the Mississippi Caledonian Society in Jackson, and members of the Natchez Society are encouraged to attend the meetings and special activities of the Caledonians, which include the Burns' Night in January, the Mississippi Highland Games in March, the Guy Fawkes Picnic in November, and the Christmas Party in December. Some Mississippi Caledonian officers and members have come to Natchez to assist in special activities.

Special activities of the Natchez Scottish Heritage Society include cooperating with the Natchez Garden Club to re-enact a Highland Scottish funeral; sponsoring a Dutch-treat breakfast for Tartan Day Celebration on April 6; constructing an April Scottish display celebrating Tartan Day at the local library; relaxing at the annual picnic on the fourth Saturday of May; sponsoring a Scottish Heritage Day the first Sunday in October at the Pine Ridge Presbyterian Church, Natchez, to celebrate Scottish Heritage Month; presenting a "Kirkin' o' the Tartans" on the second Sunday in November in cooperation with the First Presbyterian Church; cooperating with the Friends of the Armstrong Library to take up tickets for their annual Christmas Tour of Homes on the first Sunday of December; enjoying a Christmas party on the second Saturday of December; and Celebrating a Hogmanay (New Year's Eve Party).

The Society secures bagpipers for various activities, and colorful crest banners, as well as coat-of-arms banners, of members are used to decorate during monthly meetings and for special activities.

Organizational officers were the following: President, Bobby C. Scott; Vice-President, Roy King; Secretary, Carolyn Perrault; and Treasurer, Don Estes. These officers were re-elected through 1999.

Officers for 1999-2001 were as follows: President, Roy King; Vice-President, Polly Scott; Secretary, Betty Britt; and Treasurer, Don Estes.

Officers for 2001-2003 are the following: President, Dr. William "Bill" Pinney; Vice-President, John Leckie; Secretary, Betty Britt; and Treasurer, Calvin Young.

Dues are currently $6 per year, payable in January. Members and guests are encouraged to attend meetings and activities, as entertaining and informative programs are presented by members and invited presenters, delicious Scottish and American refreshments are served, and delightful fellowship is enjoyed.

Natchez Scottish Heritage Society–Bob Gordon, Installation of Officers; Calvin Young, Treasurer; Betty Britt, Secretary; John Leckie, Vice President; and Dr. William Pinney, President

The History of The *Natchez Democrat*

From steamboats to spaceships - The *Natchez Democrat* has told the stories. From the great steamboat race between the *Natchez* and *Robert E. Lee* in 1870 to man's first moonwalk some 100 years later, and even more recently the landing on Mars, Miss-Lou readers found the stories in their Natchez paper.

The Natchez Democrat was started in 1865 by Captain James W. Lambert and Paul A. Botto. Captain Lambert bought the Botto interest only a few months after the paper got its start that October, and four generations of Lamberts published the paper until 1970, when it was purchased by James B. Boone Jr. of Tuscaloosa, Alabama.

Today, *The Democrat* is owned by Natchez Newspapers Inc., which also publishes the Miss-Lou Guide, and is a part of the Boone Newspapers Inc. publishing group.

Cited as Mississippi's Best Community Newspaper by the Mississippi Press Association, *The Democrat* and its staff have garnered numerous awards for writing, photography, layout and design, including Best of Boone honors for two years in a row.

The Democrat covers Adams County and its neighboring Franklin, Wilkinson, Amite, Claiborne and Jefferson counties in Mississippi and Concordia Parish in Louisiana. It is published seven mornings a week.

JUDGE GEORGE W. ARMSTRONG LIBRARY

The Fisk Memorial Library, established March 16, 1883, and the Adams County (MS) Library (The War Information, Reference and Reading Service, a Works Progress Administration Project), established July 10, 1934, were combined into the Alvarez Fisk Memorial Public Library and Museum on July 1, 1943. This reorganization was formed to function as a free public library, an educational institution, with funds appropriated by the governing boards of the City of Natchez and the County of Adams, and domiciled in the City of Natchez, Mississippi. The Alvarez Fisk Memorial Public Library and Museum provided library service until Tuesday, May 19, 1965. The Judge George W. Armstrong Library opened its doors on Monday, May 31, 1965, as the library moved into its new building at its present location, where it continues to provide free public library service to the residents of Natchez and Adams County. The Library has been automated since 1994, and began offering public access to the internet in 1999. New computers made available for the public provide word processing capability. As the role of the public library has evolved, the Armstrong Library has also evolved, and adapted.

FRIENDS OF THE GEORGE W. ARMSTRONG LIBRARY

The Friends of the Library organization is a supporting agency for the Judge G.W. Armstrong Library in Natchez.

In the 1960s the Friends group worked to provide a new library building. Previously, the library was called the Fisk Library and was located in the old Institute Building. Once the new library was built, the Friends group was an inactive organization for several years.

The Friends group was reorganized early in 1991 as the need for community library support was again recognized. The organization works to provide funding for special projects which have not been able to be achieved through the normal funding for the library.

In recent years the Friends have provided new reference and travel books for the library, have re-carpeted the entire library, and have provided support for the summer reading programs.

Fund-raising activities have included the popular Christmas Tour of Homes and the twice-monthly book sale of discarded and donated books. All proceeds from the fund-raising projects go to help the library in some way.

The Christmas Tour of Homes gives people of the community and visitors a chance to see homes not usually open for inspection. Choosing the homes each year is a challenge. Some years new home styles have been chosen. Sometimes homes in a specific area of the city have been highlighted and sometimes, a specific area of the county provides a look at homes rich in heritage.

Book sales are held in the library meeting room on the first Tuesday of the month from 12:00-5:00 p.m. and on the third Saturday of each month from 9:00 a.m. to 12:00 p.m. The books sold range from reference to paperbacks. Most of the books are donated by persons in the community. Some are older copies of titles withdrawn from the library collection.

The Friends of the Library group is chartered as a non-profit organization under the umbrella of the state organization Friends of the Mississippi Libraries. The local group is governed by a Board of Directors, President, Vice-President, Secretary and Treasurer.

Judge George W. Armstrong Library

Natchez Community Hospital

Natchez Community Hospital is a healthcare innovator; a community hospital that dedicates its resources toward the physical and economic well-being of the Miss-Lou area. Since opening in 1973, the 101- bed facility has offered a comprehensive array of medical services and blazed new trails in leadership and community service. The hospital opened as Natchez Community Hospital under the ownership of Humana. In 1987, the name was changed to Humana Hospital-Natchez to reflect the Humana Corporation's desire to brand their 100 plus hospitals throughout the United States. In September 1993, the hospital was purchased by Health Management Associates, Inc., the premier operator of acute care hospitals in the Southeast and Southwest areas of non-urban America. The hospital once again took its original name.

Natchez Community Hospital is committed to the community and has been proud to provide participation and financial support of civic organizations, charities, education and community and cultural events. In 2002,

the hospital provided over $5,144,000 worth of charity care and employed over 300 people with an annual payroll of $10 million dollars. Over $500,000 was paid in local and state taxes. In 2003, the hospital and its eight Mississippi sister hospitals made a donation of $65,000 to the Alcorn School of Nursing.

Providing the latest healthcare technology requires a significant investment. We have a very proud record of "firsts" for Natchez. This list includes:
 • Magnetic Resonance Imaging
 • Mobile Lithotripsy
 • Labor, Delivery and Recovery Room Concept
 • Holmium Laser
 • Multi-slice Spiral CT Scanner

Natchez Community Hospital, as it appeared in 1973. A new covered entrance was added in the late 1980s and medical office buildings were added to the side of the hospital around 1975 and 1976.

Natchez Community Hospital as it appears today. The canopy was added and a side parking lot was added.

•Sports Medicine/Certified Athletic Trainer on Staff

•Friends Five-O Seniors Organization, a program designed especially for those age 50 and older

•Ultrasonic Lithoclast for the treatment of large kidney stones

•Heartburn Treatment Center

The Emergency Department is staffed with local physicians who call Natchez home. We are involved in the Mississippi Trauma Care Program as a Level III Trauma Center and we are an active member of the Southwest Trauma Care Region.

Our medical technology and state-of-the-art equipment in itself does not accurately portray all that we are. The employees of Natchez Community Hospital and their unyielding dedication and commitment to patient care are what makes us special and uniquely qualified to care. With willing hands, generous hearts, professional expertise and positive attitudes, our employees and medical staff provide the citizens of the Miss-Lou with exceptional health care. We are proud of our investments made in the Miss-Lou area and look forward to a future of continued growth.

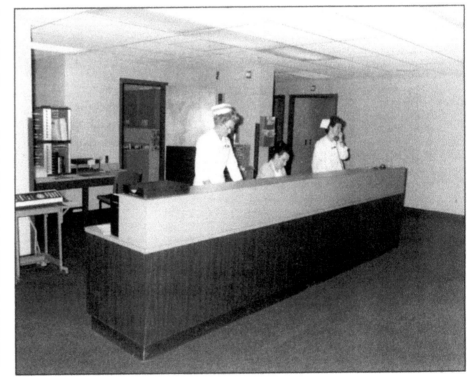

These three employees were among the first to welcome patients at the newly built hospital in 1973. They are from left, Jeanette Tisdale, LPN; Louise Woodson, Unit Secretary and still employed at NCH; and Ann Thornhill, RN and recently retired from NCH.

Natchez Community Hospital
Your Health. Your Hospital. Your Choice.

NATCHEZ REGIONAL MEDICAL CENTER

Natchez Regional Medical Center opened as a nonprofit hospital on April 18, 1960 under the name, Jefferson Davis Memorial Hospital. The name change occurred in January 1993 to establish the hospital's position as a referral center for the five Mississippi counties and two Louisiana parishes it serves. Owned by Adams County, Mississippi, the hospital is committed to serving the healthcare needs of the Miss-Lou.

Natchez Regional Medical Center is a full-service hospital offering comprehensive diagnostic and treatment services for acute, subacute and ambulatory care. Currently licensed for 205 beds, Natchez Regional Medical Center is fully accredited by the Joint Commission on Accreditation of Healthcare Organizations and is licensed by the Mississippi State Department of Health. We participate in Medicare and Medicaid, as well as commercial insurance and managed care programs. Natchez Regional Medical Center is a teaching facility affiliated with Alcorn State University and Copiah-Lincoln Community College for RN and LPN nursing programs, respiratory therapy and physical therapy programs.

Natchez Regional Medical Center's four phase $18 million renovation was completed in 1998.

In 1955, a group of public spirited Natchez citizens began to explore the feasibility of building a modern public hospital for Adams County and the surrounding area. Five years later, April 1960, the dream became reality when Jefferson Davis Memorial Hospital was dedicated.

Since that time the name has changed, but the mission is still the same - to provide quality healthcare in a compassionate environment.

Through the years many local citizens have contributed their time and talents as members of the Board of Trustees to assure that Natchez Regional Medical Center remains on the leading edge of healthcare and that the services offered are appropriate for the needs of the area. The 37 physicians who made up the original

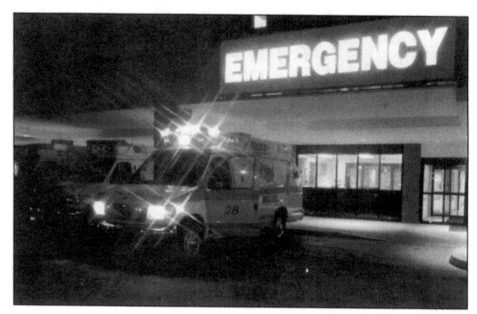

Natchez Regional Center provides 24 hour physician-staffed Level II emergency service.

medical staff began a tradition of excellence that continues today with the 50 physicians that represent the best in a broad range of medical specialties.

Renovations to the original building have altered its appearance over the years.

The addition of a state of the art Emergency Department, a fully equipped Critical Care Unit, attractive and comfortable Labor/Delivery/Recovery rooms for "modern" deliveries, and the relocation and redesign of services for easy accessibility has kept NRMC aligned with current healthcare trends. As the focus of healthcare has moved from the inpatient to the outpatient setting, NRMC has met these demands

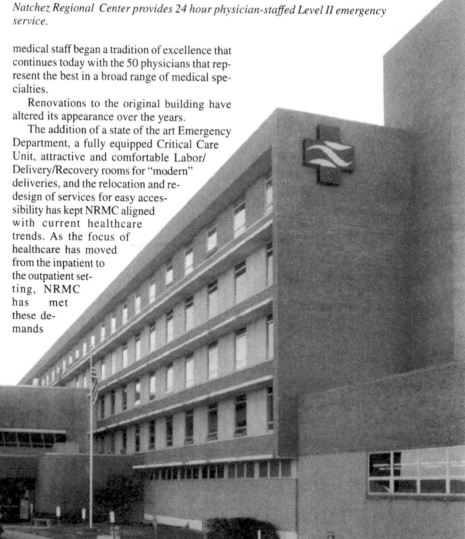

Natchez Regional Medical Center

by implementing the Cardiac Rehabilitation program and the Pre-admission Service, and by enhancing existing outpatient services such as Sleep Lab, Physical Therapy, Occupational Therapy, as well as Outpatient Surgery, Lab and Radiology Services, MRI, PET Scan, ADHD Clinic, the Women's Center, Rehab Care Unit, and Geriatric Psyche Unit.

Behind the "bricks and mortar" is the heart of Natchez Regional Medical Center, its employees. Over the years hundreds of friends and neighbors from the Miss-Lou region have joined the ranks of the well-trained, dedicated staff who provide continuous service at Natchez Regional Medical Center. Currently, 69 employees have served 20 years or more as part of this fine health care team.

In 1960, the dream of a modern public hospital to serve the people of Adams County and the surrounding area became a reality. As today's leaders continue to have a vision for the future of healthcare in the region and as local citizens continue to support their public hospital, the dream that was started in 1960 will continue to be a reality well into the 21st century.

Congratulations, Natchez Regional Medical Center on your 40th anniversary.

Natchez Regional Medical Center's 15 bed Skilled Nursing Facility fills the need between hospitalization and a return home for many patents with continued healthcare needs.

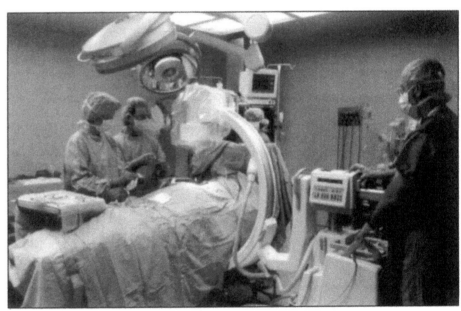

Above, Left and Right: *NRMC's surgical staff at work*

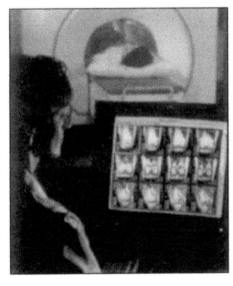

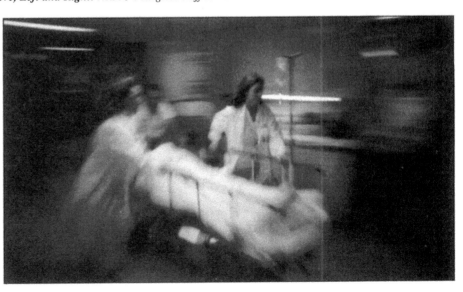

The Radiology Department provides comprehensive diagnostic imaging.

Physicians are supported by a skilled nursing staff comprised of specially trained emergency nurses who are certified in Advanced Cardiac Life Support (ACLS).

THE NATCHEZ CHILDREN'S HOME

The Natchez Children's Home is a private residential group home for neglected and abused children. It was originally named the Female Charitable Society when it was founded in 1816 by a group of Christian women. It is probably the oldest continuously operated children's home in the United States. An important goal of the organization is to draw attention to the *societal problem* that it was founded to address and has continued to address for over 187 years. The ultimate purpose of the Home today, however, is the same as it was when it first opened its doors - *to save lives, one child at a time.*

How is it possible that 187 years after a town first realized that there was a need to provide care for abused, abandoned and orphaned children, the problem is still not defeated? One answer is that people often wish to look the other way when confronted with such societal ills as abused and neglected children. To those who would never hurt or abandon a child, their stories seem beyond belief.

Many communities like to think they "don't have the problem." Better said, many don't acknowledge the problem. People who live in such dire situations simply don't figure in the community's assessment of itself. The Natchez Children's Home works to help leaders look beyond their immediate "to do" lists and recognize the profundity of the problem.

The history of the Home parallels the history of Natchez. During the glory days of the town when the millionaire planters built cotton dynasties and lived in grand mansions, many of the Territory's children, orphaned by Yellow Fever and Indian wars, lived at the Home. During the Civil War, while General Grant had his headquarters in Natchez at Rosalie, the Home was a haven to many lost children.

The Minutes of the NCH begin a year before Mississippi became a state in 1817. They tell the story of the Home and its children during the War Between the States, Reconstruction, the Gay 90s, the turn of the century, the First World War, the Roaring 20s, the Great Depression, World War II, the Civil Rights era. They are now recording the happenings of a new century.

The past generation (since about 1979) has been one of profound change for the Natchez Children's Home. The Home has reinvented itself and its operation in light of the changed circumstances of the children (most of whom are not orphans) and the area it exists to serve. This area now embraces many other counties and parishes in Mississippi and neighboring Louisiana.

The Natchez Children's Home is funded primarily by donations from individuals, churches and businesses; from corporate grants, bequests and fund raising activities. Although it is licensed by the State of Mississippi it neither seeks nor accepts large government grants.

The work of this Christian home for children extends far beyond "three hots and a cot." Dedicated couples live at the Home serving as surrogate parents and demonstrating to the children healthy family models; the children are involved in many community activities; psychological counseling is available to both the children and their estranged families; long term foster care placements are arranged and overseen. In addition staff and board members take a pro-active stand in Juvenile and Family Court matters, child abuse legislation and education issues. Although the means and methods have changed over the years, the Home's primary goal remains what it was for those founders in 1816: to provide a nourishing, Christian home for children in peril - and to save lives, one child at a time.

Natchez Children's Home, 806 N. Union St.

THE NATCHEZ LITTLE THEATRE

The Natchez Little Theatre in its present form was organized in 1948. The auditorium at Braden School was its first home.

Prior to this time theater had been important to the Natchez Community. Great stars had performed here when the city was the cultural center of Mississippi. Sara Bernhard appeared at the Baker Grand in 1917. John Wilkes Junius appeared in 1828-29 and 1838-39 as Hamlet and King Lear. William S. Hart played at the Natchez Temple Opera House before becoming America's first western movie star in 1914.

In 1932 a group of local citizens met to organize The Little Theatre of Natchez. The plays were performed in the auditorium of the old Cathedral High School on Main Street. The first one act play, *The Florist Shop*, had

been produced previously by the original little theater in the 1920s. The cast consisted of Eva Joo, Thomas Reed, Michael Kullman, Clarice George and Martin Burke.

The Natchez Little Theatre was organized in 1948. The first year's offerings were *The Cat and the Canary, Blithe Spirit* and *Ah, Wilderness.* The group used Braden School for some time, but soon outgrew it as audiences increased in size. Thoughts of building a theater occupied the NLT leaders. They had purchased the Governor Holmes House and planned to build a theater, but costs were prohibitive.

The Wesley Methodist Church on Linton Avenue was available for sale in 1969. Jack Millstein who was president said, "We paid $2,000 and assumed a $14,500 mortgage. The church took a second mortgage which we paid

off in 90 days by selling the Governor Holmes House."

The church was purchased in 1963 with the first play slated for 30 days after the deal was closed. The pulpit and choir area were ripped out, a stage was built and the original pews were used for the first play.

A glittering jewel was added to the NLT in 1963, when the Governor Holmes Players first performed *Southern Exposure.* The play has been performed each year since during the Natchez Spring Pilgrimage.

The Mississippi Medicine Show was first performed in 1976 and has been seen annually during the Natchez Fall Pilgrimage.

From 1948 to 2003 at least 220 plays have been produced by volunteers who direct, build sets, select plays, and act.

NATCHEZ COCA COLA COMPANY

Coca-Cola was first advertised on Saturday, May 29, 1886 in the *Atlanta Daily Journal*. It was a simple presentation stating: "Coca-Cola, Delicious! Refreshing! Exhilarating! Invigorating!"

The man responsible for creating Coca-Cola was a pharmaceutical chemist, Dr. John Styth Pemberton. The first batch was mixed in a three-legged brass kettle in the backyard of his two story red brick home.

In 1888, Asa G. Candler and Company, a wholesale and retail drug business, purchased one-third interest in Coca-Cola. Pemberton passed away in August 1888, shortly after Candler purchased the rights to Coca-Cola for $2,300.

In 1894, a Vicksburg pharmacist by the name of Joseph August Biedenharn was credited with bottling Coca-Cola for the first time. "Uncle Joe," as he was known, first started wholesaling the 5 gallon kegs of syrup through the Biedenharn Candy Company to various businesses who had soda fountains in the Vicksburg area. Even though Joseph Biedenharn was credited with the earliest attempts at bottling Coca-Cola in the local area, three other men were thought of as the entrepreneurs of the bottling industry. These men were Benjamin Franklin Thomas, Joseph Brown Whitehead and John T. Lupton.

In 1899, the young attorneys set up a meeting in Atlanta with Asa Candler, ensuring a contract for exclusive rights to bottle Coca-Cola. The contract simply stated that Candler would sell the Coca-Cola syrup at a fixed price per gallon and furnish all labels. The first bottling plant was opened in Chattanooga in 1899. Realizing that it was financially impossible for them to personally establish bottling plants throughout the country, the three men decided it would be more beneficial to acquire competent individuals across the country who could provide the capital and the drive to develop and manage plants in their hometown communities.

In 1901, Coca-Cola Bottling Works of Chattanooga, Tennesse was sold to James F. Johnston and William H. Hardin. This sale granted these two men the distinction of being the first to receive the franchise under the 1899 contract.

In 1906, Joseph William Kendall acquired the franchise to bottle Coca-Cola in Natchez. This was the beginning of the Natchez Coca-Cola Company. The first location for the company was 222 Main Street. After a year the plant was relocated across the street on the site of the old post office. In 1908, Joseph Kendall died, leaving the responsibility of maintaining the business to his wife, Mary. In order to take full advantage of the railroad, she moved the establishment to the corner of Wall and Monroe streets. Through the use of the railroad, she had the empty bottles delivered from Chicago, the crowns from Baltimore and the syrup from Atlanta. After the Coca-Cola was bottled, it was distributed by steamboat, horse-drawn wagons and early motorized trucks. Natchez Coca-Cola Bottling Company grew under the nurturing care of Mary Kendall. Even during the great depression, not a single employee was laid off.

During this era, the ever popular soft drink made another landmark in history. In 1916, the most recognized bottle in the world made its first debut. Some people called it the "hobble skirt" bottle named for the ladies fashions of that era. If this is the case, so be it! That unique shape went on to be granted registration as the trademark on the Principal Register by the U.S. Patent Office.

In 1945, Mary retired to let her oldest son Bill take the reigns. As an alderman, Bill had been instrumental in working with the governor's industry board and the community to bring Johns Manville to Natchez. The city was prospering! Bill died in 1961 leaving the operation to his wife Mary Louise, who later married B.F. Goodrich

In 1957, Huge Bowie retired as plant manager, after working until World War II had started and returning after the war had ended. Paul Klutts, who managed the Coca-Cola plant in Springfield, Tennessee, moved here in 1959 to manage Natchez Coca-Cola. During his leadership, Natchez Coca-Cola grew enormously. Consumption within the franchise was 100 – 6-1/2 ounce bottles of coke per person per year. Natchez Coca-Cola was among the top 10 franchises in the nation with a percentage of more than 500 bottles per person. By 1966, Vending Services was formed to service the consumer needs of the local industries.

In 1968, after acquiring the Dr. Pepper and Barqs Root Beer franchises, Natchez Coca-Cola had by far outgrown its facilities on Wall and Monroe Street. It was time again to relocate. A new plant was built at its present location, 191 D'Evereaux Drive.

In 1983, Paul Klutts retired, and John Paige from Baton Rouge, LA, became plant manager. He was here until 1984. At that time Gail Feltman, who worked as a sales manager for Natchez Coca-Cola, moved up to become plant manager.

On July 29, 1986, the Biedenharn family purchased Natchez Coca-Cola from the Goodrich family. Feltman remained plant manager until the end of the year. In 1987, Larry Clarkston left Pepsi in Shreveport, LA and came to Natchez as the plant manager for Natchez Coca-Cola.

In 1992, Natchez Coca-Cola sold its vending line, Vending Services, Inc., to Brad Fondren and Newt Willis, who own and operate Miss Lou Vending.

In January 1996, Coca-Cola Enterprises purchased Natchez Coca-Cola from the Biedenharn family. Larry Clarkston transferred and is now a Divisional Key Accounts Manager in Memphis. In that same year, Jimmy Hibbs, who had been a sales manager for Natchez Coca-Cola, became the Sales Center Manager. Hibbs retired in 2000, after 24 years of service to the company.

In September 2000, Moe LeBlanc transferred from Alexandria, LA, where he was sales manger for Coca-Cola to his present position as Sales Center Manager for Natchez Coca-Cola. As manager, Moe has an open door policy and the morale of his employees is always uppermost in his mind. Anything from Friday afternoon cookouts to Saturday, "just for fun bowling tournaments," Moe truly, "puts his people first!" Under his direction, Natchez Coca-Cola is a leading contributor of various organizations and charities throughout our city and surrounding area. We take great pride in our community and look forward to many more years of service, so, take a minute out of your busy day and "Have a Coke and a smile!"

75th anniversary publication, December 15, 1981

Moe LeBlanc, Sales Center Manager

Coca Cola Co. Building

COPIAH-LINCOLN COMMUNITY COLLEGE

1972 TO PRESENT

"We like to think of Copiah-Lincoln Community College as part of the Miss-Lou family."

That thought was expressed by Dr. Ronald E. Nettles, dean of Co-Lin's Natchez campus.

"Since the Natchez campus was founded in 1972, we have graduated more than 2,000 students and helped more than 5,000 others with their post-secondary education. Clearly, we have touched the lives of numerous families in the Miss-Lou."

Shortly after 1971, when Adams County joined six other counties to support the Copiah-Lincoln Junior College District, it was determined that due to the population concentration and relatively remote geographical position of Natchez, certain educational needs of the western-most portion of the district might better be served by a second Copiah-Lincoln facility in the Natchez area.

Prior to this time, from 1962-72, the University of Southern Mississippi had provided the first two years of higher education in Adams County. In 1972, the Mississippi Legislature passed enabling legislation to convert the USM resident center in Natchez into a degree-granting center. Certain restrictions, however, stipulated that the center could not offer freshman and sophomore courses but had to reserve such courses for Copiah-Lincoln Junior College.

Thus, Copiah-Lincoln Junior College was formally established in Natchez in the 1972-73 fall quarter with an initial enrollment of 433 students, 92 of whom were full-time and 341 were part-time. Classes were offered on both daytime and evening schedules. At that time the college was called Copiah-Lincoln Junior College, Natchez Branch, and operated on a quarter system. The name changed to Copiah-Lincoln Junior College, Natchez Campus, soon afterward, and in 1988 changed once again to Copiah-Lincoln Community College, Natchez Campus. Also in 1988 the quarter system was replaced with the semester system, offering two long semesters and a shorter, intensive summer semester.

Beginning in 1972, Copiah-Lincoln in Natchez offered the first two years of instruction in academic fields in business, health, physical education, recreation, humanities, science, mathematics, and social science (including elementary and secondary education). Also offered was an associate degree program in police science. Since that time there has been the inclusion of vocational-technical programs, Job Training Partnership Act programs, and Special Interest-Continuing Education programs. Other programs and services added include the Small Business Development Center, Elderhostel programs, Institute for Learning in Retirement, Natchez Literary and Cinema Celebration, and numerous others.

During the first year of existence of the Natchez Campus, 1972-73, classes were held in buildings owned by the City of Natchez in Duncan Park, space shared with upper division classes which were part of the University of Southern Mississippi-Natchez. Other Copiah-Lincoln classes were taught in rented class-

The annual Renaissance Faire, created in 1998, has become a big hit among students and staff.

Youngsters show off their work at Kids College, one of the more popular community programs.

Faculty and staff got together for a group photo during the Natchez campus' 25th anniversary celebration in 1996.

Copiah-Lincoln Community College in Natchez

rooms at the Natchez-Adams High School.

In 1973, the Natchez Campus was relocated to the Central School site, a vacant former elementary school building owned by the Natchez-Adams Public School System. This building was renovated for offices and library and served as the campus until 1981. In the fall of that year, the Central School building had to be vacated because U.S. Highway 84 required right-of-way directly through the school property. The Natchez Campus relocated once more in the fall of 1981, to a leased former public

Co-Lin has enjoyed participating in community events.

school building at Washington, also owned by the Natchez-Adams Public School System. This building of approximately 22,500 square feet was over-utilized almost immediately. Temporary classrooms were set up in a former gymnasium, and two offices were placed in a mobile building.

Because of growth, in 1976 a major step was taken to alleviate the problem of overcrowding of all three institutions of higher education in Adams County. That year a site of 165 acres was purchased south of Natchez on the Beltline Highway. The purchase was initially executed by a local group of individuals, who upon reimbursement of purchase price conveyed the property to Adams County and the City of Natchez for the specific purpose of consolidating higher education facilities.

In the fall of 1979, the Board of Trustees of Copiah-Lincoln commissioned the design of a comprehensive plan for development of facilities to accommodate the Natchez Campus of Copiah-Lincoln on the joint site with Alcorn State University.

Enrollment at Copiah-Lincoln's Natchez Campus in the fall quarter of 1980 had reached 455 students, of which 63 percent were part time. During the school year 1979-80, the staff included 12 full-time instructors teaching 35 classes and 21

The Natchez Literary and Cinema Celebration has earned and presented many awards since its founding in 1990. Above, from left, Emma Blissett, of Alcorn State University; William Winter, former Mississippi governor; Bill Minor, Mississippi columnist; John Grisham, Mississippi author, Gov. Ronnie Musgrove and Dr. John Guice, USM, gather at the NLCC Richard Wright Literary Excellence Award Ceremony in 2001. Minor and Grisham were the award recipients.

part-time instructors teaching 25 classes. Funding for a new building was put on hold.

However, by 1986, the vocational-technical division of the Natchez Campus had grown to the point that it required larger, newer facilities. State funds were available to build a state-of-the-art brick vo-tech building. In 1988, the vocational-technical division moved to a $2 million-plus complex near Beltline Highway (later renamed Colonel John Pitchford Parkway), about 10 miles south of the Washington site.

Many students and certain faculty members were required to commute between campus sites for classes and library use, since funds were still unavailable for the construction of an academic complex near the vo-tech building.

Enrollment continued to climb in the 1990s, with student population increasing dramatically each semester.

In the spring semester of 1995, the largest enrollment ever was attained with more than 700 students in academic, vocational, and technical classes. Approximately 1,500 additional students were enrolled during 1994-95 in other, non-credit educational programs. By the year 2000, enrollment was steady in the range of 750 to 800 full and part-time students. By 2003, enrollment consistently exceeded 800 students.

In 1993, in response to continued requests from Copiah-Lincoln, the Adams County Board of Supervisors passed an increase in millage to pay for bonds to build a $4.6 million academic complex near Copiah-Lincoln's vocational-technical building. Construction began in June 1994, with completion in January 1996.

The new building included classrooms, offices, a library, a support services area, and related areas. In June 1998, Copiah-Lincoln dedicated its first buildings in honor and memory of significant contributors to the campus. Buildings and/or facilities now bear the following names: Tom Reed Academic Center, Redd/Watkins Vocational-Technical Center, Willie Mae Dunn Library, Joey H. Paul Technology Room, W.L. Nelson Multi-Purpose Room.

Throughout its history, Copiah-Lincoln in Natchez has worked closely with other institutions of higher education, beginning in 1972 with The University of Southern Mississippi-Natchez, which closed in the early 1980s, and Alcorn State University. Leaders of Copiah-Lincoln Community College, Natchez Campus, have used the title of "Associate Dean" or "Dean" and have answered directly to either Dr. Billy B. Thames, President of Copiah-Lincoln, or, since 1980, to Dr. Eddie M. Smith or Dr. Howell C. Garner, both of whom have served as Dean of College of Copiah-Lincoln.

In 1997 Dr. Thames retired as president, resulting in major shifts in administration. Dr. Howell C. Garner was promoted from Dean of the College to President. Dr. Paul Johnson was promoted from Dean of the Natchez Campus to Dean of the College, and Dr. Ronnie Nettles was promoted from the Wesson Campus to Dean of the Natchez Campus.

Previous leaders of the Natchez Campus have included Dr. Eddie M. Smith (1972-80), Dr. Howell C. Garner (1980-85 and current president), Dr. Ed Meadows (1985-89), Mrs. Sandra Gibson (Acting Associate Dean 1989-90), Mr. Travis Thornton (1990-96), Dr. Paul Johnson (1996-97 and current Dean of the College) and Dr. Ronnie Nettles (1997-present).

In 1999, Copiah-Lincoln Community College purchased approximately 14 acres of undeveloped land adjacent to the Natchez campus. The property is the site of a proposed fine arts education and performance center, which would be jointly operated by Co-Lin and Alcorn State University.

"In the years ahead, Co-Lin in Natchez will strive to move forward on many fronts: academics, community service, and career and technical education programs," Nettles said. "We look forward to being part of the Miss-Lou family for many years to come."

The Natchez campus celebrates Black History Month, a program begun in 1996. Local pianist Alvin Shelby plays for singers Laura Winston (graduate and former staff member), Dorianna Quinones (student), and Shounda Ferguson (graduate and staff worker) during the 2001 program.

Dr. Howell C. Garner, center, Co-Lin president, and Dr. Clinton Bristow, right, president of Alcorn State University, at the purchase of 14 acres of land adjacent to the Natchez campus in December 1999. Co-Lin and Alcorn plan to create a fine arts center on the property.

Travis Thornton (now retired Natchez campus dean), left, Dr. Howell C. Garner (former Natchez campus dean and now president), and Sammy Cauthen (Adams County supervisor) during a meeting at the Natchez campus.

Churches

THE HISTORY OF THE FIRST PRESBYTERIAN CHURCH OF NATCHEZ

A number of Presbyterians drifted into the Natchez area during the territorial Government, 1798-1817, coming from the eastern seaboard across the wilderness, and down the Mississippi River from the then western states.

It is supposed that the first Presbyterian minister to labor in the south was the Rev. Joseph Bullen, who came as a missionary to the Indians in 1799. In 1801 three missionaries were sent from the Synod of North Carolina and came to Mississippi by way of Nashville, nearly perishing from lack of provisions on the long journey down the Natchez Trace. These missionaries preached in the Natchez area, seeking to consolidate the Presbyterian people and establish an organized work. One of these, the Rev. William Montgomery, later returned and settled near Natchez.

In 1804 the Bethel Presbyterian Church was organized near Uniontown; in 1807 the Salem Presbyterian Church was organized in Washington, Mississippi. The congregation, in 1811 moved to the present site of the Pine Ridge Church and the name was changed. It is the oldest Presbyterian Church organization in the state. Mississippi Presbytery was organized there March 6, 1816.

In 1807 the Rev. James Smylie from North Carolina held services for the Presbyterians in Natchez area at the Adams County Court House, and that same year the Rev. Jacob Rickhow from the Presbytery of New Brunswick in New Jersey preached several months to the Natchez people.

Under the ministry of the Rev. Daniel Smith and with the valuable help of John Henderson, elder of the Pine Ridge Presbyterian Church the First Presbyterian Church of Natchez was formally organized on March 20, 1817. He continued as Stated Supply until 1819 when the Rev. William Weir was installed as first pastor.

In November of 1812, the present lot was conveyed by John Bisland and his wife to the Committee of Trustees for building a Presbyterian brick meeting house in the city of Natchez.

Levi Weeks was contracted to design and build the brick church on the newly purchased property, which was situated on a high hill overlooking the city and the river. In June 1816, Adam Cloud delivered the first sermon in the new brick church.

Ten years later, the brick church was removed and the site was graded to its present level. A new church building, which forms essentially the present sanctuary, was constructed in 1828-29. In 1900 the Stratton Chapel was completed as a memorial to the Rev. Joseph B. Stratton who served the congregation over a span of 60 years.

In 1964 a new Educational Building was built on the half block immediately south of the church property.

This church continues to have a full program: Sunday School for all age groups, two Sunday worship services, an active Presbyterian Women's group, and a weekly Men's Prayer Breakfast. Community outreach programs include the Presbyterian Playschool Daycare Program, a Boy Scout troop, a weekly community cultural event and luncheon, and an annual blood drive. The church supports workers in the mission field in Mexico and Brazil, as well.

Our Church's Pastors:

1820-1822	William Weir
1823-1836	George Potts, D. D.
1837-1841	Samuel G. Winchester, D. D.
1843-1903	Joseph B. Stratton, D. D.
1890-1893	George W. Patterson, D. D.
1895-1898	William Hanna Neel, D. D.
1898-1915	James J. Chisolm, D. D.
1915-1921	Howard H. Thompson, D. D.
1922-1938	George D. Booth, D. D.
1938-1950	Stuart C. Henry, Ph. D.
1950-1955	J. Walton Stewart, Jr., D. D.
1955-1958	James V. Johnson, Jr.
1959-1964	J. Whitner Kennedy
1965-1974	Jac Covinton Ruffin, D. D.
1975-1979	R. Jefferson Coker
1991-1997	Matthew W. Covington, D. D.
1999-2003	David L. deVries

The First Presbyterian Church joyously welcomes all who would enter its doors.

First Presbyterian Church
Natchez, Mississippi

KINGSTON METHODIST CHURCH

Kingston was the setting for the first Protestant church in Mississippi, where the members probably met in homes. The church was organized in the Jersey Settlement in 1772 with Reverend Samuel Swayze, a Congregationalist, as pastor. The original Jersey Settlers were the families of Justus King, Obadiah Brown, Samuel Swayze and Richard Swayze. The land was surveyed by Caleb King who laid out and established the town of Kingston, about a mile from the original settlement. Caleb went back to New Jersey to marry Mary, daughter of Richard Swayze, and returned about 1775.

The Kingston Methodist Church was organized after the death of Reverend Samuel Swayze in 1800 by Reverend Tobias Gibson with seven people in the original membership: Caleb King, Gabriel Swayze, Lydia Swayze, Prudence Cory, Deborah Luce, Prudence Varnadoe and Eliza King. In 1803 Reverend Lorenzo Dow sold his watch to buy the first ground in Mississippi to be deeded for a Protestant church. The property was in Kingston, fronting on Claiborne Street and measured 40 by 60 feet in Block 2. The log building erected served the church and community as a church and school for about 20 years.

In 1822 Daniel Farrar, son-in-law of Caleb King, donated a plot of land on which a brick church was built. Trustees of this second lot were Solomon Swayze, George Varnadoe, and Daniel Farrar. The tornado of 1840 damaged this building, but it was still used until the erection of the present building.

The first meeting in connection with the present building was on November 13, 1855. On February 12, 1856, Alexander King Farrar and wife Ann Mary Dougharty "being desirous of having a new church erected in the Jersey Settlement, at or near Kingston for purposes of religious and moral culture" deeded approximately eight acres of land to the church trustees: G.W. Baynard, W.O. Foules, T.F. Davis, A.K. Farrar and Alexander Boyd.

The building began in 1856. It is a significant example of the ecclesiastical Greek Revival architecture based on its high degree of architectural finish, its excellent exterior and interior integrity, the integrity of its setting and the unique manner in which the grand temple form is employed on a small scale. It was ready for dedication on the first Sunday in May 1857; Reverend William Winans and Reverend William H. Watkins conducted the service.

An old-fashioned high pulpit adds a bit of formality and dignity. It has an upstairs gallery where slaves worshiped. An iron post through one of the pews supports the gallery, from the post to the end of the pew measures 32 inches. That is where Alexander King Farrar, a large man sat, filling the entire space.

In the 1930s and 1940s the pastor alternated Sundays with two, sometimes three, other churches: Mars Hill, Maple Street or Washington. Currently, Kingston has services each Sunday; the minister preaches first at Kingston, then at Lovely Lane.

In the 1950s the congregation saw the need of space for Sunday School classes and the first additional building was erected.

Led by the efforts of Webbie Edit, Dorothy Sojourner, and others, the church was put on the National Register of Historic Places; the acceptance ceremony was held at the church on September 12, 1982.

Desiring the comforts of central air and heat the ladies of the church participated in a variety of fund raisers and in 1994, when Charles Campbell was minister, the system was installed. During Campbell's tenure enlargement of the Sunday School building to provide a fellowship hall was begun; it was dedicated in 1999 while Mitchell Cochram was minister.

Kingston has a long and rich history, served by many notable ministers beginning with Tobias Gibson and has sent forth in the ministry two men, Boothe Poole and his brother Bill, who grew up in the Kingston church.

Each year on a Sunday in April a reunion of the Descendants of the Jersey Settlers is held at the church, followed by dinner on the grounds. In appreciation, the Descendants contribute some to the financial needs of the church. The congregation, while small in numbers, continues to put forth the effort needed to preserve the building and serve the community.

Kingston United Methodist Church (Picture courtesy of Ella McCaleb Young)

Interior of Kingston United Methodist Church (Picture courtesy of Ella McCaleb Young)

New Covenant Presbyterian Church

New Covenant Presbyterian Church in Natchez, Mississippi grew out of a Community Bible Study begun by a small group of local Presbyterians in the fall of 1993. It was their vision to raise up a new work in Natchez with an emphasis on Bible teaching, evangelism and outreach. Dr. Ligon Duncan, then assistant Professor of Theology at Reformed Theological Seminary (RTS) in Jackson agreed to lead the first lessons entitled *"The Power and Challenge of New Covenant Life - Themes in the Book of Hebrews.* Classes were held on Sunday evenings at the Howard Johnson Motel.

By January of 1994 the class had moved to First Lutheran Church, using visiting teachers and students from Reformed Seminary. In May it became a Mission Church in the Presbyterian Church in America. Thus New Covenant Presbyterian Church came into being, deriving its name from that first study of the book of Hebrews.

In August of 1994 the church sought a meeting place where a morning worship service could be held. The members of Temple B'Nai Israel were agreeable to allowing New Covenant to move to their historic sanctuary in downtown Natchez. Sunday School classes were begun and a Pastor Search Committee and Executive Committee were formed.

Throughout 1995 the church sought the man God would call to be its pastor. In February of 1996 that search led to the Rev. Mr. Dennis Flach a minister ordained in the Evangelical Presbyterian Church (EPC). A call was issued to him to become the organizing pastor of New Covenant. He accepted and moved with his family to Natchez. That fall, after much study and prayer, New Covenant requested release from the Presbyterian Church in America and came under the oversight of the Evangelical Presbyterian Church.

In the summer of 1998 Temple B'Nai Israel became a museum and it was necessary for New Covenant to find a new place of worship. Mrs. Luther Stowers owned the historic Commercial Bank building in downtown Natchez and agreed to rent it. On Sunday morning, September 13, 1998, New Covenant Presbyterian Church held the first worship service in that building which is its present home.

No longer a Mission church, New Covenant now enjoys full affiliation with the Evangelical Presbyterian denomination. Mr. Flach continues as pastor, Mr. Burnley Cook is organist and Dr. David Blackburn leads the congregational singing and special music. Worship Services are held each Sunday morning at 10:30 preceded by Sunday School for all ages at 9:15. Youth meetings with supper are held Sunday evenings at 6:00. Wednesday evening supper, song and prayer meeting begins at 5:30. At noon on Wednesdays a group meets for prayer and enjoys a brown bag lunch at the church.

New Covenant continues to attract a vital and diverse membership as it reaches into the community and surrounding area with the message of salvation through Jesus Christ alone by grace alone.

New Covenant Presbyterian Church

PARKWAY BAPTIST CHURCH

Parkway Baptist Church, originally named Fellowship, was organized in Natchez, Mississippi, on November 9, 1952. The council meeting was held in a small rented store building on Liberty Road across from the Johns-Manville plant. Rev. M. Ray Megginson, Associational Missionary of the Union Association, preached the sermon, and when the invitation was extended, 25 people came forward for membership.

On August 5, 1953, for $3,880 the church purchased from Grace McNeil (Mrs. Douglas) a building site on the 61 By-Pass just south of the Montebello subdivision. In February 1954, the first service was held in the newly-erected 76 X 35 foot building, which the men of the church had constructed entirely by themselves with donated time and materials. From that time on, Parkway Baptist Church has continued to grow and expand. During the past 50 years, six pastors have served Parkway:

Rev. M. Ray Megginson Nov. 26, 1952-June 28, 1959

Rev. Fred E. Robertson Aug. 17, 1959-Feb. 17, 1974

Rev. Gerald P. Buckley Aug. 4, 1974-Jan. 5, 1986

Dr. Randy W. Turner Sept. 14, 1986-May 10, 1992

Rev. Jimmy D. Sartain Oct. 18, 1992-Oct 6, 1996

Rev. Bart M. Walker Jan 4, 1998-

Each pastor's service has been in a different area of growth; including buildings, youth, community projects, home and foreign missions, and evangelism. Each pastor has guided Parkway to become the church it is today.

Occupying a complex of buildings on five acres of land situated on the most prominent corner in Natchez, Parkway has an annual budget of approximately $800,000 and a resident membership of 1,332. The staff includes four full-time ministers, four secretarial staff, two janitorial staff, and over 200 teachers and volunteers in many areas of service.

In addition to the regular services, special activities at Parkway include the following:

1) Wednesday Night Family Supper and Prayer Meeting

2) Monday Morning Intercessory Prayer Group

3) AWANA (Bible-centered program for children aged three through sixth grade)

4) FAITH (Evangelistic Ministry)

5) Priority (Youth Bible Study and Worship)

6) Youth Praise Band, Children, and Youth Choirs

It is the prayer of members and friends that God will continue to bless and support His Vision for His ministry at Parkway Baptist Church.

Parkway Baptist Church

TRINITY CHURCH OF NATCHEZ

"Trinity was the second Protestant Episcopal Church organized in the state of Mississippi, the first being that of Christ Church of Church Hill, in Jefferson County, which was established two years previously by the Rev. Adam Cloud. This clergyman first settled on St. Catherine Creek in Adams County as early as 1790, but was forced to leave by the Spanish government."[1] When the area became a Spanish Territory, all religions except the Roman Catholic were forbidden. Adam Cloud was exiled by the Spanish authorities for holding "discussion groups" in his home. They returned after the area became a territory of the United States.[2]

"Through the efforts of Dr. Stephen Duncan and his friends, the Rev. James Pilmore (1822-25) came to Natchez with the intention of establishing an Episcopal Church. He began his ministry on Sunday evening, May 10, 1822 in the Presbyterian Church." A congregation was established, money raised, the present building built, and the first service held in 1823. The building was an oblong red brick Federal style edifice surmounted by a large tin dome. Mr. Pilmore married Catherine Surget, the daughter of Pierre Surget, a wealthy citizen of Natchez.

"The Rev. A.A. Muller (1826-29) established the first Sunday School which boasted 35 children. The first Diocesan Convention was held there in 1826. In 1827 an organ built by Lord and Brothers from Philadelphia, Pennsylvania was installed. A place for people of color and servants to worship was created in the nave."[4]

On December 25, 1829, the Rt. Rev. Thomas Brownell consecrated Trinity Church and on Dec. 27th, he consecrated Christ Church, Church Hill.

When the Rev. Peirce Connelly was elected (1832-1835) Trinity had only 25 communicants, mostly women. By the time he resigned, the number had risen to 62. However, Rev. Connelly resigned to become a Roman Catholic, although he later returned to the Episcopal religion.[5]

In 1838 the dome was removed, the roof line reduced, an enriched Doric portico was added to the front, portland-tinted stucco was applied to the exterior. The seating capacity of the interior was enlarged and an undercroft was made for Sunday School[6] at a cost of $19,664.

The Rt. Rev. Leonidas Polk[7] re-consecrated the building on Easter April 19, 1840. A month later a tornado did $600 worth of damage to the church.

The second organ (from Hall & Laback of New York) was installed in 1851. (This organ was later replaced and is now the organ in use at the A.M.E. Church on MLK Street.)

During the Yellow Fever Epidemic of 1853 the Rev. John S. Chadbourne came from the Diocese of Louisiana to help. His father-in-law was General John A. Quitman, of Monmouth where Rev. Chadbourne died.

The Rev. Gideon Babcock Perry of Cleveland, Ohio served during the most eventful days of the Civil War. During that time General Beauregard appealed to the populace for metal, and the Vestry, believing it their duty, offered the Trinity Bell with this letter accompanying it: "Its tones are associated in our memories with peaceful Sabbath: it has summoned us and our children to the sacred temple for many years, but our land is ruthlessly invaded and we do not feel that we are desecrating a holy relic when we send it to assist in the salvation of our beloved country. In thus converting a peaceful into a deadly implement of war, we can hardly be accused of diverting it from a sacred use. Ours is a war for peace, not conquest, and our devout hope is that peace will soon be made between the two governments." The bell was never used for the purpose of warfare.

The Rev. Charles A. Dana (1866-73), found the parish greatly depressed because of the war. He had been rector of Christ Church, Alexandria, Virginia, where he had the honor of presenting Gen. Robert E. Lee to his bishop for confirmation.[8]

In 1873 the recessed chancel was added during the Rev. Alexander Mark's ministry. He and Charles Stietenroth had published *The Church News* at Trinity. Bishop Hugh Thompson transferred its publication to Jackson making it the official diocesan news paper. In 1991 it was renamed *The Mississippi Episcopalian*.

The Rev. Joseph Kuehnle (1914-46) was rector of Trinity longer than any other, with Rev. Louis O'Vander Thomas (1946-75) second. In 1918, a generous gift from Mr. N.L. Carpenter provided for restoration of the exterior to the Greek form. The Chancel Guild raised money for the interior and the ceiling of the dome was painted blue with gold fleur-de-lis symbolizing Trinity. A new rectory was purchased at 310 South Commerce. Trinity's Altar Guild, Ladies Guilds, the women of the Church, Sunday School and Young People's Service League were established at this time. The Parish House was named Kuehnle Hall as a memorial to the Rev. Kuehnle.

During the Rev. Thomas' ministry, Trinity Episcopal Day School was established. In 1970 the present school buildings were begun on its own school grounds on Highway 61 South. Its first commencement was held in 1971.

In 1976 the sesquicentennial of the Diocese of Mississippi was celebrated in Natchez.

The Rev. Limuel G. Parks Jr. oversaw the expansion and renovation of Kuehnle Hall. (David Peabody, architect) with its extension to the rear, an improved sacristy downstairs, and a choir room, office space for the organist and Master of Choristers, a music library and rooms for Christian education upstairs. His ministry was 1982-91.

In 1994 the church hosted the 167th annual diocesan council during Rev. Harry E. Allen's ministry (1991-95).

In 1996 the organ underwent extensive repair and restoration. Several new stops were added, most notable the "English State Trumpet" in the rear gallery, thus making it the largest and most versatile organ in the area.

The present rector is the Very Rev. Zabron Alfred (Chip) Davis III who was installed May 18, 1997 and the organist and choirmaster is Mr. Ignacious (Vincent Bache).

[1] *The First Hundred Years of Trinity Church*
[2] *The Righteous Rebel* by Catherine Cloud Templeton
[3] *Trinity Episcopal Church Natchez Mississippi* - Celebrating 175 years of Christian Faith
[4] Ibid #3
[5] A biography of Rev. Pierce Connelly, the father of four children, whose wife became a Roman Catholic nun –Trinity Church Library.
[6] Ibid #3
[7] *The Fighting Bishop*
[8] Rev. Dana was father of Dick Dana who lived with Octavia Dockery at Goat Castle and was wrongly accused of murder of Miss Merril, from *The Goat Castle Murder* by David Sansing & Carolyn Smith.

WASHINGTON UNITED METHODIST CHURCH

The Methodist Church at Washington, Mississippi, was organized in 1799 by Rev. Tobias Gibson, who came from South Carolina. This was the first Methodist church organized in Alabama, Louisiana, or Mississippi. It has the oldest congregation and the second oldest church building in Mississippi.

Charter members of the church were Randal Gibson and his wife, Harriet McKinley Gibson; William Foster and his wife, Rachel Smith Foster; Caleb Worley, a young man from Pennsylvania; and two servants whose identities are uncertain.

Services were held in a schoolhouse and the home of Randal Gibson until 1805. A union church was then built near the Jefferson College campus, and it was used by all denominations until it burned in 1810. The trial of Aaron Burr was held in that building. In 1812, a lot on the Jefferson College campus was secured from Lorenzo Dow, and a brick church building was erected. It was used until the present Methodist Church was constructed in 1828. This building was remodeled and the balconies were removed in 1902. A Sunday School annex, built in 1946, was removed and replaced by the current fellowship building in 1995.

Events in the church history include the wedding of Jonathan Jones and Miss Phebe Griffing, performed by Rev. Tobias Gibson on October 10, 1799. A Woman's Society was organized in the church in 1823, with Mrs. John C. Burruss, wife of the pastor, as president. Mrs. Caroline Matilda Thayer, head of Elizabeth Academy, was one of the leaders of this Society. Elizabeth Academy was established in 1818 as a Methodist school for girls. The students were an active part of this congregation until the school closed in 1845. Many of the Jefferson College students also attended this church.

A Sunday School was recorded in 1877, with Stephen L. Guice as superintendent. There was a Woman's Foreign Missionary Society active in 1887. J. Allen Lindsey, a member of the Mississippi Conference, was licensed to preach from this church. At least eleven of the pastors of the church had sons who entered the ministry.

The church records include the names of all pastors of the Washington Church since 1799. In 2003, the list included 126 pastors over 204 years of ministry. There is a small but active congregation with a choir, United Methodist Women's Group, a Ladies Circle, and Sunday School. Services are held at 11:00 each Sunday.

Washington United Methodist Church

WESTMINSTER PRESBYTERIAN CHURCH

"A FAMILY OF GOD'S PEOPLE"
33 FATHERLAND ROAD
NATCHEZ, MISSISSIPPI

In September of 1955, Mississippi Presbytery recommended to First Presbyterian Church of Natchez that consideration be given to the establishment of a second church in the area. A group of 35 Presbyterian families (mostly members of First Presbyterian) took the challenge to organize the first new church in the Presbytery in over 40 years. The plans were officially formulated in 1956.

In January 1957, Mississippi Presbytery approved these plans, and voted to call James W. Campbell as organizer of the new church in which he would later be ordained. Permission was granted for the church to use the National Guard Armory on Liberty Road for temporary worship services, and the first service was held on Sunday, July 21, 1957 with 75 people in attendance.

The Church Steering Group included: Mrs. Amanda Baker, Charles Fort, R.E. Lyon, David Aldridge, Fenner Parham, Wade Hart and Mrs. Dodie Regel. On August 25, 1957, the congregation voted to use the name Westminster. Four Elders: Charles Fort, R.E. Lyon, Fenner Parham, and Carl Regel; and six Deacons: Henry C. Doherty, David Aldridge, Holly Baker, Roger Beacham, Sidney Bunch, and Wade Hart, were elected.

The Mississippi Presbytery conducted an official Service of Organization of Westminster Church on November 3, 1957. In April 1958, through the generous gift of Mrs. Grace S. McNeil and First Presbyterian Church, property on Fatherland Road was acquired and a church building was constructed. The architect was Beverly Martin. The first worship service in the church on Fatherland Road was held on July 26, 1959, and Westminster Presbyterian Church has continuously functioned as an organized church fellowship in Natchez to the present time.

Westminster had long planned to add a sanctuary to its church plant, since the original structure was only an educational building. Rev. D.M. Mounger, a member of the Presbytery's Committee on Church Extension charged with using church properties constructively, suggested that an abandoned 1854 church building in Cannonsburg was available. On October 17, 1979, Southern Mississippi Presbytery voted unanimously to give this historic building, known as Greenwood Presbyterian Church, to Westminster.

In September 1980, Willard Builders began to move the antebellum structure from Cannonsburg. The building was then completely dismantled and reconstructed on the Natchez site. The original building was 30 x 50 feet and contained approximately 80,000 antebellum bricks, which now cover the outside of the reconstruction. The sanctuary was enlarged to 38 x 67 feet to accommodate the present congregation. Fifteen of the original pews are in use. The sanctuary was dedicated on June 28, 1981.

Pastors serving Westminster since its founding in 1957 have included:

James Campbell	1957-1962
Hallet Hullinger	1963-1967
Gordon Lyle	1968-1970
Joe Vaughn	1971-1974
Edward Page	1975-1977
Paul Mixon	1979-1987
Chris Roseland	1989-1993
Blair Cash	1995-1997
Ronald Stoker	1998-2000
Brock Watson	2002-present

CHARTER MEMBERS

October 22, 1957—The Mississippi Presbytery was presented a petition signed by 95 people requesting organization of Westminster Presbyterian Church.

December 31, 1957 Charter membership closed with 102 signatures.

Mr. and Mrs. William Arrant
Mr. and Mrs. B. David Aldridge Jr.
Mr. and Mrs. Holly Baker
Mr.* and Mrs. Robert E. Bee
Mrs. Bert V. Blake*
Mr.* and Mrs. W.L. Blick*
Miss Maria Wetzel Bowser
Mr.* and Mrs. Sidney D. Bunch Jr.
Mrs. F.L. Callon*
Mrs. A.E. Cameron
Donald Albert Cameron*
Mrs. James W. Campbell
Mr.* and Mrs. Henry Charles Doherty
James Neil Downing
Mr.* and Mrs. F.W. Eppinette*
Mr. and Mrs. L.S. Fite
Mr.* and Mrs. Charles S. Fort*
Mr.* and Mrs. J.D. Glisson
Miss Beverly E. Glisson
Miss Mary Carolyn Glisson
Mrs. R.E. Green*
Mr. Robert Hadskey
Mr. and Mrs. Wade Hart
Mr.* and Mrs. Robert E. Honnoll Jr.*
Mr.* and Mrs. A.D. Koch*
Alfred E. Koch*
Mr. and Mrs. Jason Kutack
Mr. and Mrs. D.L. Ladner
Mr.* and Mrs. Charles S. Lambert
Mr.* and Mrs. Ralph Lewis
Mr. and Mrs. Ernest Limbaugh Jr.
Miss Kendra Limbaugh
Miss Arralee Lyon
Paul J. Lyon
Miss Lattye Ellen Lewis
Mr.* and Mrs. R.E. Lyon
Mr. and Mrs. Craig McKinnon
Mr. and Mrs. Charles Mangum
Mr.* and Mrs. Charles Mayfield*
Miss Cecil McCoy*
Mr.* and Mrs. Frank McGehee
Mr.* and Mrs. Eugene Murray
Mr. and Mrs. John Rexford North Jr.
John Rexford North, III
Mrs. Martha Overby*
Mrs. Everett Paradise*

Mr.* and Mrs. Fenner Parham*
Mrs. R. Lee Parker Jr.*
Mrs. R. Lee Parker, III*
Mr. and Mrs. Robert R. Reeves
Mr.* and Mrs. Carl Regel
Mr.* and Mrs. Frank Rigell*
Mrs. E.W. Rinard*
Mrs. Lloyd Smith*
Gerald Lloyd Smith
Carroll Lee Sojourner*
Mrs. Carroll P. Sojourner
Miss Ellen Hart Sojourner
Mrs. E.P. Stone
Mr. and Mrs. C.A. Thompson
Mr. and Mrs. Sidney E. Thomas
Sidney E. Thomas, III*
Mr.* and Mrs. E.W. Torrey*
Mr. and Mrs. Alex Waites
Mr. and Mrs. Harold Waller
Mr.* and Mrs. Louis W. Willard *
Mrs. Clara S. Williams*
Mr. and Mrs. David H. Williams
Mr.* and Mrs. Sandy Woods

* Known Deceased

OLD CATHEDRAL BOYS SCHOOL

The Final Four–shown above, enjoying their Class of '35 reunion, are from left: Charles Cochran, Morris Raphael, Carl Hicks and Edmund Burke. They were the last ones to graduate from the old Cathedral Boys' School which was located on the corner of Main and Union. The Brothers of Sacred Heart ceased their operations in Natchez after the 1935 session and the Sisters of Charity took over the Catholic boys and girls schools in the city. Presently, Cathedral's modern complex on Martin Luther King Drive, stands out as an outstanding educational institution. (Extract from Morris Raphael's My Natchez Years, *used with permission.)*

Main and Union Streets during the snow of 1948. The Old Cathedral School can be seen in the background.

Bishop Oliver Gerow was loved by parishoners and others all across the Parish. He was an intellect, historian, and a very religious person. This photo was taken in later years (1950's) during the dedication of the new Cathedral High School. Shown from left, standing are: Carl Voss, Freddie Ferguson, Freddie Voss, Mayor Willie Byrne, Bennie Ferguson (hidden), Bishop Gerow, State Representative and Speaker of the House Johnny Junkin, Profilet Couillard, August Stone, Andrew Burns. Seated is Billy Sojourner. (Extract from Morris Raphael's My Natchez Years, *used with permission.)*

41

St. Mary's Orphanage for girls, located at the corner of Jefferson Street and Rankin Street (Picture Courtesy of Liz Garrity)

Natchez Area Families

ADAMS FAMILY.

Family lore states that William Adams was a wealthy landowner in Natchez in the late 1700s and was a riverboat captain, although no proof of that occupation has been found. He was supposedly a first cousin of President John Adams, and Adams County was named for this family.[1] William was listed as a native of Kentucky,[2] but a family Bible entry lists his 1755 birth in Pittsburgh, PA. William moved to Natchez with his parents, Richard and Eleanor Adams, sometime prior to 1783.[3] In 1797 he married Orpha Leonard in Natchez.[4] Orpha was already a fifth-generation American, as her great-great grandmother, Sarah Heath/Heald, was born in 1623 in Massachusetts. Sarah's husband, John Leonard, was born in England and was killed by Indians in Massachusetts in 1676.[5]

Three generations later, Orpha's parents *Joseph and Mary McIntyre Leonard, and others, were part of the General Thaddeus Lyman party who sailed from Connecticut in December 1773 for New Orleans. There they boarded flat boats that were poled up the Mississippi River headed for their claim between the Tombigbee and Bayou Pierre. It was on that trip that Mary died....*[6]

William was an active gentleman who lived to be 102 years old. His obituary states: *AN OLD MAN GONE. The oldest resident in our county, Mr. William Adams, has been gathered to his fathers. His precise age is not known, but his own recollection went back to a period considerably ante-dating the American Revolution, at which time he was living in the Yazoo Swamp Country. His reported age, which we presume is about correct, at any rate not underestimated, was 102. Mr. Adams had been a resident of this county upwards of 70 years.*[7]

Even though he could not read or write, William Adams became a prosperous farmer and slave holder. He lived to be 102...and had 12 children...Willed a granddaughter, Clarissa Fowler, a plantation, the rest of his vast holdings in Mississippi and Louisiana...he willed to his son-in-law James Ballance...Later James Ballance deeded each of the Adams boys a plantation.[8] William's estate had an estimated worth of $130,000.[9] It is interesting to note that William had 12 children, but did not remember all of them or their descendants in his will.

William had two daughters, Marcy and Catherine, who were not mentioned in the will at all. Marcy was married[10] and preceded her father in death.[11] She had two surviving children, however, William and Hiram Fowler. Catherine married David Warnock,[12] but both she and her husband had died, leaving their surviving children: Eliza, Mary, Benjamin and Joseph Warnock.[13] None of these living children were remembered in their grandfather's will. Thus it appears that Marcy and Catherine Adams and their descendants got nothing from William Adams' estate.

Obviously the family dynamics were not always smooth. There was heartache and hardship as well. William and Orpha's youngest daughter, Cordelia, died in 1819 when she was 2 years old.[14] And Orpha was an invalid for 49 years prior to her death.[15] *Submitted by Kathy Herzog.*

Note: The submitter's husband, Ben Herzog, is the great-great-great-great grandson of William Adams, and great-great grandson of Eliza Warnock Jordan Lanier.

[1]Lanier, Ethel Breland. *The Lanier, Breland and Clark Families in Mississippi*. January 1976, p. 6-7.

[2]Mississippi Department of Archives, Jackson, MS, *"True Copy of Sacramental Record of Roman Catholic Church, St. Joseph Church, Baton Rouge, LA* Item #846, p. 13: translated from Spanish, Guilermo Adams native of Kentucci (sic), eldest son of Ricardo Adams and Elenora __, and Orphy Leonard, native of this region, daughter of Jose and Maria, state their intention to contract marriage...23 Feb 1797."

[3]McBee, May Wilson. *The Natchez Court Records, 1767-1805, Abstracts of Early Records*. (Ann Arbor, Michigan: Edwards Brothers, Inc., 1953), p. 12: Richard Adams witness to estate proceedings for James Gillason, deceased, at Natchez, 10 May 1782. (Book found in Mississippi Archives, Jackson, MS, call 976.3 N19)

[4]Mississippi Department of Archives, Jackson, MS, "True Copy of Sacramental Record of Roman Catholic Church, St. Joseph Church, Baton Rouge, LA Item 846, p. 13.

[5]Saunders, M.M.; Sacramento, CA.

[6]Claiborne's History of Mississippi, written in the late 1800s.

[7]Natchez Daily Courier, Natchez, MS, 1 Apr 1857.

[8]Lanier, Ethel Breland. *The Lanier, Breland and Clark Families in Mississippi*. January, 1976, p. 6-7.

[9]Adams County Probate Court Estate packet 166 for William Adams Sr.

[10]Burroughs, Anna Sutton. Record from Adams Addenda, c/o GR&P, 6611 Clayton Road #4, St. Louis, MO 63117, has at the top of data "MS State Historical 1953 2:90f5/303": entry lists William and Orpha's children, "copied from Bible," states Marcy L. married Hiram Fower on 20 Jan. 1836.

[11]Ragland, Mary Lois. *A Partial List of Private Cemeteries in Adams County*.

[12]Mississippi Marriage Book 6, page 16.

[13]Eliza Ann Warnoc of the Old Natchez District. *Mississippi River Routes*, Vol. I, No. 1, Fall 1993, pp. 7-12.

[14]Ragland, Mary Lois. *A Partial List of Private Cemeteries in Adams County*.

[15]Lanier, Ethel Breland. *The Lanier, Breland and Clark Families in Mississippi*. January, 1976.

DAVID ALDRIDGE & BEVERLY BAKER

descend from two young adventurers, both named Thomas, who settled in the Natchez area.

Thomas Aldridge (b. 1774 in Maryland) claimed land on the Homochitto by 1803 and in 1808, married Catharine King, (b. 1789 in South Carolina), daughter of a Scotsman David King, who immigrated in time to serve America in the Revolution. Thomas owned a farm in Franklin County where he and Catharine reared their 10 children. One son was William (b. 1821) who married Caroline Massey (b. 1833) in 1858. They had two sons when he joined the 14th Cavalry in the Civil War. Eventually they had five sons, one of whom was Thomas Aldridge (b. 1862 in Hamburg, MS).

Thomas married Josephine Eliza Hart (b. 1872 in Lincoln County), a descendant of pioneer settler John Bryan Hart, a Revolutionary veteran. They inherited and farmed Hart lands in Lincoln County and had seven children, one being Byron David Aldridge I (b. 1898). Byron served in France in WWI, later marrying Carrie Starkey (b. 1896) in 1920. They had three small children when Byron, employed by Illinois Central Railroad, died following a brief illness. Carrie also died young and her children were reared by their cousin, S.J. Greer and his wife, Annie Ruth Junkin Greer, of Adams County.

David and Beverly Aldridge

One of Byron and Carrie's children was Byron David II, born in Lincoln County, MS. Following service in both European and Pacific theaters during WWII, David attended the University of Tennessee and graduated from the University of Southern Mississippi. He was vice president of Delta Delta Chapter, Delta Tau Delta fraternity. He retired as a forest engineer with International Paper Company and holds a U.S. patent in connection with his work. He is also a published novelist.

In 1950 David married Beverly Alice Baker at First Presbyterian Church in Natchez. Beverly descends from the other Thomas, Thomas Baker (b. 1791).

Thomas came to Church Hill from New Jersey in 1817 becoming a merchant in old Greenville. Thomas married Eliza McKinney Green (b. 1802), daughter of Thomas Marston Green I of Virginia, who settled near Church Hill in 1781. Their son, Everard Green Baker I (b. 1826), md. Laura Alexander (b. 1834), daughter of Amos Alexander, whose family came to the Kingston area in 1772. Their son, Everard II (b. 1853), md. Nevitt Fleming (b. 1856) at Jeanette Plantation in 1885. Nevitt descended from David Fleming of North Carolina who was in Adams County by 1802.

One of their six children, Everard III (b. 1889) md. secondly Jocelyn Dameron Parham (b. 1904 at Arcola Plantation, L'Argent, LA). Jocelyn descended from Dr. John Greenway Parham of New Orleans.

Their daughter Beverly, an honor graduate of the University of Southern Mississippi and Louisiana State University, was a librarian with the Natchez Public Schools. David and Beverly have three children: Mary Alyn Laudermilk of Gautier, Byron David Aldridge III of Atlanta, and Courtney Greenway Aldridge of Natchez, 13 grandchildren and one great-grandchild.

LYMAN DAVENPORT ALDRICH II & ELIZABETH BALFOUR FRANKLIN.

Elizabeth, known to all as Betsy, was born on Oct. 2, 1911 in Natchez, MS, to Joseph Louis Franklin and Katherine Hunt Balfour Franklin. Her family originally emigrated from Scotland in the year 1770, and her maternal ancestor, Robert Dunbar, settled at Ivy Place, three miles north of Natchez, and in 1780 made his home at Oakley Grove.

She is the great-great-granddaughter of Anne and David Hunt of Woodlawn Plantation, whose daughter Catherine married William Suggs Balfour. The Balfours built Homewood where Betsy's mother, Katherine Hunt, and her sisters Marie and Josephine were reared.

She is the granddaughter of Elizabeth Gartley Balfour and William Suggs Balfour II, a cousin who also resided at Homewood. Her parents, Katherine and Joseph Louis Franklin, were married at Homewood in 1904. Mr. Franklin was a purser on the *Little Rufus* and the *Betsy Ann*. His parents were Morris and Emma Oppenheim Franklin of New York.

Betsy lived with her family in Natchez until age 7, when they moved to New Orleans, LA. They later lived in Dallas, TX, where Betsy graduated from North Dallas High School. The family relocated to Austin, TX in order for Betsy and her brothers, Joe and Balfour, to attend the University of Texas. Upon completing her junior year of college, Betsy married Lyman Davenport Aldrich II (b. 1903, d. 1951), of Natchez and New York on ?n. 5, 1932, at the Alpha Delta Pi sorority house ? the campus of the University of Texas. Mr. ?drich's parents were Lyman Davenport Aldrich ?r. and Grace Darling Ballard of Coventry Place near Washington, MS.

Betsy and Lyman resided in New York, where he was employed with New York Life Insurance Co. While in New York, both Lyman and Betsy became accomplished photographers. It was here their children: Elizabeth Balfour (b. 1935-), Linda Buckner (b. 1939-), and Lyman Davenport III (b. 1943-), were born. They remained in New York until his retirement in 1950, when they returned to make their home in Natchez among family and friends. Within a brief year and while building their home at Point "D," a part of Coventry Plantation, Lyman suffered a stroke and died suddenly and unexpectedly in 1951 at the young age of 47. Betsy completed building their home and rearing their children at Point "D." She owned and operated a restaurant, continued her photography, educated her children and instilled in each a deep appreciation for the richness of their Natchez heritage.

Among Betsy's most cherished childhood memories were her many visits to Natchez with her brothers. They were invited each year to visit their aunt and uncle, Marie Balfour and James E. O'Kelley of Rosehill Plantation near Kingston. She and her brothers were sent by train to Natchez, where their summers were filled

Elizabeth Balfour Franklin Aldrich

with horseback riding, lawn tennis, and swimming parties at Rosehill, and enjoyed dances, community activities and visiting friends and family in the Natchez area.

Betsy, in her 92nd year, is enjoying good health and living an active life at her home in Memphis, TN, with her children, grandchildren, and great-grandchildren nearby. She is beloved and cherished by family and friends alike and is appreciated for her gracious manner, charm, and beauty.

CHARLES T. ALEXANDER & ROSE ELIZABETH CARKEET.
Charles, born about 1845 in England, owned a wholesale millinery on Main Street in Natchez. On Nov. 13, 1882, he married Rose Elizabeth Carkeet. She was born on Oct. 26, 1861 to William and Margaret (Paine) Carkeet of Natchez. She was a granddaughter of Thomas and Eliza Jane (Junkins) Paine. (See Eliza Jane Junkins and Thomas Paine.)

Charles and Rose Alexander had five children:
1) Ethel Alexander was born in Natchez and died on Dec. 14, 1922.
2) Ruth W. Alexander (b. Apr. 8, 1893 in Natchez) md. William F. Frazier on Jun. 27, 1918. Their only child, Jacqueline R. Frazier, was born on Jul. 23, 1919. On May 1, 1960, Ruth died and is buried in Natchez City Cemetery.

3) Hobson M. Alexander (b. Nov. 10, 1884) md. Anna Scheffy on Jul. 5. 1916. Anna (b. Dec. 7, 1878) was from Northampton, PA. Hobson died on May 9, 1954 and Anna died on Dec. 5, 1977. They are both buried in Natchez City Cemetery.
4) Charles F. Alexander (b. Apr. 29, 1891 in Natchez) md. Edith A. Foster on Dec. 24, 1912. Edith was a descendant of Captain A.H. and Mary Kate (Wood) Foster. Charles died on Jan. 5, 1970 and Edith died on Jan. 2, 1966. They are both buried in Natchez City Cemetery.
5) Walter B. Alexander (b. Jul. 27, 1896 in Natchez) served in WWII as a private.
On Jan. 22, 1900, Charles T. Alexander died at the age of 55 and Rose Elizabeth (Carkeet) Alexander died on Jul. 9, 1917. Both Charles T. and Rose are buried in Natchez City Cemetery.

Sources: Official Records and written family history, recorded by Hattie Kline Monsell before 1948. *Submitted by Ginga Hathaway and Marilyn Baland Gibson.*

ARNDT FAMILY.
(5) George Arndt (b. Jan. 26, 1827, Alsace, d. Aug. 13, 1882, Jackson, MS) md. Caroline Russo (b. May 11, 1832 in Germany, d. Feb. 5, 1880 New Orleans, LA), both were buried in Rodney, MS. They came from Heidelburg (had a famous uncle in Germany who wrote the song *The Fatherland*) and went to New Orleans. Children: Micheal (b. Jul. 2, 1859, d. Dec. 6, 1887), Lena, Henry, George, Emma Mayer, Bettie Brook, Mary K. O'Brien (b. Jul. 31, 1854, d. Jan 12, 1906, buried in Rodney). Emma, Bettie and Mary lived in New Orleans. George lived in Ocean Springs. They had a cousin named George Arndt living in Houston with a son Scott Arndt (b. 1967).

(4) Lena Arndt married Emile Engbarth. Lena was wealthy, spoiled (had only the best of everything, a trait Gaugau tried to emulate). Children: Minneapolis Katherine (b. 1892, d. 1970), Montana, Caroline, George, Claude, William, Charles, Joseph, Chester (died as an infant). Monty had no children; Carrie and Joe had no children; Claude had daughter, Claudia, red headed, (b. ca. 1945); George had lots of children in Michigan; Willie had Louise who had no children; Charles had Charles Jr. and Evelyn married Barrett, lived in Maine and had children and grandchildren.

(3) Minneapolis Katherine Engbarth (b. Jun. 10, 1892, d. Aug. 29, 1970) md. Dec. 25, 1925 in Ocean Springs, Stanley Melton Burkley (b. Mar. 16, 1879, d. Oct. 30, 1949) both buried in Natchez City Cemetery. Children: Stanley Engbarth (b. Oct. 5, 1926, blond); twins-Joseph Emile, red head, and Margaret Jeannette, brunette, were born Feb. 18, 1928.

(2) Margaret Jeannette Burkley (b. Feb. 18, 1928) md. first Neville Buck Marshall (b. Dec. 10, 1924, d. Dec. 26, 1990). Margaret married second Larry Ferney in 1970, no children.

Children: Margaret Katherine "Kathy" Marshall (b. Oct. 12, 1950) md. Monroe Jackson Moody Jr. Children: Monroe Jackson "Jack" III (b. Feb. 15, 1968, d. Mar. 1, 2002, Houston, TX, buried in Laurel Hill in Adams County, MS) md. Cara Winter in 1997, son Monroe Jackson IV (b. Apr. 26, 2001); Merrick Rowan Dashiell (b. Feb. 6, 1972) md. Jacqueline Passbach Jan. 13, 2001.

Marion Jeannette Marshall (b. Apr. 1, 1952) md. first Godfrey Forrester; married second John Darius Tassistro; married third Mike Holloway; married fourth Mark Drennen. Children: Angelique "Angie" Devereux Tassistro (b. May 12, 1974), Rodney Darius Tassistro (b. Feb. 21, 1976), Adrienne Marshall Drennen (b. Feb. 7, 1985). They live in St. Francisville, LA.

Charlotte Elizabeth Agnes Anne Marshall (b. Jul. 13, 1953) md. first Elliot Brumfield; md. second Alan Edmonds. Children: Charlotte Aaron

Brumfield (b. Sep. 6, 1974, married first Casey Smith, son Walker (b. Aug. 21, 1996); married second Jason Hennington, daughter Presley (b. 2001); Chesney Dawn Brumfield (b. Jun. 2, 1976) md. Jeremiah Wheeler, daughter Miah (b. Apr. 26, 2002), Elliot Buck Brumfield (b. Oct. 5, 1978), Rachel Megan Edmonds (b. May 7, 1981) md. Wesley Givens, son Marshall (b. Feb. 10, 2001).

Malquin Morgan Marshall (b. Aug. 29, 1954) md. first Salvo Piazza and married second Peter Pevonka. Children: Emily Johanna Piazza (b. Jan. 17, 1976), Jessica Conchetta Magdalena Piazza (b. May 17, 1977).

Neville Buck Marshall II (b. Sep. 12, 1957) md. Beth Anderson. Children: Charlotte Kay (b. Dec. 24, 1988), Morgan Keene (b. Sep. 22, 1991). *Submitted by Charlotte Marshall.*

RICHARD WATTS ASHTON & MARY DEVEREUX.
Mary accompanied by her daughter, Julia, came to the Natchez area between 1850-60 to live with her sister, Julia (Devereux) Kibbe at Coventry Plantation near Washington, MS.

Mary, daughter of Katherine (Keane/Keefe) and Patrick Ellis Devereux was baptized Jan. 15, 1815, St. Finbarr Catholic Church, Cork, Ireland. The family, including her sister Julia (b. ca. 1817) and brother Edward (b. ca. 1819), were forced to flee to America from Ireland in 1820 because of Patrick's having engaged in shipping grain from

Mary (Devereux) Ashton (b. 1815, Ireland, d. 1890, Natchez)

Ireland to the French army during the Napoleonic Wars. Patrick secured a position as storekeeper in the US Navy Yard in Washington, DC. A son, John Pierre, was born about 1821, Washington, DC. Patrick was killed by a fall from a horse in 1825. His widow, Catherine married second, Victor Ferren, Feb. 6, 1826, Washington DC.

Mary Devereux married Richard Watts Ashton (b. 1799, d. 1853), son of Elizabeth (Scott) and Lawrence Ashton, Aug. 4, 1835, at Warrenton, Farquier County, VA. Richard who had run away from school to fight during the War of 1812, went on to be a cadet at West Point, and was commissioned 2nd lieutenant in the Marine Corps where he served until his discharge in 1821.

Mary bore Richard six sons and one daughter. Two sons died as children; the remaining four sons fought in the Civil War.

John Devereux (b. 1836, d. 1888) enlisted April 1861, Company D, 2nd Georgia Reg. Army CSA; made captain in 1862; wounded, taken prisoner and spent two years on Johnsons Island. He married Sarah Roberts and had issue.

William Whetcroft (b. 1837, d. 1913) enlisted April 1861 in Company D, 2nd Georgia Regular Army CSA; later transferred to Company D, 2nd Louisiana; promoted to 2nd sergeant; wounded at 2nd Manassas, Chancellorsville; at Appomattox; practiced medicine, Alexandria, LA; married Nellie Holland. Their only child died in infancy.

James Scott (b. 1838, d. 1873), educated at VMI, Lexington, VA; enlisted April 1861, Pelican Rifles 2nd Louisiana Infantry CSA; elected 2nd lieutenant; promoted to captain, 1862; lost an arm at 2nd Manassas; rejoined his command; wounded again at Chancellorsville; broken in health, on the recommendation of General Robert E. Lee promoted to major; assigned to Enrollment Bureau Trans Mississippi Department. He was an attorney in Shreveport, LA; married first, Natlie Maples and second, Sallie Land; died of yellow fever four weeks after his second marriage; buried at Oakland Cemetery, Shreveport, LA. No issue.

Richard Watts (b. 1840, dsp 1862) educated Culpepper Military Institute; moved to Mansfield, LA to study law; enlisted April 1861, Pelican Rifles 2nd Louisiana Infantry CSA; elected 1st lieutenant, appointed adjutant of his regiment; was a major when killed at age 22 in the battle of Malvern Hill. He had written a letter to his sister only two weeks before his death, telling her that he thought the war would soon be over.

Julia Devereux (b. 1842, d. 1915) md. Wilmer Shields; Robert Lee (b. 1844. dsp 1852); Harrison Taylor (b. 1849, dsp l858). Mary was living with her widowed daughter, Julia Devereux (Ashton) Shields, when she died in 1890. She is buried in the Natchez City Cemetery. *Submitted by Clare Louise (Mills) Jares.*

GEORGE BACON & ARELLA GRANGER.

Arella was born Mar. 22, 1941 in Wilkinson County to Martha Shropshire (b. Aug. 18, 1905) and Joseph Granger Sr. (b. Jun. 22, 1903) of Wilkinson County. Besides Arella, they were parents of other children: Viola Chatman (b. Sep. 7, 1926); Alonzo Granger (b. Apr. 25, 1928); Joseph Granger Jr. (b. May 5, 1930); Helen Hayes (b. Feb. 25, 1932) and Dorothy Granger. They met at church, married in 1924, and moved to Adams County in 1946 to live on a plantation owned by Francis Geddes to be farmers.

After the age of 5, Arella grew up in the Kingston area where she remembers not being able to ride in a car and having to ride in a wagon to the gravel road, owned by Uncle Herod Granger. She attended a one-room school where she had to walk three miles to school with memory of the out-

Arella Granger Bacon

door toilet. She was motivated to attend college as her older sisters and brothers continued to work in the fields with crops. Later, Arella attended Natchez College for two years. She graduated from Alcorn State University with a BS in elementary education and reading in 1965.

Her first job was teaching second grade at Jefferson County Elementary School. She later married at her brother's house on Jan. 1, 1966 to George Bacon from Kingston, MS. He did body work for Jordan Auto Co. and owned his own body shop. He also did construction work. He passed away in March 2000. They had two children, Dr. Rhonda Bacon Thigpen (b. Jan. 5, 1967) and George Bacon Jr. (b. Nov. 2, 1975).

Arella has many accomplishments and community involvements. She retired in 1992 and founded and directed the Thompson After-School-Center in an old band room. She also bought a piece of land and established the Linwood Ruritan Park. She is a great asset to Jerusalem Baptist Church #2 where she is a Sunday school teacher and an usher. She has been a 4-H leader for 31 years, chairman of Keep Natchez/Adams Beautiful and a member of Alcorn State University Writing Project. She was responsible for bringing Ruritan to Natchez/Louisiana (13 clubs). She was a member of Chamber of Commerce Unification

Board and a member of the Crime Stoppers Board.

Arella's involvement has brought her over 30 awards and plaques, including the Give award, given by the state governor for dedicated volunteer work with children. She also received awards for being one of the hundred most volunteer women given by Eckerd's in Atlanta, GA. She received one of the JC Penney 250 and 1,000 dollar awards as a volunteer. She was recognized as an Alcorn State University Writing Project Mentor for motivating teachers and students to write in Jefferson County Jr. High. In addition, she has one special achievement - she has written her own book entitled *Mama, You Taught Me Well.*

Arella believes if you keep God first in your life, success is yours. *Submitted by Arella Bacon.*

WILLIAM BARLAND, son of James Barland (b. 1727) and Margaret McGuthie, was born in 1751 in Perth, Scotland. Twenty-five years later, he was in the New World and settled in New Spain, later called Natchez.

William received a British crown grant of 105 acres. When the British ceded the territory to Spain in 1779 Barland was allowed to keep his land. Around 1784 or, perhaps, a bit earlier, William gained the companionship of a young Mulatto slave named Elizabeth then owned by a Jonahs Hailer (Iler, Isler, or Eiler). The original "bill of sale" dated May 17, 1790, listed in Book B, Page 446, Natchez Court records, identifies her as a Mulatto woman, age 25, and born in America. Barland paid Jonahs Hailer $1,700 for Elizabeth and the four children fathered by Barland. The oldest of these children was born in 1785. They had 12 children.

Barland never married but his will speaks about the deep affection shared between the two. In one reference to the purchase of Elizabeth, Barland said that he had purchased the freedom of his friend and companion. That freedom had been formalized first under Spanish law and again under U.S. manumission. Barland posted a $10,000 bond to satisfy the requirements of the Legislature of the Mississippi territory for such act. By today's dollar, that would be roughly $250,000. This manumission included their children and grandchildren. It was against the law for a white man to marry a Mulatto or Black woman.

Barland worked initially as a tailor as he had in Scotland. The Barlands in Scotland were bleachers, tanners, tailors, weavers, glovers, etc. In Natchez, William Barland became a land broker by dividing his land-grant property into downtown-Natchez lots. When acreage was selling for $1 an acre, Barland sold small lots for $70. One lot in Center Square sold for $850 in June 1806.

The first Methodist church in Natchez was built on Barland land and so were Baptist and Catholic churches. The Elms sits on Barland property. With this income Barland bought more land. He purchased a parcel of 500 acres in the Douglas area from John Bisland, which was located approximately three miles from the fort in Natchez. This became his plantation in Pine Ridge where he lived until his death.

Barland had approximately 4,500 acres at the time of his death, not including land acquired for resale or his lots in Natchez. Each of his children inherited money and 320 acres. The Pine Ridge plantation was held to provide for the needs of Elizabeth until her death. A devout Presbyterian, Barland was interred on his plantation at his death in 1818.

The family home no longer stands and the family cemetery plot is no longer identifiable. The Barland name vanished from the Natchez area many years ago, but his descendants can still be found in Mississippi, Louisiana, Illinois, Michigan,

California, Texas, Tennessee and Kentucky. William Barland was a founding father of the city of Natchez. *Submitted by Francis D. Huber Jr.*

JOHN BARLOW died in Natchez of yellow fever on Sep. 17, 1829. He was probably born in the Carolinas about 1767. On Friday, Feb. 9, 1810, Bryant Barlow had a passport issued by the Gov. of Georgia to pass through the Indian lands, and we think he came to look for land for the family. On Thursday, Jan. 10, 1811 John and his son, Bryant, were issued a passport to cross the Creek Indian Lands, from Wilkinson County, GA, and moved with the help of their seven Negro slaves. We think the John Barlow who received land in the 1807 Georgia Land Lottery and the one requesting a passport to cross the Indian lands are the same as the one that lived in Perry County, MS. The land received in the lottery was in Wilkinson County, GA and the passports for John and Bryant state they were from Wilkinson County.

John and Lydia, her last name possibly may be Bryant, married about 1789 according to a lawsuit filed in Hinds County for divorce in September 1827 by Lydia. They had 10 children living at that time, seven of which were married. Oh, how I wish that lawsuit had named them, as it has been very difficult to determine all the girls. These are the children we have determined are theirs: William Bryant (b. 1791 in Robison County, NC) md. Nancy Herrington; Henry "Buck" (b. 1794, North Carolina) md. Charity Millsaps then Miranda Hayman; Missouri (b. ca. 1802) md. Southall Myrick; John Jr. (b. Sep. 15, 1804) md. Mary "Polly" Millsaps; Nathaniel Green, a twin (b. Jul. 6, 1813, Mississippi) md. Mary Byrd; George Washington, a twin, married Flora Ann Byrd, a sister of Mary's. It has been difficult, as we have not found sufficient legal documents to determine all the children. Cynthia (b. Mar. 28, 1807) may be another child, she married William Grantham.

William Bryant (called Bryant/Briant) married Nancy Herrington, said to be part Indian, about 1814. Their children were Lydia Jane (b. Sep. 22, 1815) md. Richard "Lucky" Grantham; Elizabeth (b. ca. 1818) md. Wolf Hair; Pheby (b. ca. 1820) md. Daniel McGilvary; Henry (b. ca. 1821) md. Cynthia; Narvle R. (b. Feb. 15, 1823) md. Elizabeth Byrd; Enoch (b. 1826) md. Sarah Jimmerson; Joyce may have married Mr. Culp; Martha Jane (b. 1831) md. Madison Herrington; Rebecca (b. ca. 1834) md. Colon B. Hood; Bryant P.S. (b. 1835) md. Sarah Ellen Rush; Christopher Columbus (b. Mar. 2, 1836 in Perry County, MS) md. Mary Jane Mahaffey. These are the great-great-grandparents of the compiler. Nancy (b. ca. 1838) md. Nathan Lee; Darling (b. 1841) md. Susan Crocker/Cracker on Feb. 14, 1861 in Lawrence County, MS. Until we found his death certificate in Dallas, TX we did not know the maiden name of their mother.

Christopher Columbus, called C.C. or Lum, and Mary Jane had twins as their first children, Indiana "Nan" and Louisiana "Lou" (b. Mar. 31, 1854). Nan married Charlie Johnson Eley and Lou married John Homer Tompkins; Robert Maryland (b. Apr. 6, 1856) md. Maggie Elizabeth Carroll; Nancy Virginia (b. Sep. 3 1857, d. Sep. 15, 1857); William Walter "Doc" (b. Oct. 15, 1858, was killed when a tree fell on him Dec. 9, 1901) md. Annie Henrietta Wise; Phoebe Elizabeth (b. Oct. 28,

1860, d. Aug. 24, 1958) md. Alexander Clamont Scott and are the compiler's great-grandparents. If I had only started my research five years earlier I'm sure she could have told me many tales and stories that will never be known; Mary Christopher "Crissy" (b. Jul. 5, 1862) md. Ellis Lowe in Orlando, FL where her father took the family to live; Jane Columbus (b. Mar. 23, 1864) md. Hosea Holley; John Fulks "Francis" (b. Jun. 9, 1866 in Texas, died in Orlando, FL) md. Julia Sophia Patrick; Elenora "Mamie Ella" (b. Apr. 25, 1868) md. Edward Joab Salter in Orlando, FL; Andrew Terrell (b. May 25, 1870, Utica, MS) md. Alice Lenora Hill; Susie Phelonia (b. Aug. 11, 1873, died at age 11); Dallas Mahaffey (b. Jul. 16, 1876 on the Curry Place in Utica, Hinds, MS) md. Martha Edaline Douglas. You will notice C.C. and Mary started naming their children after states, but on the fifth child they changed their pattern and possibly decided to only use family names.

This family moved from Perry County to Simpson County and then some of them to Copiah County, where the town of Barlow was established. *Submitted by Carolyn Cole*

ABRAHAM BEER & ESTHER FORCHEIMER.

Abraham came to this country in the first half of the 19th century. The exact year is not known. What we do know is that when he was 14 years old in 1853, he was in business for himself, in New Orleans. He also had a dry goods business in Liberty, MS, at the same time. He was living in Liberty when he became a citizen of this country on May 29, 1860 along with his brother, David.

Abraham also had a sister, Emily, who married Isaac Landman. Emily and Isaac had nine children. One of their daughters, Sadie, married Benjamin C. Geisenberger, son of Wolf and Fanny Geisenberger, of Natchez.

He sold the business in Liberty, moved to New Orleans, and also opened a dry goods store in Natchez. He was living in New Orleans, when he married Esther Forcheimer of Mobile, AL, in January 1869. His first two children, Rosa and Tillie, were born in New Orleans in 1869 and 1871, re-

Abraham Beer

spectively. In 1872 he sold the business in New Orleans and moved his family to Natchez, where he continued to run his Natchez company, A. Beer & Co., until his death. His son Mose Beer (b. 1872,) was followed by Clara (b. 1875), Ferdinand (b. 1876), Simon (b. 1877) and David (b. 1880).

In 1886 Abraham and Esther bought a house at 311 Jefferson St., known today as the William Harris House. Abraham lived there until his death on Oct. 2, 1903. In 1911 Esther sold the house and moved to Memphis.

Abraham's daughter, Rosa, married Solomon Myers in 1889. Mose Beer married Juanita Haas in 1895. On Feb. 15, 1899 Tillie married Robert Mayer, son of Simon Mayer, and Clara married Jonas L. Lehman. Sol, Mose and Robert joined the business. Simon married Ethel Jacobs on Jun. 4, 1902. After Abraham's death, Tillie and Robert moved to New Orleans, as did Mose and Juanita. Clara and Jonas moved to Memphis, as did Esther and David, who never married. Ferdinand married Frances Ketteringham, daughter of Frank and Ida Ketteringham, on Mar. 21, 1925. On Jul. 26, 1925 Ferdinand's mother, Esther, died.

Frances and Ferdinand met while both were working for B. Kullmann & Co. They had three children: Esther (b. 1926), Ida May (b. 1927), and Ferd (b. 1931). They were married for nine years when Ferdinand died. Frances and her three children moved in with her parents. She worked hard to support herself and her family. Among the jobs she had over the years were working as a clerk in the Quartermaster's Office of the Prisoner of War Camp in Clinton, MS; working for J.M. Jones Lumber Co. in Natchez; and for Natchez Building and Loan. Frances Ketteringham Beer died on Jul. 23, 1994. She was 93 years old. *Submitted by Bernice Beer.*

This beautiful ante-bellum home at 505 State St., Natchez, MS, owned by Mr. & Mrs. Khalil M. Raphael was built prior to 1786 during the Spanish era. It once belonged to the Spanish government and is thought to be one of the oldest homes in North America. Above her walls have flown the Spanish flag, the flag of the 13 colonies, the Bonnie Blue flag of the sovereign state of Mississippi, the stars and bars of the Confederacy, and the stars and stripes of the US.

GENE BELLE & EDNA RAPHAEL.

Edna owns and resides at 505 State Street, Natchez, MS in one of the oldest homes in North America, circa 1786, best believed to have been built prior to that date during the Spanish Era.

Edna's grandmother, Annie (Rafoul) Raphael was born in Lebanon in 1862 and died in Natchez in 1951. Around 1890 as a young widow, she migrated to the United States and to Natchez, MS, bringing her two baby boys with her. Edna's father, Kahil Monsour Rafoul, who later changed his name to Charles

Annie (Rafoul) Raphael

M. Raphael, was born in Lebanon on Jun. 21, 1882 and died in Natchez, MS on Mar. 10, 1975. The other son, Edna's Uncle Pete (Rafoul) Raphael, was born in Lebanon in 1883 and died in Natchez in 1954. He was unmarried.

Edna's father, Charles M. Raphael, as a young man went back to Lebanon in 1909 to seek a bride. He married Rose Karouze, a very beautiful and sweet young girl from a very promi-

Ota Karouze

nent family. She was born in Lebanon on Feb. 22, 1893 and died May 23, 1979 in Natchez, MS. In 1913 Edna's father and mother returned to the United States to reunite with her father's mother in Natchez, bringing back a daughter by the name of Helen, who was born to them in Lebanon on Oct. 5, 1911. Edna's father owned and operated one of the largest department stores in Natchez on Franklin Street and was a great benefactor to the poor.

Charles M. Raphael

Edna's older sister, Helen (Rafoul) Raphael, attended St. Joseph's High School and later became a head nurse at Hotel Dieu in New Orleans, LA, and then married the late Dr. J.B. Colligan in Hackberry, LA, where she still resides and lives a good life.

Rose (Karouze) Raphael

Edna Raphael Belle was the second born child, born in Natchez on Jan. 4, 1914, and had an unusually colorful life as a teenager in St. Joseph's High School. She was a star forward on the basketball team and once swam the Mississippi River and received 2nd prize in the race. Edna also wrote and produced a play called *Celebrities on Parade*. It was brought back twice by popular demand at Baker Grand Theatre.

Edna Raphael Belle, dancer on Broadway, was selected most photogenic dancer on Broadway

Edna graduated from Elizabeth Dunbar Murray School of Expression, is a graduate of Treeby Poole School of Dance, a graduate of Dominican College, where

Morris Raphael in younger years

she majored in journalism, and a graduate of Connecticut School of Broadcasting, excelling in copywriting and programming. Edna was an actress and dancer on Broadway, in movies and in television and was selected the most photogenic dancer on Broadway, but the highlight of her career was in 1953 when she reigned as Queen of Mardi Gras Ball and Parade in New Orleans, the first and only non-resident to ever have this honor. In 1967 Edna choreographed shows for the Montreal Expo 1967. Edna also worked as a disc jockey and radio broadcaster.

Edna married Gene Belle, an engineer, from Lincoln, MA on Sep. 15, 1991. He was born in Italy on Mar. 23, 1916, and was famous in his own right for many patents and inventions in aircraft. Edna was very happy living a good life and traveling, and she is quoted as saying *I traveled all over the world searching for something I found only when I came back home to Natchez.*

Morris Raphael, 2003

Edna's brother, Morris Raphael, was born Jul. 31, 1917 in Natchez, MS. He was a very talented student who became an engineer in constructing the Louisiana Causeway. Morris is involved in local politics in New Iberia, LA, has written many novels and still lives in New Iberia, LA with his sweet and talented wife, Helen. They have four children.

Edna Raphael Belle, Queen of Mardi Gras of New Orleans, Feb. 12, 1953

William is the 4th child and youngest of the Raphael family born in Natchez on Jun. 19, 1926. He was Athletic Commissioner of the state of Mississippi and a coach for St. Joseph's Rebels in Jackson, MS. William was so loved that they named the stadium in Jackson after him, the Raphael Stadium, which is a great, great honor! William is happily married to Claire, a lovely lady. They have four children and are still living in Jackson, MS.

DR. DANIEL GOULD BENBROOK & MARGARET BOYER.
Daniel and his wife Margaret came to the Natchez area around 1828, Daniel's father, John, was a farmer and Baptist preacher in Simpson County, KY and later in Tennessee. Daniel's grandfather, Ezekiel, fought for America in the Revolutionary War. Daniel was a direct descendent of John Bunyan who wrote *Pilgrim's Progress*.

Dr. Benbrook received his medical degree from Ohio State Medical College in Cincinnati, OH and was a well-known physician in Natchez for 19 years. In 1847, he moved his family to New Orleans where he became one of the founders of Charity Hospital and helped establish the Order of Masons. He died there in 1850 during a cholera epidemic. His widow and children returned to Natchez where they lived until her death in 1861. She is buried beside her husband on the Gaultney Place in Adams County. The surviving children remained in Natchez/Adams County where they married and reared families.

One son, William Gwin, married Hannah Parsons, whose father owned a brickyard and other property in the vicinity of Pearl and Madison

Streets. William G. served in the Army of the Confederacy as 1st lieutenant with the Natchez Light Infantry and later with the Breckenridge Guards. Upon returning home at the end of the war, he embarked upon a life of public service retiring from each office voluntarily to assume a new post. Over the years he served as city treasurer, Adams County Tax Assessor, Chief of Police and was president of the City School Board for 12 years.

In 1889, W.G. Benbrook was elected mayor of Natchez and held that office for 34 years until his death in 1922. At that time, he had just won another election despite the fact that he was 85 years old and had been blind for the last two years. During the hours of his funeral all downtown businesses closed. *The New Orleans Times-Picayune* ran headlines stating: *The Grand Old Man of Natchez is Dead.*

W.G. was also a 33rd degree Mason, Knight of Pythias, the oldest Past Grand Commander of Knights Templar of Mississippi and head of the state's Confederate Board of Pensioners.

Mayor Benbrook's wife preceded him in death after 64 years of marriage, but their daughter, Hannah, who married James R.C. Tate from Hot Springs, AR, continued to live in the family home.

Hannah and James' children were Gwinnette (Hancock, Rush), William (Billy) Tate, Janice (Baker, Robinson) and Mary (Lloyd). Gwinnette's daughter, Jacquelyn (Schulze), now owns Benbrook house, which was built by her great-grandfather, William Gwin Benbrook, in 1883.

THOMAS WARING BENNETT SR. & LOUISE MOULTRIE BOWEN.
Thomas "Waring" Sr. (b. Oct. 20, 1916) was the second child born to William Walter Bennett Sr. and Rebecca Mathilde Dozier Bennett of Bibb County, Macon, GA. Waring married Louise Moultrie Bowen (b. June 3, 1917) on June 15, 1940. She was the second of two children born to O. Allan Bowen Jr. of South Carolina and Louise Napier Bowen of Macon, GA. Their home, Rivoli, was built on the highest point of the Piedmont Plateau out of Macon, GA, and it burned in December 1941 (a great loss). Louise graduated from Randolph Macon Women's College in Lynchburgh, VA.

Thomas Waring Bennett Sr. graduated from Mercer University in Macon, GA. and was banker for 40 years. He was also a builder and built their barn (30' x 24' x two stories tall) and a shop and carport for two cars at 410 South Commerce. Other hobbies included the Hunt Club, Kiwanis, Santa Claus Club and Vietnam Monument, Natchez, MS.

Louise M.B. Bennett was a NPS Ranger Historian, guide and docent in 10 mansions over 13 years, and a teacher for 25 years. She was a member of AAUW and the DAR.

They had six children:

1) Louise Mathilde Bennett (b. Jan. 1, 1942), mother of two sons, divorced from NPS Ranger, has 29 years in Blue Cross Blue Shield of Roanoke, VA.

2) Thomas Waring Bennett Jr. (b. Dec. 22, 1942) was a US Marine for six years. He was the pilot of a B-52 shot down over Hanoi, Dec. 22, 1972. Maj. Bennett was MIA, no dog tags or anything ever found.

3) Jane Adger Bennett Skelton (b. Jun. 3, 1948), graduated MS State University. She had a BS and two master degrees and taught in Greenville, MS. She had a daughter and son.

4) Pat McConnell Bennett Steed (b. Dec. 28, 1952), a graduate of MS State University taught in Texas. She was the mother of two girls and one boy.

5) William Walter Bennett III (b. Nov. 11, 1955), pilot with American Airlines, spent 12 years in USN and retired as lieutenant commander.

6) Allan Bowen Bennett Johnson (b. Feb. 12, 1957), a dental hygienist. She lived in St. Louis and had no children.

Waring retired as vice president of the bank after 20 years in Macon, GA and 20 in Natchez. He and Louise then had 22 great years, traveling to all the states and all over the world. Thomas died at age 84 of heart failure.

EDWIN EUGENE BENOIST & SNODIE HOWARD TURNER.
Edwin Eugene, son of Louis Armand "L.A." Benoist Sr. and Julia Stier, was born Dec. 18, 1891, Natchez, MS and died Jul. 3, 1981, Natchez, MS. As a young man, Edwin studied at Stanton College, Culver Military Academy in Indiana and business in Poughkeepsie, NY. He later earned engineering and medical degrees at Tulane University in New Orleans. A medical officer in the U.S. Army in World War I, he set sail for France from Hoboken, NJ in April 1916, aboard a German ship which had been captured.

Upon return, Dr. Ed practiced medicine in southwest Mississippi and central Louisiana until his late 80s. His medical practice took him to all parts to deliver babies, perform surgeries, and care for victims of the Great Floods of the late 1920s. He was a Fellow in the American College of Surgeons. He took the only known moving pictures of the first Natchez Spring Pilgrimage in the early 1930s. Those movies are on deposit at the Mississippi State Archives in Jackson. Dr. Ed had a keen interest in the arts, wrote music and plays, designed lures and fishing flies, and built recreational boats. He holds several copyrights and patents. He was a member of the Natchez Public School Board.

Dr. Ed married Snodie Howard Turner on Dec. 18, 1925 at Shelby County, TN. Snodie (b. Mar. 20, 1905, Leland, Washington County, MS, d. Aug. 6, 1975, Natchez, MS) received an AB degree in bacteriology at Mississippi State College for Women on Jun. 1, 1924. She also attended West Tennessee State Normal School and was accepted into the University of Chicago for graduate studies in bacteriology but decided to forego further education and married Edwin instead. She was active in the Natchez Garden Club and in the First Presbyterian Church. Snodie, affectionately known as "Dodie" to her grandchildren, was the daughter of Enoch Franklin Turner, M.D. and Helen Howard.

Edwin Eugene Benoist, M.D. and Snodie Howard Turner Benoist

Edwin and Snodie were the parents of three children: Helen Howard Benoist (b. Sep. 5, 1928, d. Apr. 7, 1967); Edwin Eugene Benoist (b. Nov. 6, 1931, d. Dec. 18, 1988); Anne Clayton Benoist (b. Aug. 25, 1933).

Edwin and Snodie initially lived in a Queen Anne Victorian cottage at 413 South Commerce Street immediately behind the Louis Armand Benoist-Julia Stier House at 410 South Union Street. Later, they moved to 600 South Union Street, a transitional Queen Anne-Colonial Revival home, where they lived and reared their family until the 1950s, when they purchased Dunkerron Farm off the Lower Woodville Road. *Prepared Feb. 28, 2003 by Paul H. and Virginia Gerace Benoist.*

JUDGE EDWIN EUGENE BENOIST & PATRICIA JANE WHITE.

Judge Edwin Eugene Benoist Jr., the only son of Edwin Eugene Benoist, M.D. (who attended Eastman College, Poughkeepsie, NY, ca. 1912), and Snodie Howard Turner, was born Nov. 6, 1931 at the Natchez Sanatorium and died Dec. 18, 1988 at Houston, TX. His childhood homes were at 413 S. Commerce Street and 600 S. Union Street. He is buried at the Natchez City Cemetery.

Judge Edwin Eugene Benoist Jr. and Patricia Jane White Benoist

Edwin was a graduate of the Natchez public school system in 1949 where he was a member of the Natchez High School Band. He attended Culver Military Academy in Indiana and the University of the South in Sewanee, TN. He completed his undergraduate studies in history at the University of Mississippi in 1957. A 1959 graduate of the University of Mississippi Law School, he was on the Law Journal, Moot Court, served as president of his first year class, and was selected by a special faculty committee as one of four Moot Court finalists to argue a case before the Mississippi Supreme Court at Jackson.

Edwin was a Korean Conflict era pilot in the U.S. Air Force, receiving his flight training at The Vance Air Force Base, Enid, OK in 1953. He was stationed in Japan, where his first two of four sons were born. After active duty, Edwin joined the Mississippi Air National Guard stationed in Jackson. He was Natchez City Prosecutor, Adams County Prosecuting Attorney, District Attorney and Circuit Court Judge for the 6th Judicial District of Mississippi, which then included Adams, Amite, Franklin, Jefferson and Wilkinson counties. Edwin was a member of the Adams County, Mississippi State, and American Bar Associations and held memberships in the Mississippi Law Officers Association. He was a stabilizing force for the community during the 1960s.

Prior to his public service in law enforcement, he practiced law with the firms of Hicks & Benoist and Brandon, Handy, O'Beirne & Benoist. Edwin was active in fraternal and civic organizations, including Kappa Sigma Fraternity, Kiwanis, YMCA, Dixie Youth Baseball, Andrew Jackson Council of the Boy Scouts of America, American Legion, National Rifle Association, and held various chairmanships of such charitable organizations as March of Dimes and Easter Seals Foundation. He served as Chairman of the Board of Deacons of the First Presbyterian Church of Natchez and served as an Elder with the Church. He taught government and civics at Copiah-Lincoln Junior College. He was an avid hunter, fisherman and trap shooter.

Edwin married the former Patricia "Pat" Jane White (b. Dec. 10, 1931), daughter of Franklin Roe White and Emma Jane Hancock, on Jul. 25, 1953 at the First Presbyterian Church in Newkirk, OK. Patricia graduated from Newkirk High School and Oklahoma State University. She is a homemaker.

Children of Edwin and Patricia are Paul Howard Benoist, Keith Elliott Benoist, Lee Armand Benoist and Glenn Hunt Benoist. *Prepared Feb.*

28, 2003 and submitted by Paul H. Benoist and Virginia Gerace Benoist.

EUGENE BENOIST & MARGUERITE JUSTINE BELHOMME-BENOIST-MEZEIX.

Marguerite "Margaret" and Eugene Benoist married at St. Mary's Cathedral in Natchez on Mar. 13, 1850.

Justine, a milliner, was born 1815, Angouleme, France, and was baptized and made her First Communion at the Church of St. Andrew (S. Andree) in Angouleme. Justine later traveled to America as widow Madam Marguerite Justine Belhomme Marchand after losing her husband, two sons and one daughter, Rose Desiree, in France. Some history shows that she also had two other sons by Marchand.

Justine Belhomme Benoist

Eugene was born 1819 in Meaux, France. His parents were John Louis Benoist and Mary M. Benoist. His brother was Florentin. Eugene immigrated to the United States at New Orleans ca. 1848-49. He died of yellow fever at Natchez on Aug. 28, 1853 at age 34.

Felici Jobie (Jobit)

Justine then married Claudius Mezeix, previously of Lyons, France, on Dec. 2, 1860 at St. Mary's Cathedral. Claudius, son of John Mezeix and Jean Quendi, died Feb. 24, 1865 at age 40. Claudius and Justine lived on Old Palestine Road. Justine died Jul. 31, 1879, in Natchez, and is buried in the old Catholic section of the Natchez City Cemetery, between her second husband, Eugene, and third husband, Claudius.

Louise Belhomme Jobie (Jobit)

Siblings of Justine were:

1) Jerome Belhomme (b. in France, d. 1855, buried in the old Catholic section of the Natchez City Cemetery) was a French professor at Marksville, LA, and at the Moseley Academy of Second Creek in Natchez where children of planters were educated by him.

2) Marie Belhomme Labonne of Angouleme, France.

Marie Belhomme Labonne

3) Louise Belhomme Jobie (Jobit) of Angouleme, France; her daughter Felici Jobie (Jobit) was born Angouleme, France and died of yellow fever on Oct. 20, 1858 at Natchez, where she is buried in the old Catholic section of the Natchez City Cemetery. *Submitted by Paul H. and Virginia Gerace Benoist.*

Claudius Mezeix

LOUIS ARMAND BENOIST & JULIA STIER.

Louis Armand "L.A." Benoist was the only child of Madam Marguerite "Margaret" Justine Belhomme Marchand Benoist Mezeix (nee Belhomme) and Eugene Benoist. L.A. (b. Aug. 28, 1852, d. Nov. 17, 1932) is buried at the Natchez City Cemetery in the Benoist Plot.

L.A., a businessman and merchant, founded L.A. Benoist & Co., "The New York Store," ca. 1881. Previously, he worked for Donaldson & Co. and Thomas C. Perrault. L.A. was also an organizer and officer in the Natchez Building and Loan Association, held local and state offices in the Masonic Order, Eastern Star, served on the Adams County Board of Supervisors, and Mississippi State Senate. L.A. was educated at Miss Caroline de France, Cathedral School in Natchez, Jefferson College at Washington, MS, Jefferson College in St. James Parish, LA (1870), and St. Charles College Petit Seminaire of St. Sulpice (1869) in Ellicott City, MD.

Louis Armand Benoist

Early on, L.A. was described as a "good looking young merchant with a fine future" by Edith Wyatt Moore of the *Natchez Democrat* and as a "business and fraternal leader of the state for more than half a century and one of the best loved of the citizens of Natchez" in the Natchez paper on Nov. 18, 1932, the day after he died. He

Julia Stier Benoist

Marie Louise Benoist, first child of L.A. and Julia Stier Benoist

was also described as "kindly, charitable and tolerant at all times. Mr. Benoist was one of the most lovable men. He numbered his friends in all ranks of life, the highest and most humble. He was delightfully human and possessed a store of wide information on many subjects."

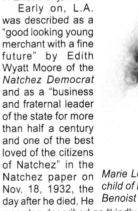

L.A. Benoist married Julia Stier, daughter of John Henry Stier and Caroline Peters, on Aug. 28, 1883, in the double parlors of Julia's family home, the Caroline Stier House, at 615 Washington Street in Natchez. At L.A.'s side was best man and life-long friend, Henry C. Norman, well-known Natchez photographer. L.A. and Julia honeymooned at Niagara Falls.

Julia Stier (b. Jul. 25, 1860, d. Dec. 12, 1951) was described as "a beloved little lady of the old school."

Children of L.A. and Julia Stier Benoist. Front: Louis A. Benoist Jr., twins-Percy Anderson and Caroline Henriette Benoist, Edwin Eugene Benoist, M.D. Back: Harold Jerome Benoist

Their first two children, Marie Louise Benoist (b. 1884, d. 1887) and Harold Jerome Benoist (b. 1886, d. 1913), were born at the Caroline Stier House. Their other children were Louis Armand Benoist Jr. (b. 1889, d. 1972); Edwin Eugene Benoist, M.D. (b. 1891, d. 1981); and twins-Percy Anderson Benoist (b. 1896, d. 1957) and Caroline Henriette Benoist (b. 1896, d. 2000). L.A. and Julia lived most of their married life at 410 South Union Street, a 1-1/2 story transitional Italianate to Queen Anne style home built by L.A. ca. 1881-1883, and later renovated post-1897/pre-1901 to its present 2-1/2 story Queen Anne Colonial Revival structure. *Submitted by Paul H. Benoist and Virginia Gerace Benoist.*

PAUL HOWARD BENOIST & VIRGINIA ANNE GERACE. Paul Howard (b. Jul. 21, 1954 at Ashiya AFB, Kyushu, Japan), the eldest son of Judge Edwin Eugene Benoist Jr. and Patricia Jane White. He married Virginia "Ginny" Anne Gerace (b. Jun. 22, 1954), elder daughter of Joseph Raymond Gerace and Norma Evelyn Ford, at Christ the King Chapel, Louisiana State University, Baton Rouge, LA, on Mar. 5, 1977. Joseph Raymond Gerace was born May 12, 1920 in Plaquemine, Iberville Parish, LA, and Norma Evelyn Ford was born Sep. 24, 1930 in Pickering, Vernon Parish, LA. Paul and Ginny had one daughter, Mary Turner Benoist (b. May 4, 1983, Metairie, Jefferson Parish, LA).

Paul graduated from South Natchez High School in 1972. He earned a BA from Louisiana State University, MBA from A.B. Freeman School of Business at Tulane University and J.D. from the Tulane University School of Law.

Ginny earned a B.A. from Louisiana State University, M.S. Southwestern Louisiana University, J.D. from Southern University Law Center. In 2003 Paul and Ginny were restoring the home built by his great-grandparents, Louis Armand Benoist and Julia Stier at 410 S. Union Street, Natchez. *Submitted by Paul H. Benoist and Virginia Gerace Benoist.*

JOHN HENRY BERRY & MARGARET ELIZABETH ROGILLIO married Nov. 8, 1845. Margaret, daughter of Emanuel and Eliza Rogillio, was born Jul. 19, 1828 at Mt. Olive, Pine Ridge, MS,

d. Feb. 25, 1908 at The Academy, Pine Ridge, MS. John Henry Berry died Mar. 30, 1901 and is buried at Natchez Cemetery, Catholic Section. The Academy house is at the cross roads of Pine Ridge, MS on land given to the Presbyterian church for a girl's school (donated by Emanuel Rogillio and Mrs. L.L. Bisland). The school was short lived due to conditions of the Civil War. Then the house was rented with funds going to the church (taken from minutes of the Presbyterian Pine Ridge Church). Margaret and Henry Berry had 13 children:

1) Mary Elizabeth "Lizzie" Berry (b. Aug. 19, 1847) md. Emanuel Mercer Rogillio Gibson, son of Tennessee Rogillio and Jordon Gibson, on May 3, 1876. They had two children.

2) Clayton Berry (b. Mar. 20, 1849).

3) Houston Berry (b. Apr. 23, 1853, d. Sep. 22, 1934 at Mt. Vernon Plantation, Pine Ridge, MS) never married and is buried beside his sister Ida Lee Rogillio, Pine Ridge Presbyterian Cemetery.

4) John Henry Berry Jr. (b. Aug. 5, 1854) md. Rosa Fowler on Jun. 14, 1886 at Trinity Episcopal Church. They have one son, Frederick W. Berry.

5) Florence Berry (b. Dec. 22, 1855, d. Feb. 26, 1857).

6) Lenora Helen Berry "Nora" (b. Sep. 26, 1857) md. Albert W. Foster on Aug. 6, 1879. They had seven children.

7) Anna Louise Berry (b. Apr. 25, 1860, d. Apr. 20, 1929) md. Walter Wade Hedrick (b. Oct. 4, 1855, d. Oct. 6. 1901) on Feb. 22, 1882. Anna and Walter are both buried Claiborne City, MS. They had eight children.

8) Lydia Arabella Berry (b. Mar. 4, 1862, d. Apr. 15, 1936) md. Charles Alexander and they ran a store at Anna's Bottom. No children. Lydia and Charles are both buried in the Natchez Cemetery.

9) Richard Taylor Berry (b. Mar. 25, 1864) left Natchez and wasn't heard from again by the family.

10) Lorissa "Rissa" Berry (b. Oct. 10, 1868) md. J.W. Sharbrough of Holly Bluff, Yazoo County, MS and they had one son.

11 & 12) twins, Emma and Ella Berry were born Dec. 17, 1870. They died unmarried and are buried at the Pine Ridge Presbyterian Cemetery next to their sister Ida Lee Berry Rogillio and brother Houston Berry. They lived at Mt. Vernon Plantation with their brother Houston Berry and handled the dairy.

13) Ida Lee Berry (b. Apr. 14, 1866, d. 1940) md. John Wesley Rogillio II (b. Aug. 20, 1865, d. 1941) on Sep. 15, 1891. Both are buried at Pine Ridge Presbyterian Cemetery.

Note: Ida Lee Berry was the granddaughter of Emanual Rogillio, and John Wesley Rogillio was the grandson of John Rogillio. John and Emanual were brothers.

Ida Lee and John Wesley Rogillio had three children:

1) Lilly Julia Rogillio (b. Nov. 1, 1894, Jefferson County, MS) became a Catholic Sister of Mercy (Sister Marie), died and buried in Vicksburg, MS.

2) Walter Samuel Rogillio (b. Dec. 1, 1897, Pine Ridge, d. Feb. 12, l957) married 1st Wilmer Wilson, two sons, Walter Samuel Rogillio and Dabney Hill Rogillio; married 2nd Vassey Johns, one son Eugene Johns Rogillio. Walter is buried National Cemetery, Natchez, MS.

3) Douglas Stampley Rogillio Sr. (b. Jan. 9, 1896, Jefferson County, MS, d. Jan. 4, 1975) md. Ethel Farmer Hughes (b. May 28, 1899, Brookhaven, MS, d. Apr. 8, 1970) on Mar. 24, 1919. They had two sons. Douglas is buried in Natchez, MS and Ethel in Brookhaven, MS.

Douglas Stampley Rogillio Jr. (b. Feb. 5, 1920,

d. Mar. 19, 1984) md. Thelma Alexander (b. Aug. 5, 1922, Maplewood, MO, d. Nov. 13, 1992), both buried National Cemetery, Santa Fe, NM. Douglas attended Natchez Public Schools, made a career in the Air Force and retired a lieutenant colonel, Albuquerque, NM. He had four children: Sylvia Ann, Douglas Stampley III, Deborah Sue, Cynthia Lee.

John Wesley Rogillo II

William Francis Rogillio (b. Jun. 26, 1922) md. Annis Elizabeth Kuehn "Betty" (b. Mar. 30, 1927) on Feb. 22, 1947, Trinity Episcopal Church, Natchez. William attended Natchez Public School and went into the Marine Corp after graduation in 1941. He served in the South Pacific in World War II, returned to the States and transferred to the Navy for flight training. In 1945 he was discharged and returned to Natchez, then went to work for Humble Oil & Refining Co. (later Exxon). He retired after 41 years and returned to Natchez. Betty attended Natchez Public Schools. After graduation in l945 she worked at Armstrong Tire & Rubber Co. until her marriage in 1947. She received a BS degree from Stephen F. Austin University, Nacogdoches, TX and MED from University of Houston, TX and taught elementary school in Texas for 20 years. She retired from HISD, Houston, TX and returned to Natchez. Bill and Betty Rogillio have two children:

Elizabeth Ann Rogillio born on July 2nd, Farmington, NM, married David Lee Anderson of Tenaha, TX on Oct. 4, 1975. They live in Carthage, TX and have three children: William Marshall, Lee Ann and Janet Laura.

William Francis Rogillio Jr. (b. Jul. 14, 1956, Huntsville, TX) md. Janet Laura Vansa on Dec. 30, 1978. They live in Fairfield, TX and have two children, Amanda Cathleen and Emily Anne.

ROBERT CARVER "BOB" BERTOLET & YVONNE PRESSGROVE. Bob met his wife, Yvonne, in Jackson. They were married at the First Baptist Church in Jackson where both were members. The Bertolets moved to the Natchez area in 1964 with their three babies: Barry Dean, Toni Jill and Robert Todd. Bob was born and reared in Bethlehem, PA, where he attended schools from the first grade to the completion of a geology degree from Lehigh University in Bethlehem.

He started his employment with Standard Oil of Indiana, now Amoco, working in the Wichita, KS, District for one year. He was then drafted into the Army where he served two years in Japan in the topographic engineering battalion. He returned to Amoco and was sent to the Jackson, MS, office. He was then hired by the R.A. Campbell Oil Co. of Vidalia, which brought him to this area.

Bob was a member of Rotary Club, served on the Board of Directors at Natchez Regional Hospital, was in the Vidalia Jaycees, on the Vidalia Planning Commission, on Natchez Opera Board of Directors, on the Board of Directors for Trinity Episcopal School and served as President of the American Cancer Society in Natchez.

Yvonne was born and reared at Charleston, MS, where her great-grandfather settled in 1835. After graduating from Charleston High School, she received a degree in nursing from the University of Mississippi. She worked as a surgical nurse and in-service education instructor at the Medical Center, taught nursing at St. Dominics School of Nursing and the USM Natchez branch School of Nursing.

Yvonne has served as president of the Nursing Alumni, on the Ole Miss Board of Directors, served on the Ole Miss Campaign, established a nursing scholarship at the Med Center, and provided a nursing research lab. She was involved with the Natchez Mayor's War on Drugs, Pilgrimage Garden Club and the American Cancer Society as publicity chairman. She likes to write, play the piano, read, and has a number of collections.

Their older son, Barry, graduated from Trinity Episcopal School, the University of Mississippi, and the University Medical School. He interned and did a residency at Shands-University of Florida in Internal Medicine and Cardiology. He is an invasive cardiologist in Tupelo, MS. He is married to the former Bethany Buckley of Jackson. They have two children, Sam and Sarah Elizabeth.

Their daughter, Toni, graduated from Trinity Episcopal School, the University of Mississippi, and the University Medical School. She interned and did a residency at the University of Mississippi Medical Center. She has a practice in Jackson, MS, and she is also an associate professor at the Medical Center. She is married to Harold Henthorn of Denver, CO.

Their younger son, Todd, graduated from Jackson Prep of Jackson and the University of Mississippi with a master's degree in petroleum geology. He also attended the University of Texas in Austin. In 2003 he had offices in Natchez and Jackson where he was an independent geologist. He married the former Rhonda Lynn White of Vidalia, LA and they live in Ridgeland, Ms.

WILLIAM ALEXANDER BISLAND & CAROLINE LOUISE BAKER.

Leaving Mt. Repose, the home he built on Pine Ridge in 1824, William Bisland migrated with his family to Terrebonne Parish, LA, in 1846 when crop land in Adams County had become exhausted. He had a previously established interest in the sugar business in south Louisiana where he would assume management.

Bisland died the following year and was succeeded in business on his plantation, Hope Farm, by his son William Alexander Bisland, who married Caroline Louisa Baker in 1848. Six children were born to this union before 1861 when their mother died.

Caroline Louise Bisland

William enlisted in the Confederate Army Apr. 11, 1862, serving as captain in Company H, 26th Louisiana Infantry; paroled Jun. 10, 1865 at Franklin, LA. On Sep. 16, 1865, he married Caroline Cerelia Pride. William, his health broken by the trials and privations of war, returned with his bride to a devastated Hope Farm and the challenge of providing for a family, three children of the first union surviving.

A son, Ralph, was born Nov. 24, 1868. It was into this setting of reconstruction that Caroline Louise Bisland was born May 4, 1874, followed by Sarah Stelle, William Witherspoon and Elizabeth Williams.

The Bisland Family connection was extensive in Louisiana and Mississippi, a source of strength which, undergirded by their Christian faith, prevailed through the years.

Unable to restore his plantation business and with bodily afflictions, William Alexander Bisland

died Feb. 12, 1889. His son, Ralph, struggled for several years to retain the family holdings while his mother and siblings moved to New Orleans where they found employment and schooling. Louise taught school to help provide for the family.

Inevitably Hope Farm was lost to creditors. In 1901 the family migrated back to Mississippi where relatives were established. Daughter, Sarah, had married Dr. Joseph Dunbar Shields, resident physician at Pine Ridge. They lived at Mt. Repose, Sarah's ancestral home, where the Bisland refugees found a haven until 1903 when Mrs. William A. Bisland purchased The Cedars at Church Hill, MS, near lands that her son, Ralph, managed. She moved into this home with her two daughters, Louise and Elizabeth. Louise taught the neighborhood children in a one-room school, also teaching Sunday School at Christ Episcopal Church. Her students were Shields, Fauntleroy, Valentine and Hornsby children.

After Elizabeth's marriage in 1904 and her mother's death in 1911, Louise moved back to Mt. Repose joining Sarah, Dr. Shields and their children: Ralph, Caroline and Dunbar Jr. A classroom was designated in the home where Louise taught children of the family and neighborhood until the Pine Ridge School was built nearby, where she was employed as principal assisted by one teacher.

Industrious by nature, Louise raised violets which she packaged, selling orders by mail. She assisted in honey production working with bees in the apiary and faithfully helped with domestic chores. She inherited a gift for writing, evidenced by manuscripts unpublished but kept among private papers. Her spiritual life was strengthened by daily devotion to Scripture reading, study and prayer. "Auntie" was a popular visitor in homes of the extended family, compatible with young and old. Seldom in the limelight she impacted many lives with education, encouragement and her example of steadfastness through the challenges of life.

Familiarly known as Miss Louise Bisland, she died Sep. 24, 1961. Funeral services at Pine Ridge Presbyterian Church were followed by burial within the Bisland enclosure where lie her grandparents, William and Mary L.L. Bisland and others of their progeny. *Submitted by Mrs. L.R. McGehee.*

DR. DOUGLAS STARKE BISLAND.

Douglas (b. May 14, 1828, d. Apr. 26, 1896) was buried in the Natchez City Cemetery. He was the fifth of eight children born to James Bisland of Adams County, MS, and his second wife Mary King, daughter of Moses King and Elizabeth Starke of Franklin County, MS. Douglas was baptized in the Pine Ridge Presbyterian Church; he attended Oakland College in the years 1835, 1836, and 1837. It is not known where he attended medical school or if he apprenticed under another doctor. An oil portrait of him is owned in 2003 by his great granddaughter Nan Meyer, Richmond, VA.

Douglas married his second cousin, Sarah Ruth Harriet "Sallie" Kirkland, on Jun. 15, 1853, in Concordia Parish, LA; they lived on Oak Pond Plantation in Catahoula Parish. The marriage was performed by Reverend Benjamin H. Williams, minister of Pine Ridge Presbyterian Church. Sarah (b. 1835) was the older of two daughters of Zachariah Tucker Kirkland and Harriet Perry. Harriet's mother, Judith King, was a sister to Douglas' maternal grandfather, Moses King. In 1862 Sarah died without issue and was buried in the Pine Hill Cemetery, near Sicily Island, LA.

Douglas married Anna Elliott Conner Dunbar on Oct. 7, 1869, daughter of Jane E.B. Gustine and Dr. William Carmichael Conner, and the

widow of Robert Chotard Dunbar who died in a Civil War Battle of Winchester, VA. To them were born two sons; both died young before her marriage to Bisland.

Three children were born to Anna and Douglas: Jane, Douglas and Henry.

Jane Gustine (b. 1870) died of a ruptured appendix in 1895. She was engaged to be married and was buried in her wedding dress in the Natchez City Cemetery.

Douglas Starke Jr. (b. Feb. 8, 1872) was called Starke and married Oct. 22, 1896 in Adams County, MS, to Hulda Rawle (b. Sep. 24, 1873), daughter of Elizabeth Helm Stanton and John Rawle. Her grandfather, Frederick Stanton, was the builder of Stanton Hall. Starke died Sep. 27, 1908 of a gunshot wound

Dr. Douglas Starke Bisland

while hunting. Hulda died Jan. 28, 1920, in Touro's Infirmary, New Orleans, LA; she and Starke are buried in the Natchez City Cemetery. He died intestate; her will is filed in the Adams County Courthouse, Natchez, MS.

Starke and Hulda had four children: a daughter, Huxley, died young.

Elizabeth Stanton Bisland (b. Sep. 6, 1897, d. Aug. 17, 1978 in Michigan) md. Dec. 7, 1920 in Carencro, LA, Dracos Alexander Dimitry, son of Dracos Anthony Dimitry and Elizabeth Dimitry Ruth. They had four sons: Douglas B., Dracos Jr., D. Donald, and John Randolph. Elizabeth died Aug. 17, 1978 in Michigan.

Anna Elliott (b. July 1899, d. Jul. 20, 1977) md. Edward K. Thompson Jr. in 1916 in Natchez, MS. They had one child, Nan Bisland Thompson and were divorced. She married Arthur Duvic, no issue. Anna died in New Orleans Jul. 20, 1977 and was buried in Metairie Cemetery, Metairie, LA.

Henry Conner (b. Mar. 3, 1874, d. Apr. 4, 1874), buried in the Natchez City Cemetery. *Submitted by Ella McCaleb Young.*

JAMES BISLAND,

the fourth child of John and Susanna Rucker Bisland, was born Sep. 23, 1790, died Jun. 17, 1842 and was buried in the Pine Ridge Presbyterian Church Cemetery. He farmed land he bought and sold land in Franklin, Jefferson and Adams County. He was a Presbyterian and was on the membership of Union Church and Pine Ridge at various times.

James was a lieutenant in the Adams Troops during the War of 1812. He rode horseback for six days bringing the first news to Washington, MS, that the war had ended. He married three times: first to Mary Abigail Ross in 1817. She was born 1798, died 1819 and is buried near Bunkley, Franklin County, MS. They had two girls: Jane P. and C. Elizabeth; both died young in August 1822 and are buried in the Mount Airwell Cemetery, Adams County, MS.

On Mar. 8, 1821 he married in Franklin County to Mary King (b. Jan. 8, 1799, d. Mar. 12, 1835), the oldest of six children of Moses and Elizabeth Starke King. She is buried in the Mount Airwell Cemetery. Her tombstone confirms the date of her death which differs in various publications. She had eight children:

1) Martha Jane (b. 1822, d. 1900) md. James Franklin McCaleb in 1846. See her biography.

2) Susannah H. (b. 1823, d. 1827).

3) William David (b. 1825, d. before 1835).

4) Peter King (b. 1826, d. 1829).

5) Douglas Starke (b. 1828, d. 1896) md. first Sarah Kirkland in 1853; she died, and he married Anna C. Dunbar in 1869. See his biography.

6) Thomas Alexander (b. 1829, d. after 1860) attended Oakland 1835, 1836 and 1837, when his brother Douglas also attended. When Douglas married Sarah Kirkland, Thomas signed their marriage bond. In 1860 he was farming and living with Mary Bisland, widow of his uncle William. He served in the 4th Louisiana Infantry. No marriage or death record known for him.

7) Susannah Elizabeth (b. 1831) md. in 1850 to Thomas Bradford of Jefferson County, MS; they had two sons, James and Alexander, both baptized in the Pine Ridge Church. They moved to Tennessee, probably about 1859, as she was "dismissed" from the Pine Ridge Church at that time. Dismissed was a term then used when a member left for another church.

8) Mary Louise (b. 1835, d. 1892) was 12 days old when her mother died. Susanna, Mary's parental grandmother, who died later that year, was sponsor for Mary when she was baptized in the Pine Ridge Church. In l858 Mary married Robert Fulton McGinty of Jefferson County, MS, at Peachland, the home of her sister Martha McCaleb. In 1860 McGinty was sheriff in Jefferson

Tombstone of Mary King Bisland (b. Jan. 8, 1799, d. Mar. 12, 1835), wife of James Bisland. Courtesy of Ella McCaleb Young.

County and in 1865 circuit court clerk. They had four children: Thomas, Newton, Hugh and Margaret.

James married third, Catherine Gates Apr. 21, 1836; they had one child John James (b. ca. 1837). Catherine stated at his death that James left five children by Mary and one by her. James' property in Natchez reverted to the seller; little is know of Catherine and her child after James' death. *Submitted by Ella McCaleb Young.*

SUSANNA RUCKER BISLAND was born Feb. 2, 1767 in Culpepper County, VA, the youngest of five children of Peter and Sarah Wisdom Rucker. The others were Colby, Jonathan, Catherine and William. On Jul. 10, 1784, she married John Bisland (b. Mar. 24, 1742, Glasgow, Scotland). She died Oct. 12, 1835 and he died Apr. 10, 1821. She and John are buried in the cemetery on Mount Airwell Plantation, Adams County, MS, where they had a home before 1790. All 11 children were probably born there.

The Bisland family were founding members of the Pine Ridge Presbyterian Church, first called Salem and located at Washington, MS. Three of their daughters and a granddaughter married men who served as ministers of that church. None of her five daughters lived beyond 30 years of age, and some left infants that died and are buried in the Mount Airwell Cemetery.

Alexander (b. Apr. 10, 1786, d. Feb. 2, 1811) was single.

John Jr. (b. Aug. 17, 1787, d. Nov. 2, 1814) was single.

Peter (b. Mar. 17, 1879, d. Aug. 31, 1829) md. Barbara Foster, Jan. 15 1808. Their nine children were John James, Clarissa Ann, Susannah, John, Elizabeth, James Rucker, William Gardner, LeVisa Rolston, Mary Jane.

James (b. Sep. 23, 1790) md. Mary Abigail Ross on Mar. 13, 1817, and she died Aug. 29, 1819. They had two daughters, Jane P. and C. Elizabeth. On Mar. 8, 1821 he married Mary King (b. Jan. 8, 1799, d. Mar. 12, 1835) and they had eight children. He married Catherine Gates Apr. 21, 1836. James died Jun. 17, l842, leaving a widow and one child by Catherine and five by Mary King. Elizabeth (b. Apr.

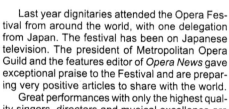

Susanna Rucker Bisland (b. Feb. 2, 1767, d. Oct. 12, 1835). Courtesy of Ella McCaleb Young.

4, 1792, d. Sep. 14, 1822) md. James Dunbar Feb. 18, 1808. They had seven children: Susan, Ann Matilda, Alexander Bisland, James Jr., Jane P., Martha Jane, and Catherine Elizabeth.

Sarah Ann (b. Sep. 17, 1793, d. Oct. 12, 1823) md. Reverend James Smylie on Feb. 2, 1815. Of their five children only Alexander M. lived to have progeny.

Jane Patterson (b. Jan. 20, 1795, d. Aug. 10, 1816) md. John Isaac Wayne Ross on Mar. 7, 1816; no issue.

William (b. Jan. 7, 1797, d. Aug. 20, 1847) md. Mary Lavinia Louise Witherspoon on Oct. 19, 1820. Their six children were Jane McClary, Susannah Elizabeth, William Alexander, John Rucker, Thomas Shields and Leonora Witherspoon.

Katharine (b. Sep. 10, 1798, d. Dec. 20, 1823) md. Reverend John Patterson Jul. 18, 1822; Their only child, Susanah Rucker, was born Dec. 16, 1823.

Susannah (b. Feb. 12, 1802, d. Sep. 28, 1825) md. Reverend Samuel Hunter May 11, 1824. They had one child, Catherine Ann (b. Mar. 9, 1825, d. Sep. 8, 1827).

David (b. Nov. 22, 1805, d. Nov. 23, 1805). Written in the Session book when Susanna died: *A member of this church when first organized at Washington in the year 1807, having sustained an unblemished Christian character through out the whole period, departed this life at an advanced age in full hope of a glorious resurrection at the last day. Submitted by Ella M. Young.*

DAVID S. BLACKBURN. It was 13 years ago that Dr. Blackburn visited Natchez, staying at Monmouth Plantation where he heard the owners, Mr. and Mrs. Ronald Riches, sharing with friends their excitement of hearing *La Boheme* at the Sante Fe Opera the previous evening. Upon meeting, Dr. Blackburn shared that two singers who were in his New York Studio were leads in that performance. The rest is history.

It so happened there was a meeting the next day with the mayor on how to have an Opera Festival in Natchez. Dr. Blackburn was asked to attend. There was great enthusiasm even after failure on three previous occasions. The mayor asked Dr. Blackburn to provide guidance, or a syllabus on how such an undertaking could be successful in Natchez. After doing so, he was asked to come back and help organize a group of leading citizens.

He fell in love with Natchez, the need, challenge and opportunities. For the past 13 years he has dedicated his life to achieving a world class Opera Festival that would receive positive national acclaim, enrich the cultural life of Mississippi, inspire and enhance the life of thousands of children in the Arts, and make a lasting financial impact on Natchez and Adams County.

Last year dignitaries attended the Opera Festival from around the world, with one delegation from Japan. The festival has been on Japanese television. The president of Metropolitan Opera Guild and the features editor of *Opera News* gave exceptional praise to the Festival and are preparing very positive articles to share with the world.

Great performances with only the highest quality singers, directors and musical excellence are delivered by Dr. Blackburn each season. He designed a two level national training program: 1) Young Artists, 2) Artists in Residence. Twelve are admitted in each program to present recitals, coach with leading assistant directors on his staff, sing secondary roles, and cover lead roles in a special performance.

Each year in October, hundreds of singers make application for an audition in New York for this program. Agents also request auditions for their finest singers for leading roles. Dr. Blackburn, with his wonderful training and unique talent, selects only the best to contract with the Natchez Opera Festival. This is a valuable training tool for outstanding young singers from around the world who he encourages and helps move on to the next level in their career,

Dr. Blackburn has insisted on a strong Educational Opera Outreach Program which now reaches performances to over 15,000 children in schools throughout Mississippi. An outstanding children's opera is prepared and double cast by some of the finest young talent in America. Out of this

David S. Blackburn

program Dr. Blackburn has taken those of extreme interest and talent, working with many of them on a weekly basis. He has helped many young singers go on to receive full scholarships in colleges and universities in vocal music and countless others whose lives have been enriched by music.

BENJAMIN SEBASTIAN BLEDSOE, eighth son of Benjamin and Sarah Harris Bledsoe (b. Nov. 20, 1807 in Campbellton, GA) went to Natchez, MS, where he married Mary Anne Gustine Postlethwaite (b. Apr. 24, 1819) on Feb. 13, 1838 (Family Bible Record). Benjamin Sebastian died in Natchez, MS, Sep. 20, 1847, aged 39 years and 10 months. Mary Anne died in Natchez, MS, Aug. 28, 1905.

Benjamin and Mary Ann Bledsoe had issue: 1) William (b. Aug. 5, 1839, Natchez, MS, d. _); 2) Elizabeth Postlethwaite (b. Nov. 29, 1845, Natchez, MS, d. Jan. 1, 1930); 3) Mary Ann Gustine (b. Jan. 31, 1847, Natchez, MS, d. Sep. l3, l924).

Mary Ann Bledsoe, daughter of Benjamin Sebastian and Mary Ann Postlethwaite married Zimri McDonald of Marley's Mills, NC, on Sep 28, 1865 and had issue: Mary Ann Gustine McDonald (b. Aug. 18, 1866) and Emily Postlethwaite (b. Aug. 1, 1868). Mary Ann Gustine Bledsoe McDonald died Sep. 13, 1924.

1) Mary Ann Gustine McDonald, daughter of Zimri and Mary Ann Gustine McDonald, married Aaron Culipher Register of Tensas Parish, LA, on May 8, 1891, died Natchez, MS, Jan. 16, 1954. Aaron Culipher Register died Natchez, MS, in March 1930, age 62 years. Mary Ann McDonald Register and Aaron Culipher Register had issue:

(1a) Jean Marie Register (b. Dec. 2, 1892) md. Byron Robert Modesitt of Grand Island, NE, Jan. 9, 1931, no issue.

(2a) Hilda Culipher Register (b. Apr. 2, 1894) md. Thomas Edgar Young of London, England, 1921, died Natchez, MS, May 29, 1926, age 32 years, had issue: Anabel Register Young (b. Jul. 28, 1922) and Thomas Edgar Young (b. Jun. 28, 1924).

(3a) Anabal Postlethwaite Register (b. May 13, 1896) md. William Homer Bowman of Catahoula Parish, LA Aug. 18, 1918, has issue: Nedra Register, Aaron Charles, Jean Elizabeth, John William and William Homer.

(4a) John Aaron Register (b. Feb. 2, 1899) served as Special Courier to Pershing during World War I at Chaumont France. Served to the end of World War I. He died at Natchez, MS, as a result of an automobile accident, Oct. 5, 1924, age 25 years.

Bledsoe

Bledsoe Coat of Arms

2) Emily Postlethwaite McDonald, daughter of Mary Ann Gustine McDonald and Zimri McDonald, married Sanford Peabody Hulbert of New York at Natchez, MS Feb. 8, 1891. Emily died at Houston, TX June 4, 1944, age 75 years 10 months and 4 days, no issue.

GREGORY SEELEY BOOTH & SHIRLEY DARLEEN CRAIG.

During the mid-1980s Gregory Seeley Booth and Shirley Darleen Craig Booth made their residence on Windemere Plantation in Concordia Parish, LA.

Gregory Seeley Booth and Shirley Craig Booth

Greg was born in Bridgeport, CT Oct. 29, 1943 to Raymond Seeley Booth and Julia Benedict Smith Booth (See separate biography).

He graduated from Bridgeport Central High School in 1961 and attended Wesleyan University in Middletown, CT where, like his father, he was a member of Beta Theta Pi fraternity. In 1964 he joined the U.S. Navy and in 1966 he was awarded Naval Aviator Wings and was commissioned as an Ensign.

Shirley Darleen Craig was born in Natchez Feb. 20, 1942 to Wadley D. Craig and Josephine Elaine Richardson Craig (See Craig biography). She graduated from Natchez High School in 1960 and in 1964 received a BA in journalism from Louisiana State University where she was a member of Alpha Chi Omega sorority.

She spent two years as an editor for the *Pensacola (FL) News-Journal* and the fall of 1966 traveling in Europe. On Jan. 14, 1967 she and Greg were married in the chapel at NAS Miramar, San Diego, CA.

From 1967 through 1980 Greg made five West-Pac cruises, flying U.S. Navy F-4 and F-14

jet aircraft in the Vietnam War and making 628 carrier landings, including 158 night landings.

In 1971 he received a BS in engineering science and in 1972 a master of science degree in physics from the U.S. Naval Postgraduate School in Monterey, CA.

In 1969 Shirley spent 10 months traveling in Asia, returning home at the end of Greg's second West-Pac tour. Ryan Seeley Booth was born to the couple Dec. 13, 1972 in La Jolla, CA. On Oct. 29, 1975 Ashley Craig Booth was born in Portsmouth, VA. Scott Seeley Booth was born in Pensacola, FL Oct. 19, 1978, and Lori Craig Booth was born in Corpus Christi, TX Feb. 20, 1982.

Commander Greg Booth retired from the U.S. Navy in 1984 and harvested his first cotton crop on Windemere Plantation that same year. In January 1985 the family completed its move from Kingsville, TX to Concordia Parish, LA.

On Aug. 15, 1998 Ashley married Christopher Alan Chamberlin, son of Aubrey Adrian and Lanell Farr Chamberlin of Rambin, LA. Daniel Jackson Farr Chamberlin was born to the couple in Metairie, LA Jul. 13, 2000, and Katherine Ward Benedict Chamberlin was born in Brandon, MS Jul. 23, 2002.

On May 27, 2000 Ryan married Heather Dawn Simmons, daughter of Donald Quinon and Chong Ok Yun Simmons. Grace Elaine Booth was born to the couple Nov. 15, 2001 in Baton Rouge, LA.

On Aug. 7, 2003 Scott was commissioned as a second lieutenant in the U.S. Marine Corps, and Lori was a student at Louisiana State University.

Greg continued to grow cotton on Windemere Plantation and spent non-farming months working as a paramedic. A full-time homemaker, Shirley was an active member of the Natchez Garden Club and had served as chairman of the Preservation Society of Ellicott Hill.

RAYMOND SEELEY BOOTH & JULIA BENEDICT SMITH.

Raymond and Julia Booth moved to Magnolia House in Natchez in 2002 after having spent 35 years of retirement in Phoenix, AZ, the Hawaiian Islands, Fiji, Tonga, and American and Western Samoa.

A descendant of Governor William Bradford

Ryan Seeley Booth

Ashley Craig Booth

Scott Seeley Booth

Lori Craig Booth

of the *Mayflower*, Raymond was born in Washington, CT Sep. 25, 1905 to Earle Buckingham Booth and Mariette Elizabeth Seeley. Earle (b. Dec. 28, 1868 in New Haven, CT) was the son of Watson Cooler Booth and Julia Buckingham. Mariette (b. Aug. 2, 1874 in Washington, CT) was the daughter of Benjamin Nichols Seeley and Anna Apluma Hunt.

Raymond graduated as valedictorian in 1927 from Pennington School for Boys, a Methodist prep school in Pennington, NJ, and received a BS degree in chemistry from Wesleyan University in Middletown, CT in 1931. He was employed as an executive with the Borden Company until his retirement in 1967.

Julia (b. Oct. 29, 1906 in Roxbury, CT), daughter of Lincoln Charles Smith and Susan Hatch Pierce, was a noted artist, writer and lecturer. Lincoln (b. Nov. 6, 1878 in Woodbury, CT) was the son of Charles Kirtland Smith and Julia E. Benedict. Susan (b. Dec. 11, 1878 in Roxbury, CT) was the daughter of Frank H. Pierce and Elizabeth Van Ness Hatch.

Julia Booth

Julia graduated from Philadelphia School of Design in 1932 and traveled that year to Egypt, Greece, Turkey and other parts of the Mediterranean in the first of many tours that were to include two around the world.

Ray and Julia were married Oct. 14, 1933 in Roxbury, CT. They had two children, Mariette Seeley Booth (b. Nov. 6, 1940 in New Haven, CT) and son Gregory Seeley Booth (b. Oct. 29, 1943 in Bridgeport, CT).

Mariette graduated from Bassick High School in Bridgeport, CT in 1958. In 1962 she received a BS degree from Tuffs University and a master of science degree in 1971. She married Steve Vogel Jun. 3, 1963, and Roger Booth Vogel was born Jul. 20, 1966. Mariette taught biology at Clemson University.

Ray was an avid investor for most of his life and enjoyed spending his spare time charting investments and keeping track of events on Wall Street. Upon his retirement in 1967, he and Julia moved to Phoenix, AZ. They found refuge during the colder months each year in Hawaii or parts of the South

Raymond Booth

Pacific where Julia prolifically recorded local scenes and landscapes in watercolor.

THE BRABSTONS OF ADAMS COUNTY.

The first Brabs(t)on documented in the United States was John Brabson as referenced in a 1715 tax list in East Nottingham, Chester County, PA.

In the 1790s, two Brabston boys, John and Thomas, arrived in Adams County, MS, to live with their aunt, Mrs. Jessie (Elizabeth) Greenfield. It is believed that John and Thomas were the sons of Thomas Brabson, son of John. Thomas died in Lancaster County, PA in 1792. While there are numerous Brabsons in the United States, it appears that the alternate spelling, Brabston, was adopted by John and Thomas.

Jessie Greenfield married Elizabeth Holiday on May 13, 1773 at Old Swede's Church in Philadelphia, PA. Jesse's first land entry in Mississippi was 1789 on Bayou Pierre (now in Claiborne County). In 1792 Jesse was listed as a resident of the Natchez District. Jesse died in 1806, burial spot unknown. In 1807, Elizabeth was living on Second Creek in Adams County. On Feb. 11, 1811, Elizabeth married Benjamin Roach. This marriage was short lived. In 1818, Elizabeth donated land and buildings for Elizabeth Female Academy at Washington, MS. On Jul. 11, 1845, she was buried at Grace Episcopal Church in Philadelphia, PA.

John Brabston married Mary "Polly" Bullen in 1804 in Jefferson County, MS. Mary was the daughter of the Rev. Joseph Bullen and Hannah Moore. In the 1820s, John relocated to Warren County, MS and he and Mary are buried in an unmarked, abandoned cemetery near the corner of Gibson Road and China Grove Road in Warren County.

One branch of the family (Virginia Brabston Cook and family) still resides in Warren County.

Thomas married Anna Eldridge, daughter of David Eldridge of Adams County in 1810.

Thomas died Sep. 18, 1832, probably in Adams County, but his final resting place is unknown. Anna died Oct. 14, 1847 and is buried in Woodlands Cemetery, Philadelphia, PA. Thomas had extensive land holdings in both Adams County and in Concordia Parish, LA. Thomas and Anna had three children. Ann Marie (b. 1812, d. 1835) md. John Wesley Vick and they established Linden Plantation near Mount Alban (SE of Vicksburg) in Warren County, MS.

Upon her death in 1835 (final resting place unknown, but presumed to be with her father), her brother James Mickell (Mickle) (b. 1815, d. 1876) assumed control of Linden. He married Roche Robinson (b. 1816, d. 1895) who was probably living with her sister, Mary Downs, of Beech Grove Plantation, adjacent to Linden. James and Roche are buried at Linden.

The third child, Elizabeth Roach Brabston (b. 1816, d. 1889) md. William J. Ferguson (b. 1801, d. 1876). Both are buried in Machpelan Cemetery in Lafayette County, MO.

James M. and Roche Brabston had five children, only one of whom, William Henry, had issue. William married Agnes E. Willis in 1879, daughter of Edward Bryan Willis and Margaret E. Irwin. James Roche, William (b. 1857, d. 1889) and Agnes (b. 1859, d. 1943) are also buried at Linden.

This history is respectfully submitted by Bryan Willis Brabston Jr., grandson of William and Agnes and son of Bryan Willis Sr. (b. 1884, d. 1957) and Sarah Natalie Newell (b. 1906, d. 1989), daughter of Sally Hoggatt Newell. Bryan Sr. and Natalie are buried at St. Albans Episcopal Church, Bovina, MS.

Bryan Jr. and his wife, Joy Banks, are the current residents of Linden Plantation. *Submitted by Joy and Bryan Brabston.*

ADAM WADE BRADY & JESSICA JOY. Adam (b. Apr. 14, 1982) was the third child of four children born to Henry Brady Sr. and Rebecca "Carol" Wade of Adams County, MS. He married Jessica Joy on June 28, 2002. She was the fourth and last child born to Steve Joy Jr. and Sharon Lewis Joy.

Adam graduated Natchez High School and attended Copiah-Lincoln College. He has worked as a teller, December 2000 to present, and enjoys writing and astronomy. Jessica graduated

Adam, Jessica and William Noah Brady

ACCS and also attended Copiah-Lincoln College; she is a housewife. They have one son William Noah Brady (b. Jan. 11, 2003). They live in the Morgantown area and attend Lighthouse Baptist Church.

HENRY BRADY SR. was the fourth and last child born on Jul. 23, 1947 to Lafayette Brady and Eva Mae Mercer Brady of Natchez, MS. He married Rebecca "Carol" Wade on Jul. 2, 1971. Carol was the fifth child of six born to Cliff and Doris Wade.

Brady Family

Henry attended Port Gibson High School and worked for the MDOT from 1967 to 2002. He enjoys reading and going to church. Carol attended Martin and is a housewife. They have four children: Jenny (b. Sep. 27, 1972); Henry Jr. (b. Jun. 15, 1975); Adam (b. Apr. 4, 1982); and Matthew (b. Aug. 7, 1983). Henry and Carol live on Pine Ridge Road and attend Lighthouse Baptist Church.

HENRY BRADY JR. & BERTHA FRANKLIN. Henry Jr. (b. June 15, 1975) is the second of four children born to Henry Brady Sr. and Rebecca "Carol" Wade Brady of Adam's County. He married Bertha Franklin on Mar. 9, 1996. Bertha was the fifth and last child born to Cecil and Georgia Franklin.

Henry Brady Jr., Bertha Franklin Brady and Shelby Brady

Henry attended Natchez High School and began working as a butcher in 1995. He enjoys going to church and hunting and fishing. Bertha attended ACCS. She is a housewife and enjoys reading. They have one child, Shelby Brady (b. Apr. 19, 1997).

BRANDON FAMILY. The Brandon family has been in Adams County, MS since about the year 1786 with the arrival of the immigrant, Gerard

Brandon. Gerard was born in County Fermanagh, Ireland around 1750. He purchased 640 acres in Washington, MS and built his home "Selma." There he raised his family of nine children which included the first native born Governor of Mississippi - Gerard Chittoque Brandon.

Gerard Chittoque Brandon received his education from private tutors, Jefferson College in Washington, MS, Princeton College in New Jersey, then entered and graduated at William and Mary College in Virginia. He was elected a trustee of Jefferson College in Washington, MS in 1812. He was a lawyer by profession and for a while had his office in Washington until he lo-

Gov. Gerard C. Brandon

cated as a planter to Wilkinson County, MS. He was a representative (1815) from Wilkinson County in the Territorial Assembly and a delegate in the First Constitutional Convention of Mississippi (held in Washington, MS) and adopted the Constitution under which Mississippi became one of the States of the United States of America. He was a member of the Mississippi Legislature in 1821, 1822 and in 1823; and Speaker of the House in 1822. He was elected Lieutenant Governor of Mississippi for the terms of 1824-25 and 1826-27 during which time he filled the unexpired terms of Governors Leake and Holmes as Governor. He was elected Governor of Mississippi for the terms 1828-29 and again for 1830-31. He was offered the U.S. Senatorship but declined and retired from politics to the private life of a planter. Gerard married twice. He had two sons by his first wife, Margaret Chambers, and six sons and two daughters by his second wife, Elizabeth Stanton.

Gerard C. Brandon's son, Dr. James Chambers Brandon, by his first wife Margaret, married Anna Virginia Monette who was the daughter of well-known physician, Dr. John Wesley Monette. Dr. Monette's ancestors originally came from Poitou, France. Dr. Monette and his wife lived at Sweet Auburn in Washington, MS where they reared their family.

Dr. Monette was

Dr. John Wesley Monette

noted as a historian, naturalist, poet and writer as well as physician. Some of his works are titled *Floods of the Mississippi River, The History of the Discovery and Settlement of the Valley of the Mississippi,* and *Observations on the Epidemic Yellow Fever of Natchez and of the Southwest.* In the 1820s several epidemics of yellow fever broke out in Natchez and Washington, MS, which started Dr. Monette's investigation of the disease. At this time Dr. Monette suggested the use of quarantines in restricting the disease. This was the first step in controlling yellow fever which later contributed to finding a "cure."

Dr. James Chambers Brandon and Anna Virginia Monette had eight children. One son, Gerard Brandon, was a prominent attorney in Natchez. Gerard was born at Sweet Auburn in 1861. He attended Jefferson College. Gerard graduated with a degree of Bachelor of Arts at University of

Mississippi in 1882 and received the degree of Master of Arts in 1884 from the University.

Gerard was principal of the public school of Natchez in the old Natchez Institute from September 1882 to September 1889. Gerard read law under the direction of Richard E. Conner of the Natchez Bar and began to practice law in September 1891. From 1887 to 1891 Gerard was one of the owners and publishers of the *Natchez Evening Banner* and from 1889 to 1891 was teller and assistant cashier of the Natchez Savings Bank & Loan & Trust Company. Gerard's law firms have been Reed & Brandon; Brandon & Bowman; Reed, Brandon & Bowman; and last, Brandon & Brandon.

Gerard married Daisy Patterson and they reared four children: Ethel Monette Brandon (b. Dec. 3, 1894, d. Dec. 4, 1948) md. David Lawson Lemmon Smith and second Robert S. Dixon; Gerard Hamilton Brandon (b. Sep. 12, 1896, d. Mar. 8, 1961) md. Kate Doniphan Prichard (b. Jul. 31, 1899, d. May 11, 1983); Sara Patterson Brandon (b. Jun. 18, 1902, d. Oct. 3, 1993) md. Harry Wynn Rickey; James Monette Brandon (b. Jan. 26, 1904, d. Dec. 4, 1977) md. Frances Marie Mahier. Gerard H. and his brother, James, were both attorneys and practiced law with their father in the law firm Brandon & Brandon.

Gerard Hamilton Brandon was baptised and confirmed in Trinity Episcopal Church in Natchez. Gerard H. attended public schools in Natchez then graduated from Branham & Hughes School for Boys at Spring Field, TN. Gerard H. completed the freshman and sophomore classes at University of Mississippi then entered the law school at the same university.

During World War I he was assigned to the first class in the Officers Training School at Fort Logan H. Root in Little Rock, AR. He was commissioned 2nd lieutenant in 334 Field Artillery. For eight months he attended the Artillery Training School at Lar Sourge in France. Gerard was transferred to 107 Field Artillery and moved "to the front" when the Armistice was declared Nov. 11, 1918. After the Armistice, Gerard was honorably discharged from military service and returned to the United States and to the University of Mississippi to complete his law studies and to receive a degree of bachelor of law in June 1920. Gerard practiced law in Natchez and was for four years county prosecuting attorney.

Gerard H. and his wife, Kate Don, reared four daughters: Kate Doniphan Brandon who married first George Lawrence Adams (b. Oct. 10, 1913, d. Jul. 16, 1994) and second John Green; Mary Ann Brandon married Lester Kenneth Jones (b. May 2, 1925, d. Sep. 12, 2001); Daisy Patterson Brandon married Wilton Rogers Dale; Barbara Gerard Brandon married Charles Hayden Kaiser II.

Descendants of Gerard H. and Kate Don Brandon still residing in Natchez in 2003 were Mrs. Kate Don Brandon Green, Mrs. Mary Ann Brandon Jones, Mrs. Daisy Patterson Brandon Dale, Mrs. Barbara Gerard Brandon Kaiser, Mrs. Kim Monette Jones Garrett, Mary Ann Cartwright Jones, Mrs. Elizabeth "Betsy" Dale Holleman, Elizabeth Holleman, John C. Holleman, Lindsay Holleman, Hayden Kaiser III, Caroline Kaiser, Chase Kaiser, Mrs. Kate Doniphan Nations Seale, Peyton Gore, Fleming Gore Stout, Adrian Sandel, Ashley Sandel, and Will Sandel. *Submitted by Kim M. Garrett.*

VIOLA & MARCELLUS BRANICKS.

Viola was a cook associated with the Quitman family at Monmouth as a slave. Marcellus, also a slave, worked for the McMurran family as second waiter. Viola served as bridesmaid for the August 1856 wedding at Melrose of slaves Patrick and Mime.

The records of Trinity Episcopal Church indicate that Marcellus and Viola (colored) were married at Monmouth on May 14, 1857 by the Rev. Charles Dana.

The 1886 Natchez city census lists the Branicks family living in the South Suburban district where Melrose and Monmouth were both located. At that time, Marcellus, age 69, was working as a gardener. His wife Viola was listed as 55, and the children living with them were Viola (14), Joseph (11), Cassie (8), David (6), and Edward (5). It is unclear whether these are children or grandchildren. Rosalie Quitman Duncan sold a portion of the Monmouth property to Viola Brannick on Apr. 15, 1903.

PAUL BRITT & BETTY ANNE TARVER.

Betty Anne Tarver (b. Jul. 22, 1937 on Smithland Plantation, Natchez, Adams County, MS) is the daughter of Mary Louise McCaleb and Roy Howard Tarver. Mary Louise (b. Oct. 30, 1918 in Adams County), the daughter of Anne Matilda Farrar and Sidney Briscoe McCaleb Sr., who owned Smithland Plantation in the Kingston Community, Adams County. Roy (b. Aug. 10, 1911 in Smithdale, Amite County, MS, d. Jan. 4, 1985 in Natchez) was the son of Frances "Fannie" Elizabeth Thornton and Isaac "Ike" Ham Tarver of Lincoln County.

As a Natchez native, Betty is descended from several very early settlers in the Natchez District. These include the following: Richard Swayze, Caleb King, William McCaleb, Alexander Farrar, George Dougharty, William Collins, Windsor Pipes, John Bisland, Moses King, Peter Rucker, Morris Custard, John Robson Sr., Eliza Sojourner, Joseph Thomas, Dr. Henry Kirk White Ford, and both Alexander Boyd and his sister Mary Boyd.

The siblings of Betty Anne Tarver are William John Tarver (b. Aug. 16, 1938 in Natchez); Pauline "Polly" Tarver (b. Feb. 26, 1940 in Natchez); George David Tarver (b. Apr. 24, 1941 in Natchez); Daniel Howard Tarver (b. Jun. 26, 1943 in Natchez); and Benjamin Edward Tarver (b. Jul. 30, 1944 in Natchez).

On Nov. 25, 1955 in Natchez, Betty Anne Tarver married Paul Britt (b. Mar. 31, 1927 in Copiah County, MS), the son of Bessie Hudson and Carl Britt. They are the parents of seven children, all born in Natchez: Charlotte Britt (b. Sep. 12, 1956 (see separate biography); Karen Delores Britt (b. Oct. 17, 1957); Patricia Kaye Britt (b. Jul. 3, 1959); Terry Lee Britt (b. Sep. 26, 1960); Andrew Duane Britt (b. Dec. 13, 1964); Michael Lynn Britt (b. Jun. 18, 1971); Angela Michelle Britt (b. Oct. 18, 1975).

Paul Britt worked for many years for Billups Petroleum Co. and for Southland Oil Company in Natchez.

Betty Anne Tarver, November 1989

Betty Anne Tarver attended schools in the Natchez Public School System, including Carpenter #1, Carpenter #2, Natchez Institute, and Natchez High School, graduating in 1955. While she was in high school, she took business courses. During her last two years, she worked for attorney Frank W. Walden and continued working for him for more than a year after graduation. For the past 18 years Betty has worked in the law office of Natchez attorney, Daniel J. O'Beirne.

Betty has fond memories of helping her grandfather, Sidney B. McCaleb Sr., in his little country store in the Kingston area. Before she was even school age, at night he allowed her to help him count his money from the store. He started her off by counting pennies, and when she could count them correctly, he moved her up to other coins. By the time she was in the third grade, she could easily count all of his money accurately.

ANDREW BURNS & ALICE EVELYN WILKINS.

Andrew was born in Natchez on Jun. 21, 1923, the seventh of eight children born to Honora Grady and Francis Parnell Burns. He passed away on Jan. 31, 1999. He was widely known as "Uncle Doc" to his nieces, nephews, and many of their friends. He was also known as "Doumy" to many of his friends.

Andrew and Alice Burns at 50th wedding anniversary, 1997 and Tim and Carla Burns

His siblings: Patrick Parnell Burns (b. Dec. 28, 1911), Anthony Grady Burns (b. Oct. 11, 1913, d. Dec. 9, 1991), Mary Agnes Burns Frye (b. Nov. 28, 1915, d. Dec. 15, 1995), Honora Burns Aubic (b. Nov. 1, 1917, d. Jan. 25, 1985), Margaret Burns (b. Oct. 13, 1919), Peter Theophile Burns (b. Oct. 19, 1921), and Ann Elizabeth Burns Garrity (b. Jan. 17, 1925).

Andrew was a lifetime member of St. Mary's (Basilica) Parish. He was also a member of the Knights of Columbus. He graduated from St. Joseph High School in 1941.

During his high school years, Andrew began working in the family business, Burns' Shoe Store. His grandfather Patrick Burns (who had come from Ireland and settled in Natchez) established Burns' Shoe Store in 1893. The business was in continuous operation for 105 years, until Oct. 31, 1998.

After serving in the Army Air Corps during World War II, Andrew returned to Natchez and the family business.

On Feb. 10, 1947, he married Alice Evelyn Wilkins, from Tensas Parish, LA. She was born on Jun. 3, 1923, to Lily Souter and William Lee Wilkins.

Andrew and Alice had two children: Carla Marie Burns (b. Jan. 4, 1955), and Timothy Thad Burns (b. Feb. 14, 1957).

During his lifetime, Andrew enjoyed many summers on Lake St. John. His maternal aunt, Mary Agnes Grady, had built a cottage on the lake and it became a family get-away. In the autumn months, Andrew enjoyed following Cathedral football. He was also an avid hunter, preferring deer and rabbit.

MARGARET BURNS

(b. Oct. 13, 1919) was born at 812 Main Street, Natchez, MS, the fifth of eight children. Her siblings: Patrick Parnell Burns (b. Dec. 28, 1911), Anthony Grady Burns (b. Oct. 11, 1913, d. Dec. 9, 1991), Mary Agnes Burns Frye (b. Nov. 28, 1915, d. Dec. 15, 1995), Honora Burns Aubic (b. Nov. 1, 1917, d. Jan. 25, 1985), Peter

1st Reunion of descendants of Patrick Burns

Theophile Burns (b. Oct. 19, 1921), Andrew Burns (b. Jun. 21, 1923, d. Jan. 31, 1999) and Ann Elizabeth Burns Garrity (b. Jan. 17, 1925).

Her paternal grandparents were Patrick Burns (b. Mar. 17, 1837, d. Mar. 17, 1909) and Mary Welch (b. 1844, d. Feb. 26, 1982) and her maternal grandparents were Anthony James Grady (b. 1850, d. 1909) and Mary Ann Davis (b. 1854, d. 1913). Her parents were Francis Parnell Burns (b. Feb. 24, 1880, d. Aug. 5, 1946) and Honora Grady (b. Jul. 11, 1886, d. Oct. 5, 1955). Her grandfather Patrick Burns, who was born in Ireland, founded Burns Shoe Store and his sons and grandsons continued the business for 105 years. She has lived her lifetime in Natchez. She graduated from St.

Margaret Burns

Joseph School in 1936 and MSCW (Columbus, MS) in 1940 with a BS degree in elementary education. She taught school in Lake Charles, LA, 1940-43. She taught in Natchez Public Schools, 1943-77. She is a lifetime member of St. Mary's Basilica. *Submitted by Margaret Burns.*

SAMUEL BURNS, master carpenter and furniture maker, came to Adams County in 1840 from what is now West Virginia. His son, also a master carpenter and furniture maker, was the father of Samuel Burns, about whom this story is written.

Saturday, Mar. 14, 1908, began quietly enough, but by mid-afternoon, Natchez, MS was under martial law, 11 people were dead or dying, a five-story business (the tallest building in 1908 Natchez) was rubble and at least 18 homes had burned to the ground or sustained fire damage.

Mrs. Bernard (Rosa) Moritz owned one of those homes. On March 14, she was showing needed repair work to a young plumber, Samuel Joseph Burns, when he received a phone call that he should report to the Natchez Drug Co. to find and repair a gas leak in plumbing that had been recently completed.

The Masons had erected the building that housed the Natchez Drug Co. in 1892 for use as a Masonic Temple Opera House. The Natchez Drug Company bought the building in 1904 and remodeled it for use as a laboratory. Mr. Burns proceeded to the fourth floor of the building. A survivor, Miss Myrtle Simms, later testified: *He carried a lighted candle in his hand and made a test of the gas fixtures. I heard him remark: 'The leak is not here; it must be somewhere below.' Mr. Burns then went to the second floor with a lighted candle to look for leaks.*

The ensuing explosion left 11 people dead: Ada White, Cleveland Laub (chemist), Inez Netterville, Willie Kates, Mrs. John P. Ketteringham, Carrie H. Murray, Sam Burns, Luella Booth, Lizzie Worthy, John Carkeet and Uriah Haskins.

After an "exhausting" inquest, Sam Burns was exonerated from all liability. An editorial that appeared in the Mar. 19, 1908 edition of Natchez's *The Daily Democrat* stated, *The decision is all that could have been expected... that he (Burns) employed the same method that has been the practice for years and years by old and experienced men, known to all plumbers and to many who are not."* P.W. Mulvihill, a competing plumber, testified during the inquest that "young Burns," a former employee of his, was regarded as a "sober, intelligent and efficient workman" and that he would have entrusted Burns with such a job as the one at the Natchez Drug Co.

Although only 21 at the time of his death, Sam Burns was well known and respected in the Natchez Community. He was a member of Company B, Third Regiment, State National Guard. Sam's brother, Joseph Stratton Burns, was a first lieutenant in Company B. Sam was also a member of Eagle Hook and Ladder Co., No. 2, Natchez Volunteer Fire Department. His funeral cortege started at the family home on Orange Avenue, where his great-great-nephew now (2002) resides. Two military companies of the SNG led the procession to the gravesite. A volley was fired across the flower-covered mound and taps were blown by the bugler." The firehouse bells tolled, as well.

Sam's brother, Joseph Stratton Burns, was married to Bessie Kellogg Burns. Bessie was pregnant at the time of Sam's death and witnessed the explosion's billowing smoke from a distance. She later named her own son Samuel Bentley Burns. Rosa Moritz, who had called Sam Burns (the plumber) to her home on the morning of Mar. 14, 1908, had a daughter, Edith Elizabeth, who later married Samuel Bentley Burns. Their son, Samuel Bentley Burns Jr., is the author of this article.

CHARLES AVERY BRYAN & SUSAN JEANNETTE CLARK. Capt. Charles Bryan (b. Apr. 23, 1838, in Maryland) was a Confederate soldier in Co. B. 1st Maryland Cav., captured in Virginia, prisoner of war at Camp Chase, Columbus, OH. After the war he bought a plantation in Franklin Parish, LA. He died at his home on South Rankin St., Natchez, MS. and was buried in Natchez Cemetery. In 1877 he was a vestryman, Trinity Episcopal Church.

He married Susan Jeannette Clark (b. Dec. 29, 1841, Natchez, MS), daughter of Col. Robert Clark and Margaret S. Crane of Newark, NJ. They were married May 19, 1869 by the Rev. Charles B. Dana of Trinity Episcopal Church, Natchez. She died May 27, 1893.

Col. Bryan and his wife, affectionately called Nettie, had two surviving children:

Charles Myer Bryan (b. Jul. 4, 1877) md. Lotta Ventress, daughter of Mr. and Mrs. L.T. Ventress, Woodville, MS. They had three children: Charles C. Bryan, Thomas Bryan and Charlotte Bryan.

John Kausler Bryan (b. Mar. 10, 1875 on the plantation in Franklin Parish, LA) was baptized and confirmed at Trinity Episcopal Church, Natchez. He died Sep. 14, 1919 in Natchez, MS.

Married by the Rev. Josiah H. Perry of Trinity Church, Natchez, MS on Apr. 5, 1904.

Annis Dunbar Johnstone (b. Aug. 6, 1868, Rye Westchester County, NY), was the daughter of Mary Dunbar Jenkins "Mamie" (born at Elgin Plantation, Natchez, MS, daughter of John C. Jenkins and Annis Dunbar Jenkins) and Louis Morris Johnstone (New York, NY). An 1886 Census Natchez, Adams County, MS: L.M. Johnstone, Planter; M.D. Johnstone, Housewife; A.D. Johnstone, daughter. There home was on St. Charles Ave., Natchez, MS.

John and Annis Bryan had two children:

John Kausler Bryan Jr. (b. Feb. 7, 1907, d. Apr. 25, 1994) md. Clarice Lambert George, daughter of Benjamin James George and Beatrice Lambert George, at Trinity Episcopal Church, Natchez on Jun. 25, 1934. Three children: John K. Bryan III, Clarice Lamar Bryan, Ann Lambert Bryan.

Annis Dunbar Bryan (b. Jun. 24, 1912, d. Apr. 19, 1995) md. Charles August Kuehn Jr., son of Charles August Kuehn and Annie Elizabeth Annis. Three children:

1) Annis Elizabeth Kuehn "Betty" (b. Mar. 30, 1927) md. William Francis Rogillio on Feb. 22, 1947, Trinity Episcopal Church, Natchez. Two children, Elizabeth Ann Rogillio and William Francis Rogillio Jr.

2) Charlotte Rose Kuehn (b. Oct. 25, l929) md. Ralph Oswald Thompson Jr. on Sep. 3, 1949, Trinity Episcopal Church, Natchez. Two children, Janice Kay Thompson and Ralph O. Thompson Jr.

3) Effie Scott Kuehn (b. Nov. 8, 1931) md. Robert Ray Gough, San Rafael, CA, Aug. 21, 1952. One child, Bryan Ray Gough.

Peter Buttross Sr. family siblings: Janice Walker, Marilyn Emfinger, Peter Buttross Jr., Patricia Kenner, Margaret Brinegar, Jayne Buttross

The three girls attended Natchez Public Schools, baptized and confirmed Trinity Episcopal Church, Natchez.

PETER BUTTROSS SR. & WADDAD HABEEB BUTTROSS are both children of Lebanese immigrants who came to America at the turn of the 19th century. In both of their families there are six sons and two daughters. Peter and Waddad had six daughters and one son:

1) Patricia Ann Buttross Kenner holds a degree in speech pathology from the University of Southern Mississippi, Hattiesburg (USM). She has practiced the greater part of her career in New Orleans public schools. She has two children, Katherine Alexis and Brian Patrick.

2) Catherine Louise died in infancy.

3) Peter Buttross Jr. holds a Ph.D. in political philosophy from Louisiana State University; a master's in international management from The Thunderbird School, Glendale, AZ; a double BA from the University of Dallas, Irving, TX. He was recipient of a Fulbright Fellowship to France, a

Rotary International Fellowship to Belgium and the LSU Alumni Federation Scholarship in politics. He has worked as a domestic and an international banker and a teacher. He is a writer/poet. He has two children, David Alexander and Matthew Ryan.

4) Marilyn Alexis Buttross Emfinger holds an AB degree in business administration from Southwest Junior College, Wesson, MS. A self-taught horticulturist, Marilyn owns and manages a green house and garden center operation in Lafayette, LA. She has three children (with Charles Ray Emfinger, deceased): Charles Ray Jr., William Lockwood, and Christopher Jude; and two grandchildren, Noah and Kylie.

5) Janice Marie "Bunny" Buttross Walker holds a master's degree in special education from USM. She has taught Special Ed for 23 years, mostly in the Lafayette public schools. She is married to Glen Walker and has two children, Jonathan Marshal and Erin Marie.

6) Margaret Waddad Buttross Brinegar holds a bachelor's degree in speech pathology from USM and a master's from the University of North Carolina, Chapel Hill. For 23 years, she has co-directed, practiced and taught at The Child Development Center on the campus of the University of Southern Mississippi, Hattiesburg. Her late husband Roger Brinegar was a ceramic artist, member of the Mississippi Arts Guild, and a longtime employee in the public relations office of USM.

7) Jayne Louise Buttross holds a bachelor's degree in political science from USM and a law degree from the University of Mississippi, Oxford, MS. She has maintained a private law practice, has been Dean of Students at the Mississippi School for the Deaf, and has held high-level non-elective state governmental offices, including general counsel to the governor and deputy director of the state Department of Environmental Quality.

Peter's parents, David and Freeda Buttross, began their life together in New Orleans and ended in Canton, MS.

Waddad's parents, Alex and Loretta Habeeb, began their life in Jamestown, PA, and, after returning to Lebanon where they were detained by WWI, returned to settle in Vicksburg, MS, where Waddad was born. Waddad attended Vicksburg public schools, as well as All Saints College. Peter attended Canton public schools, as well as Saint Stanislaus in Bay Saint Louis.

Peter Buttross Sr. and Waddad Habeeb Buttross

In 1941, they were married in Vicksburg and lived in Canton until 1947 when, with their two young children, Patricia and Peter, they moved to Natchez where they became part of the town's then-thriving business community. For two years they were in business with Peter's brother Alphonse in Buttross Wholesale at 112 North Pearl Street. In 1949, Peter and Waddad opened their department clothing store, Cradle Thru College, at 500/502 Main Street. The store was co-managed by them and sustained by their five daughters all of whom "worked in the shop." Though the business changed locations twice and though its name was changed to Peter's Children's Boutique, their store remained in continuous operation from 1949 until 1991 when they retired. Peter also bought, developed, and managed light commercial real estate.

Peter was twice president of the Natchez Lions Club and twice president of the Natchez Jay-

cees, as well as a Fourth Degree in the Knights of Columbus. He was campaign manager for southwest Mississippi for Governor John Bell Williams, and a volunteer state-wide campaigner for Governor Bill Waller. He has two holes-in-one, both on #6 of the Natchez Duncan Park Course. He is also a member of Beau Pre Country Club.

Waddad is author of *Waddad's Kitchen,* a cookbook of both American southern and old family Lebanese recipes. Another cook booklet is in production, *Cooking With Bulgar Wheat.* She is a member of the Natchez Garden Club and a former member of the Altar Society of Saint Mary's Basilica of which they are members.

Josephine Richardson Craig and Wadley D. Craig

WADLEY D. CRAIG & JOSEPHINE ELAINE RICHARDSON. Wadley D. Craig and Josephine Elaine Richardson were married Aug. 21, 1940 and until 1946 owned and operated The Pilgrimage Inn, a popular hangout for Natchez High School students on Homochitto Street where Braden School was later located.

Wadley was born Nov. 11, 1915 in the Craig Settlement area of Rapides Parish between Libuse and Kolin to Samuel Green Craig and Mary Rosella Brown. The progenitor of the Craig family in that area, Joseph Craig of Scotland, had settled there with his Irish wife, Anna Margaret Devereaux, in 1849.

Their son, Joseph Jr., married Anna Adeline Thompson, granddaughter of Lemuel Thompson and Frances Robertson who had come into Louisiana's Florida parishes in 1811. Green was born to Joseph Jr. and Anna on Nov. 20, 1880, and on Dec. 18, 1901, he married Mary Rosella Brown (b. Oct. 28, 1882), daughter of Richard Duncan Brown and Louisa Smith of Grant Parish, LA. They were descendants of Richard Stone Brown and Priscilla Wainwright of Franklin County, MS and William Henderson Smith and Mary Louise Cook of Smith County, MS.

In 1932 at the height of the depression, Green and Rosella's 17-year-old son Wadley set out to find his way in the world. His path eventually took him to Natchez where he met Josie who was visiting friends in the city. Josie (b. May 8, 1919) was

Wade Wadley Craig (age 3) and Shirley Darleen Craig (age 5), children of Wadley and Josie Craig

the daughter of Lee Thomas Richardson and Mary Virginia Ward of Yazoo County, MS.

Lee's paternal great-grandparents, Joseph and Frances Banks Richardson, had come to Yazoo County from South Carolina in the 1830s. All four of Josie's great-grandfathers, William J. Richardson, John W. Wilson, James T. Ward, and Richard M.L. Evers, and one great-great-grandfather, Henry H. Tisdale, were Confederate veterans.

On Feb. 20, 1942 a daughter, Shirley Darleen Craig, was born to Wadley and Josie, and on Jun. 2, 1944, a son, Wade Wadley Craig (See separate Craig and Booth biographies).

In 1946 Wadley and partner Jake Brown opened The Sports Center at 118 N. Union Street in Natchez. Several years later Wadley bought out his partner when Jake was elected Adams County supervisor. Wadley and Josie maintained a home for many years at 712 North Rankin Street.

An avid sportsman, Wadley enjoyed the outdoors and from 1950 the couple maintained a second home on Lake St. John in Concordia Parish, LA. They moved there in 1960. In 1973 ownership of The Sports Center was passed to their son Wade, and Wadley and Josie purchased Windemere Plantation on the Ferriday to Lake St. John Highway. Wadley grew cotton there for nine years. In 1984 Wadley and Josie built a house on Windemere Plantation and retired there.

A full-time homemaker, Josie enjoyed working in her garden and became well known in the community for her expert flower arranging. A member of both the Natchez Garden Club (from 1951) and the Ferriday Garden Club, she brought home numerous awards from the annual flower shows.

WADE WADLEY CRAIG. Wade (b. Jun 2, 1944, Natchez) was the son of Wadley D. Craig and Josephine Elaine Richardson Craig. He graduated from Natchez Adams County High School in 1962 and in 1966 received a Bachelor of Business degree from Western Kentucky University in Bowling Green, KY.

In 1971 Wade opened a sporting goods business in Meridian, MS and in 1973 purchased the Sports Center at 118 N. Union Street, Natchez, from his father. He opened the Sports Center in the Natchez Mall in 1981, and in 1983 he purchased a competing downtown business, Rex Sporting Goods, and combined the two businesses into the Rex Sporting Goods location in 1987. In the fall of 2002 he combined the two businesses under the Sports Center name and moved to a new location on Seargent S. Prentiss Drive.

He also operated Rex Team Sports which supplied team uniforms and equipment to schools and civic organizations across the states of Mississippi and Louisiana. The Sports Center joined Nation's Best Sports buying group in 1969. Wade became one of the five national directors in 1998 and was named chairman of the Finance Committee in 2002.

Wade was also active in local youth sports programs, coaching numerous youth baseball and basketball teams and serving as head coach for the Trinity Episcopal School soccer program.

On Apr 10, 1968 Wade married Teri Lynn Balint (b. Sep 18, 1945) in West Palm Beach, FL. Teri was the daughter of Joe and Margaret Balint. They were divorced in 1983.

He married Elizabeth Anne Rhodes, daughter of Roland Eugene Rhodes (b. Jan 21, 1928 in Union Parish, LA) and Elsie Mae Roberson (b. Nov 29, 1932 in El Dorado, AR) on Dec 11, 1985 at the Jefferson Street Methodist Church in Natchez. Elizabeth was born Nov 14, 1958 in Laurel, MS. She brought into the marriage Robert "Bobby" Tucker Craig, born Virgil Brooks Tucker IV Apr 2, 1982 in Memphis, TN. Wade

Wyatt Craig was born to the couple in Natchez Feb 9, 1987 and attended Trinity Episcopal School.

Elizabeth attended the University of Mississippi in Oxford where she was a member of Delta Gamma sorority. She was active in many aspects of Natchez community life including the Natchez Garden Club, the Miss Hospitality Pageant, and the Jefferson Street Methodist Church youth program.

Wade and Elizabeth Craig with Wade Wyatt (seated) and Bobby (standing)

She was founder in 1995 of the New Life Renewal cancer support group. She died in Natchez Feb 23, 1998 and is buried in Natchez in Greenlawn Memorial Park.

Wyatt, Wade and Bobby Craig

On Sep 23, 2000 Wade married Rebecca Lynn Williams Adams in Natchez. Rebecca was born Aug 22, 1960 in Shreveport to Charles Marvin Williams Sr. and Janette Eason. She received paralegal certification from LSU Shreveport in the early 1980s and was also a Notary Public for the State of Louisiana.

CAUSEY FAMILY. The Causeys in Mississippi and Louisiana largely descend from the two marriages of Revolutionary War Captain William Causey Sr. who was born Jul. 17, 1744 at Grant's Causeway, County Galway, Ireland (family legend) and died Jul. 3, 1828 at his Causey Springs Plantation, established 1805 near Berwick, Amite County, MS.

William Cawsey (sic, Causey) apparently arrived at Charles Town, SC aboard the Brigantine *St. Peter* from London on Feb. 10, 1768. This may not have been his first crossing, and he may have had close relatives in Maryland.

He lived in Maryland at the start of the Revolutionary War and joined the 14th Maryland Battalion of Militia in 1776, later serving under General Francis Marion, the famed "Swamp Fox," in South Carolina from 1779-82. He enlisted as a private, was elected an ensign and promoted to captain before the war's end. He was thereafter called "Captain" in honor of his patriotic service. After the war he moved his wife and family to near Beaufort, SC and remained there, it is said, until the children of his first marriage were grown.

William reportedly married his unknown first wife in Maryland and reared a family of 11 children. She died ca. 1803 in South Carolina. He married secondly to Susannah Jackson, daughter of Patriot Isaac Jackson, on Sep. 2, 1805 in Wilkinson/Amite County, MS and reared a second family of eight children.

For his Patriotic Revolutionary War service he was granted 320 acres of land in Amite County, MS on the west fork of the Amite River between Liberty and Centreville, one-half mile north of Berwick, Amite County, MS. Given the natural freshwater springs on the property, his plantation became known as Causey Springs. Over time, he increased his acreage significantly, at one time holding in excess of 2000 acres.

CAUSEY LINEAGE: The E.R. Killian family is dually descended from both of William's two marriages; his second marriage to Susannah Jackson through their son, Seaborn Tarrant Causey (b. 1817, d. 1858), their grandson, Garnett Taylor Causey (b. 1846, d. 1917), and their great-grandson, Edward Edison Causey (b. 1880, d. 1951) md. Helen Daisy Causey.

Helen Daisy Causey (b. 1879, d. 1936) is a daughter of Henry Rufus Causey (b. 1846, d. 1926) and the granddaughter of Josiah Chelson Causey (b. 1808, d. 1850). Josiah Chelson Causey is a son of Thomas Causey (b. 1778, d. 1853) and a grandson of William Causey's first marriage.

Edward Edison and Helen Daisy Causey's daughter, Victoria Hinton Causey (b. 1913, d. 1988) md. Jewel Royce Killian (b. 1909, d. 1983). Victoria and Jewel are the parents of E.R. Killian. *Submitted by E.R. Killian.*

MARY ELIZABETH MCMURRAN & FARAR BENJAMIN CONNER. Mary Eliza (b. 1835, d. 1864) lived at Holly Hedges in downtown Natchez when she was a girl, then at the Melrose estate on the eastern edge of town. She was about 11 when they moved to the suburbs near her Quitman cousins at Monmouth.

In the parlor at Melrose on Jan. 24, 1856, Mary Eliza married Farar Benjamin Conner (b. 1834, d. 1904) of Linden, the younger brother of her aunt Fanny's husband Lemuel P. Conner. Though no photographs of her have survived, a beautiful pink and white silk dress manufactured by famed dressmaker Charles Worth of Paris that was part of her trousseau has been passed down through the Conner family.

The children of Mary Eliza McMurran and Farar Benjamin Conner were: Benjamin Farar Conner ("Fazee," b. January 1857); Mary Louisa Conner ("Soulie," b. at Melrose Dec. 28, 1858, d. of dysentery at Melrose, May 20, 1864); and John McMurran Conner (b. 1861, d. of dysentery at Woodlands, May 21, 1865). Fazee, the first-born, endured a surgical procedure for a club foot in New Orleans as an infant, and remained somewhat crippled for the remainder of his life.

Farar Conner had studied at Yale, then he and his wife received Killarney Plantation on Lake St. John in Louisiana from his father-in-law, John T. McMurran. In her mid-20s, Mary Eliza began to show signs of a debilitating illness that affected her spine and her mental faculties. She deteriorated to the point where she was described as having the body of an old woman and the mind of a child. She died in her Melrose bedroom in March 1864. All the family women and slave women stood watch around her bed that night, then her mother wrote to her brother John McMurran Jr. in Maryland the details of his sister's death: "Eleven o'clock, April 1st, was named as the funeral hour - ere that the precious clay was robed in white, in simple but full dress of Swiss muslin - kind friends sent beautiful flowers - a crown of white Azaleas encircled her head, a bunch of snowdrops in her hand and then strewn with other pure white flowers - it was like decking a bride - but the bride of death!" Mary Eliza's daughter died of dysentery within a month of her mother.

In 1861, Farar Conner had joined a company of Confederate cavalry, the first company to leave Natchez. He was a private in the Army of Virginia, promoted in 1863 to become a member of Bragg's army on the staff of General William T. Martin, his brother-in-law. He was wounded and captured at the Battle of Shelbyville, then held in a military prison at Johnson's Island for 13 months. He returned home in 1865 to find his wife and daughter dead, and the son born after he left for war dead also within days of his return. Farar Conner continued to farm at Killarney, and later married Maria Chotard.

ELIZABETH FRANCES TURNER & LEMUEL PARKER CONNER. Lemuel Parker (b. 1827, d. 1891) was born to William Carmichael Conner (b. 1798, d. 1843) and Jane Elizabeth Boyd Gustine (b. 1803, d. 1883) who married in 1823. Conner grew up as a boy on a plantation in the vicinity of Second Creek, then his mother bought the suburban Linden estate after his father's death. Elizabeth Frances "Fanny" Turner was born at her family home, Franklin Place, on Dec. 4, 1829, the daughter of Elizabeth Baker and Edward Turner.

Lemuel P. Conner married Fanny Turner at Franklin Place on Jan. 6, 1848. Their children were: Elizabeth Frances "Fanny Eliza" Conner (b. 1848, d. Sept. 28, 1860); Jane Gustine "Janie" Conner (b. Apr. 3, 1850 at Franklin Place, d. Sept. 24, 1944) md. Moses Liddell Randolph (b. 1842, d. 1907) ca. 1874, lived at Blythewood and had four children; Mary Louisa "Minnie" Conner (b. 1851, d. 1863); Elizabeth "Zizie" Turner (b. 1853, d. 1877) who married Mr. Eustis; Rebecca Parker "Nannie" Conner (b. 1854, d. 1913) md. John H. Gay III of Colorado in 1877 and moved to Hollywood, CA; William Edward "Willie" Conner (b. 1856, d. ca. 1863); Theodosia Turner Conner (b. 1858, d. 1909) md. William L. Shaw and had a daughter named Theodosia; Edward Turner Conner (b. 1860, d. 1871); Lemuel Parker Conner Jr. (b. 1861, d. 1943) md. Mary McCrery Britton (b. 1863, d. 1936) on Dec. 12, 1888; and Elizabeth Frances "Little Auntie" Conner II (b. 1864) md. Rev. R.W. "Walt" Bailey (d. 1901).

Lemuel Conner attended Yale College, then read law with his brother-in-law John McMurran but became primarily a planter in Mississippi and Louisiana. Fanny and Lemuel maintained a winter residence at their plantation Innisfail on Lake St. John in Louisiana and a summer home in the Natchez suburbs that was called Sedge Hill, then later, Roselawn. In 1854 they constructed a pair of Greek Revival dependency buildings identical to those at Melrose, the next-door home of Fanny's sister, Mary Louisa McMurran. The sisters hoped to be able to wave to one another from their balconies. But the Civil War intervened before the Conners were able to construct the mansion house. The Conners later moved across the lane to Woodlands, home to Fanny's mother, Eliza Turner.

In 1860 Lemuel Conner owned 256 slaves and two plantations, together worth $240,000. He took an active part in Louisiana's secession convention in January 1861, and recorded the testimony of the slaves accused in the Second Creek conspiracy that led to the hanging of at least 27 slaves. Conner served with the Confederate Army at Tullahoma as a lieutenant colonel on Gen. Braxton Bragg's staff in the Army of Tennessee. In 1866 and 1867 Conner borrowed heavily and ended up in bankruptcy. In 1884 he began his law practice as "Conner & Son." He died Mar. 24, 1891 at Woodlands. Fanny died Sept. 25, 1910 at Blythewood, in Bayou Goula, LA.

ROUTH WILLARD SMITH CROWELL. Routh Willard was born Jul. 11, 1913 at Oakley Grove Plantation, Natchez, MS, to Mamie Willard Foster (b. Oct. 24, 1896 at Hermanville, MS) and Davidson Routh Smith (b. Dec. 16, 1880 at Pascagoula, MS), son of Clara Ann Montgomery and Austin W. Smith and a descendant of Job Routh, builder of Routhland in Natchez.

Mamie and Davidson met at a ball at Stanton Hall, Natchez, where Mamie was a student.

Davidson was attending Jefferson Military College, Washington, MS. They married Sep. 25, 1912 at the Presbyterian Manse, Natchez. Davidson farmed and raised livestock on his Natchez plantation, Saragossa. Besides Routh, Davidson and Mamie were the parents of Austin Williams Smith (b. Jul. 18, 1914); Katherine Willie Smith (b. Sep. 23, 1915); Mamie Montgomery Smith (b. Apr. 18, 1917); Georgia Barnes Smith (b. Jul. 3, 1921); and Walton Pembroke Smith (b. Mar. 3, 1925).

Routh grew up at Saragossa, where a memorial event of her childhood was the funeral of Caroline Burkes, who was her "Mammy." The services were held from Saragossa house, with her father and some of Mammy's church members carrying the wooden coffin to the Smith Family Graveyard on Saragossa. Following the coffin, a choir, dressed in white, sang *Swing Low, Sweet Chariot*, making a very spiritually moving scene for the children.

For the first three years, Routh was taught by "Miss Claudie," who was paid $25 a month plus her room and board, living in one room of a separate cottage near the house. The children were taught in the other room. From the fourth through the ninth grades, Routh attended a one-room school, also on Saragossa. After attending the tenth and eleventh grades at Natchez High, she graduated from Bryan Technical High School, Dallas.

Routh's first job, at Walgreen Drug Store, Dallas, was temporary. Her permanent employment began at Sanger Brothers, Dallas, where she handled the Peggy Sage line of nail and hand beauty preparations; and in a sales contest in 1938 she won a week in New York City. In 1957 she became buyer of cosmetics and boudoir accessories at Sanger until she retired in 1977. Her best promotion was bringing to Sanger all the inaugural ball gowns of the American First Ladies.

On Aug. 20, 1940 in Dallas, Routh married Porter Crowell, who had attended Texas A&M until he was injured and had to go to work. At first, weighing cotton seed on the dock for Trinity Cotton Oil Co., Dallas, he eventually became superintendent. Surviving three company mergers, he retired there after 41 years.

Porter died Aug. 6, 1981 in Dallas, and having no children, Routh returned in 1996 to Natchez, where she spent six years restoring an old house on Main Street. An avid gardener, she specialized in raising watermelons, one weighing 106 pounds.

A member of the First Presbyterian Church, the Natchez Chapter DAR, and the Colonial Dames XVII Century, Routh is presently deeply involved in a "Stop Litter" campaign in Adams County.

GEORGE MALIN DAVIS & ELIZABETH SHUNK.
Elizabeth (b. 1823, d. 1877, Natchez) md. George Malin Davis (b. 1820, d. Oct. 11, 1883, Natchez) on Oct. 19, 1842. She brought to the marriage several Louisiana plantations, including Vaucluse. He was born in Pennsylvania and came to Natchez as a child with his mother and brothers. He studied at Oakland College in Claiborne County. Their two children were Francis Davis (b. Jul. 15, 1844, Natchez, d. January 1848, Natchez) and Julia Davis (b. 1846, Natchez, d. Jan. 29, 1883, Natchez).

Julia Davis, who attended boarding school in New York, married Stephen Kelly in New York in 1873. He was the son of Richard Kelly, founder and president of the Fifth National Bank in New York. Though trained as a medical doctor, Stephen Kelly followed his father into the banking field.

George Malin Davis was one of the members of the Natchez planting aristocracy who seems to have survived the Civil War in good financial shape. While many planters were mortgaging and selling property, he was acquiring it. His purchases included Concord and Choctaw which was the primary Davis family home. Davis was described as a "fire-eater" and secessionist. During the Union occupation of Natchez, Choctaw was appropriated by Gen. Brayman for his Natchez headquarters. On Dec. 8, 1865, John T. McMurran sold his law office to Natchez attorney George Malin Davis, and Melrose to Davis' wife, Elizabeth. The purchase price of Melrose was recorded as $38,000.

After the Civil War, Elizabeth and George Malin Davis returned to Choctaw. Their daughter Julia Davis and her husband Stephen Kelly divided their time between New York and Melrose in Natchez. They had one child, George Malin Davis Kelly (b. 1876, d. 1946), who was born in New York but baptized in Natchez by Episcopal Bishop William Green. In 1883 Julia Davis Kelly contracted tuberculosis from a servant and died in Natchez. Later that same year, her father, George Malin Davis, also died.

Julia's son, G.M.D. Kelly, inherited a vast estate amassed by his grandparents, including Melrose, Concord, Cherokee, and Choctaw as well as several plantations in Louisiana. Stephen Kelly returned to New York so that his son could be reared by family there, though they made at least two trips back to Natchez during George's boyhood. During this time, the Melrose estate was cared for by former Davis house slaves, Alice Sims and Jane Johnson, who lived with their families on the property. Alice Sims lived above the dairy, and Jane Johnson lived in a 3-room former slave house.

In 1900 George M.D. Kelly married Ethel Moore (d. 1975), a childhood friend from New York. He brought his bride to Natchez, and they rehabilitated Melrose for their family home - considered the first historic preservation efforts in the state of Mississippi. They were members of the First Presbyterian Church, where he led the choir. She belonged to the Natchez Garden Club and opened Melrose for public tours beginning with the first Natchez Spring Pilgrimage in 1932.

MILDRED LOUISE "CANDY" DAGGETT & JOHN DAVIS YOUNG.
Candy (b. Nov. 17, 1947 in Boston, MA) was the granddaughter of Fred L. Daggett and Mildred Jones Daggett. She is named for her grandfather's Daggett Chocolate Co. She is the daughter of Richard Charles Daggett and Eula Routh Wurster Daggett. She is also the granddaughter of Emeline Dayton Wurster and Oscar Rodney Wurster from Jonesville.

Emeline Dayton had attended Stanton College and Oscar Wurster had attended The Natchez Institute. He stayed with Wiggins relatives in Natchez while he attended. He also was christened at the First Presbyterian Church in Natchez by Rev. Stratton. Candy married John Davis Young in 1971 in Jonesville, LA, divorced 1990. They have three children: Ella Ruth Young (b.

Oscar R. Wurster Christening, First Presbyterian Church, Natchez, MS, June 12, 1898

Apr. 18, 1972, Natchez, MS); John Davis Young Jr. (b. Dec. 25, 1973, Natchez, MS) and Sarah Louise Young (b. Jun. 30, 1975, Natchez, MS).

Ella Routh and her husband Roy Spinks live in New Orleans and have two small children. John Davis Young Jr. "Johnny" and his wife Brandi Nichols Young live in Winnsboro and have one child. Sarah Louise and her husband Clint live in Monroe and have one child.

Candy is a teacher and is descended from the following Natchez District ancestors: Jeremiah Routh, Ebenezer Dayton, Edward Cochran, George Cammack, on her mother's side as well as Joseph Swayze, Joshua Smith and David Edwards who were from New York, through Ebenezer Dayton's wife, Phebe Smith, who

Oscar R. Wurster, Natchez Institute, senior picture

came to the Natchez District and is of the same family as the Swayze family who also came here from New England. Candy is a descendant of Dolar Davis and John Winchester from Boston, MA on her father's side who are the same ancestors of the Winchester and Davis family of Natchez.

Candy has lived and worked in Natchez. She has taught school and also worked in retail. She presently teaches and lives in the Jonesville area. Candy has one sister, Linda Routh Barrett and her husband Tom Barrett, who live in Vienna, VA and have two children. She has one brother Rod Daggett and his wife Penny Calhoun Daggett who live in the Jonesville area and they have three children. Her daughter Sarah Louise and her husband Clint married in December 2001 in Natchez,

JOHN DAVIS came from Sorento, Italy as a stowaway. He lived with a sea captain in New Orleans, LA and married Honora Haley (b. 1831, d. 1890) from County Cork, Ireland. He ran an Oyster Bar on Bourbon Street in New Orleans, LA. They moved to Natchez after the August 1856 hurricane that destroyed Last Island. John Davis made sure his wife and children were safe on the island, then sailed a small boat out to get help for the survivors.

His daughter, Mary Ann (b. 1854, d. 1913) md. Anthony J. Grady (b. 1850, d. 1909) from Norco, LA. They had six children: Anthony, Daniel, Honora, Mary Agnes (whose twin died) and John. Anthony served in WWI and settled in Oregon. The other children remained in Natchez. In 1902, Honora was Queen of the Fireman's Ball at 16 years of age. In 1910 Honora married F. Parnell Burns (b. 1880, d. 1946), son of Patrick P. Burns (b. 1837, d. 1909) who was born in Clonaig, County Armagh, Ireland. Patrick's wife was Mary Welch (b. 1844, d. 1882) from Ireland. His two brothers, Francis and Peter, also lived in Natchez. Francis and Patrick both served in the Confederate Army with the Louisiana Miles Brigade.

Patrick was born and died on March 17. He opened a Mercantile Store at the triangle of Pine and St. Catherine Streets; the business was later moved to Main Street as a shoe store. Patrick gave shamrocks to all on St. Patrick's Day and the tradition continued for the 105 years of the business.

Patrick's sons, Parnell and Peter, continued the business. They reared eight children in Natchez: Patrick P. md. Edith Profilet and reared their eight children in Natchez; Anthony G. md. Louise McNeely and reared their daughter in Natchez and Florida; Mary Agnes md. Charles L. Frye and moved to Starkville, MS; Noreen md.

Front, l-r: Sarah Garrity, Derrick Garrity, Shaun Hollywood, Benjamin Hollywood, Thomas Garrity. 2nd row: Curtis Maier, Daniel Garrity, Liz Garrity, Garrett Maier, Joseph Garrity. 3rd row: Michael Hollywood, Marie Hollywood, Elodie Maier, Mary A. Shell, Dorothy Garrity. Back row: Robert Hollywood, Paul Maier, Robert Shell, Byron Garrity. (Timothy Hollywood is not pictured)

Conway Aubic and reared their son in Natchez and Vidalia, LA; Margaret never married, taught school in Natchez for over 30 years; Peter T. Burns md. Therese Chouset and reared their eight children in Natchez; Andrew md. Alice Wilkins and reared their two children in Natchez; Ann E. "Liz" md. William B "Billy" Garrity in 1949 and reared their six children in Natchez.

Billy served during WWII in the Air Force (two brothers in the Navy and one in the cavalry). Liz's four brothers served in WWII, Coast Guard, Seabees, Infantry and Army Air Corps. Their children are W. Byron Garrity Jr. DVM married Dorothy Gillette from Arkansas and reared their four children: Derrick, Sarah, Thomas and Daniel, in Natchez. M. Elodie married P. Paul Maier of Natchez and reared their two sons M. Garrett and W. Curtis in Natchez; F. LeRoy Garrity died Feb. 1, 1977; H. Marie married Robert F. Hollywood of McComb, MS. Their four sons: Timothy, Michael, Benjamin and Shaun, were reared in Mississippi and Louisiana; Mary Agnes married Robert S. Shell of Vidalia, LA and lived in Memphis, TN; Joseph G. Garrity married Belinda Daniels and was a lieutenant with the Natchez Fire Department.

Billy's father was F. LeRoy Garrity Sr (b. 1889, d. 1976) who married Katherine Elodie Butchart (b. 1889, d. 1931). Their six children were reared in Natchez. LeRoy's parents were William H. Garrity and Louisa Rizzi; their children remained in Natchez. Byron B. Butchart (b. 1863, d. 1930), father of Elodie, came to Mississippi from Owens Sound, Ontario, Canada, originally from Dundee, Scotland. He married Mary Meath (b. 1860, d. 1925) and their children were also reared in Natchez. Most of the Butchart family remained in Canada.

Louisa Rizzi was the daughter of Geosephe (b. 1819, d. 1961) and Johanna. They lived around the Rodney and Bayou Petite areas of Mississippi. William was reared in Natchez by his mother Mary and his stepfather Patrick O'Brien. His father Michael was killed in a wagon accident in 1838. William had a sister Catherine. The Garrity (Geraghty) family came from Ireland. Their home was where the Natchez Landing restaurant was located.

DAVID LELAND DOW & ROSALIE MAST.
David (b. Jun. 16, 1956) and Rosalie Mast (b. Dec. 7, 1957) were married in Dover, DE on Jan. 6, 1979. David was born in Greenville, SC to Harley and Miriam (Westburg) Dow. Rosalie (called Rosey) was born in Dover, DE to Daniel and Rebecca (Hershberger) Mast.

David and Rosey met at Elkton Baptist College in Elkton, MD in September 1975. Later, they transferred to Pensacola Christian College in Pensacola, FL. They were married during their senior year. David graduated with a BS in Bible in 1979. Rosey majored in elementary education with a minor in English but did not continue her studies after their marriage.

After graduation, they returned to Elkton, MD where David taught at a Christian school. The couple first arrived in Natchez in July 1982, when they attended candidate school at Maranatha Baptist Mission, a ministry of West Side Baptist Church at 306 Oak Street in Natchez. From 1982 to 1986, the Dow family came to Natchez each summer for further missionary training.

They moved to Grenada, West Indies on Jan. 9, 1987 where they did mission work until December 2000. In January 2001 David became the pastor of West Side Baptist Church after James W. Crumpton retired. The Dow family moved to Natchez on Jan. 28, 2001.

For 10 months they lived in church housing at 804 Myrtle Ave. then they purchased a home in Washington, MS just north of Natchez at 82 Farr Road. David resigned his position as pastor on Mar. 13, 2002. In Jul., 2003 he accepted a position on staff at Capitol Baptist Church in Dover, DE.

In 1982 Rosey began writing, a hobby which turned into a career. Her first book, *Megan's Choice*, was a reader's favorite in 1996 and began a series of four frontier romantic mysteries including *Em's Only Chance, Lisa's Broken Arrow*, and *Banjo's New Song*. Her novella in *Fireside Christmas* became a national best seller, and her historical novel, *Reaping the Whirlwind*

Dow family: David Sr., Darrell, David Jr., Nathaniel, Steven, Jonathan, Miriam, Rosey, James

won the coveted Christy Award in 2001. Her other titles include *Betrayed, Face Value*, and *An Unexpected Surprise*. She has published several articles on writing craft in *Cross and Quill*. Her work also appeared in *Chicken Soup for the Christian Woman's Soul, Tea Cups for Women*, and *Tea Cups for Mothers*, anthologies of true heartwarming stories. Rosey also conducts writing workshops and is a nation-wide public speaker. She appeared on the television series, *Encounters with the Unexplained*, and on dozens of radio broadcasts. She has a web site at www.roseydow.com.

While in Natchez, Rosey became very active in local affairs. She held memberships in the Progressive Study Club, the Historical Society (where she chaired the Natchez Family History Book Committee), and the Friends of the Library. She also worked with the Natchez Garden Club to help them polish their short history of the Henderson family.

The Dows have seven children: David Livingstone Dow (b. Sep. 12, 1979); Darrell Champlin Dow (b. Aug. 13, 1980); Miriam Rebecca Dow (b. Nov. 17, 1982); Jonathan Goforth Dow (b. Mar. 4, 1984); Nathaniel Saint Dow (b. Mar. 4, 1984); Steven Edward Dow (b. Oct. 9, 1988); and James Elliot Dow (b. Sep. 28, 1991). *Submitted by Rosey Dow.*

WILLIAM CLIFTON DUKES FAMILY.
In the early 1920s, William Clifton Dukes (b. Mar. 14, 1895, d. Jul. 10, 1960), his wife Lillie Mae Dukes (b. Mar. 2, 1897, d. Jan. 22, 1970) and two daughters, Cora Lee (b. Oct. 17, 1916, d. May 21, 1980) and Juanita (b. Nov. 19, 1919, d. Jan. 3, 2002), entered Natchez on their wagon from Louisiana. They did not have enough money to buy supper so Willie, as he was called, cut a man's yard in order to buy bologna and crackers for their supper. Willie and Lillie were ambitious young people, and they both got jobs. One of their first jobs was milking cows twice a day at St. Mary's Orphanage. Willie later worked at the Natchez Box Factory. Desiring to better himself and his family, he went to work for Oppenheimer Department Store. He had found his calling and he loved it.

Lillie had found out that she did not like housework. In order to avoid that chore, she got a paper route with *The Times Picayune* to earn the money to pay a maid to do the work.

Eventually, they were able to buy Oppenheimer's out and Dukes Department store was birthed. With two teen-age daughters and a new son-in-law, Venton Lloyd Watson (b. Sep. 7, 1915, d. Jan. 9, 1995), this became a family business.

The first store was on the corner of Commerce and Franklin Streets. The black tiles that the Dukes put on the front of the store are still on the Franklin Street side. Business was great and they opened a store in Ferriday, LA.

This family business operated on the same motto as the post office. Neither rain nor sleet nor snow could keep the store closed. There was a flood in Ferriday in the mid-1940s, but Dukes was open for business as usual. Some of the family, and a dedicated employee, Winnie Goza, battled the flood in order to keep the doors open.

During WWII, they opened a store at Centerville in order to accommodate Camp Van Dorne. This store closed at the end of the war. The 1950s brought many changes to this family as well as Natchez. The original store moved across the street on Franklin into a building that the Dukes owned. (A tornado took the roof off this building about four years ago. There is a vacant lot there now.) The Watsons opened Dukes at Nosser City.

One thing that never changed was Lillie's dislike for housework. She would work in the yard from sun up to sundown at her house on Ashburn Park, but the inside work was left to her housekeeper, Edna Williams, lovingly called Cook. (The Dukes had lived at 204 South Commerce before moving to Ashburn Park. The library is now in that location). Lillie's outside work paid off as she had a show place yard. Dr. Homer Whittington was the only person allowed to cut her flowers, and he used them at Twin Oaks during the Pilgrimage.

If one was part of the family, one was part of the business. It became the training ground and the launching pad for the grandchildren: Clifton Lloyd Watson, Patricia Lynn Campbell, and Ronald Keith Watson, in that order. Jobs were varied such as sweeping, dusting, etc. but the fun job was being able to use the cash register. Papa, as he was called by the grandchildren, always kept a close eye on them when he heard the ring of the register.

The stores were open until 8:00 p.m. on Saturday, and the family would eat supper in the store, which could be bologna and crackers (we've made a complete circle).

By the 1960s, downtown business was not what it used to be and the Franklin Street store closed. A few years later, the store at Nosser City closed the doors to Dukes Department Store forever. *Submitted by Patsy Collins.*

ROBERT DUNBAR, THE ANCESTRAL ROOT OF THIS FAMILY TREE

Robert Dunbar emigrated from Scotland with his father, mother and brother about the year 1770. They made their first home in North Carolina, some accounts say Virginia; at least he married Ann Beaver, a Virginia Lady. His brother left the family for parts unknown and was never heard of afterwards. From this first home they moved to West Florida, accompanied by Mr. Dunbar's father. From thence they moved to Butler's Plains in East Louisiana. There they resided for some time struggling with poverty and difficulties. Not owning a servant at that time, Mr. Dunbar cleared with his own hands the land he cultivated and was reduced to such straits in consequence of having cut his leg severely, that he had to eke out a living by mending shoes for his neighbors.

Robert Dunbar Family burial ground

He then moved to the Ivy Place about three miles north of Natchez. Here his father is said to have died and to have been buried at the Spanish Fort below the city. This was about the year 1780, when the country was under the Spanish Regime. From the Ivy Place he moved with his family to Oakley Grove, the plantation where he and his wife spent the balance of their lives and reared a large family, six sons and three daughters. His wife passed before him to the Silent Land.

The Ivy Place spoken of above is now owned by Geo. M. Marshall Esq. who married Mr. Dunbar's great-granddaughter, Charlotte Hunt. The above Family Tree will show how numerous are their descendants. They are widely scattered in the region around Natchez and across the River in Louisiana. They can point proudly to the record of these their worthy ancestors, who lie buried in the family burial ground at Oakley Grove which was so long their home and now owned and occupied by Wm. McCaleb, who married their great-granddaughter, Bettie Buckner. Mr. Robert Dunbar was a prudent, industrious and useful citizen, an affectionate husband and father and a conscientious and consistent Christian.

The above account was transcribed from the base of an artistic portrayal of the Robert Dunbar Family Tree drawn in 1891 by Olivia Dunbar Archer, a great-great-granddaughter of Robert and Ann Dunbar who are represented by the trunk of the tree. The inscription copied from their tombstone at Oakley Grove and posted on the trunk of the tree is as follows: Robert Dunbar, native of N. Caroline; Aged 78 years, Died 13th March A D 1826, Wife, Ann Beaver, native of Virginia, Aged 71 years Died 29th Aug AD 1822.

Numerous references to land conveyances in Adams and Jefferson counties testify to Robert Dunbar's widespread holdings of property acquired from the Spanish Government as early as 1782. Purchases of slaves are recorded beginning in 1786. He is named among early settlers who raised indigo and tobacco, later found to be unprofitable.

Robert Dunbar Family tree

Listed in the Spanish Census of the Natchez District in 1792 he is recorded as having subscribed to an Oath of Allegiance to the United States in 1798/1799.

Robert Dunbar named in the Natchez Court Records 1767-1805 as a "respectable inhabitant of this country" was faithful in civic duties as a witness, executor, party to settling disputes, appraiser, juror, an "overseer of the poor;" appointed in 1801 supervisor of highways in the Pine Ridge Twp.

The Robert Dunbar Family supported the organization of the Pine Ridge Presbyterian Church; records evidence continued active membership of descendants.

The Dunbar home, Oakley Grove, was located on what is now property of the Natchez-Adams County Airport. Near the home site the Family Burial Ground, restored 1979-83, honors Robert and Ann Dunbar, six of their nine children and three spouses, seven grandchildren and nine great-grandchildren.

Although their backgrounds have similarities, and names suggest a kinship between Robert Dunbar of Oakley Grove and William Dunbar of The Forest, no evidence has as yet been found to prove a family connection other than intermarriage in subsequent generations.

WILLIAM DUNBAR FAMILY. Although much has been written about William Dunbar, his name is not recognized by most Americans and no biography about him has been written. He is probably best known as the inventor of the screw press used in baling cotton and as the man chosen by Thomas Jefferson to lead the first exploration expedition of the southern Louisiana Purchase. Jefferson, with whom William corresponded for seven years, also sponsored him for membership in the American Philosophical Society. William contributed 12 publishable manuscripts to the Society between 1803-10.

Arthur H. DeRosier Jr. states in an article he wrote for *The Journal of Mississippi History,* "William Dunbar was one of the most brilliant American Scientists of the post-Revolutionary War period." DeRosier also says that the scientific contributions which William Dunbar made from 1771 until his death, deserve for him a preeminent place in histories dealing with the old Southwest.

William Dunbar

William Dunbar (b. ca. 1750/51, Elgin, Morayshire, Scotland) was the eldest son of Sir Archibald Dunbar and his second wife, Anne Bayne, who married in 1750. William had a younger sister, Peggy, and a brother, Thomas, in addition to older half brothers and at least one half sister.

William's early schooling was provided by tutors. It has been said that William graduated from Glasgow University. Records show, however, he entered Kings's College, Aberdeen, in the fall of 1763, and graduated Mar. 30, 1767, with a MA degree. He came to Philadelphia, PA in 1771, not for his poor health as has been reported, but to make his way in the world, there being no future for him in Elgin. He spent two years trading with the Indians, and in 1773 he formed a partnership with John Ross for the purpose of opening a plantation. William traveled to Pensacola to obtain a land grant from the British Governor. He lived on this grant near Baton Rouge until 1784 when he removed to Natchez.

In 1785, he married Dinah Clark, niece of his business partner. Their nine children were born at The Forest Plantation near Natchez: Anne (b. 1786, d. 1864) md. Samuel Postlethwaite; Margaret (b. 1788, d. 1851) md. James Dunlop; Eliza (b. 1791, d. 1864) md. Francis Surget; William (b. 1793, d. 1847) md. 1st, Annis Stockton Field and 2nd, Mary Field, daughters of Robert and Abigail (Stockton) Field; Helen (b. 1796, d. 1845) md. Henry Huntington; Archibald (b. 1798, d. 1850) unmarried; Thomas (b. 1801, d. 1808), unmarried; Robert (b. 1803, d. 1840 dsp) md. Elizabeth Holmes; Alexander (b. 1806, d. 1852), unmarried.

William and Dinah's tombstones in The Forest cemetery, Adams County, MS bear these inscriptions; hers - "In memory of Dinah Dunbar consort of the late William Dunbar, born at Whitehaven, England 20 Oct 1769, died at the Forest 15 Nov 1821, Aged 52;" and his - "Sacred to the memory of William Dunbar. His wife laments a tender husband. His children an affectionate parent,

Dinah (Clark) Dunbar, wife of William Dunbar

his friends a valuable acquaintance. His country a most useful citizen and science a distinguished Votary." "William Dunbar of the Forest was a native of Scotland and son of Sir Archibald Dunbar of Thunderton near Elgin. He died the 16 Oct 1810 in the 62 year of his age." *Submitted by Julia Ann Dunbar.*

WILLIE MAE SEAB DUNN has lived in Natchez since 1960. She was born in Holden, LA and attended elementary and high School there. In 1944 she graduated from Southeastern Louisiana College with a BA degree and received a master's degree in library science from Louisiana State University in 1947. After working in several Louisiana Parish Libraries for 14 years she moved to Natchez, MS and worked in the school libraries in Adams County. In 1972 she became librarian of the Natchez Branch of the Copiah Lincoln Junior College. After working there for 17 years she retired in 1990. In 1999 this library was named the Willie Mae Dunn Library.

Dunn is descended from William Calvit who came to the Natchez District in the 1780s with many family members. His mother, Mary Calvit Higdon and three brothers: Joseph, Frederick and Thomas, all received Spanish Land Grants and today have many descendants in this area as well as in Louisiana and Texas.

William's Land Grant was on what is now the border of Franklin and Adams counties along Sandy Creek. He gained notoriety by being divorced during the Catholic Spanish Period by his second wife, Phoebe Crawford Jett. Phoebe went on to obtain her own Spanish Land Grant in downtown Natchez, Lot 3 Block 13 on Jefferson Street where the Harris House now stands.

William's sons scattered but his grandson, another William, returned to run the plantation and was very successful in adding to the original 800 acres. His son Charles Brantley Calvit was even more successful and is listed in the 1860 Census as owning $10,000 in real estate and $97,000 in personal property.

Charles Brantley's youngest daughter Mary "Mollie" married James Zebedee Rowland. Their youngest daughter Clara Katie married Willie Bryant Seab. Clara and Willie Seab are the parents of Dunn.

Dunn married Lemuel A. Dunn Jr. in 1961 and was divorced in 1972. She has two adopted stepchildren, Leecie Jane who lives in Natchez, MS and Harvey Earl who lives in Mathiston, MS. She also has a sister Jimmye Seab Crews who lives in Centreville, AL.

CHARLES STIETENROTH EIDT FAMILY. William Eidt was born in Dhierkiem-On-The-Rhine, Germany in the year 1838. He and a brother arrived in America in 1858, by way of New Orleans. They made their way to Natchez where they settled. William fought in the Civil War and returned to Natchez and reared a family. He was a barber for many years.

One of his sons was named Samuel Graff. He too was a barber for some years but he was a printer for the *Natchez Democrat* for 62 years. His oldest son was Sam Joseph, and he was a typesetter for the *Natchez Democrat* and later for the *Natchez Times* newspaper. Sam married Jeanerett Harlow of Natchez and they had only one child. A son named Charles Stietenroth was born July 8, 1927.

Charles attended school at Cathedral School and was taught by the brothers. During school years he worked after school at the Natchez Printing and Stationery Co., which was owned by his mother. He worked for a short time at Armstrong Tire and Rubber Co., then went into the Navy, and served in the South Pacific until the end of WWII. On returning home he worked again for the Natchez Printing Co. which was now owned by Walter Abbott.

When the *Natchez Times* paper started publishing here, he was the head pressman and remained so just until before it closed. He then went to work for the U.S. Postal Service as a letter carrier and stayed there until he retired. Charles married Webbie Jo Burnham from Rankin County

on Jun. 29, 1950. They moved to the Kingston Community in 1951, the year of the big ice storm. They were without electricity for 31 days; that also meant no water as the well pump was electric. Water was brought up from the pond for bathing and for the toilet. Jugs of water were brought from town each day for drinking and cooking; kerosene lamps were the only light they had.

Daughter Nancy Maurine was born Aug. 7, 1951.

Nancy attended school in Natchez then Louisiana Tech at Ruston. She married Walter Willis and has one son, Matthew Isaac. She has been employed at International Paper Co. for 24 years as a mechanic.

From left: Charles Maurice Eidt, Charles Stietenroth Eidt, Jeanie Dell Cauthen, Webbie Jo Eidt, Maurine Edit

Son Charles Maurice (b. Jan. 18, 1955) attended Natchez School and has been employed for Chevron Oil Co. for 25 years. Charles married Yvonne Cavin of Wilkinson County and they have two boys, Johnathan Charles and Joseph Adam. Charles has a daughter by a previous marriage, Destiny Hope.

Second daughter Jeanie Dell (b. July 23, 1959) attended school in Natchez. She married Todd Cauthen of Natchez. They have no children. They own Delta Rental Co. of Natchez.

Charles and Webbie still live in the Kingston Community and attend the Kingston United Methodist Church, where she teaches the adult Sunday school class. *Submitted by Webbie Eidt.*

GEORGE THOMAS EISELE was the first of three children born to Johan Georg and Barbara (Schwartz) Eisele of Natchez, MS. George (b. Jun. 6, 1844) md. second, Ellen Virginia Scothorn on Jun. 25, 1883. Ellen was the sixth and last child born to Isaac William and Emily (Hays) Scothorn.

George worked as city clerk of Natchez and as alderman for two terms from 1902 to 1914. He also enjoyed owning a hardware store at No. 12 Union Street. His wife, Ellen Virginia, spent her time rearing a family and with church work. They had six children: Ruth Barbara (b. Apr. 14, 1884); Nancy Catherine (b. Dec. 6, 1885); William Conrad (b. Dec. 31, 1887); Harry Lee (b. Jul. 27, 1890); Florence LeClerg (b. Dec. 12, 1892) and Estelle Rosemary (b. Sep. 5, 1894).

Other interesting facts: George Thomas served in Co. B, 10th Mississippi Regiment CSA. Both of his grandparents were born in Rosenfeld, Germany. Nancy C. "Nan" taught 1st grade for 40 plus years in Natchez. Florence "Dolly" was librarian at Fisk Library and Braden School.

Conrad and Harry died as 3 and 4-year-olds due to yellow fever; Ruth died in Natchez Mar. 4, 1973; Nancy died in Natchez Jul. 8, 1979; Florence died in Natchez Oct. 14, 1979; Estelle Rosemary "Daisey" died in Gulfport, MS Jan. 10, 1986; George Thomas Eisele died Nov. 18, 1915 and Ellen Virginia Scothorn Eisele died Feb. 27, 1937.

ENGBARTH LINE (7) Johannes Engbarth married Anna Margaretha Koch (b. 1755, d. 1793) and had children: Johann Jakob, Maria Chritina, Maria Franziska, Anna Maria, Johann Petrus, Ludwig.

(6) Ludwig Engbarth (b. Oct. 12, 1792, d. Nov. 2, 1852) md. Anna Katharina Scheuer (b. May 18, 1791, d. Sep. 14, 1848), daughter of Philipp Joseph Scheuer and Anna Maria Kurtz. Children: Katharina; Franziska; Maria Ann; Elisabeth; Wilheim (b. May 27, 1824); Anna Maria md. Philip Bader; Christina; John md. 1st, ?? and 2nd, Adelia Knapp; Katharina Elisabeth.

(5) William Engbarth (b. May 27, 1824) md. Pauline Schmidt (widow) on Oct. 25, 1853. Children: Emile (md. Lena Arndt), Pauline (md. Kaiser), Edward (died young of tuberculosis), Josephine (md. Eidt), Idella (md. Wagner - no children), Sophia (no information).

(4) Emile Engbarth (b. Port Hudson, LA, d. 1897) md. Lena Arndt. His family moved to Rodney, MS when he was young. She was born in Rodney - he was a politician (Republican) at Rodney; after his death she was made postmistress at Rodney (wrote to President Polk for the position, then sent to Ocean Springs, also as postmistress (her brother, George, was there) left everything in Rodney except their cow, who would only let Grandma milk her. Gaugau sneaked her kitten on the boat. When Katherine was born while her father was at a political meeting in Minneapolis, the other politicians named her for the city and gave her father a chest of silver flatware for the baby. (Katherine had her forefinger cut off by her uncle, Edward Engbarth, who died of consumption. Lena was wealthy and spoiled. Children: Minneapolis Katherine (b. 1892, d. 1970); Montana; Caroline; George; Claude (b. Dec. 10, 1896); William James (b. Aug. 24, 1881); Charles Edward (b. Aug. 12, 1885); Rodney Joseph (b. Jun. 28, 1889 in Rodney, MS); Chester (died as an infant).

Monty, Carrie and Joe had no children; Claude had daughter Claudia, red headed born about 1945 and has one child; George had lots of children in Michigan; Willie had Louise who had no children; Charles had Charles Jr. and Evelyn (md. a Barrett, lives in Maine and has children and grandchildren).

(3) Minneapolis Katherine Engbarth (b. Jun. 10, 1892, d. Aug. 29, 1970) md. Dec. 25, 1925 in Ocean Springs, Stanley Melton Burkley (b. Mar. 16, 1879, d. Oct. 30, 1949) both are buried in Natchez City Cemetery. (Children: Stanley Engbarth (b. Oct. 5, 1926) is blond; twins (b. Feb. 18, 1928), Joseph Emile (red head) and Margaret Jeannette (brunette).

(2) Margaret Jeannette Burkley (b. Feb. 18, 1928) md. first Neville Buck Marshall (b. Dec. 10, 1924, d. Dec. 26, 1990). Margaret married second Larry Ferney in 1970, no children. Children: Margaret Katherine "Kathy" Marshall (b. Oct. 12, 1950) md. Monroe Jackson Moody Jr. Children: Monroe Jackson "Jack" III (b. Feb. 15, 1968, d. Mar. 1, 2002 in Houston, TX) buried at Laurel Hill in Adams County, MS, married Cara Winter in 1997, son Monroe Jackson IV (b. Apr. 26, 2001); Merrick Rowan Dashiell (b. Feb. 6, 1972) md. Jacqueline Passbach (Jan. 13, 2001).

Marion Jeannette Marshall (b. Apr. 1, 1952) md. (1st) Godfrey Forrester, (2nd) John Darius Tassistro, (3rd) Mike Holloway, (4th) Mark Drennen. Children: Angelique "Angie" Devereux Tassistro (b. May 12, 1974); Rodney Darius Tassistro (b. Feb. 21, 1976); Adrienne Marshall Drennen (b. Feb. 7, 1985). They live in St. Francisville, LA.

Charlotte Elizabeth Agnes Anne Marshall (b. Jul. 13, 1953) md. (1st) Elliot Brumfield and (2nd) Alan Edmonds. Children: Charlotte Aaron

Brumfield (b. Sep. 6, 1974) md. (1st) Casey Smith, son, Walker (b. Aug. 21, 1996), married (2nd) Jason Hennington, daughter, Presley (b. 2001); Chesney Dawn Brumfield (b. Jun. 2, 1976) md. Jeremiah Wheeler, daughter Miah (b. Apr. 26, 2002); Elliot Buck Brumfield (b. Oct. 5, 1978); Rachel Megan Edmonds (b. May 7, 1981) md. Wesley Givens, son, Marshall (b. Feb. 10, 2000).

Malquin Morgan Marshall (b. Aug. 29, 1954) md. (1st) Salvo Piazza; married (2nd) Peter Pevonka. Children: Emily Johanna Piazza (b. Jan. 17, 1976); Jessica Conchetta Magdalena Piazza (b. May 17, 1977).

Neville Buck Marshall II (b. Sep. 12, 1957) md. Beth Anderson. Children: Charlotte Kay (b. Dec. 24, 1988), Morgan Keene (b. Sep. 22, 1991). *Submitted by Kathy Moody.*

EARL EMERICK & CAMILLA MOORE. Camilla
(b. 1906, d. 1985) and Virginia (b. 1910, d. 1990) were born in Tunnel Hill, GA to Edith Wyatt and Frank Moore. The family moved to Natchez about 1915. Camilla married Clyde Crothers (b. Mar. 3, 1897, d. Mar. 4, 1942) about 1926. Clyde owned Natchez Tire and Battery Co., and for a while was city clerk and Adams County supervisor. Camilla was bookkeeper for Clyde until his health caused the business to be sold in 1939. She then became the secretary at the ICRR freight office.

Camilla Emerick leaning over behind Connelly's Tavern. This picture appeared in the 1941 Sears Catalog which led Earl Emerick to Natchez to marry her.

In 1941 her picture was in the Sears Roebuck catalog, showing her in ante-bellum attire behind Connelly's Tavern. An ICRR engineer Earl Emerick (b. 1905, d. 1973) from Terre Haute, IN, fell in love with the girl in the picture; he transferred to Vicksburg and brought an engine to Natchez, meeting Camilla at the freight office. Clyde died in 1942.

Earl and Camilla married May 9, 1943 in St. Francisville. They had one son Earl Evan "Buddy" Emerick Jr. (b. Sep. 20, 1945) who married Judy Daniels (b. Jun. 5, 1946) in February 1965. They have three daughters: Jeri Jolyn; Julie Jordan (b.

Linda and Earl Evan "Buddy" Emerick

Nov. 17, 1967); Mary Jane "Janie" who married Danny Richards (b. May 13, 1962) on Sep. 30, 1981; one son Hayden Spencer Richards (b. Oct. 20, 1990).

Buddy and Judy divorced in 1980. He married Linda Miller Young (b. Jul. 28, 1947) on Jan. 28, 1983. Linda has two children, Jerry Lynn Young (b. Mar. 25, 1968) and Miranda Lee Smith (b. Apr. 28, 1967). Jerry married Donna Roberts (b. Aug. 8, 1968) on May 5, 1992 and have three children: Amanda (b. Nov. 21, 1989), Jessica (b. Apr. 23, 1992) and Jeremy (b. Feb. 21, 2002).

Miranda married Brian Smith on Jun. 17, 1995 and has three daughters: Abigal (b. Oct. 25, 1997), Bethany (b. Dec. 17, 1999) and Arianna (b. Mar. 5, 2002).

FIELD FAMILY. The Field family came to the United States from England, when Henry Field came to Jamestown, VA in 1635 aboard the ship *Expectation.* Osborne King (O.K.) Field was born on Sep. 17, 1812 in Jefferson County, KY, son of James Lewis Field and Elizabeth Stevens. O.K. came down the Mississippi River on a flat boat, and arrived in Natchez at the age of 22 and decided to make his home here. He met his first wife, Mary Hamilton, and they were married. After her passing several years later, he remarried to one of the younger Hamilton sisters, Virginia Hamilton.

The Hamiltons were from Port Gibson and lived in a beautiful home called Highland. O.K. and Virginia bought the home Shadyside which was on the outskirts of Natchez and had several children, one of which was Levi "Lee" Benjamin Field. In the mean time, O.K. started a brick company on Canal Street, the only brick company in Natchez. He had a booming business in 1850 where they made the bricks for several of the antebellum homes in Natchez, including Longwood.

He also began to buy land reaching from Mississippi to Louisiana. In 1880 he bought the home Glenfield and the Majorica Plantation from the Cannon heirs. Glenfield was a working farm, where they also spent a great time entertaining on part of the property called Park Place. The Field family was very prominent and they also attended the Episcopal Church. O.K. Field passed away at Glenfield in the late 1880s.

Dr. James S. Meng (whose ancestors were Flemish) was born in Wilkinson County, MS, in 1824 and spent the majority of his life in both Natchez and Vidalia. He graduated from a New York Medical College and studied in Edinburgh, Scotland, and Paris. He married Caroline Gibson of Gibsons Landing in Concordia parish on Lake St. John. He was ranked highly in his profession and his skill as a physician was acknowledged by all. In addition to serving as a physician, he also filled several Republican offices, and was known as a honest and trustworthy man. However, after the downfall of the party, Dr. Meng continued with his work as a physician, helping anyone who needed his expertise, whether they could afford his services or not. He died at his home on Jan. 14, 1891.

Lester Joseph Meng Jr. was the son of L.J. Meng Sr. His brother was James Carol Meng. His mother was Sue Marsh Meng, of the Dardens of Fayette, MS, who married into the Marsh family from Waterproof, LA. *Submitted by Marjorie Field Meng.*

ELIZABETH (DUNN) McCULLER. Her ggg-and gggg-grandparents were Richard Fletcher, a captain in American Revolutionary War, and his wife, Rebecca Hunnicutt, who moved from Virginia to Washington, MS, in 1803 with their three sons: Lionel, a private in MS Militia War of 1812 (md. Pheobe T. Dewell); Robert Richard (md. Mary

Margaretta Malbrity); and Flavius Felix Flores (md. Amanda D. Cable); and their daughter Lavinia (md. Godfrey Glassburn, a captain in MS Militia, War of 1812 in 1814; John L. McLendon in 1819; and Andrew Williams in 1833). His other two daughters were born in Adams County: Rebecca Hunnicutt (md. John Branch, M.D.) and Amanda Melvina (md. Tobias Gibson).

Lavinia Fletcher and Godfrey Glassburn had a son, Evander Lycidies, who married Margaret I. Wilson, and a daughter Lavina G., who married David G. Dunn, son of Richard L. and unknown Dunn in Adams County.

Lavinia and David Dunn had nine children, the oldest being Dr. Richard L. Dunn. There is a write-up on him in *The Biographical and Historical Memoirs Of Mississippi* that stated his parents were natives of Mississippi and his paternal grandfather, a native of Ireland, was one of the oldest families of Adams County. In 1866 Dr. Dunn married his cousin, Stella M. Gibson, daughter of Amanda M. Fletcher and Tobias Gibson, and settled in Yazoo City, MS, where his family had moved to in 1841.

HUGH JUNKIN FOSTER FAMILY. In 1910, Hugh Foster, a sixth generation Mississippian, was born in a farmhouse on Foster Mound Road northeast of Natchez. His parents, Harry Penny and Ruth Junkin Foster, had lived in the house since their marriage in 1898.

Known as Sterling Plantation, the property encompassed approximately 165 acres of land. In the late 18th century, it had been part of a Spanish land grant awarded to William Foster, Harry's great-great uncle. Harry grew up at Glen Mary Plantation in a house built for his father, William Peter Smith Foster, at the time of his marriage to Laura Penny. Ruth Junkin Foster, born in County Antrim, Ireland, immigrated to Natchez as a toddler. She spent much of her childhood at Sunnyside, near the intersection of the Steam Plant Road and Pine Ridge Road.

The earliest members of the Foster family arrived in the Natchez area about 1783. They traveled overland from South Carolina where James Foster had served as a private during the Revolutionary War. The family's extensive land grant included what became known as Foster's Mound in the Pine Ridge area. More than 200 years later, James Foster's descendents continue to live along Foster Mound Road.

At the time of Hugh Foster's birth, there were already four children in his immediate family and he would be followed by two additional births. For a while, his father, Harry, taught school in a one-room building located across the road from the farmhouse. When that assignment ended, the schoolroom was moved and attached to the house. Other family enterprises included a grocery store in Natchez on Pine Street and a dairy that operated from the huge wooden barn near the house.

Hugh ended his formal education at tenth grade. Subsequently, he worked in the family dairy and for Excelsior Laundry. In the 1930s, the four Foster brothers: Harry Jr., Frank, Hugh, and T.J., became partners in the Natchez Steam Laundry and Dry Cleaners on St. Catherine Street. The laundry offered extensive services including fluff dry, industrial linen rentals, home pick-up and delivery, tailoring, and storage.

Employing up to 100 people, the business flourished in an era when home laundry facilities were uncommon. In the late 50s, arson destroyed the building and its contents. Within a year, a new facility had been constructed at the original site. For over four decades, the laundry remained a family business. In 1977, Hugh, the only remaining Foster owner, sold the laundry and retired.

Throughout his life, Hugh much preferred working on the farm where he raised cows, pigs, horses, and chickens. Among his crops were hay and the occasional field of cotton. Gardens produced abundant vegetables and, along with beef, pork, and chicken grown on the farm, resulted in a nearly self-sufficient family diet. Milk arrived in the kitchen each day, not by delivery, but directly from the barn in a non-pasteurized state.

Hugh Junkin Foster Family, l-r: Hugh Junkin Foster, Annie Mae Carter Foster, Jacqulyn Foster Weiss, Hugh Carter Foster, 1958

During World War II, Hugh was a private in the U.S. Army. He trained under Gen. Patton in the California desert and then guarded German war prisoners in south Georgia. While overseeing prisoners in a peanut patch, Hugh met Annie Mae Carter. They were married in March 1944 and shortly thereafter Hugh was sent to England to await the European mainland invasion. With the 7th Armored Division, he marched through France, liberating villages. During the Battle of the Bulge, Hugh became separated from his unit and suffered frozen hands and feet. After a lengthy recuperation in a Parisian hospital, he returned to the United States on the *Queen Mary*. Hugh's children, Jacqulyn and Carter, were born in 1946 and 1947 respectively. The family attended Pine Ridge Presbyterian Church, where Fosters had worshipped since its founding in 1807. Hugh served as a deacon for the church and Annie Mae taught Sunday School.

The farmhouse itself continued as a gathering place for extended family and was regularly visited by Granny Ruth, numerous aunts and uncles, and several generations of cousins. The ample screened back porch was a natural location for talking and eating. Metal rockers sat alongside ancient wooden chairs, often occupied by the most senior relatives. Children made endless trips up and down the concrete back steps, seeking food, tattling on one another, or pausing long enough to gather energy for another foray to the pastures. Huge pecan trees shaded the house, an ancient cistern yielded unlimited cool, pristine water, and the location atop a small knoll ensured an unrestricted view of the surrounding land. Horses were always available for riding, blackberries nestled in profusion along the barbed wire fences, and the ponds promised bream in abundance. Several wooden structures housed hundreds of chickens whose eggs were sold each week to families in Natchez.

Both Jackie and Carter attended Pine Ridge School through the sixth grade. Hugh served as a member of the Board of Trustees and Annie Mae was president of the PTA. A two-story white-framed building, the small school featured two grades in each classroom. Despite limited resources, students were exposed to art, music, and regional travel, along with more traditional subjects.

Beginning at age 6, Jackie volunteered to "receive" at an antebellum home during spring Pilgrimage. Dressed in a hoop-skirted costume featuring tiny blue flowers, and with her lace pantaloons revealed as befitted a child, she stood in Mt. Repose's nursery and regaled visitors with stories about antique toys and furnishings belonging to children of another time. Plates of sugar cookies and all the Coke Jackie could drink rewarded her efforts each day. As a teenager, with her skirts lengthened and pantaloons discreetly hidden, Jackie volunteered at Mistletoe. This antebellum home originated as a honeymoon cottage for her ancestor, Barbara Foster, and Peter Bisland. Public speaking abilities were honed during these years of volunteering, as was a profound appreciation for the historical significance of the Natchez area.

Jackie graduated from Natchez-Adams High School in 1963 and was followed by Carter in 1965. Jackie worked as a "page" at Fisk Public Library during her high school years. Miss Eleanora Gralow, Library Director, became a mentor and role model. Through her encouragement, Jackie completed college coursework in library science and a professional career as a librarian followed. In 1975, Carter served as a member of the court during his cousin Marty Junkin's reign as Pilgrimage Queen.

Today, three members of the Hugh Foster family are buried beneath a towering oak tree adjacent to the Pine Ridge Presbyterian Church. They sleep in peace close to the home they loved so well. Future generations will visit this hallowed place and understand the indelible Natchez connection. *Submitted by Jacqulyn Foster Weiss.*

JAMES FOSTER. The date of arrival and port of entry in America of this branch of the Foster family is undetermined, but tradition places the time in the 17th century. These Fosters were Cromwell supporters who were exiled to the New World upon the restoration of King Charles II to the English throne. One of the Fosters moved to the colony of Virginia and is believed to be the progenitor of James Foster. By late 1783, James Foster (b. Aug. 2, 1752, d. Nov. 24, 1835) had arrived in Adams County. He had traveled from South Carolina with members of his family including his widowed mother, Mary (b. 1727, d. 1819) and siblings Nancy Foster (Gilbert) (b. ca. 1755, d. 1820); John (b. May 25, 1757, d. Jan. 26, 1837); William (b. September 1759, d. Jul. 12, 1834); and Thomas (b. Sep. 10, 1762, d. Sep. 1, 1829).

Foster Mound Plantation

Both James and Thomas had served at Fort Moultrie during the early days of the Revolutionary War. James' young wife, Charlotte, died soon after the family's arrival in the area and he later married Elizabeth Smith Brassfield (b. Feb. 25, 1763, d. Dec. 13, 1837). James and Charlotte had one daughter, also named Charlotte (b. May 5, 1778, d. Aug. 24, 1833). There were seven daughters and one son born to James and Elizabeth:

Rachel Elizabeth (b. Nov. 26, 1786, d. Sept. 17, 1814); Frances (b. Feb. 17, 1788, d. Jul. 21, 1833); Eleanor (b. Nov. 16, 1790, d. 1826); Barbara Foster (b. Apr. 6, 1793, d. unknown); Miriam Foster (b. Jan. 25, 1796, d. 1815); William James (b. Apr. 15, 1798, d. Jan. 15, 1870); Sinai Amelia (b. Sep. 18, 1800, d. Aug. 24, 1881); and Mary Ann Foster (b. Nov. 5, 1803, d. Jun. 4, 1834).

Harry Penny Foster Sr. (1872-1939)

In April 1784, James petitioned the Spanish government for a grant of land located on the north side of St. Catherine Creek, about six miles northeast of Natchez. Additional grants were received for Mary Foster as well as James' three brothers. Sister Nancy Gilbert settled nearby and began development of Muddy Fork Plantation. By 1788, James had bought his father-in-law Zacariah Smith's land, which included Foster Mound. He moved his family into the log cabin Smith had built atop a burial mound constructed many years previously by the Natchez Indians. In 1803, James and his brother John, along with Randal Gibson, donated land for Jefferson College, one of the nation's first publicly funded institutions of higher learning. The Foster Mound dwelling, significantly enlarged and stuccoed, still survives.

William James Foster married Mary Maury (b. Feb. 10, 1811, d. Nov. 11, 1883), a Canadian girl who came to Natchez in 1820 with her mother. Mary's father was a British officer serving in Canada who died when Mary was a young child. William Foster and Mary Maury Foster had seven children: Ezilda Roszilla Foster (b. Jan. 17, 1826, d. Jul. 31, 1846); James A.J. Foster (b. Jan. 2, 1828, d. Sep. 9, 1879, a Confederate soldier); Mary E. Foster (b. Oct. 22, 1830, d. Mar. 20, 1914); Virginia Foster (b. Jan. 13, 1833, d. Sep. 25, 1834); Frances A. Foster (b. Dec. 22, 1835, d. Sep. 17, 1863); William Peter Smith Foster (b. May 21, 1837, d. Apr. 20, 1881); and Erastus Bridgers Foster (b. Oct. 10, 1842, d. May 20, 1923, a Confederate soldier).

Ruth Junkin Foster (1872-1961)

Erastus Bridgers Foster married his cousin Josephine B. Rogillio in 1865. They had two children, William J. Foster and Minnie Foster. His second wife was Leonora Chambliss with whom he had no children. Erastus inherited Foster Mound Plantation and lived there until he sold the property at the end of 1892.

In 1855, William Peter Smith Foster, brother of Erastus, married Laura Penny (b. Apr. 25, 1835, d. Aug. 6, 1891). William and Laura had 12 children: Mary Elizabeth, Albert, Annie, Olive, Lorena, Jessie, Laura, Harry Penny, Medora, Ella, Effie, and Maude. When William and Laura married, they lived at Glen Mary across St. Catherine's Creek from Foster's Mound. Later, they moved to Arunda in Jefferson County but subsequently the family returned to Glen Mary. Harry Penny Foster grew up at Glen Mary and attended Jefferson College with his sisters and brothers.

Harry Penny Foster (b. Jan. 24, 1872, d. Jul. 19, 1939) md. Ruth Junkin (b. Oct. 25, 1872, d. Dec. 28, 1961) in 1898. She was the ninth of 10 children born to David Junkin and Jennet McKinstry Junkin. Ruth came to the U.S. at age 2 from Larne, County Antrim, Ireland. Harry P. Foster and Ruth Junkin Foster had seven children: Ellen (md. Gordon H. Rowe, had five children); Harry (md. Nan Druetta, no children); Frank (md. Otimese Brown, one child); Jennie (md. Reginald Lowe, three children); Hugh (md. Annie Mae Carter, two children); Bessie (md. Joseph E. Smith, two children); Thomas James "T.J." (md. Flora E. Atkinson, one child; md. Agnes Wilson, three children).

Harry P. Foster was a teacher and for many years owned a grocery store located on Jefferson St. next to King's Tavern called H.P. Foster Grocery. The building is now a tavern. The Harry Foster family lived in a farmhouse perched on a small knoll on Foster Mound Road about one mile east of the Pine Ridge Road intersection. The property was known as Sterling Plantation and remained in the Foster family until 1997. *Submitted by Jaqueline Weiss and Agnes Foster.*

THOMAS JAMES FOSTER. Thomas James "T.J." Foster was born on May 30, 1913 near Foster's Mound in Natchez, MS to Harry Penny Foster (b. 1872) and Ruth Junkin Foster (b. 1972). T.J. was the youngest child of seven children in the family. He married Flora Edith Atkinson (deceased) and had one daughter, Nan Erle Foster Schuchs.

Later, he married Agnes Wilson on Mar. 3, 1940 and they had three girls: Katherine, Jessie, and Elizabeth "Bette." They had 12 grandchildren and 17 great-grandchildren. With his three brothers, T.J. owned Natchez Steam Laundry at the original site on St. Catherine St. in Natchez. Upon his retirement he worked for nine years as site administrator during the restoration of historic Jefferson College on Hwy. 61N near Washington, MS. He died of a heart attack on Dec. 14, 1997.

T.J.'s wife, Agnes Wilson Foster, was the daughter of Otis L. Wilson and Jessie Porter Wilson. Otis was the fifth child of nine children born to William H. Wilson and Annie Delaney Wilson. Born in Natchez, Otis worked at Benoist Clothing Store on Main Street in Natchez all his life. Jessie was born in Windsor, Ontario and came to the United States as a teenager.

Otis and Jessie had two children: Samuel (b. 1917) and Agnes (b. Dec. 26, 1915). When Samuel was six months old, Jessie died of thyroid disease. On Jan. 23, 1920, 3-year-old Samuel

T.J. Foster family, 50th anniversary photo

choked to death. Still a young man, Otis was suddenly left alone with his small daughter, Agnes, to rear. He moved into his family home at Mt. Airy Plantation on Liberty Rd. where his sisters could help him rear his little girl. Agnes has fond memories of life with her aunts.

Agnes's grandfather, William H.H. Wilson, was the fifth child of Joseph Wilson and Catherine Anderson. Adams County records show the 1833 marriage of William and Annie Delaney from St. Francisville. They had nine children: Bessie D., Henry E., Katie I., Hannah E., Otis L., Annie, William W., Charlotte, and Maurice W. For many years William worked at Learned Lumber Co. He also built Mt. Airy house in 1907. He fought for the Confederacy in the Civil War and had a distinguished record. *Submitted by Agnes Foster.*

GREG LEE FOWLER & MELISSA "MISSY" ANN TARVER, daughter of Jean Ruth Campbell and Benjamin Edward Tarver, was born on Aug. 5, 1965 in Vicksburg, MS. She grew up in Natchez, MS, and Pearl, MS, graduating from Pearl High School. Jean Campbell, daughter of Maurine Ester Small and James Curtis Campbell, was born Nov. 3, 1945 in Vidalia, LA. Maurine (b. 4 Dec 1919 in Princeton, IL) was the daughter of Elizabeth J. Lange and Albert Orange Small. James (b. Feb. 28, 1908 in Ruston, LA) was the son of Cora Albritton of Georgia and Larkin Albert Campbell of Alabama.

Ben, the son of Mary Louise McCaleb and Roy Howard Tarver, was born Jul. 30, 1944 in Natchez; Mary Louise (b. Oct. 30, 1918 in Kingston, Adams County, MS) md. Roy on Jul. 10, 1936 in Roxie, Franklin County, MS; Roy (b. Aug. 10, 1911 in Smithdale, Amite County, MS, d. Jan. 4, 1985 in Kingston). Mary Louise was the daughter of Anne Matilda Farrar and Sidney Briscoe McCaleb, and Roy was the son of Frances "Fannie" Elizabeth Thornton and Isaac "Ike" Ham Tarver.

Ben is descended from several early settlers of the Natchez District, including names such as the following: Swayze, King, McCaleb, Farrar, Dougharty, Collins, Pipes, Bisland, Rucker, Custard, Robson, Sojourner, Thomas, Ford and Boyd.

Jean and Ben Tarver were the parents of the following children: Melissa "Missy" Ann Tarver (b. Aug. 5, 1965 in Vicksburg, MS); Benjamin "Benji" Tarver (b. May 25, 1971 in Natchez); James Isaac "Ike" Tarver (b. Oct. 2, 1969 in Natchez); and Samuel Tarver (b. May 25, 1971 in Natchez).

Missy first married on Oct. 20, 1990 in Nortonville, KY, to Michael Don Warren (b. Nov. 8, 1962), the son of Patsy Hill and Robert Don Warren. Missy and Michael are the parents of two daughters, Danica Devon Warren (b. Apr. 5, 1991 in Hopkinsville, KY) and Christian Nicole Warren, (b. Jun. 28, 1994 in Hopkinsville). Both are honor students, and both are active in soccer and Girl Scouts.

After divorcing Michael in 1997, Missy married on Nov. 8, 1998 to Greg Lee Fowler (b. May 15, 1966), the son of Helen Lack and James Fowler. Missy and Greg are the parents of Keelan Paige Fowler (b. Nov. 19, 2001) in Hopkinsville, KY.

Missy received a BS degree from Austin Perry in 1996 and master of education degree from Tennessee State University in 2000. She teaches special education at Whitthorne Middle School. Greg works for Robeson Sewing Machines, a textile machine liquidator. He, Missy and their daughters live in Culleroka, TN.

IDA ELIZABETH "COOKIE" (GREER) GATHINGS. Ida Elizabeth was born in Natchez to Carey and Lucy Greer on Jul. 2, 1943. She was welcomed by two brothers, Carlton and Amos. She went to school at Washington School and was graduated from there in 1961. After High School she went to the University of Southern Mississippi at Hattisburg and graduated from there in 1964. She went into internship in medical technology at Baptist Medical Center Princeton for a year in Birmingham, AL. She worked at Baptist Medical Centers for 33 years. When she wanted to come home for the weekend she would catch the train in Birmingham and come to Vicksburg where she would be met by a member of her family.

On May 28, 1965 she married Jerry Milam in Birmingham and they had two sons, Greer Milam (b. Aug. 26, 1968) and Jeffrey Scott Milam (b&d. Mar. 22, 1969). Their marriage lasted about 12 years and in 1985 she married Jim Gathings. She and Jim had no children. Even though their marriage lasted only nine years, they remained friends.

She left Baptist Medical Center and went into Real Estate. She is now employed with Reality South in Birmingham.

After high school in Birmingham, Greer, her son, graduated from Samford University with a BS degree in math and physics. He then entered the Southern Theological Seminary in Louisville, KY and received a master of divinity degree there.

He now teaches math and is assistant math team instructor at Vestavia Hills High School in Birmingham, AL. This math team has been National Champions for 11 out of the last 13 years.

B. CLARENCE GEISENBERGER FAMILY. B. Clarence (b. Dec. 2, 1892 in, Adams County, MS, d. Oct. 13, 1948, Natchez) was a businessman greatly involved in the civic and social welfare of the Natchez Community. He was vice-president of the Interstate Coffee Co., part owner of Simon Mayer Insurance Agency, served as president and on the Board of Directors of the Association of Commerce and he along with other members of the industrial committee was instrumental in bringing badly needed industry, Blue Bell Globe a garment factory, to the Natchez area in the 1940s.

After serving as a lieutenant in WWI, he was a charter member and post commander of Herbert J. Remondet Post of the American Legion, being an active member until his death.

Of vital interest to him was the public schools of Natchez and their expansion program that he was part of, having served for many, many years on the Natchez School Board, and as trustee of the Agnes Carpenter Fund. During WWII, he served as chairman of the Adams County Selective Service Board.

He was a member of Temple B'Nai Isreal, a member of Harmony Lodge No. 1 and Natchez Lodge of Elks.

He married Kate Shields (b. Mar. 31, 1896, d. Jan. 16, 1954) of Brandon, MS on Jul. 18, 1927. They had two children, Harriet S. Geisenberger (b. Mar. 10, 1929, d. Mar. 17, 1988) md. Ralph B. Shields Jr., Vidalia, LA on Jun. 7, 1952 and had two sons, Ralph B. Shields, III and Clarence D. Shields, both of Vidalia, LA. Clare B. Geisenberger (b. Dec. 2, 1931) md. David L. Eidt on Jul. 2, 1960 and has two children: David L. Eidt Jr., who lives in Brandon, MS, and Kate S. Eidt who lives in Jackson, MS.

His grandparents were Wolfe Geisenberger (b. Jul. 2, 1819, d. Dec. 9, 1899) of Weisenburg, Alsace and Fannie Nettre Geisenberger (b. Dec. 25, 1836, d. Dec. I3, 1904) of Schwindratzheim, Alsace. Wolfe received his naturalization papers in April 1856 making him a citizen of the United States of America. He and Fannie had seven children: Alexander, Benjamin and Abraham, all born in Port Gibson, MS, while Florence, Samuel, Leon and Albert were all born in Natchez, MS.

His father was Wolfe's second son, Benjamin C. Geisenberger (b. Jul. 24, 1860, d. May 5, 1935) md. Sadie Landman (b. Apr. 2, 1866, d. Dec. 30, 1926) of Magnolia, MS. Their four sons were Alex, Maurice, Clarence and Robert E. Lee Geisenberger.

Clarence's daughter, Clare, and her husband live in the family home on Main Street in Natchez, MS which was built and lived in by Benjamin and Clarence and their respective families. *Submitted by David Eidt.*

NORMA HAMMETT WATSON GEISENBERGER.

Norma was born Feb. 17, 1939 in Natchez, MS, to Mamie Montgomery Smith and David Arthur Hammett. Mamie (b. Apr. 18, 1917 at Saragossa Plantation, Natchez) and Arthur (b. Feb. 12, 1911 in Natchez) met through a friend and were married May 9, 1936 at the Presbyterian Manse, Natchez. Together as a team, they built, owned, and operated Hammett Supply Co., beginning in 1945. After Arthur's death in 1978, Mamie and Norma continued to run the business until June 1990, when they closed it.

Five generations at Saragossa. Mamie Foster Smith on her 85th birthday. Mamie Smith Hammett, Norma Hammett Watson Geisenberger, Carol Lee Watson Mathias and Jenni Mathias

Mamie and Arthur had two other children, Joseph Montgomery Hammett (b. 1943) and David Arthur Hammett (b. 1944), but both died at birth.

As an only child, Norma grew up in Natchez, attending Natchez public schools, from kindergarten through 12th grade. Her childhood was one of "Country Mouse and City Mouse." She lived in Natchez, upstairs over the family business, where there was always much activity, with people coming and going. She was around people all the time and enjoyed meeting them. Then, she would go to Saragossa, her grandmother's home in the country, and enjoyed being with her grandmother in the country, never seeing another person. Norma spent many days outdoors riding her horse or fishing. In the evenings, she and her grandmother would sit under the gallery of Saragossa and listen to the whippoorwills and the owls.

Norma attended Hinds Junior College and the University of Southern Mississippi, and she worked at the USM-Natchez Branch in the late 1970s.

She married Clifton Watson (b. Jun. 2, 1957, Natchez) and they had two daughters, Carol Lee

Davidson R. Smith and Mamie Willard Foster at Saragossa, 1910

(Watson) Mathias (b. Apr. 17, 1958) and Connie Lynn (Watson) Bradshaw (b. Oct. 5, 1960). In 1978 Norma divorced Clifton Watson.

Attending Westminister Presbyterian Church, Natchez, Norma enjoys the women's circle and other church activities.

After closing Hammett Supply Co. in 1990, Norma worked at the Adams County Chapter American Red Cross, becoming executive director. In June 1999 she retired and is enjoying retirement at this time. In 1966 she married Wilfred W. Geisenberger, also born and reared in Natchez. He, too, is retired having practiced law in Natchez for 34 years.

GIBSON FAMILY OF THE NATCHEZ DISTRICT, settlers who arrived from South Carolina about 1779-80. The Gibson family had existed in South Carolina for several generations, and before that in the state of Virginia. Details of this enormous clan may be found in the book *Jordon and Hannah Gibson's Descendants,* by Beulah Kenisell Waller, Litho USA Quality Press, Englewood, CO, 1978. Before that large volume was made available, the early Gibsons were detailed in Boddie's *Historical Southern Families.* Invariably, there must have been some errors in both volumes, as such occur in any book of genealogy.

While there are ample details available about the hundreds of Gibson descendents, there is little printed about the early South Carolinans who immigrated to Natchez. Oddly, we find that a newspaper obituary of Edna Gibson Bullen, daughter of one of the first families to arrive reads as follows:

"Died last day of September 1839 at the residence of her son, David Bullen, Mrs. Edna Bullen, in her 82 years of age. She was a native of South Carolina, but had been in Mississippi upwards of 60 years. She was one of the original eight members of the first Methodist Church in the West, about 50 years ago." Printed in *The Rodney Telegraph.*

This obituary indicates that Mrs. Bullen and her parents arrived in Natchez about 1779. Her parents were Gideon/Gibeon Gibson, born ca. 1720 in South Carolina or Virginia and Mary O'Connell, born ca. 1725, Ireland. Mr. Gibson's given name is curiously spelled Gideon in one spot, and Gibeon in the next. Perhaps this is a misreading of old handwriting. Of his wife, Mary, we know little.

The original Registry Book of Prince Frederic Winyaw Parish, Episcopal Church of South Carolina lists a number of the children of this couple and their birth dates.

One of the first written records of Gibeon Gibson in Natchez is his petition to the Natchez Court Oct. 16, 1781 seeking payment for some work on a deceased man's estate. He owned at least 630 acres on the St. Catherine's Creek area. We know very little of the man before or after he came to Natchez. Boddie states that Gideon

Gibson participated in the regulator uprising in South Carolina in 1768. He further states that Gideon did not serve in the Revolution but that several of his sons did.

There were several men with the name of Gideon Gibson. This may account for the confusion and errors that can be found concerning men with this name. Gideon and Mary O'Connell were the parents of numerous children:

William Gibson (b. Sep. 15, 1743, probably South Carolina)

Sarah Gibson (b. Jan. 19, 1744, Williamsburg District, SC) md. John Foster and John Ferguson.

Jordon Gibson (b. 1747) md. Mary Middleton.

Gideon Gibson (b. 1750).

Reuben Gibson (b. Nov. 29, 1751, Williamsburg Dist., SC) md. Mildred Dulin. He died Oct 9, 1816.

Mary Gibson (b. Oct. 2, 1752, Charleston, SC) md. Joseph Harrison of South Carolina and Natchez ca. 1773.

Samuel Gibson (b. 1755). We are not certain whether this is the Samuel Gibson who founded Port Gibson, MS.

James Gibson (b. 1757).

Elizabeth Gibson (b. 1759) md. Daniel Whitaker.

Edna Gibson (b. ca. 1757, md. ca. 1775, d. Sep. 30, 1839) md. first, John Holstein and second, John B. Bullen.

Rachel Gibson (b. 1763, d. 1851) md. John William Foster.

Cynthia Gibson (b. 1765) md. Henry G. Holstein.

Randal Gibson (b. Sept. 17, 1766, Pee Dee, SC, d. Apr. 13, 1836 in Warren County, MS) md. Harriet McKinley on Feb. 7, 1792.

David Gibson (b. 1768, Mars Bluff, SC, d. Dec. 12, 1858, Jefferson County, MS) md. Frances McKinley on Feb. 2, 1792.

Two notable Gibsons were Rev. Randal Gibson, Methodist Minister and one of the founders of Jefferson College, at Washington, MS. He gave a large portion of the land that was set aside. Rev. Tobias Gibson was a Methodist Minister who brought the Methodist Faith to the Old Southwest for the first time, arriving in 1799 on assignment by Bishop Francis Asbury. His first church was at Washington, MS and his original eight members included several of his Gibson relatives. His parents were Jordon Gibson and Mary Middleton. He died a young man and his remains are located at the Crawford Street Methodist Church in Vicksburg. *Submitted by Harold C. Fisher.*

THOMAS GILBERT FAMILY. Thomas and Tillman Gilbert of Ohio County, KY, married Louisa and Elizabeth Guice, daughters of Jonathan Guice and Anna Stump of Franklin County, MS. By the 1830s, the two couples had settled on adjoining properties in Catahoula Parish, LA, Tillman on Maitland and Thomas on Mayhew Plantation. In 1854 Thomas (b. Jan. 3, 1803, d. Jun. 5, 1855) and Louisa (b. Jan. 19, 1807, d. Oct. 23, 1898) purchased what is now known as the Dorsey House at 305 North Pearl Street, Natchez. Following Thomas' death, the family maintained the country residence on Mayhew and the Natchez home. In 1860, with Louisa's move to historic Oakley in Franklin Parish, LA, she established the Gilbert family which for 125 years would consistently yield community and political leaders in that parish.

The surviving children of Thomas and Louisa Gilbert were Clara Louisa (md. Nelson Hower); Barbara Salome (md. William W. Richardson); Thomas Benjamin (md. Adeline Cornelia Norris); Jacob (md. Ellen Daniels); Sarentha (md. Charles Thacker); and Rachel Josephine (md. Dr. W.W. Lee). Rachel and Dr. Lee became the grandparents of Gen. Claire Lee Chennault, American aviation pioneer and leader of the WWII era volunteers, the "Flying Tigers."

Thomas Benjamin Gilbert's wife Adeline Norris of Pine Hill Plantation, Sicily Island, Catahoula Parish, LA, was the daughter of Harriet Perry and her second husband Dr. Richard Henry Norris. Harriet, like Louisa Guice, had ties to Franklin County, MS. She was the daughter of Judith King Perry, a young widow, who married Franklin County planter Bartlett Ford in 1808.

Of the nine children of Thomas and Addie Gilbert, son Daniel married Mary Emma Carr in 1893. Their three children were Jess, Fred and Irma. Jess and Fannie Adams' son, Jess Carr Gilbert, married a distant cousin, also a descendant of Harriet Perry, but through her first husband Zachariah Tucker Kirkland. Before his death in 1835, Zachariah and Harriet had two daughters, Sarah Harriet Ruth (md. Dr. Douglass Stark Bisland) and Patience Julia (md. John Henry Lovelace of Ferry Place Plantation, National Register of Historic Places). John and Patience were the parents of Florence Lovelace who married William S. Peck I of Battleground Plantation, National Register of Historic Places. It was their granddaughter, Barbara Jane Peck, who became the wife of Jess Carr Gilbert in 1946; hence, the great-great-granddaughter of Harriet Perry Kirkland Norris married Harriet's great-great-grandson.

Barbara Peck Gilbert Haigh is the daughter of Jess C. "Sonny" Gilbert and Barbara Jane Peck of Sicily Island, LA. She and her husband Thomas David Haigh resided in Adams County for a number of years before moving to neighboring Jefferson County in the 1990s. They have remained active in Natchez activities and organizations, with Barbara currently serving the Natchez Historical Society as president (See Haigh family history).

For this genealogy and family history, descendants are indebted to Frances Gilbert Martin, great-great-grandaughter of Thomas Gilbert and Louisa Guice. Her dedication to family research has yielded invaluable information, and she is an inspiration to her family. *Submitted by Barbara Gilbert Haigh*

GRAFTON-BELCHER-DOWNING, the Grafton brothers: Daniel, Thomas, John, Stewart, Allen, and one sister who married a McKown first entered South Carolina. They came to Adams County, MS Territory: Daniel by 1783, John by 1791, Stewart and Allen in the early 1800s. Thomas died in 1798 and his family remained in South Carolina.

Daniel married Mary Barr, had eight children and died by 1801.

John Grafton married Janet Allen, had five children, and died in 1821. They lived at Pine Ridge in Adams County.

Allen Grafton was in Adams County when he died in 1809. He had nine children.

Stewart Grafton (b. ca. 1760, in Ireland, d. Apr. 13, 1837 in York Twp. Ontario, Canada) md. first a Miss Shaw and had a daughter, Margaret (b. May 22, 1788). He married second Mary McCool in 1794 and had nine children.

Margaret Grafton, daughter of Stewart, married her first cousin, Thomas Grafton, son of John at Pine Ridge Feb. 7, 1808.

In 1811, Stewart decided to move to Canada because he did not want to live in any country fighting England, War of 1812. He left Adams County in November 1811, taking all his family and his daughter Margaret and her husband Thomas Grafton and was in Canada by May 14, 1812.

On the way to Canada, Thomas Grafton died Apr. 11, 1812, Sugar Creek, Venango County, PA. He had two children, Jenny (b. 1810, d. 1826) and Stewart (b. 1812, d. 1825).

Margaret (Grafton) Grafton married second in 1814 or 15 in Canada to John Belcher, as his second wife and they had six children. John Belcher died in 1834 and Margaret Grafton Belcher died Mar. 9, 1840. Three of their children: William Shaw (b. 1816, d. 1860), Hannah Rachel (b. 1825, d. 1905) and Katherine (b. 1828, d. 1900), and their half brother, Alexander Belcher, left Canada in the early 1840s and moved to Raymond, Hinds County, MS.

Hannah Rachel married Gerard Brandon Downing May 30, 1847 in Raymond. Gerard (b. 1815 in Adams County, MS) was the son of Thomas Downing and Ann (Newman) Whitaker Downing.

Hannah and Gerard had six children: Margaret Ann (b. 1848, d. 1926) md. Henry Brainard; William Walter (b. 1851, d. 1918) md. three times; James Douglas (b. 1853, d. 1932) md. Artie Wright; Gerard Newman or Gerard Brandon Jr. (b. 1858, d. 1936); Thomas Alexander (b. 1862, d. 1931) md. twice; Edgar Lee (b. 1865, d. 1900). Gerard Brandon served in the Civil War.

Thomas Alexander Downing (b. Jul. 8, 1862 in Raymond, d. in Jackson, MS) md. first, Emma Kennedy Feb. 7, 1888 in Raymond. Their children: Emma Hugh (b. 1889, d. 1945) md. John Roberts; Thomas Joseph (b. 1891, d. 1891); Marie Rachel (b. 1891, d. 1980) md. Ernest Alley and Margret (b. 1894, d. 1979) md. Edgar Wilson.

Thomas Alexander married second, May Estelle Flewellyn (b. 1881, d. 1954), daughter of James H. Flewellyn and Virginia B. Herron. Their children: Mae Estelle (b. 1903) md. Robert Barksdale; Katherine Virginia (b. 1904, d. 1985) md. Harold J. Hewitt (b. 1898, d. 1984) on Oct. 6, 1925 in Jackson, MS, had two daughters, Virginia (b. 1932) md. Edwin Jones and Sarah May (b. 1935) md. Roy Parker; Edmond Lee Downing (b. 1909, d. 1958) md. Nell McRaney and had one daughter, Ann Morris. *Submitted by Sarah H. Parker.*

RICHARD GRAHAM & ADELE GAUDET are descended from Colonial English and French Acadian forbears respectively. Richard's Walworth ancestors in America started with William Walworth "The Pioneer" who arrived at Fisher's Island off the coast of the Connecticut colony in 1689 and his son John Walworth. Adele's Gaudet ancestors trace their presence in North America to Jean "Old Jean" Gaudet through his son, Denis Gaudet, who arrived in Port Royal prior to his 1644 marriage to Martine Gauthier.

Richard's parents were Alice Gordon Walworth Graham (whose Walworth forbears arrived prior to Mississippi statehood) and Richard Norwood Graham (whose Graham forbears were from Greenwood, SC). Adele's parents were John Valery Gaudet (from New Orleans, LA) and Emma Pauline LeBlanc Gaudet (from Franklin, LA).

Richard and Adele were married in New Orleans in June 1962 where both families lived. Richard had just graduated from Tulane University Engineering School and Adele had completed three years at Tulane University Newcomb College. They moved to Maryland with the Air Force until 1967, then returned to New Orleans until 1972. Richard took a position with Ingalls Shipbuilding in Pascagoula, MS and they moved to Gautier, MS.

In 1976, Richard got a wonderful chance to work as an engineer with Aramco in Saudi Arabia. They moved overseas with their children (Madeleine born in 1963 and John born in 1967) and stayed for a decade enjoying the culture and travel opportunities. Both children went to an Aramco-run American style school in Saudi Arabia and then went to boarding schools, Madeleine to Marymount in Rome, Italy and John to Kent

School in Connecticut. Adele worked in the school library.

Dick and Adele Graham

The Grahams moved back to Natchez in 1986 for a year and a half, then they got another position in the Middle East; this time it was in Yemen working for the U.S. State Department building a new American embassy.

On completion of the embassy in late 1989, they returned to Natchez and have remained until the present. They came back to be close to Richard's father and mother and provide their children with a home base. Richard obtained a fine engineering position with Alcoa World Chemicals in their Vidalia, LA adsorbents and catalysts plant. He retired in April 2002.

Madeleine graduated from Tulane University in 1985 and John also graduated from Tulane in 1990. Adele's father and mother had also attended Tulane. Richard's father graduated from Clemson University as an engineer, his mother attended MS University for Women, LSU, and Columbia studying writing.

Madeleine married Michael P. Hallal, USN in 1985 and they traveled around the U.S. as a Navy family. They have two sons, Patrick and Nicholas.

John was commissioned in the USAF on graduation from Tulane. He married Andrea Holliday of Twin Falls, ID and they also have two sons, Brenden and Reilly.

ALTON WAYNE GRAY & DONNA GAIL WRIGHT. Alton was the second of five children born to Alton Earl Gray and Georgia Franklin Huff of Natchez, MS on Feb. 4, 1965. He married Donna Gail Wright on Jan. 11, 1985. Donna Gail was the first child of three born to Bobby Joe Wright and Patsy Wright.

Wayne and Donna Gray with children Daniel and Caleb

Alton Wayne worked as a target D.C. in 2002. His hobbies are hunting, fishing and going to church. Donna enjoys reading and doing puzzles. They had two children, Daniel Burnes (b. Mar. 18, 1983) and Caleb Gray (b. Jan. 30, 1987).

The family lives in Florence, AL and they attend Loretto Baptist Church. Wayne Gray attended Coffee High School and Donna Gray, Rodger High School.

AMOS SHELDON GREER & HILDA MAE RAWLS GREER. Amos was born Dec. 7, 1915, at the Greer homestead just north of five corners near Ruth, Lincoln County, MS. He was the seventh of nine children born to Amos Nelson and Ida Elizabeth Summers Greer and is the grandson of Frank Greer, who established the original homestead in 1869 on present-day Hwy. 583 where it remains intact today. He spent his childhood and formative years working the family farm and experimenting with higher yield crops and raising hogs. He graduated from Ruth High School in 1934, attended Copiah Lincoln County Junior College in 1935 and Pearl River Junior College in 1936. Because of his father's illness, he had to return to the family farm in the spring of 1936 to help harvest the family crops. Known by everyone as Shell, he left home on Christmas day, 1938, to work at Armstrong Tire and Rubber Company in Natchez, MS.

Amos Sheldon Greer, Hilda Mae Rawls, taken in 2001

Hilda Mae Rawls was born on Jan. 26, 1915, at the Rawls homestead just east of five corners near Ruth, Lincoln County, MS. She was the fourth of four children born to Cicero Clifton and Iva Nora Hodges Rawls. Her childhood was also spent on the family farm. As a teenager, she became the pianist and youngest member of the Sweetwater Choir, an award winning gospel choir founded by Cicero Rawls which performed all over Lincoln County in the late 1920s and early 1930s. She graduated valedictorian of the Class of 1933, Ruth High School and graduated from Copiah Lincoln County junior College in 1936.

Amos and Hilda were married Jun. 28, 1940, in Brookhaven, MS and resided in Natchez where Amos spent 12 years at Armstrong Tire, then three years in private business. They were Sunday school and Training Union teachers at the First Baptist Church in Natchez. Amos joined the Masonic Lodge in Natchez in 1942 and remains a current member. A son, Amos Sheldon Greer Jr., and a daughter, Elizabeth Greer, were born in 1942 and 1947 respectively in Natchez. Due to their son's illness, the family moved to Grand Prairie, TX, where Amos worked for Chance Vought Aircraft.

The family moved to Littleton, CO, in the summer of 1960, where he worked for Martin Marietta Co. until the summer of 1965 when they returned to Grand Prairie, TX. He worked at Print Pak Inc. from 1966 until his retirement in 1998, having completed 59 years working in industry. Amos and Hilda presently reside in Grand Prairie, TX. They have four grandchildren and three great-grandchildren.

AMOS SHELDON GREER JR. & NANCY LANGFORD. Amos Sheldon Greer Jr., the eldest of two children born to Amos Sheldon and Hilda Mae Rawls Greer, was born on Jul. 21, 1942, in Natchez, MS. From his home on Ouachita Street in Natchez, he made many trips with his family back to the Greer homestead in Bogue Chitto to visit his paternal grandmother, Ida Elizabeth Greer, and his maternal grandparents, Cicero and Iva Nora Rawls at the Rawls homestead in Bogue Chitto.

He entered public school at Braden Elementary School in Natchez and remained a student

there through the sixth grade. Although contracting asthma at an early age, he began his athletic career at the age of 7 in the Natchez Little League Association. As a pitcher and shortstop, he qualified for three All-Star teams, including a trip to the 1954 Mississippi Little League Regional Tournament in McComb, MS.

In the winter of 1954, his illness becoming chronic, his family moved to Grand Prairie, TX. He graduated from Grand Prairie High School in 1960 as an Honor Merit Student in science and a three-sport letterman in baseball, track and basketball. As a senior, he was captain of the 1960 basketball team and an All-City honoree in basketball and State Regional Finalist in track. He entered Texas Tech University in the fall of 1960 on a basketball scholarship and graduated in 1966 with a BS degree in engineering physics.

His professional career spanned 33 years beginning as a research engineer at Bell Helicopter Co. in Forth Worth, TX and ending as Director of NDE Research for Southwest Research Institute in San Antonio, TX. On retiring from SWRI, he spent five years as a professional consulting engineer. While most of his career was spent in the Nuclear Power Industry, he participated in numerous Defense, Manned Spaceflight, Medical and Power Generation programs and was a member and officer of 15 professional and engineering societies. During his career, he was fortunate enough to visit every state in the continental USA and 21 foreign countries in pursuit of engineering programs.

Amos, or Little Shell as he was known in Mississippi, married Nancy Langford in 1963. They have two children, Terry and Kay Lynn, and three grandchildren. They presently reside in Grand Prairie, TX.

AMOS CAREY GREER SR. & LINDA FAYE MYERS. Amos was born on Nov. 17, 1940 to William Carey Greer and Lucy Carlton Greer, in Natchez, MS. Amos was known to many of his friends and family as Butch, attended school at Washington, MS under the watchful eye of his mother who taught school there.

Greer Family Reunion in October 1992. Standing l-r: Amos Carey Greer Jr. and wife Susan Seyfarth, Jennifer Sue Breithaupt, Lucie Maria Greer Breithaupt, William Quinn Greer holding daughter Sarah Lynn Greer, Ida Elizabeth Greer Gathings and her son Jerry Greer Milam, and Carlette Greer Williams. Seated row is (little boy standing is J.C. Greer), Amos Carey Greer Sr., Lucy Edna Carlton Greer, and William Carlton Greer Sr. Kneeling in front is Theresa Ann Breithaupt and John Maxwell Breithaupt Jr.

Amos had one older brother, William Carlton, and a younger sister, Ida Elizabeth "Cookie." He loved animals as a young boy, often raising such pets as raccoons, bobcats and alligators.

Upon graduation from high school, he attended Southwest Community College where he became friends with Gerald Day. On a weekend trip with

Gerald to visit family, Amos met Linda Faye Myers and they were married in early 1961. They built a small house on his father's property in Natchez. Amos worked for Armstrong Tire and Rubber and retired after 26 years of service.

Amos and Linda had two sons, Amos Carey Greer Jr. and William Quinn Greer. Amos and Linda divorced in the mid-70s. After two other marriages, he married his old high school sweetheart, Myra Johnson. After a brief time, which was the happiest time in his latter years, he became ill and passed away on Dec. 5, 1992, in the Community Hospital in Natchez. He is buried in Greenlawn Memorial Cemetery.

He lived for his grandchildren, Cara L. Greer and John C. Greer, the children of Carey his oldest son; Sarah Greer and Molly Greer, the daughters of the youngest son Bill. Amos also enjoyed the outdoors and spent many hours hunting and fishing. He passed this hobby to his sons, whom are avid outdoorsmen as well. He was a good father, grandfather, and is missed by all that knew him.

AMOS "CAREY" GREER JR. Amos was born on Jul. 13, 1962 in Natchez, MS to Amos C. Greer and Linda M. Greer. He attended school in the Natchez public schools and graduated high school in 1980. In 1982 he was married to his high school sweetheart Susan R. Seyfarth, the daughter of John and Rosie Seyfarth. In October of that year their first child, Cara Louise Greer, was born. On Feb. 14, 1990 their second child, John Carey Greer, was born. Carey and Susan have lived in Natchez all their lives.

Carey enjoys hunting, motorcycle riding and spending time on the family's estate, which is located in Lincoln County just a few miles from Ruth, MS. As a young boy he spent many hours there with his grandfather, W.C. Greer. He and his grandfather were very close, he being the oldest grandson. He and his grandfather spent many hours fishing and hunting. In 1980 he moved into his grandfather's home and lived with his grandparents while finishing high school.

His mother had remarried and moved to St. Francisville, LA. Wanting to graduate with the classmates which he had been growing up with he stayed behind. He lost his grandfather in 1981, leaving behind his grandmother, Lucy Carlton Greer. Carey has one brother William Quinn Greer who is married to Debbie Miller and lives in St. Francisville, LA. They have two daughters, Sarah and Molly.

Carey is employed by ALCOA Vidalia and works as an I&E technician. He has always worked in the electrical field and has an industrial electrical degree from Copiah-Lincoln Junior Collage.

Carey and Susan are both members of 61 South Church of Christ, where Carey teaches the teenage Sunday school class. This is the same church that they were married in on Apr. 30, 1982. To God be the glory.

LUCIE MARIA GREER was known as Maria and the oldest of three children born on Sep. 10, 1959 to William Carlton and Mary Grace Greer. She has a sister Carlette Williams of Natchez and Carl Greer of Alvin, TX.

Starting at an early age, she was an avid horse lover. She rode in the horse shows at Pine Ridge every weekend and won several trophies for her fun.

She attended South Natchez-Adams County High School and was in several clubs there. She married John Breithaupt and they had three children: Jennifer, Maxwell (known as Max) and Theresa. For a while, she and John lived in a trailer on her parent's property on Old Washington Road, now known as Newman Road. They then moved to an apartment in Natchez owned by his father.

Maria and John's marriage ended and she is now living south of Houston, TX where she is assistant manager at a Dollar Tree Store. Theresa, her daughter is working there with her.

Jennifer married Brandy Davis and they have one son, Cody. She now lives in Ferriday and is dispatcher for AMR Ambulance Service in Monroe.

Max and his daughter Sarah reside in Houston, TX also.

SEDLEY JOSEPH "S.J." GREER & ANNIE RUTH JUNKIN

SEDLEY JOSEPH "S.J." GREER & ANNIE RUTH JUNKIN were married in Natchez on Sep. 3, 1926. S.J., descendant of a pioneer Mississippi family, was born on May 7, 1889 in Lincoln County, MS, the son of Thomas Ezekiel Greer and Hannah Elizabeth Reeves. Annie Ruth (b. Jan. 14, 1899) was the daughter of Hugh Junkin and Annie Yeager of Quitman Plantation in Adams County, MS.

S.J. received a degree in horticulture from MS State University and, after teaching school for several years, came to Natchez as county agent. He soon met Annie Ruth Junkin, who was educated at Whitworth College and Millsaps College. After they were married S.J. and Annie Ruth lived at the Mississippi State Experiment Station at Foster Mound where S.J. was director.

They were soon actively involved in Adams County life. Devout Methodists, they were members of Jefferson Street Church where both taught Sunday school for most of their adult lives. S.J. served on the Board and Annie Ruth was a leader in the women's group. Over the years S.J. was a member of the Board of Trustees of Judge George Armstrong Library, a member and officer of the Rotary Club, a member of the Natchez-Adams County School Board, head of the Draft Board during WWII, and was a member of the Mississippi State Alumni Association. Annie Ruth was an active member of many groups in Natchez, among them the Pilgrimage Garden Club, the Rosecraft Club, the United Daughters of the Confederacy, and the Adams County Homemakers Extension Club. S.J. enjoyed gardening and always made time for his favorite hobby of fishing while Annie Ruth devoted her spare time to her flower garden, sewing, canning, and travel.

After S.J. left the experiment station, he opened a feed and seed store on the corner of Pine and Franklin Streets. Afterward he was head of the Adams County Welfare Department. Annie Ruth taught in the Natchez and Adams County Public Schools before her marriage and again in later years.

S.J. and Annie Ruth Junkin Greer and two of their grandchildren, Ann and Rae Wise

In the early 1930s during the Great Depression, S.J. and Annie Ruth, unable to have children of their own, adopted newly born twins whose mother, S.J.'s cousin, Carrie Starkey Aldridge Cannon, had died. They named the twins Sedley

Joseph Jr. and Carolyn Ann and soon set out to get the twins' older siblings. First they were successful in bringing sister Mary Jo Aldridge into their home and about a year later brother David Aldridge. Later they were able to bring all the children together when sister Evelyn Montae Aldridge came to live with them. The family, now complete, spent many happy years at the Foster Mound house and later at a home S.J. built near Washington.

Throughout the years S.J. and Annie Ruth Greer served the community generously with their time and money and, in return, they were highly respected throughout Adams County.

WILLIAM CAREY "CARO" GREER & LUCY EDNA CARLTON

WILLIAM CAREY "CARO" GREER & LUCY EDNA CARLTON. Carey was born on Mar. 19, 1906 to Amos Nelson and Ida Summers Greer. He walked to the one-room school at Topisaw, a distance of about three miles. His parents were poor farmers so he left school in the third grade to help on the farm. As a young adult he went to work on the Mississippi Central Railroad as bridge foreman working out of a camp car in all areas of the railroad. He would only get the chance to get home on some weekends. He passed away Mar. 20, 1981.

Lucy Edna Carlton (b. Apr. 18, 1908) was the daughter of George Martin and Ella Pearl Johnson Carlton. Her parents passed away at a very early age and she was reared in several foster homes, going to several different schools and colleges. She was an elementary school teacher having taught in a number of Adams County Schools in her 33

Lucy Edna Carlton and William Carey Greer, the day they married on Sept. 1, 1935

years of teaching. She taught 22 years at Washington School. She passed away Jul. 5, 1998.

They met at his home when she came to spend the weekend with one of his sisters who was going to Whitworth College in Brookhaven with her. They married on Sep. 1, 1935. In 1938 their first son, Carlton, was born. Soon afterward he got a job with the construction company that was building Armstrong Rubber Co. They moved to Washington in 1939 in a house on the S.J. Greer property. They soon started building a house closer to Natchez.

On Nov. 17, 1940, their second son, Amos Carey Greer, was born. He attended school at Washington, where he graduated. He passed away on Dec. 5, 1992. Amos also worked for Armstrong for many years.

Their daughter, Ida Elizabeth "Cookie" Greer was born Jul. 2, 1943. She graduated from Washington and graduated from the University of Southern Mississippi and interned at Baptist Medical Center Princeton in Birmingham where she worked as medical technologist for 33 years.

Caro was an avid fisherman, loving to fish white perch. Many mornings he would get with his two sons and would be on Old River with pole in hand when the sun came up. A lot of times they would be waiting for the sun to come up.

When he retired from Armstrong Rubber Co. in 1971, he and Lucy bought a trailer and moved it to his old home place south of Brookhaven, MS. Here he revitalized some of the old fields and planted vegetables that he gladly gave to anyone that wanted them. He was instrumental in planting some of the fields in pine timber.

WILLIAM CARLTON GREER SR.

WILLIAM CARLTON GREER SR. is the oldest son of Carey and Lucy Greer, both now deceased. He was born on Jan. 3, 1938 in Brookhaven, MS at home. His dad went around the corner to get the doctor and when they got back he welcomed them. It was always joked that the doctor and Carey stopped for a stiff drink to reinforce them and they waited too long. Aunt Claudia, a midwife and sister to Carey, had taken care of everything.

He came to Natchez with his parents at the age of about 2. He started school at Washington High School in the fall of 1943. Carlton graduated from Washington School in the spring of 1954 and was the second youngest, at that time, to enroll in Mississippi State in the fall of 1954. He studied engineering and forestry for two years and came home.

He went to work at Armstrong Rubber Co. on Sep. 10, 1957. He married Mary Grace Lowry in June 1958 and they had three children: Maria (b. 1959), Carlette (b. 1961) and Carl Jr. (b. 1968). Their marriage ended and on Aug. 13, 1981 he married Helen Eudora Rasberry Brown.

They combined the two families: Marla, Carlette and Carl with William, Rieta, Helen, Monica and Esther. They now have 23 grandchildren and four great-grandchildren. Carlton retired from Armstrong after 30 years and now serves as deputy sheriff in Concordia Parish where he and Helen now live. He is also captain in the Concordia Parish Fire Protection District #2 and co-ordinator of the Deerpark Neighborhood Watch in the Deerpark, LA area of the parish, where they now reside.

Helen is a volunteer radio dispatcher for the Concordia Parish Fire Protection District #2, having an office in their home with all the radio equipment needed to maintain emergency radio contact and message delivering to the 16 fire units and several ambulances and Sheriff's Office as the need arises.

Shortly after Carlton and Helen married, they moved to Carlton's fishing camp to make a retirement home. It is located at Fairview Landing, 20 miles from town almost at the end of a road that is unbelievably bad. They reared their last three children there. During high water, the water would get under their house which is 14 feet off the

Helen E.R. Greer and William Carlton Greer taken in July 1998

ground. Travel then would be about a mile to the vehicle by boat—good weather or bad weather. In 1997 they bought a trailer and moved it under a huge pecan tree at Deerpark, LA on the safe side of the levee.

Carlton and Helen dedicated their lives to God at Bougere Baptist Church at Deerpark and promised God they wanted to help others in life. Although both now have some medical problems, *With God's help and guidance we still maintain a 24/7 life dedicated to helping others*, Carlton says.

WILLIAM CARLTON GREER JR.

WILLIAM CARLTON GREER JR. was born on Feb. 9, 1968, son of William Carlton Greer Sr. and Mary Grace Lowry in Jefferson Davis Memorial Hospital. As the youngest child and the only boy in the house, he soon became a toy for his older two sisters, Lucie Maria and Carlette. The family lived on Old Washington

Road (now known as Newman Rd.) on US 61 north towards Washington.

Carl, as his family called him, went to Morgantown Elementary School, then to Washington Jr. High and graduated from South Natchez High School, by the skin of his teeth, in 1986. His parents were divorced in 1981 and Carl took turns staying with his father in Ferriday, LA and with his mother in Natchez, but always attended school in Natchez. He liked to spend his summers and any other chance he got fishing and playing in Ole River at the family's camp at Fairview, LA.

From l-r: Dylan Jarrell Greer, Tracie Lynn Watson Greer, William Carlton Greer Jr., and Dakota Robert Greer. The dog's name is Star.

After graduation in 1986, Greer, as he wanted to be called, joined the US Coast Guard and was in Cape May, NJ in boot camp for Christmas that year. After boot camp his first duty station was the CGC Northland, a 270 foot cutter based in Portsmouth, VA. There he spent the next couple years sweeping and swabbing the decks as a fireman apprentice. From there he went to Yorktown, VA where he attended training school to be a machinery technician. During school he married Mary Darlene Hall, also of Natchez, but they were soon divorced.

Greer's next duty station was the CGC Valiant, a 210 foot cutter based in Galveston, TX. He was assigned to the engine room and worked mostly as a diesel mechanic. In September 1990 he married Tracie Lynn Watson from Kemah, TX, and they moved to Elizabeth City, NC. There Greer had more technical training, this time to be an aircraft mechanic. After completion of training, he was assigned to CG Air Station Savannah, Ga. He flew in the backseat of the HH-65 search and rescue helicopter, known as the Dolphin, and helped maintain the station's six helos.

While in Savannah, he and Tracie had three children: William Carlton III (b&d. Aug. 7, 1992); Dakota Robert (b. Apr. 7, 1994) and Dyllan Jarrell (b. Aug. 1, 1995).

In 1996 Greer got out of the Coast Guard and moved just south of Houston to Alvin, TX. After several jobs he settled with an aircraft mechanic job at Hobby airport. He worked there for a couple years and when the U.S. Postal Service offered him a job, he accepted it. He hired on in March 1998 as a clerk and when his 90 day probation was up he asked to switch crafts to a city carrier. His first post office was LaMarque, TX. Greer was there for a couple years, then transferred to Webster, TX. As of December 2002 Alvin, TX is still where he calls home and he still drives more miles a day in the right seat of a mail jeep than in the left seat of his old 72 Chevy pickup.

HAIGH FAMILY. Marian and Norman Haigh moved to Natchez in the 1980s upon his retirement as manager of Louisiana Delta Plantation, a 90,000-acre farming operation in Catahoula Parish, LA. Devoted to the restoration of productivity of farmlands, he has also consistently sup-

ported wildlife conservation. In 1993 Haigh was named the Goodyear/NACD Conservationist of the Year, and his Sibley Farms was named Conservation Farm of the Year in Adams County. Haigh was the 1999 recipient of the National Wetlands Award in Land Stewardship and Management. Continuing to purchase and restore undeveloped farms (his current project being Dixie Plantation in Tensas Parish, LA), Haigh has also patented a four-wheel-drive hydraulically-driven excavator, recently donated to Mississippi State University.

Marian Myers Haigh spent her early years in Arkansas, while Norman is a native of Kansas. He earned his degrees from Kansas State University and is a veteran of the Korean War. The Haighs have four children: Marian "Bunny," an accomplished artist and sculptor in Austin, TX, who is married to Peter Van Bavel; Barbara Lynn Bamer, who is employed by her father and is the mother of two sons, Kenny and Stephen Bamer; Stephen Kelly, Manager, Consolidated Grain and Barge Co., Olney, IL, who is married to Melinda Ewing of Harrisonburg, LA, and is the father of Katie Jo; and Thomas David, a resident of Jefferson County.

Thomas David Haigh and Barbara Peck Gilbert of Sicily Island, LA, married in 1988 and moved to Sibley Farms, where he held the position as farm manager. Ill health forced David's early retirement, and currently he enjoys reading, gardening, and maintaining their property between Cole's Creek and Folkes' Creek in Jefferson County. He has an interest in antiques, especially bottles, of which he has quite a collection. Both Barbara and David are members of the Natchez Scottish Heritage Society; David has become especially curious about the Haig Clan, and they are researching his ancestry.

Both Barbara and David have sons by previous marriages. David's son is Thomas Andrew Haigh, who is serving in the U.S. Army as Specialist, U.S. Army Apache Helicoptor Unit. Barbara's son is Thomas L. Enright, an attorney with the Louisiana Department of Justice. Thomas, a former Marine who served in Desert Storm, is a captain in the U.S. Army Reserves currently stationed in Afghanistan. He is married to Erin Elizabeth Bernard of Baton Rouge, and they have two young children, William Thomas and Eleanor Jane "Ellie" Enright.

Barbara has a MA degree in English and has taught English for 30 years. She developed the Gifted Program for high school students in Catahoula Parish, LA, taught at Louisiana Tech University and Alcorn State University, and is currently in the English Department at Copiah-Lincoln Community College in Natchez. She serves the Natchez Historical Society as president and the George Harlan Chapter of the Colonial Dames 17th Century as vice-president. She is an avid genealogist and has done substantial research on her ancestral families, which include Peck, Gilbert, Lovelace, Kirkland, Holstein, McKinnie, McNabb, Woodward, and Bacot.

CLINT HANCHEY & SARAH YOUNG were wed in a festive holiday wedding on Saturday, Dec. 29, 2001 at the First Presbyterian Church in Natchez, MS. The bride is the daughter of "Candy" Mildred Daggett Young of Jonesville, LA and John Davis Young Sr. of Ferriday, LA. She is the granddaughter of Richard Daggett of Jonesville, LA and the late Eula Routh Daggett and "Pete" Ella Mae Young of Ferriday, LA and the late Leo Young Sr.

The bridegroom is the son of Ben and Linda Hanchey of Monroe, LA, and the grandson of the late Elizabeth Wood Atkinson of Monroe, LA and the late Ben Atkinson and the late Mr. and Mrs. Clinton W. Hanchey of Lake Charles, LA. The Rev.

David DeVries assisted by Father Tim Hurd performed the double-ring ceremony at 6:30 in the evening. The church was decorated with lavender, pink and white flowers consisting of English Roses, Hydrangea and Casablanca Lilies. Organist Anna Rose Davis played traditional wedding music for the occasion and accompanied the groom's aunt, Camille Wood, in a solo performance of Ava Maria and The Lord's Prayer.

Escorted by her father, the bride entered the church wearing a white sleeveless satin gown with a square neckline and a full skirt embellished with embroidered flowers accented with seed pearls. A flowing train fell from the bodice. The bride wore a silver tiara with a floral jewel design consisting of seed pearls and rhinestones complemented by a chapel length veil of silk illusion. The bride carried a bouquet of beautiful hand tied white southern Hydrangeas, Lilies, Roses and Tulips.

Serving her sister as matron of honor was Ella Ruth Young Spinks of Birmingham, AL. She wore a strapless champagne two piece floor length dress of satin brocade. Her other attendants wore the same matching outfits. They were Brittany Squyres of Baton Rouge and Brooke Squyres of Dallas, TX, stepsisters of the bride and Alicia Hanchey Kelly, sister of the groom of Baton Rouge; Rebecca Bernard Breland of Baton Rouge; Natalie Crow Schwager of Jackson, MS; Rebecca Rabb and Heather Denning. The bridesmaid's bouquets consisted of roses, lilies and tulips in pink, white and lavender.

Flower girls were Betsey Lee and Ginny Calhoun Daggett, first cousins of the bride. Ring bearer was Barrett Lancaster Young, brother of the bride. Tea Girls and Greeters, who passed out programs and baskets of wedding bubbles, were Lindsey Elizabeth and Stephanie Routh Barrett, first cousins of the bride. Candle Lighters were Ashton Myles Hanchey and Robert Taylor Hanchey, cousins of the groom.

Groomsmen were Trent Crawford, Jay Sciro, Bill Dunn, Michael MaHaffey, David Catter, David Summersgill and "Johnny" John Davis Young Jr., brother of the bride. Ushers were Rodney Daggett, first cousin of the bride, "J.P." James Patrick Kelly, brother-in-law of the groom, Spencer Usrey, Jason Hall, Neil Faulkner, and Ricky Raven.

Sarah Young and Clint Hanchey
on wedding day, Dec. 29, 2001

For her daughter's wedding, the mother of the bride, "Candy" Mildred Daggett Young, wore a floor length dress with a bronze bodice and a satin bronze floor length circular skirt with matching jacket. The mother of the groom, Linda Hanchey, wore a floor length dress with a platinum colored bodice and a satin platinum floor length straight skirt with a matching jacket. Millie Lancaster Young, stepmother of the bride, wore a cranberry floor length dress with matching jacket.

Scripture readings were read by Emalie Dunn and Francis Leo "Buddy" Young Jr., uncle of the bride. Following the double-ring ceremony, a reception was held at the Carriage House Restaurant on High Street in Natchez, MS. The bride's table featured a white, tiered wedding cake decorated with sugar flowers and ribbons. The bridegroom's cake was a chocolate confection decorated with a law motif. Guests were served a variety of party foods and danced to music provided by a band. Serving the cake were Linda Routh Daggett Barrett, aunt of the bride; Penny Calhoun Daggett, aunt of the bride; Rosemary "Toni" Chandler Turner, Jeanne Craddock Shively, Emeline Reeder, cousins of the bride; Bobbie Bass Calhoun, Fontaine Cook Gremillion, Peggy Davis Crow and Joanna Henry Bernard. They will take a honeymoon cruise to the Caribbean following the wedding. The couple will live in Baton Rouge after the wedding where Clint is in Law School at LSU and Sarah is employed at the Union Planter's Bank.

HARRISON FAMILY - SETTLERS IN NATCHEZ.

There was more than one Harrison family in Natchez during the time of the American Revolution and afterwards. Information about this family is still developing, many generations after the immigrant, Joseph Harrison, died in 1823. Several ladies have been accepted into the DAR on the basis of this man's service to the American Cause. Mrs. Frances Ebaugh of Florida was one of the first, if not the first to "prove" this line and she is continuing to submit supplemental information in 1980 and later.

Mrs. Ebaugh maintains that Joseph Harrison of Natchez had a brother by the name of James Harrison. Supplemental records sent by Mrs. Ebaugh to the DAR in Washington, D.C. included a notarized photocopy of the original papers of Mrs. Mary Greenwood Anderson, which stated that Joseph and James Harrison, brothers, immigrated from South Carolina to Nashville and then to Natchez.

James Harrison had a son by the name of Nathaniel Harrison, and this individual is frequently confused with a son of the same name, belonging to his brother, Joseph Harrison. James Harrison's son married Letitia Gibson on Sep. 11, 1804, at Washington, Adams County, MS.

Other children of Mr. James Harrison are purported to have been James, George, Henry, Cynthia, Rhoda and Susan. We are not positive where these children settled, Nashville, Natchez or both.

Our data about Mr. Joseph Harrison is well documented and we have ample evidence of this family's association with Natchez. His first marriage was to Mary Gibson, daughter of Gideon/Gibeon Gibson and Mary O'Connell. Records of South Carolina Land Grants show that James Harrison was in Craven County about 1751, and they show that Joseph Harrison was also in Craven County about 1773. The children from the marriage of Joseph and Mary Gibson were:

Sarah Harrison (b. 1778 in Nashville, d. 1868, Yazoo County, one mouth short of her 19th birthday) md. John Wesley Bradshaw (b. ca. 1774, d. 1831 at Rodney, Jefferson County, MS). Indians kidnapped Mr. Bradshaw during his childhood and he was never sure who his parents were. He apparently took the surname of people who reared him.

Nathaniel Harrison (b. 1783, in Washington, Adams County) was a bachelor who took the responsibility of rearing the orphan children of his brother, James G. Harrison. A much mutilated copy of a newspaper obituary praises the man for his devotion to his nieces and nephews. He died at the family residence in Jefferson County, Home Hill on Jul. 3, 1873. The obituary indicates that his father was a native of Virginia, that he immigrated to South Carolina and was married there, and finally came to Washington, MS, where

he, the father, spent most of the last years of his life. Nathaniel Harrison served under General Claiborne during the War of 1812. The newspaper mentions his great financial loss, as well as family deaths in what it oddly calls The States Struggle. At the time of his death the state was still under the heel of the Federal Government's Reconstruction Plan. Newspapers were careful of what they had to say regarding the late war.

Rosanna Harrison (b. 1784, d. August 1862, in Rapides Parish, LA) md. Joseph Francis Henderson on Mar. 12, 1798. She is buried in Henderson Hill Cemetery. She left nine children.

James Gibson Harrison (b. ca. 1786, d. Jun. 4, 1833) md. Elizabeth Lick Norris on Jul. 15, 1811. Six children survived.

Cynthia Harrison (b. ca. 1790 at Natchez, d. Jul. 29, 1829, Rodney) md. Michael Hooter on Nov. 10, 1810. He was born 1791 in Louisiana and died Nov. 30, 1867 in Yazoo County, MS. Six children survived her.

Harriet Letitia Harrison (b. ca. 1790, d. after 1842) md. Thomas C. Vaughan. Five children survived her.

Mary "Polly" Harrison (b. 1791) md. Samuel Brannan. Three children survived her.

Mercy/Marcie Harrison (b. ca. 1792, d. Oct. 26, 1869) md. John Carnahan (b. 1779, Westmoreland County, PA, d. Mar. 11, 1867) on Oct. 9, 1808.

Elizabeth Harrison (b. Oct. 8, 1801, d. Aug. 8, 1872) md. Charles Perkins on Feb. 11, 1819. Three children survived her.

The second marriage for Joseph Harrison was with a Nancy Nichols, which occurred on Oct. 15, 1809. There was no issue from this marriage.

The third and final marriage of Joseph Harrison was with Mrs. Sarah Perkins. That marriage occurred on Jul. 30, 1815, and a son, Thomas Harrison, was born. He did not reach manhood, and instead died sometime before 1824 in Jefferson County. Just prior to his marriage to Mrs. Perkins, Mr. Harrison issued a document in both Adams County and Concordia Parish. The document, which named each of his children by Mary Gibson, apparently an effort to protect these children's' inheritance.

The will of Joseph Harrison is filed in Adams County, MS, and it names all of his children and his sons-in-law. The will is also on record in Concordia Parish, LA where he owned a large tract of land just across the river opposite Natchez. Submitted by Harold C. Fisher.

MARY M. HARSON & JOHN HODGKINS HIGGINS.

John Hodgkins Higgins was born about 1819 in Trenton (now Lamoine), ME. He was the son of Theophilus and Sarah (Hodgkins) Higgins; the grandson of the Revolutionary soldier, Lieutenant Levi Higgins, who served in the 7th Company, 6th Lincoln County Regiment of the Massachusetts Militia; and a direct descendant of William Brewster and Thomas Rogers of the Mayflower.

By 1842, John Higgins had migrated from Maine to Wilkinson County, MS, where his sister Eunice (Higgins) Lewis resided. She was the wife of Colonel John South Lewis. On Jun. 7, 1842, John Higgins married Mary M. Harson. Mary was born in Wilkinson County about 1822 to Joseph and Mary "Polly" (McCullock) Harson. She was the granddaughter of Matthew McCullock, an early settler of the Mississippi Territory. Matthew took the oath of allegiance to Spain between December 1788 - July 1789 and in the Spanish Census of 1792 he is listed as Mateo MacCullock of Homochitto.

In June 1848, when John and Mary Higgins mortgaged 52 acres of land (three miles from Cole Springs in Wilkinson County) they stated that they

resided in Adams County. And the 1850 Adams County Census shows John and his family living in Natchez. John and Mary Higgins had three children: Sarah Jane Higgins (b. Oct. 5, 1843, Natchez) md. Thomas A.B. Paine (see Sarah Jane Higgins and Thomas Aylette Buckner Paine); Marshall A. Higgins (b. ca. 1847); and Richard Higgins (b. ca. 1850).

By 1853 John Higgins had moved to Rodney, MS, where in November 1855 he was elected Constable of District 5, Jefferson County. Then on Nov. 8, 1855 the Natchez Courier reports: Murder at Rodney - There has been an outrageous murder committed in Rodney, Dr. Greenfield shot Higgins, and then cut his throat while groaning in death. Greenfield will soon be arrested, the Sheriff is on his way to Rodney.

After John's death, Mary Harson Higgins moved back to Natchez. Three years later, on Jan. 22, 1858, Mary married her second husband, William M. Conner.

William M. Conner enlisted in the CSA at Corinth, MS on May 5, 1861 as a private in Captain Thomas A. Wilson's Company G of the 12th Regiment of Mississippi. On Mar. 9, 1862, Marshall Higgins (John and Mary's oldest son) was about 15 years old when he enlisted at Natchez as a Private in Company B/new Company G, 12th Regiment of the Mississippi Infantry. Three months later tragedy once again came to Mary. On May 31, her second husband and her oldest son were both fatally injured in the Battle of Seven Pines (Richmond, VA). William died on Jun. 8, 1862, and Marshall died on Jun. 14, 1862.

Mary Harson-Higgins-Conner remained in Natchez, where in 1870 she and her youngest son, Richard, were living in the household of her son-in-law, Thomas A.B. Paine. Mary died in Natchez on Jan. 18, 1873; she was buried in the Natchez City Cemetery, Plot 3, Lot 466.

Sources: Official Records, Natchez Courier and the Eben M. Hamor Manuscript (Hancock County, ME). Submitted by Ginga Hathaway.

ALEXANDER HENDERSON.

Uncle Alec (b. 1794, d. 1865), as the family lovingly referred to Alexander Henderson, was the second son of John Henderson. He was named after John Henderson's older brother. The first Alexander had been granted land on St. Catherine's Creek in 1788.[1] He was also mentioned as a tobacco grower in the Mississippi Territory.[2] Little is recorded of this second Alexander. However, the family ties were extremely close, as revealed in the business transactions (see his brother Thomas's will) and the following comments in the diary of Ellen Newman who was the wife of John Waldo Henderson, Alexander's nephew:

1864 May 11 Uncle Alex sent George in today - all Negroes are allowed to come out, Oct. 24th Alex is here - he is so much company for me - but oh I am so lonely at times Nov 15th Alex is gone home with Johny

1865 Mar 26 Uncle Alex is very unwell today May 1st Poor Uncle Alex is gone - he died last Wednesday - how happy he is now - this is a sad place and I don't care if I never come back - where is my darling husband now - I can not hear from him - what is there to keep me here I feel as if I were all alone now, Uncle Alex is gone - he has been a father to me - and I loved him - where will be my home-home -

Ellen's parents were living in New Orleans at this time. She had lost her little girl (Julia), her brother, her father-in-law (Thomas) and now her dear Uncle Alex with whom she had been living at the Grove Plantation while her husband was away at the war.

The following inscription is on the back of a

71

picture in the possession of a descendent of the Henderson family:

Ambershome photograph on glass of Alexander Henderson

Portrait of Alexander C. Henderson Grove Plantation, Adams County, MS.

A Christian gentleman whose whole life, with a heart full of love, was devoted to his brothers and sisters, their children and grandchildren who gathered yearly in his home to enjoy his royal hospitality. He was a veteran of the War of 1812 and actively engaged in the Battle of New Orleans.

Portrait by Anderson, Artist and Photographer, New York City, 1858 or 1859.

Alexander remained a bachelor and upon his death stated in his will:

It is my will that all my property or the proceeds thereof after paying all my debts shall be distributed in equal shares to my sisters, Susan Henderson, Mary Peale, Celia H. McDannold, and my brothers J.D. and Isaac Henderson, and the children of my deceased sisters Isabella A. Browder, Elizabeth Semple, Anna M. Chase and brother Thomas Henderson. The children of each to receive jointly their deceased parents share.[3]

And so this kindly benevolent man with a fairness that was inborn, left all of his assets to be divided equally between his much-loved family.

[1]American State Papers p. 363, 366-369

[2]Residents of the Mississippi Territory Book 2B-Strictland and Edwards

[3]Will probated Adams County Courthouse January 1866

JOHN HENDERSON (b. 1755, d. 1841), Planter and Broker, Linguist, Author, Postmaster, Territorial Treasurer, and Church Founder. John Henderson was a man of high moral principles and integrity, whose life was grounded in his unshakable faith in God, tireless work ethic and devotion to his family and friends. In his business dealings as a planter, broker, and mercantile owner, he was recognized for his honesty and fairness. John envisaged a thriving and prosperous Natchez community tempered by laws of state to protect hearth and home and a strong Christian foundation for living. He was an active and concerned citizen who promoted religious freedom, public education, and the general welfare of the less fortunate.

John was born into a family of very devout Covenanters (Calvinists who signed the Covenant during the Protestant Reformation). As he records in his own hand in the Henderson family bible:

John Henderson

I was born in Grenock, Scotland, on the twenty third of January in the year 1755 and educated in Stirling. My father named William Henderson, physician in Grenock, son of William Henderson of Saughy near Thornhill and Ruskin. My mother was named Isabella Allen, the only daughter of William Allen, Baillie in Stirling, son of Walter Allen who suffered much in the persecution of the church, as did my grandfather, in the time of Mr. Erskin and Mr. Fisher's Secession.

This moral upbringing of commitment and dedication set the tone for the rest of his life.

At the age of 15, John left his native Scotland to seek a new life in a new country. He continues to relate in the family bible:

I left Scotland on the fifteenth of September 1770 and arrived in Norfolk, VA on the first of November of 1775 and arrived in Baton Rouge on the Mississippi that September.

During that time he signed on as Supercargo (an officer on a merchant ship whose duty it is to manage the commercial concerns of the voyage) to Havana, Cuba where he contracted black fever (malaria). After a time, he returned to Baton Rouge, and continued to work there for a number of years. On Apr. 30, 1787, at the age of 32 years, John departed for the Natchez District where his brother, Alexander Henderson, a tobacco and cotton planter had already settled. He was to begin a new chapter in his life.

The Natchez District was under a permissive Spanish rule when John arrived in Natchez. The Spanish government was eager to encourage settlement of the area and liberally awarded land grants and encouraged land purchases to would-be citizens. They maintained a tolerant and conciliatory government to accommodate the predominately Protestant British and American populace.

Against this backdrop, John quickly found financial support and purchased a small business at the old port of Natchez-under-the-Hill. He soon established himself as a successful mercantile owner, cotton broker and auctioneer. He purchased 250 acres of fertile planting land from his brother Alexander.

A year after John's arrival, he met Miss Selah Mitchell, young daughter of Isaac Mitchell and Mary Nettles, formerly of South Carolina. John discovered that Selah had a very strong Christian faith and was an industrious young woman. His letters indicate that he fell deeply in love with Selah as

Selah Mitchell

their friendship grew. A man of decision, he wasted no time in asking for her hand in marriage. On Jul. 28, 1788 John and Selah were wed at John's plantation on St. Catherine's Creek near Natchez. From this union the couple were blessed with 13 children.

Their first child, Isabella, arrived on Jan. 30, 1790. Thomas, their fifth child, born Jan. 9, 1798, was the builder of Magnolia Hall.

Because of John's linguistic skills, he became a translator and interpreter for the Spaniards of the district. From his business profits and the land grants, awarded him by the Spanish for his services, John began to acquire much property.

In addition to his mercantile business, he owned six plantations over his lifetime, among them, Saughy (named for a place in Scotland), Clairmont, The Point, The Cliffs, and the Grove (acquired from Isaac Mitchell's estate). In 1801 John Henderson acquired land on which he built a house known today as The Elms.

As his faith remained steadfast and his family and livelihood flourished, John's interests and influences abounded. A man of conviction, in 1797, John wrote the first book published in the Mississippi Territory, Paine Detected. This was his response to Thomas Paine's essay, The Age of Reason.

In 1798 the Spanish relinquished the territory to the United States, and John emerged as a prominent businessman, planter and Protestant leader. John committed himself to building a better community and took an active role in civic and community matters. He was appointed treasurer of the Natchez Territory by the Territorial Gover-

Magnolia Hall

nor and in 1806 served as Natchez Postmaster. He did not, however, waiver in his religious principles as evidenced by his refusal to deliver mail on the Sabbath! He served on several community boards, including the bank and the first established community hospital in Natchez. While John was recognized as a community leader, he was most revered for his devotion to the Presbyterian Church. In 1803, he and three of his neighbors founded the Salem Presbyterian Church near Washington, MS.

In 1817 John relocated his ever-growing family from The Elms to a house located on the present site of Magnolia Hall. It was in John and Selah's parlor on Mar. 20, 1817 that they and eight other members founded the First Presbyterian Church of Natchez, As dedicated Presbyterians, John and Selah selflessly pledged their time, energy, and monetary support to the church. Selah was particularly concerned with the unfortunate plight of destitute widows and their children. She believed that it was the responsibility of the church to extend Christian charity to those unfortunate families. To address the situation, she was among the founders of The Female Charitable Society in 1816. It has been in continuous operation since its inception and today is known as the Natchez Children's Home.

John remained devoted to his beloved Selah and their family throughout his life, as evidenced by an excerpt from his letter to his wife:

My Dearest Lover,

I am almost ashamed to tell you how weak I am, You are hardly an hour out of my thoughts by day or by night, and were it not from the expectation that every mail will bring news...

Pleasant Hill

As a loving husband and father John instilled his Christian principles and moral ethics in his children. His will was a testament to that legacy. John's children, who had financial security, generously relinquished their claims to his estate, so that their siblings might have a more generous share of the inheritance. A greater epitaph could not be written.

JOHN WALDO HENDERSON & ELLEN NEWMAN. John was born on Oct. 16, 1832, to Thomas and Bathsheba Henderson. Their first son, he was baptized at the First Presbyterian Church in Natchez when he was 10 years old. John graduated with distinction from Oakland College in 1832. He earned both an A.B. and an A.M. degree. Oakland is now Alcorn State University.

On Jan. 30, 1856 John married Ellen Newman, daughter of Jane Miller and Samuel Brooks Newman, a wealthy and well-known New Orleans cotton broker. Before moving to New Orleans, the Newmans were prominent in business, civic, and religious life of Natchez. Samuel, Ellen's father, was named for

John Waldo Henderson

his grandfather, Samuel Brooks, who was the first mayor of Natchez.

Young Samuel Newman had assumed the responsibility of his household at age 16, owing to the ill health of his father. Upon reaching his majority he married Jane Miller of Natchez. In his 20s he was urged by leading citizens to take the office of Sheriff of Natchez and Adams County, which he filled for 13 years with great credit. He had also served as an Elder in the First Presbyterian Church of Natchez. The family moved to New Orleans in 1853 where Samuel engaged in the cotton industry. He lost his great fortune late in life. Death came on Feb. 3, 1893.

Ellen Newman and John Waldo Henderson had been married six years when John enlisted in the Breckinridge Guards serving as a lieutenant under Longstreet and Bragg. John kept a diary during the war years. In it he mentions William, his faithful slave, who went to war with John and stayed throughout the entire conflict with him. It was not uncommon for a Southern officer to have a servant who cooked his meals and tended his horse. John left from Washington, MS, on Aug. 12, 1862, to join General J.C. Breckinridge in Port Hudson, LA.

John W. Henderson family

With her three young daughters: Julia Bathsheba, Ellen Newman (called Nellie) and Corinne, Ellen made her home at the Grove south of Natchez while John was at war. It was here that Julia contracted diphtheria and died on May 29, 1862. After the war this family moved to Belvedere and were blessed with four more children: Ellen "Nellie" married John Ayres and lived at Melmont in Natchez; Corinne Miller never married and lived with Nellie; Waldo Putnam Henderson (b. 1867); Florence Putnam Henderson (b. 1869) md. John Marshall Kelly, lived at Belvedere and was a librarian at the Fisk Public Library; Anna Brooks Henderson (b. 1871) md. John Liddell Young and they made their home

in Little Rock, AR; Thomas Newman Henderson (b. 1874) lived in Natchez.

Very active in the Presbyterian Church, he served as a Sunday School leader and an elder. In 1903 he was ordained as an evangelist and preacher serving at Carmel, Greenwood and Pine Ridge Churches in Adams County, at Hermanville Church in Claiborne County, and at Fayette Church in Jefferson County. At the last two he was entrusted with the power to ordain ruling elders and deacons.

The Hendersons were married for 60 years. John Waldo died Aug. 16, 1916 at his home, Belvedere on Homochitto Street. Ellen lived another seven years and died at the age of 87 in 1923.

JULIA PUTNAM HENDERSON (b. 1830, d. 1870) lived at home with her father, Thomas, and her aunt, Susan. As a schoolgirl, Julia had a quick mind and a sincere love of knowledge. When she was about 16 years of age she joined the First Presbyterian Church of Natchez. Just as Julia reached womanhood, her health failed, and she never regained it completely. The loss of her health limited her activities. She had loved music and had excelled as a performer, but she was forced to give this up. Sometimes her illness affected her eyes and her hand, so she had to give up some of her literary pursuits. Finally the war plunged her into poverty.

It was under the pressure of these times that Julia conceived the idea of using her pen to have a Christian influence on others. However, Julia shrunk from notoriety and did not like to be spoken about in public. So, using the pen name "Theta" she wrote many stories and articles for Christian publications. Her writings appeared in *The Children's Friend and The South Western Presbyterian* to name a few. She became a Sabbath School teacher and used many of her stories in her teachings at her church. One of her books, *Annie Balfour*, is in the Archives of the Natchez Garden Club.

At the age of 33 Julia wrote an account of her father's illness and death. In this account which began on Jan. 27, 1863, and continued until the death of Thomas Henderson on Mar. 6, 1863, several friends and relations of the Henderson family are mentioned: Aunt Susan (Susannah), Thomas's sister, who lived with them at Magnolia Hall; Susan Chase who had breakfast with Thomas on the day he became ill; Mr. Postlethwaite, who helped Thomas out of his carriage and into his home; Rev. Stratton, the minister of The First Presbyterian Church to which Thomas and Julia belonged; Uncle Alick, Thomas's brother, who discovered that Thomas could not move his left side; Thomas and John who were Thomas's sons serving in the Confederate army; Cousin James, possibly James Carradine; Dr. Foster who was a consulting physician; Uncle Waldo Putnam, who came from Tennessee to see Thomas; and Cousin Mary Carradine who was the daughter of Thomas's sister Elizabeth.

Julia continued to write until she died at Belvedere on Aug. 5, 1870. She was 40 years old. Julia's faith in God was the driving force in her life.

SUSANNAH HENDERSON (b. 1808, d. 1865) was born in Natchez to Selah and John Henderson. As her father recorded in the family Bible: *Susannah, my tenth child was born on Saturday, Jan. 9, 1808 between 6-7 a.m.*

Upon her father's death in 1841 unmarried Susannah inherited the family home, now known as Pleasant Hill. Probated in the May term, 1841, John Henderson's will read:

(Fourth) I bequeath to my Daughter Susannah Fifteen thousand Dollars with lawful interest until paid in Shares of Stock in the Commercial or

Planters Bank in Natchez or cash at the option of my Executors.

(Ninth) I hereby bequeath to my Daughter Susannah my negro man Jordan and my negro woman Harriet during their normal life as slaves also my Dwelling House in which I reside with the Out houses & two Lots on which they are situate with the appurtenances thereunto belonging to her proper use. [sic] benefit and behoof [sic] during her lifetime and at her death to revert to Alex C. and Thomas my sons or their heirs…

(Thirteenth) I bequeath to my Daughter Susannah one four wheeled carriage and two horses

(Fifteenth) I wish my Kitchen & House-hold Furniture including Beding [sic] Raiment, trinkets & ca to be equally divided between Susannah, Mary & Elizabeth S.D.H. as they may agree

[Spelling and capitalization as written in the original]

In 1844 Susannah's sister-in-law, Bathsheba Henderson, passed away leaving Susannah's brother, Thomas, with several young children to raise. Still single, Susannah (sometimes called Susan) raised many of her nieces and nephews.

As the name suggests, Pleasant Hill stood on a steep hill at the southwest corner of South Pearl and Washington Streets. In the same square, the Home of the Catholic Sisters and its garden were at the same height until 1858 when Thomas Henderson decided to erect the mansion now known as Magnolia Hall. With this in view, he purchased the Pleasant Hill property from his sister, Susannah. He had the original house lowered and moved down Pearl Street on logs to its present location at 310 South Pearl Street.

The deed seemed to be an exchange wherein the sister retained the old house but relinquished her life tenure in lot number one and lot number three of the Pearl and Washington square. The document was signed in June 1858, before the house was moved. After the house left its original site Thomas Henderson excavated the lot down to street level to make way for the new mansion, Magnolia Hall. In doing so not one tree was destroyed. Workmen lowered them all with the same loving care they had shown for the house.

Susannah continued living with her brother's family until her death in 1865. As recorded in the diary of Julia P. Henderson, Thomas suffered a stroke, and Aunt Susan attended him until his death on Mar. 6, 1863. Susannah Henderson passed away two years later at the age of 58 on Jun. 23, 1865.

THOMAS HENDERSON (b. 1798, d. 1863) was John and Selah Henderson's fifth child and the first of their children born into this new nation, the United States. With his ever-increasing fortune, Thomas's father, John had moved his family from their early Spanish, The Elms (1782) to their new dwelling Pleasant Hill. This home was located within sight of the Mississippi River, one short block from Main Street and three short blocks from the river docks. In the parlor of this home in 1817, John and three other ruling elders established the First Presbyterian Church of Natchez.

Prior to 1830 Thomas became acquainted with the Putnam family of Port Gibson. The Putnams, descendants of Major General Israel Putnam of Revolutionary War fame, had left their native Connecticut and made the westward trek to the "Crossroads of America," Ohio. It was there that Thomas met Bathsheba, the daughter of Aaron Waldo Putnam and Charlotte Loring. They were married at the home of Bathsheba's brother, A.W. Putnam on Feb. 11, 1830. They were married for 24 years until her death on Jun. 11, 1844.

The couple was blessed with five children: Julia Putnam (b. Nov. 25, 1830, d. Aug. 5 1870);

John Waldo (b. Oct. 16, 1832, d. Aug. 18, 1916); Selah (b. Jan. 7, 1835 d. May 11, 1836); Thomas Alexander (b. Mar. 23, 1837, d. Nov. 26, 1904); William Putnam (b. Jan. 11, 1839 d. Jun. 28, 1839)

In the 1840 census Thomas appears as head of household with three white males (Thomas, John Waldo and Thomas Alexander) and two white females (Bathsheba and Julia Putnam). In the 1850 census after the death of Bathsheba, Thomas's household consists of his unmarried sister Susannah age 42, daughter Julia 19, son John 17, son Thomas Alexander 15, Daniel P. 18 (possibly a Putnam cousin), Charlotte Henderson 9, Selah Henderson 3, Elizabeth Henderson 1/2, and M.E. (Mary Elizabeth) Browder 26, daughter of Thomas's sister Elizabeth. Charlotte, Selah, and Elizabeth are presumably the children of John Henderson, Thomas's brother. Elizabeth Henderson died in 1849.

A close personal and business relationship existed between the brothers—John, Thomas and Alexander. A portion of Mt. Hope Plantation was purchased jointly in 1828 by Thomas and Alexander. These holdings were eventually enlarged to 1,050 acres. The Cliffs was built on the property in 1850 and deeded to John Waldo, Thomas's son. Thomas and Alexander also jointly owned Ashley in Concordia Parish, LA. Lands in Carroll Parish, LA, were owned jointly with John. Other lands in Washington, Rankin and Scott counties in Mississippi were owned jointly by all three brothers.

Elias Peale married Thomas's sister, Mary. Thomas and Elias Peale were engaged in the commission business known as Henderson and Peale in the city of New Orleans at 3 Common Street. In Natchez the firm was known as Henderson and Co. According to family tradition, Thomas—who at the time was an officer in the Commercial Bank of Natchez—was in the vault when the devastating hurricane of 1840 hit Natchez. Busy in the vault, Thomas emerged unaware of the destruction around him. Thomas was a Ruling Elder, ordained and elected in 1838; Superintendent of the Sabbath School until his last sickness; a Commissioner to the Presbytery, Synod and General Assembly; true confidant to the Rev. Stratton; and a staunch supporter in the building of the beautiful edifice the First Presbyterian Church which stands today a few yards from his home, Magnolia Hall.

At the age of 60 Thomas began the construction of Magnolia Hall. Thomas enjoyed his beautiful home but a few short years. Suffering a cerebral hemorrhage in January 1863, Thomas died Mar. 23, 1863.

THOMAS ALEXANDER HENDERSON was born in 1837, the second son of Thomas and Bathsheba Putnam Henderson. After the death of his mother when he was 7, Thomas was reared by his father Thomas and his maiden aunt Susan.

Thomas's name first appears in April 18, 1861, when he enrolled in Capt. W.T. Martin's company, Mississippi Volunteers. This company subsequently became Company A, Jeff Davis Legion of the Confederate Army, and so the war went on. Thomas Alexander with his comrades from Natchez was in the very center of the Virginia campaign. On July 3, 1863, Thomas Alexander was wounded at Hunterstowns, PA as the troop was moving to the battle of Gettysburg. He was transferred to a Confederate hospital in Lynchburg. By November and December he was back in service.

The following year, in September 1864, he was again in hospital in Raleigh, NC and was eventually transferred to Kittrell Springs Hospital. On Dec. 3, 1864, Thomas Alexander was captured

at Stony Creek Station, VA with a large contingent (163 privates and seven officers). He was confined to Point Lookout Federal Prison in Maryland, located at the tip of the peninsula where the Potomac River joins the Chesapeake Bay. Prisoners lived 16 to a tent and were habitually short on rations. The physical conditions of the location were subject to extremes of weather, from blazing heat to bone-chilling cold. Four thousand prisoners died in over 22 months.

Fortunately for Thomas Alexander, the war was over six months after his imprisonment. He was released on June 5, just six days short of four years after he left Natchez.

Thomas Alexander spent the years that followed engaged briefly in the grocery business and then as a bookkeeper in Britton and Koontz Bank. He *"had been there so long he seemed almost a part of the institution, having at all times the fullest confidence and esteem of those connected with the bank. He was unmarried, and during his long life was a devout member of the Presbyterian Church, whose teaching he followed in giving that charity to aid and succor the needy, distressed and sick.*

He has left a legacy to all men, especially to the young, the example of a pure and blameless life, faithful to every duty, ever practicing the golden rule, and seeking no reward other than that of the Master 'Well done thou good and faithful servant.' More precious than perishing marble of capricious earthly fame" (Obituary, Natchez Democrat).

DAYLON H. HICKS & LYNOLA WILSON. Daylon (b. Jun. 22, 1937) was the third of five children born to parents who lived in Texas. He married Lynola Wilson (b. Aug. 18, 1940), the second of three children born to Nina Samanatha (Carroll) McCartney.

Daylon worked as a missionary from 1967 to date (Jan. 26, 2003). He enjoyed carpentry, painting and writing. Lynda spent her time with the children, cooking, sewing and taking care of her home.

Daylon and Lynda had six children: Kathryn (b. Mar. 14, 1960), Toscha (b. Apr. 16, 1963), Daylinda (b. Feb. 3, 1965), Daylon Jr. (b. Jun. 23, 1967), Mark (b. Feb. 12, 1969) and Timothy (b. Jan. 3, 1974).

The Hicks were missionaries to Haiti for 17 years and returned to Natchez in 1991. At present they travel to churches to encourage mission and prayers for the world. Daylon Jr. lives in Natchez and married Nancy Gagnard. They have one daughter Kelsey (b. 1998). They attend Trace City Baptist. Mrs. Hicks' mother died at home in 2000.

HOLSTEIN FAMILY. Tradition says that, with the exception of Native Americans, it was the adventurer-explorer Stephen Holston who first settled the area of the Holston River before 1749. Acknowledgement of Holston's early settlement is found in the 1750 journal of Dr. Thomas Walker of Virginia. Stephen Holston (the grandson of Matthias Claesson of Holstein, Sweden, who immigrated to Pennsylvania before 1700, and the son of Henry Holstein) was in Virginia before settling in South Carolina, and by this time the family's surname had become Holstein for its place of origin. A 1753 South Carolina document records Holston's request for governmental compensation after Indians terrorized his wife and stole household items.

Stephen Holston married Judith King, and the family tradition of naming a son of each generation "King" began with them. Traveling down the Mississippi River with their nine children, Stephen II, Henry, King, Sarah, Delilah, Rebecca, David, John, and an unknown daughter, Stephen and

Judith settled in the Natchez Territory and Rapides District of Louisiana. In a 1781 statement to the Natchez governor, Holstein described himself as old and "very sick." He died in the Natchez area soon afterward.

Of interest in Natchez records are references to this Holstein family, the most significant being their part in the 1781 Natchez rebellion against the Spanish regime. Judith Holstein's name appears as one of those arrested and detained in New Orleans. Other Holsteins were forced to flee Natchez, returning when it was safe.

Stephen Holstein's spirit of adventure showed itself in his sons and grandsons, who were instrumental in the exploration and settlement of Stephen F. Austin's settlement of Texas. Along with their close relatives, the Lovelace family, they met with Austin in Natchez, helped finance Austin's search for the mouth of the Brazos River aboard the *Lively*, led land explorations west, and scouted ahead of Austin's settlers, supplying them with bear, turkey, venison, and honey from the new frontier. One cousin's journal describes his 1822 journey to "Saint Antonio" and the "fandango" he attended there. Later, alone and starving on the western frontier, he is forced to kill a nursing doe and suckle her for survival.

It is from son Henry Holstein and his wife Cynthia Gibson (a collateral ancestor of renowned Methodist minister Tobias Gibson) that some Natchez residents descend. The four daughters of Gerard Hamilton Brandon and Kate Doniphan Prichard are from this line.

Barbara Peck Gilbert Haigh descends from Henry Holstein's daughter Louisa, who married Richard Lovelace of Ferry Place Plantation on Sicily Island, Catahoula Parish, LA. Their son John Henry Lovelace married Julia Patience Kirkland (See The Kirkland Family); daughter Florence Celeste (b. 1845, d. 1881) md. a cousin William Smith Peck I (b. 1842, d. 1910); son William Smith Peck II (b. 1873, d. 1946) md. Barbara Estelle Woodward (b. 1893, d. 1983); daughter Barbara Jane Peck married a cousin Jess Carr Gilbert II. These are the parents of Barbara Haigh (See The Gilbert Family).

Barbara and husband, Thomas David Haigh, residents of Jefferson County, maintain ties to Natchez through involvement in numerous social and historical organizations (See The Haigh Family). *Submitted by Barbara Gilbert Haigh*

JOHN MICHAEL HOOTER FAMILY. Michael Hooter was born in Germany in 1727, per the Census of Opelousas (Louisiana) in 1777. His wife Mary Barbara Kemble was also born in Germany in 1733. He arrived in Philadelphia, PA on the ship *Edinbergh* Sep. 16, 1751. We think that he met and married his wife after reaching America. His name is listed in a book by the name of *A Collection Of Upwards Of Thirty Thousand Names Of German, Swiss, Dutch And French Immigrants*, by Prof. I. Daniel Rupp.

We hear of Michael Hooter next on Dec. 12, 1755, when he appeared in the County of Northampton, PA. He reports an Indian attack on a settler's house, among other events. The incident is found in report of the commission to locate the site of the frontier forts of Pennsylvania, Harrisburg, PA, 1916. The report refers to him as John Michael Hute.

In the book, *History Of Fayette County, PA* by Ellis, he discusses the settlement of that part of Pennsylvania by white settlers on land that belonged to the Indians. An uproar occurred in May 1768, near the settlement of Redstone. Some 50 or more white settlers were mentioned. Among the names were Michael Hooter, Richard Harrison and Lawrence Harrison. Other names listed were several that can later be found as settlers of the

Survey plat for Michael Hooter, Sep. 1, 1772

Natchez District. The English government apparently promised land at faraway Natchez to any settler who would leave the disputed countryside.

In the publications of *The Mississippi Historical Society, Vol. V,* we find an account by Daniel Huey. He said that in the month of April 1770, he was at a place called The Muskingham River, which ran into the Ohio. He found there a considerable number of English Families who told him that they came from Red Stone Creek by way of Ft. Pitt, and that they were en route to Natchez on the Mississippi, in the Province of West Florida where they proposed to make a settlement.

There were some 79 white persons and 18 Negroes. They had tools, implements, seed, saw mills and grist mills. Huey later saw the settlement at Natchez and was very much impressed with it. The entire group apparently went down the Mississippi River on flat boats, and per Edward Mease, they arrived in July of 1770.

Sarah Bradshaw

The Mississippi Archives Department has the original copy of the British Land Grant of the 450 acre site given to Michael Hooter. That government had a number of blank grants printed up, and the variables were simply inked in, such as the settler's name, quantity of land, description thereof, etc. The document for Michael Hooter was printed with the date 176_. Over the top of that date was written First day of September ANNO DOM. 1772, (signed by) Peter Chester, Esquire, Governor General of West Florida, Pensacola.

The Hooter property was described as being on Second Creek, about 10 miles east of Fort Natchez.

Again, in the same volume mentioned above, *Publications of The Mississippi Historical Society,* we found a narrative by Edward Mease on his travels through the Province of West Florida during 1770 and 1771. On Feb. 23, 1771, he went to several of the settlers' houses near the fort. He wrote glowing accounts of the settlers' industriousness and of the extreme richness of the soil of the area. He counted 64 individuals, including eight in the Hooter family.

The Hooter family remained in the Natchez District for some years, eventually departing for Avoyelles Parish, LA, where the immigrant died about 1787. His wife died there about 1796. The family did not entirely leave the Natchez area for some three generations. We found their names upon various legal papers for nearly 100 years after arrival. The probate papers of both Hooters name their children. They were:

Michael Kemble Hooter (b. 1755, d. 1815 in Catahoula Parish, LA) md. Nancy Lovelace.

Mary Barbara Hooter (b. 1758, d. 1814, Avoyelles Parish, LA) md. John Louis Lacroix and Hugh Bailey.

Elizabeth (Isabelle) Hooter (b. 1762) md. John Jean Baptiste Lejeune.

Joseph Hooter (b. 1765, d. 1809 in Avoyelles Parish, LA) md. Sarah Clark. This couple were the parents of Michael Hooter (Jr.) who located in Yazoo County, MS about 1829. He left countless descendants in the Yazoo and Mississippi areas.

Phillippe Joseph Hooter (b. 1767, d. bef. 1824) md. Genevieve Guillory.

Louis Hooter (b. 1771, probably in Natchez, d. 1799) md. Marie Louise Valdrick.

Jacques Hooter (b. 1774).

Marie Josephe Hooter (b. 1776, d. aft. 1826) md. Laste Landerman.

In addition to the sources mentioned above, information about this family may be found in the book *Oath Of Allegiances (PA), Natchez Post Scripts,* and several of the early colonial census reports of Mississippi and Louisiana. *Submitted by Harold C. Fisher.*

PRINCE ABD AL-RAHAHMAN BARI (BARRY)

was the son of Ibrahima Sori "Mawdo" (the Great) Bari the Almaami or "King" of Futa Jallon. Futa Jallon was an independent nation for 150 years until the late 1880s when it was colonized by the French. Futa Jallon is now part of the Republic of Guinea.

Prince Abd Al-Rahahman is commonly known in Natchez by his father's name, "Ibrahima" or Abraham. Prince Ibrahima was born in 1762 in Timbo, then capital of Futa Jallon. In 1788 he and his friend Samba were captured in war, sold into slavery and brought to Natchez where they were purchased by Thomas Foster Sr., a man of Ibrahima's own age.

Together these three, their families and other enslaved African-Americans, developed Foster's Fields, a plantation on Pine Ridge later known as Greenwood Plantation. As such, Ibrahima and Samba were no different from thousands of other enslaved Africans and African-Americans who labored in Mississippi.

However, in Ibrahima's case, the anonymity of slavery was pierced by his chance meeting in 1807 at Washington, MS with Dr. John Cox. Cox recognized Ibrahima as the son of the Almaami who had taken care of him 26 years earlier when Cox became ill in Africa. As a result, the story of Ibrahima's origins in Africa and his enslavement in Mississippi became widely known.

Ibrahima's family is representative of thousands of African-American families who were living in Mississippi both before and after statehood. His family history connects African-Americans living in the Natchez vicinity today with a specific place and family in Africa.

Ibrahima's family is a symbol of the enormous contributions made to the development and history of the Natchez vicinity by other enslaved African-Americans, even though their names and family origins are usually not known to us.

Ibrahima had a wife and son, Al-Husayn, left in his native land of Futa Jallon. It is believed he had nine children in America. Only the names of three of five sons are known for certain: Simeon (Simon), Levi (Lee) and Prince.

The most likely candidates for the remaining children based on their position in the Foster estate papers, their naming patterns and their descendants, are Charles, Samuel, Esther, Susy, Sarah and Kate.

One of Ibrahima's sons was taken to St. Mary Parish in Louisiana by Thomas Foster's son, Levi. That son was most likely Charles, probably by a woman named Sylvia. Charles and Sylvia were both allotted by Thomas Foster's Estate to Levi Foster. Their absence from the inventory taken at Foster's Fields indicates they were already living in Louisiana when Thomas died in 1829.

Charles had four children by his wife Mary named Briget, Abraham, Jeff and James. Briget was probably named after the wife of Ibrahima's son Prince. Charles and Mary also reared a child named Charity.

Briget's children were Margaret, William, Robert, Charity and John. They are listed in 1857 in the Estate of James M. Muggah. William was probably the William Foster listed in Iberia Parish in the 1880 census with children named Lucy, Jane, Henry, Eliza, Ada and Patrick. Present day descendants of Charles and Mary have not yet been identified.

It is possible that a man named Jerry Foster was also a son of Charles by a woman other than Mary. Jerry did not know where his own parents were born, but he named his second son "Charles" after naming his eldest son after himself. Jerry Foster has descendants living in Franklin, Louisiana.

About 1794, Ibrahima married Isabella. She was brought from South Carolina by Robert Stark and sold to Thomas Foster with her children, Jacob, Anaky and Limerick.

Thirty-six years later in 1828, Ibrahima and Isabella were freed after 40 years of his enslavement on the condition they return to his homeland. Ibrahima returned to Africa in 1829 with Isabella, but he died shortly thereafter in Liberia. Thomas Foster died the same year.

En route to Africa via northern states, Ibrahima raised enough money to purchase freedom for his sons, Simon and Levi, and Simon's family. They went to Liberia in 1830. Today Simon's descendants live in both Liberia and the United States because some of them named Gaye and Innis immigrated to America during the past 25 years.

Drawing of Prince Ibrahima by Henry Inman held by Library of Congress

These Liberians knew of their descent from Simon's son, Simon, but their descent from Ibrahima was discovered by Artemus Gaye only after his arrival in the United States.

Ibrahima's son Prince was allotted with his family to Mrs. Sarah Foster. Later Prince's wife Bridget and most of their children: Alfred, Eli, Edmund and Elijah (Lee), were allotted by Sarah Foster's Estate to her daughter, Frances Foster Wells, wife of Samuel Wells who owned Dry Bayou Plantation in Franklin County.

Wiley Wood of Wilkinson County purchased Dry Bayou in 1843, but he later sold it without its enslaved people. Those people were probably taken to Wilkinson County where some descendants may still be living. They have not yet been clearly identified, although one may be the Prince Collins at Percy's Creek who married Maggie America Collins.

The oldest child of Ibrahima's son Prince named Ferriby was allotted by Thomas Foster's Estate to Barbara Foster Barnard (later Brooks), wife of Col. William Barnard. Upon Col. Barnard's death, Ferriby was allotted to Barbara's son, Henry Clay Bernard. The names of Ferriby's children, if any, are not known. However, it is possible that some African-Americans named Bernard or Brooks from Pine Ridge are Ibrahima's descendants.

Prince's daughter Violet was allotted by Sarah Foster's Estate to Thomas Foster Jr. along with Joe and Sarah and their son George. When Thomas Jr. died in 1830, James Carson Jr. became guardian of Thomas's three minor children. Carson eventually took Violet, Sarah and Joe to St. Mary Parish, LA, after Thomas's daughter, Pamela Foster, married Felix Demaret of that parish.

Violet had two sons in Louisiana named Morrison and Alfred, but the names of their descendants are as yet unknown. *Written by David S. Dreyer and submitted by Artemus Gaye.*

IBRAHIMA'S DESCENDANTS.

A woman enslaved at Foster's Fields on Pine Ridge in the early 1800s named Esther is a likely candidate for one of the four daughters of "Prince Ibrahima" of Futa Jallon. In the inventory of Thomas Foster's Estate, Esther and her children: Ben, Margaret, Daniel, Parker and Spencer, are listed immediately before the families of Ibrahima's sons, Simon and Prince, and immediately after Ibrahima's friend Samba, Samba's wife Celia and their children, Andy, Solomon and Samba.

Esther is the only woman at Foster's Fields with children who is listed without a husband. Her listing immediately after Samba and Celia suggests the possibility that Esther may have been another wife of Samba's.

Descendants of Ibrahima and Isabelle Barry

Esther's family was allotted to Mary Foster Collins whose husband William K. Collins owned Pine Grove Plantation north of Liberty Road on Second Creek. In 1840, this plantation was purchased by Wiley Wood of Wilkinson County, then resold without its enslaved people.

Margaret American Collins and Parker Lyons are almost certainly Esther's children. They appear in the 1870 census at Percy's Creek in Wilkinson County among a group of 23 individuals bearing names such as Benjamin, Spencer and Prince, all of whom appear to be related.

However, the 1880 census reports that both parents of Margaret American Collins were born in Africa. That would be consistent with Samba being her father, but not with her mother Esther being a daughter of Ibrahima born in America. While this record is inconsistent with Esther's descent from Ibrahima, it could easily be in error.

Margaret American Collins' daughter, Maggie America Collins, married a Prince Collins, possibly a grandson of Ibrahima's son Prince. The family of Prince and Clarketta Jarvis Collins is one of many families descended of Clarketta's great-grandparents, Prince and Maggie America Collins Collins, both of whom might be Ibrahima's great-grandchildren.

Parker Lyons was almost certainly Esther's son, Parker, and he had many descendants who later lived near Whitestown, then went to Coahoma County in the early 1900s before leaving there as well.

Other descendants of Esther through Esther's son Daniel, Daniel's daughter Esther, and granddaughter Esther's son Daniel, are still living near Pine Grove on Cranfield Road. They include descendants of Josephine Collins Brown, one of the children of Esther's great-grandson Daniel.

Professor Terry Alford, author of *"Prince Among Slaves,"* believes that "Susy," the enslaved mistress of Thomas Foster Jr., was a daughter of Ibrahima. His reasoning is based on the belief that Ibrahima made his last bid to obtain freedom for his family in response to Thomas Foster Jr.'s treatment of Susy. Furthermore, Ibrahima's son Simon named his first daughter "Susan" probably after his likely sister, "Susy."

However, shortly before he died in 1830, Thomas Jr. sold "Susy" and her three children named Lize, Peg and Judge (all born prior to her liaison with Thomas) to his brother Levi Foster in Louisiana.

It is possible that Thomas Jr. also had a child by Susy, and that he did not want his child enslaved or reared by Susy. Consequently, he may have made some alternative arrangements for such a child before he died. If such a child existed, she was probably the "E." Collins, a 40-year-old mulatto woman living in Vicksburg in 1870.

"E." Collins appears to have a 12-year-old daughter named Susie Collins living nearby in Vicksburg who later married Stewart Foster of Pine Ridge. The Bible of Stewart and Susie Collins Foster gives Susie's maiden name and lists a large number of descendants. The Bible is presently held by granddaughter Pearl Harris.

Thomas Foster's son Isaac remained on Pine Ridge unmarried, and he received a large inheritance of enslaved people from Thomas Foster's Estate. However, 10 individuals, several with Old Testament names, are listed separately from other enslaved people in the distribution to Isaac.

These 10 include Samuel, the most likely remaining son of Ibrahima who is listed with his wife Phillis and children, Tilda and Allen, immediately after Simon and Prince in the estate inventory.

There is also among the 10 a man named Abram or Abraham with no wife or children who is listed next to Ibrahima's son Lee in the inventory. He could be a grown son of one of Ibrahima's children. There is also a possible daughter of Ibrahima named Kate with her husband Ned and son "Little Abram."

Finally there is Kezziah, the daughter of Joe and Sarah, and a man named Dick who is probably Kezziah's husband. Joe, Sarah and their two children, George and Kezziah, are listed immediately before the families of Samba, Esther, Prince and Samuel in the initial inventory. Sarah is likely daughter of Ibrahima, probably named after Thomas Foster's wife, Sarah.

While the evidence linking each of these individuals to Ibrahima is not that strong, the fact that they are all listed as a group significantly supports the case of each of them. Thus Samuel, Kate and Sarah make the list of Ibrahima's likely children.

Descendants of these three have not yet been identified, although Allen Henderson of Pine Ridge, who is listed as 65 in the 1880 census, could conceivably be Samuel's son Allen.

The first family-wide reunion of descendants and possible descendants of Ibrahima's family and other people living at Foster's Fields occurred at the "Ibrahima Fest" held at the Natchez Community Center in April 2003 on the 175th anniversary of Ibrahima and Isabella's liberation from slavery.

There are thousands of descendants of Ibrahima living today, most of whom do not know about their "Roots" in the village of Timbo, Futa Jallon. Yet everyone who attended that event became instant "descendants" of Ibrahima and Isabella's international, interfaith and interracial legacy. *Submitted by David S. Dreyer for the descendants of Ibrahima and Isabella Barry.*

JERRY W. ILES & BETTY JOE THORNHILL.

Jerry (b. Oct. 18, 1932) is the son of the late Tessie Esther Shirley Iles and Percy Joseph Iles Sr. of DeRidder, LA. Betty Joe Thornhill Iles (b. Dec. 31, 1934) is the daughter of Codie Viola Thornhill and the late Joseph Francis Thornhill of Crowville, LA. Percy and Shirley Iles spent their last years in Natchez, and Codie Thornhill lives in Natchez at this time.

Jerry W. Iles family: Jerry, Greg, Betty and Geoff

Jerry graduated from Northwestern State College in Natchitoches, LA in 1954 and entered LSU Medical School, graduating in the Class of 1958. Betty graduated from Northwestern State College in 1956 with a degree in education. They married Aug. 12, 1956 in Crowville, LA.

After a year of internship in Shreveport, LA, Jerry entered the U.S. Army for a tour of four years, three of them spent in Germany.

Mark Gregory "Greg" Iles (b. Apr. 8, 1960) and Michael Geoffrey "Geoff" Iles (b. Aug. 25, 1961) were both born in Germany. Both sons graduated from Trinity Episcopal High School in Natchez and from Ole Miss in Oxford.

Greg is married to the former Carrie Martha McGee. He is a published author and Carrie is a successful dentist. They have two children, Madeline Marcantel Iles (b. Oct. 21, 1993 and Mark Gregory Iles Jr. (b. Dec. 6, 1996).

Geoff is married to the former Saundra Simmons Williams. He is a dental practice consultant and also business manager for Hero's Journey Media Corp. Simmons earned a BS degree in nursing and is currently employed at Natchez Regional Medical Center. Their two children are Mary Catherine Iles (b. Aug. 2, 1991) and Michael Geoffrey Iles Jr. (b. Aug. 29, 1995).

Jerry Iles began his medical practice in Natchez in 1964 and is still active in the practice of medicine today.

JOHN DORSEY IRELAND & VIRGINIA "JENNIE" ROBSON.

In October 1878, Robert Ireland wrote his brother John, congratulating him on his forthcoming marriage, adding that he had ordered from St. Louis a buggy as a wedding gift. The couple pictured are mature, but the buggy could have been the wedding gift from his brother Robert.

John Dorsey Ireland (1854-1919) and Virginia Fox Robson (1860-1932)

John Dorsey Ireland (b. Oct. 16, 1854, in Jefferson County, MS, d. Apr. 11, 1919, at Stephania) was one of three children born to Stephen Ireland (b. Jul. 1, 1811) who married Jan. 31, 1845, Martha Owens (b. Apr. 18, 1824, d. Feb. 5, 1882), both were born in Maryland and buried at Christ Episcopal Church, Jefferson County, MS.

On Jan. 15, 1879 John Dorsey Ireland married Virginia Fox "Jennie" Robson (b. May 18, 1860, at Greenwood Plantation, Adams County, MS, d. Jun. 13, 1832, Ensley, AL, at the home of her daughter, Virginia). Jennie was the sixth child of seven born to John and Carolyn Boyd Robson. They married at Magnolia Hill, the ancestral home of her mother. John and Jennie are buried in the Natchez City Cemetery.

John and Jennie were members of the Washington Methodist Church where he was a steward, trustee, lay leader and Sunday School Superintendent. He was a farmer and Jennie was a typical homemaker of the day. Her sister Josephine often remarked about the preserves, jelly and sweet butter made by Sis Jennie as being better than any she could produce.

The major portion of Spring Hill was sold in 1913, but 125 acres called Stephania, was retained until 1922. Jennie, then a widow, sold the property and went to live in Ensley, AL, where she bought a house and operated a boarding house for a number of years. Born to John and Jennie were three children, all born at Spring Hill Plantation on Pine Ridge Road.

The children were Virginia Robson Ireland (b. Jan. 20, 1890, d. Jul. 23, 1958) md. John Henry Cook (b. May 18, 1885, d. Nov. 26, 1954) on Jun. 27, 1928. Both are buried in Elmwood Cemetery, Birmingham, AL. For 17 years Virginia taught school, first in Mississippi and then in Alabama, and John Henry was an insurance salesman. They had one child, John William.

Josephine Thorn Ireland (b. Apr. 11, 1891) md. Herman August Hunderup, a Baptist minister, on Aug. 22, 1917, at the Washington Methodist Church; reception at Jefferson College. He was born Oct. 26, 1891, died Sep. 3, 1970, and buried in Portland, OR. She died Jan. 27, 1927, giving birth to a stillborn child who is buried with her in the Natchez City Cemetery. They had three children who lived to maturity: Anna Josephine, Herman August Jr. and John Ireland.

Martha Olivia Ireland (b. Aug. 22, 1895, d. Feb. 7, 1960) md. William Alva Brown (b. Jan. 7, 1879, d. Oct. 28, 1961) on June 19, 1915 in Natchez. Both are buried in Lakewood Cemetery, Jackson, MS. They had one child Mary Virginia. *Submitted by Ella McCaleb Young.*

JOHN CARMICHAEL JENKINS FAMILY. John Carmichael (b. Dec. 13, 1809, Churchtown, PA) was the son of Robert Jenkins (b. Jul. 10, 1767, d. Apr. 18, 1848, Churchtown, PA) and Catherine Mustard Carmichael (b. Jul. 23, 1774, Brandywine, PA, d. Oct. 23, 1856, Churchtown, PA), daughter of Rev. John Carmichael and his second wife, Catherine Mustard and granddaughter of Daniel and Elizabeth (Alexander) Carmichael who came to America with their family in 1737 from Tarbert, Argyllshire, Scotland. The Jenkins family is descended from David Jenkins who emigrated from Wales to Pennsylvania in 1700.

John graduated in 1833 from the Medical School, University of Pennsylvania and moved to the Natchez area to assist in the plantation management and medical practice of his uncle, Dr. John Flavel Carmichael.

Dr. Carmichael (b. Oct. 14, 1765, d. Oct. 21, 1837) was the son of Rev. John Carmichael (b. Oct. 17, 1728, Tarbert, Scotland, d. Nov. 15, 1785, Pennsylvania) and his first wife Phoebe Crane. After his graduation from the University of Pennsylvania, Dr. Carmichael entered and served in the Army for 17 years as a surgeon. At the end of his Army service, in 1798, he settled near Fort Adams, Wilkinson County, MS, becoming one of the pioneer cotton planters of the South.

John Carmichael Jenkins was one of the outstanding scientific planters in the lower Mississippi Valley and proved to be an astute manager of plantation finance. His uncle's estate at the time of his death was in debt over $150,000. In 20 years time, John had paid off the entire debt, met his own obligations, purchased Elgin Planta-

John Carmichael Jenkins (1809-55)

tion near Natchez, accumulated a fortune and turned his scientific training to horticultural experimentation and cultivation.

He met and married Annis Field Dunbar (b. Oct. 2, 1820, Forest Plantation), daughter of Annis Stockton Field (b. Jul. 27 1799, Princeton, NJ, d. Oct. 12, 1823, Forest Plantation), first wife of Dr. William Dunbar (b. Jun. 19, 1793, d. Dec. 8, 1847, Forest Plantation). After their marriage, John and Annis made their home at Elgin Plantation where their five children were born: Annis Dunbar (b. Aug. 19, 1840, d. Oct. 23, 1840); Alice (b. Dec. 14, 1841, d. Mar. 25, 1929) never married; Mary Dunbar (b. Jul. 27, 1843, d. Nov. 16, 1927) md. Lewis Morris Johnstone; John Flavel (b. Dec. 13, 1846, d. Feb. 13, 1927) md. Helen Louisa Winchester; William Dunbar (b. Sep. 18,

Annis Field (Dunbar) Jenkins, wife of John Carmichael Jenkins

1849, d. Mar. 12, 1914) md. Henriette Koontz.

At the time of his death, John Carmichael Jenkins owned four plantations: Elgin, Adams County; River Place and Eagle Bottom Place, Wilkinson County; and Stock Farm in both Wilkinson County and West Feliciana Parish, LA, a total of 5,394 acres, producing cotton, corn, oats, millet and hay. His orchards at Elgin produced cherries, apricots, figs, strawberries, plums, raspberries, pears and grapes. In addition, he had introduced six new varieties of apples and 18 new varieties of peaches.

Both Annis and John Carmichael Jenkins died in the same year of Yellow Fever, she on Sep. 16 followed by John on Oct. 14, 1855, leaving their young children orphans. They are buried at Elgin Plantation, Adams County, MS. *Submitted by Julia Rae (Mills) Erhardt.*

JOHN FLAVEL JENKINS FAMILY. John Flavel Jenkins (b. Dec. l3, 1846, Elgin Plantation, d. Feb. l3, 1927, Natchez) was the son of John Carmichael Jenkins and Annis Field Dunbar. His childhood years were spent at Elgin Plantation. He was 9 years old when his parents died. He was 16 when the Civil War broke out and he ran away from his guardian, Josiah Winchester, to enlist as a private in the Breckinridge Guards. Although he took part in the battles of Murfreesboro and Chickamauga as well as other engagements, he was never injured. After the War he attended Washington and Lee University, graduating in 1868. He then returned to Natchez and on Nov. 7, 1872, at Elms Plantation (sometimes known as Glen Burnie), the country home of Judge Josiah Winchester and his wife, Margaret Graham Sprague, he married their daughter, Helen Louisa Winchester (b. Oct. 28, 1849, Glen Burnie, d. Jan. 11, 1917, Natchez).

John and Louisa were the parents of nine children, all born at Elgin: John Carmichael (b. Aug. 7, 1873, d. Jan. 30, 1908) died unmarried; Margaret Graham "Meta" (b. Oct. 5, 1874, d. Apr. 19, 1937) md. Eugene Montgomery; Winchester "Jim" (b. Dec. 25, 1875, d. May 15, 1949) md. 1st, Margaret Allison Young and 2nd, Anna Clothilde Smith; Julia Dunbar "Jule" (b. Mar. 4, 1877, d. Apr. 24, 1908) md. Devereux Shields; William Dunbar "Dunny" (b. Apr. 6, 1878, d. Jan. 23, 1914) died unmarried; Sturgis Sprague "Hassie" (b. Dec. 26, 1881, d. Sep. 5, 1938) md. 1st, Grace Peebles and 2nd, Bertha Harris; Louise "Bo" (b. Apr. 12, 1885, d. Sep. 15, 1968) md. Harrison Louis Winston; Francis "Frank" (b. Aug. 4, 1890, d. Jul. 31, 1909) was unmarried; Hyde Rust (b. Jun. 7, 1894, d. Mar. 12, 1973) md. Helen Ferriday Byrnes.

John was elected Adams County Chancery Clerk on the Democratic ticket in 1895 and held this office for 20 years. In a letter dated Dec. 16, 1898 addressed to his daughter, Mrs. Col. Devereux Shields, Columbia, TN, he wrote, ...*you are in a fertile and prosperous country - and in that beautiful part of Tennessee where I spent the most roseate days of my existence, a soldier of the Confederate Army. How I used to love to dash down those beautiful pikes on my Cavalry horse for a morning skirmish of the enemy's pickets, and hear the sharp crack of the rifles ring out on the morning air. So that from this dull prosaic existence here, when I read your dear letter about the pleasant times you were having up on those scenes 'Where the Battle was Fought,' it brought back to my mind the halcyon days of my own youth.*

In later years, John lived with his daughter, Margaret Montgomery in the house she had inherited from her maternal grandmother, Margaret Graham (Sprague) Winchester, after whom she had been named.

At the time of his death, John was Natchez

The John Flavel Jenkins family ca. 1897. Standing l-r: Sturges Sprague "Hassie" Jenkins, Winchester "Jim" Jenkins, John Carmichael Jenkins, William Dunbar "Dunny" Jenkins. Seated l-r: Margaret Graham "Meta" Jenkins, Louise Winchester "Bo" Jenkins, John Flavel Jenkins, Helen Louisa (Winchester) Jenkins with Frank Winchester Jenkins, Julia Dunbar Jenkins with her brother, Hyde Rust Jenkins on her lap.

City Clerk, manager of four large plantations, commander of the Natchez Camp UCV and secretary of the Riparian Land Owners' Association. He was a charter member of the Gaillard Sporting Club and a member of the Presbyterian Church. *Submitted by Julia Rae (Mills) Erhardt.*

WILLIAM TILER JOHNSON & ANN BATTLES.

William (b. Natchez 1809, d. 1851) was the son of Amy Johnson (freed 1814). He was freed in 1820 by the white plantation owner, Capt. William Johnson, who was probably his father. The petition to the Mississippi Legislature specified that the 11-year-old boy would be educated and maintained by the plantation owner until he reached the age of 21.

William Johnson learned barbering from his brother-in-law, James Miller (born free in Philadelphia 1816, d. July 8, 1865, New Orleans) who married his sister Adelia (b. 1806, d. Jan. 8, 1848) in 1820. In 1830 Johnson began working in a Port Gibson barbershop, then he bought out James Miller's shop on Main Street in Natchez when the couple relocated to New Orleans. In 1834 he expanded his barbering business to include bathhouses. He also began lending money at interest. In 1835 he purchased his first tract of land, and the same year married Ann Battles (b. 1815, d. 1866), the daughter of Harriet Battles (b. circa 1792, freed by Gabriel Tichenor in 1822, d. 1873) who owned a home on State Street. Fire destroyed almost the entire city block in October 1839, followed by a devastating tornado in May 1840. Johnson then used salvage from Parker's Hotel to rebuild a house on the Battles' property for his family.

The children of William and Ann Johnson were William Jr. (b. Jan. 24, 1836); Richard (b. Oct. 11, 1837); Byron (b. June 22, 1839); Anna (b. Mar. 25, 1841); Alice (b. Apr. 16, 1842); Catharine (b. Dec. 22, 1843); Phillip (b. 1844, d. shortly after birth); Eugenia (b. Jan. 2, 1845); Louis (b. Nov. 28, 1846); and Clarence (b. May 16, 1851). The children were well educated, and were baptized in the Roman Catholic St. Louis Cathedral in New Orleans.

In 1851, William Johnson was murdered at the age of 42, leaving his wife to assume responsibility for her large family - though at the time they were among the most wealthy free people of color in Mississippi and owned a number of slaves themselves. Ann Johnson sold the farm property, rented out rooms in her home, and managed the barbershops where their sons William, Richard, and Byron worked. However, William went insane after his mother's death in 1866, Richard suffered

from a heart condition, and Byron was murdered in 1872. Eugenia married Juanito Garrus, a barber who boarded with the family. Anna, Catharine, Alice and Josephine purchased Peachland Plantation in 1874; Anna and Catharine also became second-grade teachers at Union School and at Ravenwood. Clarence, a blacksmith, married Catherine Lynch, the sister of John R. Lynch. Their son, William R. Johnston (d. 1938), a Howard University graduate, practiced medicine in Natchez. His wife Sally (d. 1975), a renowned seamstress, continued to live in the family home on State Street.

In 1951 LSU Press published the diary of William Johnson, which provides the most complete account of the life of a free black man in the antebellum South.

JOSEPH "JOE" MONTGOMERY JONES & BESSIE LENA JONES-MITCHELL.

Joe (b. Nov. 21, 1877 in Loudon County, TN), the son of Rufus and Belinda (Montgomery) Jones. Joe married Bessie Lena Jones-Mitchell of Greeneville, TN on Apr. 24, 1907 in Concord, Knox County, TN. Bessie was the daughter of Mahlon Marcus and Nannine Alice (Arwood) Jones and was later adopted at age 16 by Samuel Newton and Caroline Mitchell.

When Rufus died in 1898 he left his land to his two youngest children, Joe and his sister Mattie. In 1906 Joe placed his timbered land for sale receiving only unacceptable offers. Joe then realized he could cut the timber himself, produce and sell the lumber. He spent the next five years acquiring stumpage, producing and selling lumber until in 1911 he suspended activities in Tennessee. Joe decided to name his business J.M. Jones Lumber Co. and for the next 10 years or so he moved his operations through Arkansas and Louisiana, until building a plant in Ferriday, LA in the early 1920s. In 1930 this plant was totally destroyed by fire and in 1935 the present J.M. Jones Lumber Co. was built in Natchez overlooking the Mississippi River.

Jones Family, 1947. Seated: Kenneth Jones, Audrey Jones, Joe Jones, Bessie Jones, Shirley Jones, Howard Jones. Standing: Raymond Jones, Eva Deane Jones, Mary Dell Jones, Newton Jones.

Joe and Bessie were members of the First Baptist Church where Joe served as deacon and trustee. They had 11 children, nine of which lived to adulthood. They are Raymond Mitchell Jones (b. Jan. 28, 1908, d. Dec. 28, 1960) md. Josephine Feltus; Joseph Montgomery Jones Jr. (b. Jul. 2, 1909, d. Sep. 25, 1912); James Newton Jones (b. Aug. 31, 1911, d. May 28, 1985) md. Janie Day Butler; twins which died shortly after birth; Shirley Teresa Jones (b. Jan. 24, 1914, d. Jul. 11, 1990); Howard Lee Jones (b. Feb. 8, 1915, d. Mar. 18, 1981) md. Mildred Elizabeth Redell; Audrey Lynn Jones (b. Aug. 18, 1918, d. Sep. 24, 1977) md. Marion Herbert Tobias; Mary Dell Jones (b. Feb. 6, 1920, d. Feb. 27, 1999); Eva Deane Jones md. William "Billy" Marvin Simonton; and Lester

Kenneth Jones (b. May 2, 1925, d. Sep. 12, 2001) md. Mary Ann Brandon.

Descendants of Joe and Bessie Jones who are still living in Natchez today are Kim Monette Jones Garrett and her husband Milton Garrett, Ann Jones, Mrs. L. Kenneth Jones, Eva Deane Jones Simonton and her husband Billy Simonton, Cindy Simonton Cooke, Brad Simonton and son Will Simonton, Emily Virginia "Pokey" Jones O'Beirne and her husband Tommy O'Beirne, Meg O'Beirne, Ryan O'Beirne, H. Lee Jones Jr. and his wife Sherry Scarborough, Kay Jones Cole, Howard L. Jones III and wife Sally Mullins and their two children Lee and Liza, Joey Finley Wilson and her three children: Ally, Tanner and Peyton, Scottie Cole Barlow and her husband Jeff Barlow and their two children, Kathleen and Joseph. *Submitted by Kim Jones Garrett.*

PEGGY JUNE

was born on Dec. 23, 1948 at the Natchez Sanitarium Hospital that was located on Franklin Street, the block over from where the Convention Center is now. Her mother is Dorothy Curtis Skates (b. Jan. 27, 1927 at her home near Rocky Springs, which is this side of Utica, MS) and her father is Herman Bankston Skates (b. Nov. 2, 1922 in Utica, MS) but was reared by his grandparents in Learned, MS.

Her mother's sister, Margie, and her daddy's sister, Dolly were friends. When he came back from WWII, they introduced Herman and Dorothy to each other. When they met, Dorothy thought he was the best looking guy she had ever seen. They married on Oct. 12, 1946, then moved to Natchez. Her daddy worked as a body repairman at Natchez Equipment Co., Dossett Olds, and his own shop, Skates Body Shop.

Her mother stayed at home and reared four children, but when Peggy was a senior at Natchez High School, her mother started to work at the Adams County Health Department and worked there until she retired in 1990.

Peggy's brothers and sisters are Ray Herman Skates (b. Oct. 3, 1950), Barry Lester Skates (b. Nov. 25, 1956) and Charlotte Dorene Skates (b. Mar. 11, 1959). Peggy grew up on Pine Ridge Rd. and went to school at Pine Ridge School. When the schools consolidated, she had to go to Braden Elementary. She continued on to Martin, then the new Natchez High. She felt that she had gotten a wonderful education with the Natchez Public Schools.

Peggy's first job was during high school at the Fisk Public Library. In fact, she had the dubious job of helping to pack all those books to be moved to the new Judge George Armstrong Library. She was married to Kenneth Jordan the August after she graduated. Charles Jr. was born one week before their first anniversary on Jul. 26, 1967. Two and a half years later, on Mar. 6, 1970, Keith Herman was born. She worked part-time for Deposit Guaranty as a bank teller where she was once robbed. On Nov. 8, 1977, her third son, Douglas was born.

She received her degree in elementary education in 1980 from USM Natchez. Her first teaching job was at Trinity Episcopal School as a junior high math teacher. After three years there, she started teaching for the Natchez Public Schools. In 1998, she earned her master's degree from Alcorn in guidance counseling. Four years later, she got her National Board Certification. She has enjoyed being a guidance counselor at Morgantown Elementary School.

On Aug. 2, 1986, she married Jimmy June. They have six beautiful grandchildren who are the love of their lives and have hopes of having even more. God has truly blessed her in so many ways throughout her life.

DAVID JUNKIN & JENNIE MCKINSTRY sailed with their seven children from the port of Larne in County Atrium, Ireland and arrived in Natchez about 1872. Two more children were born to David and Jennie after arriving in the U.S. Their children are as follows:

1) Thomas James (b. Oct. 25, 1854, d. 1932) md. Mary O'Neill (b. 1854, d. 1928), had six children: David, O'Neill, Nellie (md. Willie Hugh Wilson), Sam (md. Marie Zurhellen), Jennie (md. D.N. Piazza), Mamie.

2) Eliza Jane (b. Oct. 21, 1856, d. 1931) md. John W. Meath (b. Mar. 8, 1863, d. Jan. 19, 1906), two children, Jennie (md. John Borden) and T.J. Meath (md. Martha Bridges).

3) Ellen (b. Apr. 20, 1859, d. Nov. 4, 1942) never married.

4) William (b. Sep. 1, 1861, d. Oct. 10, 1946) md. Mary Ratchford (b. Sep. 11, 1871, d. Apr. 19, 1956), four children: Wm. J. Junkin (md. 1st, Bertha Zurhellen and 2nd, Jennie Smith); John R. Junkin (md. Sophie Dix); Mary Junkin (md. John Bellan); Richard Junkin (md. Rose Lambert).

5) Hugh (b. Sep. 14, 1863, d. 1925) md. Annie Yeager (b. Sep. 19, 1877, d. Nov. 1, 1974), four children: Annie Ruth (md. S.J. Greer); Hugh Y. (md. Clarabel Kaiser); Sarah (md. A.W. Graning); Jennie (md. W.H. Kisner).

6) Sarah Ann (b. Apr. 7, 1866, d. Jun. 6, 1916) md. Charles Ratchford, no children.

7) Francis "Frank" (b. Apr. 13, 1868, d. Mar. 29, 1942) md. first, Ella Foster (b. Aug. 5, 1873, d. Feb. 9, 1917), four children: Frank Watkins Junkin; David (md. Evelyn Lawrence); Laura (md. 1st, Clifton Blankenstein and 2nd, Alex Lott); Ellen (md. W.L. Billups).

8) Samuel (b. May 25, 1870, d. Jul. 11, 1884), not married.

9) Ruth Junkin (b. Oct. 25, 1872, d. Dec. 28, 1961) md. Harry P. Foster (b. Jan. 24, 1872, d. Jul. 19, 1939), seven children: Ellen (md. Gordon H. Rowe); Harry (md. Nan Druetta); Frank Junkin (md. Otimese Brown); Jennie Junkin (md. Reginald Lowe); Hugh Junkin (md. Annie Mae Carter); Elizabeth Ruth "Bessie" (md. Joseph E. Smith); Thomas James "T.J." (md. 1st, Flora Edith Atkinson and 2nd, Agnes Wilson).

10) John Russell (b. Aug. 14, 1876, d. Jan. 14, 1896) not married.

The oldest Junkin son, Thomas James, came to America first and worked for his Uncle James Junkin in his blacksmith and wagon shop on Main Street. The shop is believed to have been on the corner of Main and Rankin, where the old First Baptist Church stands today. Money earned by the eldest son was sent to the family in Ireland to assist them in making the passage. Upon arrival from Ireland, the Junkin family lived on Palestine Road in a plantation house that resembled Dunleith that later burned.

The David Junkin family began to buy land and farm. They acquired about 30,000 acres around Anna, which they operated as Junkin Brothers. The 30,000 acres consisted of Williston of Kirkland Plantation, Williston Plantation, Mercer Plantation and Quitman Plantation. They also acquired two smaller plantations, Foster Mound and Sunnyside. Cotton and corn were their main crops, but at one time they also grew potatoes and lettuce which they shipped from the railroad platform at Foster Mound. Junkin Brothers also dealt in cattle.

When Junkin Brothers was dissolved, the lands were divided among the brothers: William, Frank and Hugh. William Junkin got Mercer Plantation and Foster Mound Plantation, where he lived; Hugh Junkin got Quitman Plantation, where he lived; and Frank Junkin got Williston of Kirkland Plantation, Williston Plantation and Sunnyside. The oldest son Thomas continued to operate his blacksmith shop. All the children married except Ellen, who lived with family members. They are all buried in the Natchez City Cemetery.

JAMES KEMPE, born about 1760, Ireland, is on the 1795 Prince William County, VA property tax roll. He married Margaret (Graham) Bird, widow of Thomas Bird, August 1801. They moved to Natchez, MS Territory in 1809. James Kempe as Captain, Adams Troop of Horse, Hind's Battalion, MS Dragoons led his troop at the Battle of New Orleans, War of 1812, later being promoted to colonel, Mississippi Cavalry. The six surviving Kempe children were Jane Rawlston (b. Sep. 3, 1802) md. first, Francis Spain Girault and second, Charles N. Rowley; Frances Elizabeth (b. Apr. 24, 1804); Margaret Louisa (b. Jan. 16, 1806) md. William Burr Howell (their daughter Varina was second wife of Jefferson Davis); James (b. ca. 1810) md. Elizabeth __; Thomas Byrd (b. ca. 1812) md. Margaret P. Lee; David Beckett (b. ca. 1815, d. September 1832) was unmarried.

Margaret Kempe died Jul. 10, 1818 and James Kempe died Sep. 18, 1819. Marengo Plantation, LA was part of the large estate they left.

On April 24, 1823, Frances Elizabeth Kempe married Sturges Sprague (b. ca. 1799, New York, d. Oct. 5, 1838, Shreveport, LA). Sturges's ancestry remains untraced. His first record is Head of Household, 1820 Adams County, MS Census. He was an attorney-at-law, bank cashier, merchant, and plantation owner. He was Colonel of the 1st Louisiana Regulars and served as an officer of Harmony #1 Masonic Lodge, Natchez. He was also one of the eight founders of Shreveport, LA. The Spragues' six children were Margaret Graham

Margaret Graham Sprague (b. Nov. 18, 1824, d. May 19, 1906)

(b. Nov. 18, 1824); Frances Louisa (b. ca. 1829, d. Feb. 18, 1869) md. James T. Pugh; Maj. Sturges (b. ca. 1831, d. Aug. 27, 1865, Vicksburg); Capt. David Kempe (b. ca. 1833, d. Apr. 4, 1862, Shiloh); Pvt. Thomas Beckett (b. Feb. 16, 1835 and the only son to survive Civil War) md. Julia Walton; William Howell (b. ca. 1838, d. Aug. 20, 1861).

On March 31, 1846, Margaret Graham Sprague married Judge Josiah Winchester (b. May 22, 1814, Salem, MA, d. Sep. 30, 1887, Natchez, MS), a descendant of John Winchester (b. May 19, 1611, Cranbrook, County Kent, England), arrived in Boston Apr. 6, 1635 on the *Elizabeth* with his wife Hannah Sealis (b. Jan 1614, Bidden

Judge Josiah Winchester (b. May 22, 1814, d. Sep. 30, 1887)

den, County Kent, England). Josiah came to Natchez to practice law with his uncle, George Winchester. The Winchesters had 12 children: Francis Kempe (died unmarried), Virginia Dunbar (md. Frederick Stanton), Helen Louisa (md. John F. Jenkins), Mary Hannah (died unmarried), George (md. Courtney Leathers), Sturges Sprague (died unmarried), Margaret Sprague (md. Frederick Clark), Josiah (md. Emma L. __), Sprague (died unmarried), Thomas Kempe (md. Emma Kate Montgomery), Robert Lee, John Maxwell (md. Mrs. Mamie Patterson).

Robert Lee "Bob" Winchester (b. Jul. 25, 1865, Natchez, d. Dec. 23, 1917, Memphis, TN) md. Clara Frances Schmieding (b. Apr. 27, 1875, Fort Garland, CO, d. Nov. 10, 1939, St Louis, MO) on Jun. 28, 1909 in St. Louis, MO. They had four daughters: Dorothy, Clara Louise, Margaret Graham, and Elizabeth Lee. *Submitted by Jayne Eannarino, granddaughter of Robert Lee Winchester.*

FRANCIS KENDALL KETTERINGHAM & ELIZABETH PALMER. Francis (b. Oct. 1, 1802) and Elizabeth (b. May 23, 1806) were married April 6, 1829 in Norfolk, England, where both were born. They had three children born in Norfolk: Matilda (b. Feb. 19, 1830), John Palmer (b. Jul. 3, 1832), and Lavinia (b. Sep. 13, 1834).

In 1825 Francis bought his way out of Queen Victoria's Army, and in 1836 Francis and his family sailed from England to the United States. On Oct. 4, 1836, while on board the ship, *Berwick,* Elizabeth gave birth to her fourth child, Charles "Captain" Berwick Ketteringham. They arrived in New York on Nov. 20, 1836.

They made their way to Natchez and in June 1840, twin sons, Francis "Frank" Kendall and Fred Palmer Ketteringham were born. On June 11, 1844 Francis Kendall Ketteringham became a U.S. citizen. On April 5, 1845, another child, William Kendall, was born and Mary Hannah was born Nov. 17, 1847.

On Sept. 5, 1853 Francis died of yellow fever.

The David Junkin Family, Christmas 1903. Top Row: Willie Hugh Wilson, Charlie Ratchford. Second Row: Jennie Junkin Piazza, O'Neill Junkin, Nellie Junkin Wilson, Sarah Junkin, Ella Foster Junkin, Franklin junkin (in arms David Junkin), Ellen Junkin, Ruth Junkin Foster (in arms Harry Foster Jr.). Harry Foster Sr., (in his arms Ellen Foster Rowe). Third Row: Annie Yerger Junkin (in arms Sarah Junkin Graning), Hugh Junkin Sr. (in lap Hugh Junkin Jr.), Mary O'Neill Junkin, Thomas Junkin, Jennie McKinstry Junkin, David Junkin Sr., Eliza Junkin Meath, Johnnie Meath (in lap Thomas John Meath), Mary Ratchford Junkin (in arms Richard Junkin), William Junkin Sr. (in arms Mary Junkin Bellan). Bottom Row: Annie Ruth Junkin Greer, Mamie Junkin, Sam Junkin, Jennie Meath, William Junkin, John R. Junkin.

After his death, Elizabeth opened a boarding house in Natchez. She died on Feb. 14, 1878.

Three of their sons, Frank, Captain, and Fred all served in the Civil War. Frank was in Co. E of the 4th LA Battalion, while Captain and Fred were in Co. D of the 16 MS Volunteers.

Matilda married Harvey S. Wilkins on Dec. 23, 1847 but later divorced him when he left Natchez and his family in search of gold. Matilda and their three daughters moved into the boarding house with her mother and helped to support them as a seamstress. Matilda died on Aug. 19, 1911.

John was married three times. He married Angelina Mann Nov. 18, 1851. This marriage ended in divorce. He later married Maria Louisa Holmes on June 2, 1875. This marriage also ended in divorce. On Aug. 17, 1885, John married Eliza Jane Alexander. Eliza died in the tragic Natchez Drug Company explosion, March 14, 1908. John was a machinist by trade. He died July 5, 1902.

Lavinia married David Kirk Jan. 16, 1851. Their two sons died as infants and Lavinia died March 11, 1858.

Captain married Margaret Tucker on Nov. 1, 1859. His trades included printer, photographer and the grocery business. Captain died in 1881.

Fred married Mary Caroline Popkins in 1859. They were married less than a year when she died. Fred died Dec. 18, 1877.

Frank married Rachel McClutchie on Aug. 30, 1859. Frank lost his eyesight and was legally blind, but still managed to go about his daily life. They had seven children, though one only lived three days, and two were twins. Rachel died April 12, 1887 and Frank on June 19, 1919.

William's trade was carpentry. He married Isiline Parsons Hackler on April 27, 1863. They had nine children, two from her previous marriage. Isiline died Feb. 26, 1905 and William on March 10, 1927.

Mary Hannah married Leroy L. Key on Sept. 4, 1866. She died June 2, 1877.

OSCAR KIBBE & JULIA DEVEREUX.

Julia's story like that of many other Adams Countians was an intricately woven tapestry of relationships. She was born about 1817, Ireland and emigrated with her family to Washington, DC in 1820. Her first Mississippi record is her marriage to Oscar Kibbe on Aug. 24, 1853, Jefferson County as his second wife.

The first Mississippi record for Oscar (b. May 8, 1808, Kentucky) is his marriage on Feb. 14, 1839, Jefferson County, MS to his first wife, Elizabeth Kemball (Newman) Tucker, widow of Pennington Tucker. Elizabeth Newman married Pennington Tucker on Apr. 27, 1829 as his second wife. Pennington Tucker married his first wife, Susan Wade, on Jan. 2, 1813.

Susan (Wade) and Pennington Tucker had a son, George W. Tucker (b. ca. 1826), who was reared by his step-mother, Elizabeth. He married May 1, 1852 to Margaret S. Glover (b. ca. 1829, England). There may have been other children of this union. Susan died before 1829.

Elizabeth (Newman) and Pennington Tucker had a daughter, Sarah Louise Tucker (b. ca. 1830) md. Oct. 20, 1857 to William K. Douglas, and a son, Paschal Edward Tucker (b. Nov. 21, 1831, d. Mar. 20, 1899). Pennington Tucker died before 1839.

Oscar Kibbe was step-father to Sarah and Paschal Tucker. He and Elizabeth had three children: Harriet O. Kibbe (b. ca. 1840) md. F.A. Gorton Nov. 8, 1870; Victoire S. Kibbe (b. Sep. 6, 1842, d. Jul. 3, 1887) md. __ Wailes; and Alice L. Kibbe (b. ca. 1844) md. Samuel J. Gilmore (b. Apr. 18, 1870). Elizabeth Kibbe died before March 1848.

Circa 1840-80, the families of Amos and Eupaphus Kibbe were also in the Natchez area. Their exact relationship to Oscar has not yet been found. (Were they brothers? cousins? uncle/nephew?)

Amos Kibbe (b. ca. 1817, Missouri) md. Henrietta Tucker (b. 1821, d. 1844) on Nov. 5, 1840. Henrietta was possibly a daughter of Pennington and Susan Tucker? When Amos died in 1852 in Louisiana, Oscar was appointed administrator of his estate and undertutor for his children, Oscar Alonzo Kibbe (b. ca. 1841) and Henrietta Kibbe (b. ca. 1844).

Julia (Devereaux) Kibbe (1817-93)

Eupaphus Kibbe (b. ca. 1828, Kentucky) is referred to as "Cousin Paph" in a letter from Miss Lizzie Douglas dated 1942. He married Sep. 28, 1865, Susan Caroline Rawlings (b. ca. 1843), daughter of John Thomas Rawlings and Caroline Matilda Dix. Their children were Caroline (b. ca. 1868); Elizabeth (b. 1870, d. 1952) md. George Baker Mock (b. 1858, d. 1949) on Oct. 10, 1889; Julia Gorton Kibbe (b. 1873, d. 1902) md. Joseph Robert Marchand on Jan. 25, 1891, Fayette, MS; Ralphine (b. 1876, d. 1880).

Julia and Oscar lived at Coventry Plantation near Washington, Adams County, MS. Although they never had children, Julia mothered Oscar's three daughters and two of his step-children. They also provided a home to Amos Kibbe's children and to Julia's sister and niece. Oscar died May 23, 1881.

When Julia died Oct. 29, 1893, at the home of her niece, Julia Devereux (Ashton) Shields in Natchez, she had been a resident of Adams County for more than 50 of her 75 years. Her obituary says that her death was the source of the deepest grief to her numerous relatives and friends. Submitted by Clare Louise (Mills) Jares

KILLIAN FAMILY.

The Killians in Mississippi and Louisiana primarily descend from George Killian (b. 1740, d. 1830) who immigrated to the Natchez District from Burke County, NC about 1783. The youngest son of Andreas Killian's (b. 1702, d. 1788) first marriage, George, served in the Burke County Militia which saw duty at Cowpens, King's Mountain, Ramsour's Mill and Yorktown during the Revolutionary War. He held two British Crown Land Grants and several claims near Morganton, Burke County, NC.

After immigrating to the Spanish Natchez District, George Killian achieved two Spanish Land Grants of 1,000 acres east of Natchez, MS and later migrated south to the Spanish West Florida Province in 1804, settling near Montpelier, St. Helena Parish, Louisiana at Killian's Cross Road. He and his sons, Joseph and George Jr. held 4,000 acres of Spanish Land Grants.

George and his wife Mary Ann reared a family of eight children. George Killian associated with many Revolutionary War Patriots and many of his children married sons and daughters of Patriots.

While most of his family moved with him to St. Helena Parish, Louisiana in 1804, one son, David, remained in Natchez. David's descendants migrated to Claiborne County, MS about 1830 and later to Franklin Parish, LA about 1863, pioneering on the Bayou Macon at Killian's Ferry.

George Killian's children and their spouses are: Joseph (b. 1768) md. Mary Ann Hughes of Maryland in 1799; John (b. 1770) md. first, Elizabeth __ in 1790 and second, Mary Goodrail/Goodail; Sara Ann (b. 1780) md. George Lawing in 1795; David (b. 1781) md. Nancy Ann Hughes in 1802; Nancy Ann (b. 1782) md. first, Abraham Galtney in 1797 and second, Abram Buckles/Buckholtz; George Jr. (b. 1782) md. first, Barbara Hooter in 1821 and second, Mary McRae in 1822; Priscilla Ann (b. 1786) md. first, Samuel S. Lewis in 1815 and second, John Wright in 1830; Mary Ann (b. 1788) md. Jason Plant in 1815.

Mississippi counties of interest include Adams, Amite, Claiborne, Copiah, Franklin, Hinds, Jefferson and Warren.

Louisiana parishes of interest include the Florida parishes of East Baton Rouge, East Feliciana, West Feliciana, Livingston, St. Helena and Tangipahoa; and the northeast Louisiana Parishes of Franklin, Madison, Ouachita, Richland and Tensas.

Early families connected to the Killians include Batchelor, Buckles (Buckholts, Bucholtz), Calvit, Causey, Coleman, Flowers, Galtney (Gwaltney, Gaultney), Hall, Haslip (Hazlit, Hazlip), Hughes, McRae (McCrae), McVoy, Newcomer, Noland, Packwood, Pettiss, Plant, Rheames, Rhymes, Skipwith, Wheat and Womack.

More genealogical details and extensive histories on 4,000 direct descendants of George Killian, 1740-1830, can be found on-line at: http://familytreemaker.genealogy.com/users/k/i/l/Ed-R-Killian

KIRKLAND FAMILY.

Although few of the Kirkland name are found in the area today, the marriages of two Kirkland brothers to McKinny sisters in South Carolina and the subsequent settlement of many of their children in Louisiana and Mississippi near the end of the 18th century explains why the name Kirkland is found in both Jefferson and Adams County records.

The marriage of Martha, the daughter of Joseph Kirkland (b. ca. 1734, d. 1790) and Laminda McKinney to Thomas Marston Green (b. 1758, d. 1815) began a series of alliances that would confuse any family historian. Martha (b. 1760, d. 1805) was the mistress of Springfield Plantation in Jefferson County, where Andrew Jackson married Rachel. After Martha's death, Green married Priscilla Kirkland Llewellyn, niece of his deceased wife. During her widowhood in 1810, Priscilla married Charles Burr Howell, the widower of her stepdaughter Mary Green.

William Kirkland (b. ca. 1735, d. 1806) and his wife Elizabeth McKinney remained in South Carolina, but their son Zachariah (b. 1761, d. 1823) and wife Martha Raiford (b. ca. 1765, d. ca. 1829) settled in Jefferson County well before 1802, when Governor W.C.C. Claiborne appointed him Major of the Jefferson County 2nd Regiment Militia. Their daughter Sarah married William, the son of Cato West and Martha "Patsy" Green (sister of Thomas Marston Green) and after his death, she became the wife of William E. Parker, who acted as Jefferson County Clerk for a number of years in the early 1800s. Zachariah Kirkland's friendship with Cato West is evidenced by his being the first witness to West's will.

Zachariah's sister Elizabeth was the wife of Everard Green, the brother of Thomas Marston Green. His brother Archilaus married Thomas Marston Green and Martha Kirkland's daughter Jane.

Zachariah's daughter Patience married William M. Smith of South Carolina. One of their daughters was given the name Laminda, as was a daughter of her cousin Martha Kirkland Green. Although the location and death of the first Laminda are unknown, the murder of her husband

Joseph Kirkland in southern Alabama gave a nearby creek the name Murder Creek.

Zachariah's son Zachariah Tucker Kirkland (b. 1799, d. 1935) md. Harriet Perry (b. 1803, d. 1881) of Franklin County, MS. They settled on Kirkland property and built Pine Hill Plantation near Sicily Island, Catahoula Parish, LA.

Barbara Peck Gilbert Haigh descends from Harriet Perry through both her mother and father (See The Gilbert Family). Barbara is the wife of Thomas David Haigh (See the Haigh Family).

In addition to the above alliances with the Greens, the Wests, and the Howells, the Kirklands married into numerous other families with Mississippi heritage, among whom are the Winns, the Ellises, the Scotts, and the Bislands. *Submitted by Barbara Gilbert Haigh*

LOUIS KOERBER & BARBARA HAILE. Louis
(b. ca. 1810) and Barbara (b. 1813) of Bavaria had 10 children: John (b. 1833), Louis (b. 1840), Amelina L. (b. 1842), Barbara Regina (b. 1844), George Adam (b. 1847), Francis M. (b. 1848), Louisa (b. 1851), Leonard (b. 1853), Rosanna (b. 1855), and William Henry (b. 1857).

George Adam Koerber md. Anna E. Noyes (b. 1849) and had two children, Robert H. (b. 1870), and George Joseph (b. 1871, d. 1924) who md. Leonore Guetreux-Grubin (b. 1884, d. 1973) and had five children:

1) Leonore Anna Koerber (b. 1906, d. 1992) md. Arthur Leon Moritz (b. 1904, d. 1984). Daughter Leonore Marie Moritz (b. 1931) md. Paul Vincent O'Malley (b. 1930). See their descendants in the Leopold Moritz & Sophia Mars biography.

2) George Joseph Koerber (b. 1909, d. 1912).

3) Oliver Wilds Koerber (b. 1913, d. 1997) md. first Mary Neal and had Carolyn, md. second Helen and had George Oliver, md. third Geri Tullos, and md. fourth Gertha Johnson.

4) Edith Marguerite Koerber (b. 1915) md. Thomas Louis Piazza (b. 1915, d. 1991) and had two children:

a) Thomas Louis Piazza Jr. (b. 1938) md. first Mary Elizabeth (b. 1943), md. second Lillian Abrams and had Sharon (b. 1963), Greg (b. 1965), Elizabeth (b. 1966), Robert (b. 1969), and Andrea (b. 1970).

b) George Koerber Piazza (b. 1943) md. Nancy Farish (b. 1946) and had Michelle Charisse (b. 1967) who md. Michael Ciaravino (b. 1965) and had Angelina Michelle Ciaravino (b. 2002) and Gianna Charisse Ciaravino (b. 2002).

5) Vera Georgette Koerber (b. 1917, d. 1969). Current Natchez residents are Mrs. Oliver Wilds Koerber (Gertha), Mrs. Thomas Louis Piazza Sr. (Edith), and Paul and Leonore O'Malley.

CHARLES AUGUST KUEHN & ANNIE ELIZABETH ANNIS. Charlie (Charles August) Kuehn
(b. Sep. 17, 1883 in Natchez, MS) was the son of A.P. (William August Paul) Kuehn and Maggie (Margaret Jane) McConchie. Maggie (b. Oct. 28, 1855 Natchez, d. Apr. 29, 1888) was the daughter of William Mitchell McConchie of Kirkcudbright, Scotland and Ann Lester, native of England. William and Ann married in Natchez Dec. 28, 1847.

A.P. Kuehn was a watchmaker and jeweler (b. ca. 1835 in Bavaria) and came to the U.S. in the late 1850s. A.P. and Maggie were married in Natchez Jul. 19, 1881, and their children were Rosa, Charlie and Robert Henry.

Charlie Kuehn was a grocer from a very early age, owned his first store as a teenager, and operated numerous stores in Natchez and Adams County until his death Dec. 8, 1945.

The Kuehns were parents of six children born in Natchez, five of whom lived to marry and have children. The oldest child is Florence (b. Jan. 18, 1908) is still living at 94, and enjoys visits from her children, grandchildren, and great-grandchildren. She married Coyne Connell Miller Sr. July 1, 1928 in Natchez and they had two children, Connell Miller Jr. and Mary Jean Miller, wife of John Leckie. The other children were Brother (Charles August Jr.); Paul William (b. Oct. 5, 1910, d. Nov. 30, 1914 in Natchez); Bob (Robert Jasper); Nan (Annie Elizabeth); and Mary (Mary Annis). Brother Kuehn (b. May 19, 1909, d. Jun. 1, 1974) md. Annis Bryan Dec. 16, 1926. Their children are Betty (Mrs. Billy Rogillio), Rose (Mrs. Ralph Thompson) and Effie (Mrs. Bob Gough). Bob Kuehn (b. Sep. 1, 1914, d. Dec. 20, 1978) md. Kathleen in 1936. Their children are Bobby, Don, Dick and Karen (Mrs. Gene Clements).

Nan Kuehn (b. Jun. 8, 1916) md. Webb Carter Jan. 9, 1936. Their children were Hattie Marie and Webb Jr.

Mary Kuehn (b. Nov. 16, 1918, d. Oct. 3, 1995) md. Andrew Bryant on Jan. 2, 1937. Their children are Sonny (Charles Andrew), Sissy (Mary Annie) and Hattie Vermel. Mary married Bud Wilkinson about 1944. Their children are Jimmy, Johnny and Barry.

Annie Elizabeth "Daisy" Annis (b. Mar. 31, 1886 Baton Rouge, d. Nov. 22, 1935 Natchez) md. Charlie Kuehn Apr. 30, 1907. Daisy Annis was the daughter of William Crawford Annis and Annie McCarthy (nee Wright).

W.C. Annis (b. Jul. 12, 1840 St. Martin Parish, LA, d. Oct. 21, 1903 in Baton Rouge). He was the son of John Morris Annis (b. 1810 in Vermont) and Sara Elizabeth Brister (b. 1815 in Amite County, MS). W.C. Annis learned the printing trade in Baton Rouge, LA and published several small weekly newspapers in St. Francisville, Bayou Sara and Baton Rouge. He sold the *Weekly Advocate* in the late 1880s and served as the city editor until his death. He enlisted in the Confederate Army at Camp Moore on Jul. 5, 1862 in Co. B, 9th Bn. of Louisiana Infantry and served at Port Hudson, LA.

Sara Elizabeth Brister was the daughter of George Brister (b. in the late 1770s in Virginia) and Anna Sullivan (b. ca. 1791 Edgefield District, SC). George Brister's forebears were in Middlesex County, VA in the late 1600s.

ARTHUR EDWARD CAVELIER DE LA SALLE
was born in New Orleans Aug. 9, 1930. His father, René Robert Cavelier de La Salle was also born in New Orleans on Dec. 28, 1890 and his mother, Jeanne Matelde Senac was born in New Orleans Jan. 3, 1891. His father's family is from Normandy and his mother's from Lourdes, France. Her mother was born in New Orleans in 1854. Her father's home still stands on the corner of Bourbon and St. Louis streets. They met when she was 14 and he was 15 at a party in a mansion on Esplanade Ave. René La Salle graduated in chemical engineering from Tulane University, with post-graduate studies at Louisiana State University. He entered the sugar industry in Louisiana, but eventually this took him to the British Empire, especially the West Indies, with off season in Europe. At one point, he did not return to this country for seven years.

Jeanne Senac attended Newcomb College and became a school teacher. Eventually, the Houston Public Schools asked her to come there and establish the teaching of French in the Houston schools, and she was the first to do so.

Returning to America after the seven year absence, René called Jeanne when his ship docked in New York, and said, *Jeanne, lets get married!* She said OK. So he took the train to New Orleans, transferred there to the Southern Pacific, and they were married in Houston at the Sacred Heart Church, now a Houston historic landmark and a cathedral. The honeymoon was along the Southern Pacific Railroad with one stopover at the beautiful old Hotel Beaumont, three days in New Orleans, and off to Antigua, British West Indies. They were later in Central America and Cuba, before returning to America. Their first child, David, was born in New Orleans in 1925, but died at three months from pneumonia.

Arthur was born in New Orleans in 1930, attended Holy Name of Jesus School, Audubon School, and Newman School. His father was killed in an automobile accident March 19-20, 1945. Arthur was nearly killed, and chose recovery on a 20 day cruise from New Orleans to Cincinnati and return, on the steamer *Gordon C. Greene*, the boat still seen in *"Gone With The Wind."* The *Greene* stopped in Natchez, April 1945, and Arthur and his mother toured Stanton Hall, Linden and Longwood. The Nutt family were still living at Longwood then, and allowed visitors to climb all the way to the dome, if they wished.

Arthur chose private education after his father's death. He likes to say that he was born a historian, not a child, and felt that from the very beginning he was not being taught true history in American schools.

He and his mother traveled extensively. He had great interest in architecture and studied the buildings of New Orleans and Louisiana plantations at a time when many plantation houses such as Uncle Sam and Belle Grove, now legends, were still standing. His mother bought and owned, for five years, the Hermitage plantation house on the River Road at Darrow, LA. An interest in transport brought an extensive western railroad trip and study in 1949, now preserved on film. Also purchase of a historic 1882 locomotive, in 1949, and its restoration. This led to the business part of Arthur's career in history, the restoration and preservation of period railroad equipment and the establishment of the American Railroad Equipment Association, Inc. and the building of its museum, *Trains of Yesterday* at Hilliard FL. The work had to be moved to the Pittsburgh area of Pennsylvania, and at Irwin, about 20 miles east of that city, Arthur purchased one of the earliest mansions west of the Eastern mountains, Col. John Irwin's great stone mansion, Brush Hill, and its restoration and placement on the National Register of Historic Places. In Pennsylvania, Arthur married Patricia Maureen Flansbaum (Coover) and adopted his two sons from their mother's previous marriage, Carl Alan, 6, and Adam David, 5, and together they produced Jeanne Ambre Victoria.

During this time period railroad equipment was supplied for the Henry Ford Museum, Opryland, and the Lahaina, Kaanapali & Pacific Railroad, Maui, Hawaii. However, Natchez area and Springfield Plantation House were always on Arthur's mind. He had read about Springfield in New Orleans in 1947, when he was only 16 years old. He finally visited the plantation when 26. His great interest was not, as so many writers have said, the fact that Andrew Jackson was married there, but rather, its great columns, perhaps the first great columns west of the Atlantic Seaboard. As a teenager, he could not understand why great columns were in the Natchez area so early, while in the lower Louisiana area they did not appear until much later with the arrival, about 1830, of the American Greek Revival period. This was, of course, because of British West Florida, the 14th colony. American history does not teach of the two colonies loyal to the Crown, Florida and West Florida.... "We find no argument with good King George." This resulted in much immigration to this area by loyalists, people loyal to the Crown who wanted no part in treason. So they went to Canada, the islands, Britain and here, West Florida.

They brought with them Georgian architecture, and especially with Springfield 1791. Here was Arthur's principal interest in the great plantation house. It had been offered as a gift to the American people by the plantation's absentee ownership, but politics prevented that. The ownership, the James H. Williams Estate of St. Louis, then planned destruction by neglect. They did not want to sell, so Arthur, watching the situation from his own mansion, Brush Hill, could not bear to see one of the most important buildings in American architectural progression, destroyed. Visiting James H. Williams Jr. in St. Louis, 1976, Arthur proposed a lease on the house and grounds in exchange for the restoration at his (Arthur's) cost. This was accepted and Mr. Williams requested the formation of the Historic Springfield Foundation, with a view to the donation to that for the long term purpose. But Jim Williams died suddenly in 1980 and that donation was never made. Arthur La Salle has donated most of the magnificent furniture that he has collected through the years, some of which are family pieces, to the Foundation, but the donation of the house and grounds has never yet, at this writing, been made. The restoration was carried out in three stages and is now, except for removing main hall floor over-lay, re-producing shutters, and a few other items, nearly complete. Arthur does not want to see over-restoration on Springfield, which is so original.

Arthur has continued his studies in history. He, along with a student guest were inaugural passengers for 16 days on the *American Queen*. In 1996, to Europe for two months, both ways on the *Queen Elizabeth* II. To Galveston in December, 1999, round trip, on the *Delta Queen*. And to Australia and New Zealand in March 2000 for the royal victory over the republicans, to be with The Queen during Her Majesty's tour. Arthur was an official guest for The Queen's arrival ceremonies in Sidney. He had met The Queen on July 1, 1997 in Ottawa for the 150th anniversary of Dominion status for Canada. "The most gracious person that I have ever met."

Queen Elizabeth has read some of Arthur's work, which has been published in Great Britain, and expressed Royal Command appreciation of his work.

Arthur has been listed in *"Who's Who in America"* for 28 years, and by the International Biographical Institute in Cambridge, U.K. He did serve in the U.S. Army for a short time in 1951, but a kidney condition caused an Honorable Discharge. He is a member of the International Monarchist League, and that of Canada, Australia and New Zealand. He is an absolute monarchist. Eighteen students from the United States, including Mississippi, Mexico, Argentina, United Kingdom, France, Germany, Chech Republic and Japan have been hosted at Springfield, as has the entire Mississippi Supreme Court and five former governors.

GEORGE YOUNG LATHAM JR. & LEONA RUTH FLETCHER

married April 15, 1955, Natchez, MS. George (b. Jun. 3, 1932), the son of Florence Eugenia Nichols, daughter of Bennie Rebecca Jones and Thomas Nathaniel Nichols and George Y. Latham Sr., son of Mary Louise Fletcher and Benjamin Watkins "Alex" Latham.

The first Latham to the Natchez area was James Latham (b. 1810 in England) married 1st, Nancy Smith and 2nd, Allison Latham. In 1860, James, a carpenter, owned 1,200 acres and was a neighbor of William F. Smith and Jane Selmon Smith. James and Nancy's son, John Phineas Latham (b. Oct. 9, 1839) married on Feb. 27, 1868, neighbor, Martha Jane E. Smith (b. Mar. 13, 1843). John died Mar. 1, 1919 and Martha

Jane died Sep. 17, 1926. Both buried at Christ Church, Church Hill, MS.

Benjamin Watkins "Alex" Latham (b. Sep. 3, 1883), son of John P. and Martha Jane S. Latham, married Mary Louise Fletcher (b. Jun. 30, 1884), daughter of Jane Donoho (b. 1847, d. 1895) and John Evandu "Van" Fletcher (b. Aug. 13, 1839, d. Apr. 17, 1894). John E. Fletcher served in CSA, Adams Troop, Co. A, Jefferson Davis Legion. John Evandu Fletcher, the son of Flavius Felix Flores Fletcher (b. Dec. 20, 1803, Petersburg, VA) and Amanda D. Mardis (b. Oct. 10, 1805, Louisville, KY). Both F.F.F. Fletcher and Amanda Mardis buried Christ Church.

Jane Donoho, daughter of William Carroll Donoho (b. Dec. 27, 1814, Bedford County, VA, d. Mar. 17, 1865), buried at Margin Church Hill. William Carroll Donoho married Francis Dade Davis (b. 1822) Fairchild Plantation. She married 2nd, John Mozart Rohboch. She died ca. 1894, Amite, LA.

George Latham Jr.'s mother, Florence Eugenia Nichols (b. Nov. 5, 1912, d. Mar. 13 1996), buried Greenlawn, Natchez.

The first Nichols to the Natchez District was Nathaniel Nichols (b. Jul. 22, 1769, New Rowan, CT) who married three times: 1) Grace Sherman (b. Sandorn, VT), 2) Isabella Cochran Miche, widow of David Miche, 3) Orlando Lane.

Nathaniel Sherman Nichols (b. ca. 1814), son of Nathaniel and Isabella Nichols, married Mar. 3, 1835 to Flora Flowers (b. ca. 1822), daughter of Uriah and Elizabeth Watson Flowers. Nathaniel died at Eldergrove Plantation, Tensas Parish, LA), buried Natchez Cemetery.

Henry Sherman Nichols (b. Dec. 24, 1835), son of Flora Flowers and Nathaniel Sherman, married Apr. 9, 1862, Harriet Reynolds. Henry died Feb. 8, 1908, Sicily Island, LA.

Thomas Nathaniel Nichols (b. Oct. 28, 1870), son of Henry Sherman and Harriet R. Nichols, married Jun. 12, 1900, Catahoula Parish, LA to Bennie Rebecca Jones (b. Oct. 23, 1882, Wayside Plantation, Waterproof, LA), daughter of Frank A. Jones Sr. and Ellen Olivia Wailes. Frank Sr., son of the Rev. John G. Jones, author of *A Complete History of Methodism*, Vols. I and II, 1799-1846, ca. 1966. Olivia Wailes, daughter of Edward Lloyd Wailes and Olivia May Elizabeth King. Both Ellen and Frank Jones were Jersey Settler descendants. Swayzes, Colemans, Griffings and Kings connections found in *The Descendants of the Jersey Settlers of Adams County, MS, Vols.* I and II edited by Frances Preston Mills, ca. 1981 and Vol. III, edited by Ruth Fletcher Latham ca. 1996.

Ruth Fletcher Latham (b. Dec. 28, 1933, Ville Platte, LA), daughter of Alma Carter (b. Jan. 13, 1908, Coldwater, LA) and Evan Corbitt Fletcher (b. Mar. 4, 1909 Winnfield, LA). Evan and Alma Fletcher with their four children: Leona Ruth Fletcher, William Everett Fletcher, Paul Douglas Fletcher and James Carl Fletcher, moved

George Young Latham Jr.

to Natchez in September 1948, where Evan was employed by California Company. All four children graduated from Natchez High School.

George and Ruth Latham have one child, Karen Rebecca Latham (b. Jan. 28, 1975) md. Charles J. O'Quinn. Children: Ryan Daniel O'Quinn (b. Jun. 5, 1997) and Madison Sage O'Quinn (b. Sep. 27, 1999).

JOHN ANDREW LECKIE & MARY JEAN MILLER.

John Leckie (b. May 4, 1931 in Kitchener, Ontario, Canada) completed seven years with the Royal Canadian Navy as a US trained pilot. While in flight training in Pensacola, FL, he married Mary Jean Miller of Natchez, MS on Aug. 12, 1956. John and Jean returned to Canada in early 1957.

Jean Andree was born in September 1957 and John Miller was born in May 1959. The family left the Navy in 1961 to return to Mississippi. John started working with the partnership of Miller and Webb Oil Co. (AMOCO) and at the same time entered USM resident center to complete a BS degree in education. One of four to be the first graduates from the center in 1966. He went on to complete a MEd in 1969. This was the year that Charles Edwin was born. John retired from the Natchez Public School System in 1993 after 27-1/2 years.

Mary Jean Miller was born on Feb. 23, 1931 to Florence E. Kuehn Miller and Coyne C. Miller Sr. Florence Miller is a native of Natchez born in 1908 to Charles August Kuehn, a noted grocer in Natchez. His father had been a well-known watchmaker and jeweler in Natchez. Mary Jean graduated from Natchez High

John Andrew and Mary Jean (Miller) Leckie

School in 1949, then from Stephen College for Women in 1951. She completed her teaching degree at Oklahoma State University in 1953 and taught in Lawton, OK for two years prior to moving to Pensacola, FL in late August 1955, where she taught in the lower elementary grades at Pleasant Grove School. A month after their marriage in Natchez, they were transferred from Pensacola to Kingsville, TX until completion of flight training and receipt of flight wings in March 1957.

Jean Andree Leckie married Joseph Robert Gamberi Jr. in 1979. Joe graduated from Mississippi State in petroleum engineering in 1983 and is currently employed as a petroleum engineer with the Callon Oil Co. Andree also graduated from MSU in 1979 and completed her teacher certification in 1981 and is currently the art teacher at Cathedral High School. They have four boys: Joseph Robert Gamberi III attending USM; James Andrew Gamberi is in the 11th grade; Jonathan Taylor Gamberi is in the 8th grade; and Joshua Miller Gamberi is in the 6th grade at Cathedral School.

John Miller Leckie married Madelyn Ann Rosiek in 1986. He attended MSU and understudied the farming operation under his grandfather C.C. Miller Sr., then went into partnership with his uncle C.C. Miller Jr. and since has partnered with his cousin C.C. Miller III. They currently farm Bougere Farms which property was purchased in 1947 and cleared by C.C. Miller III. C.C. Miller Sr. Lynn started her degree in accounting and business at Texas A&M but completed at LSU in 1989. She completed her requirements for CPA and accepted employment with Silas Simmons Accounting firm. She met the requirements for CPA and in 2002 became the first female partner with Silas Simmons.

Doctor Charles Edwin Leckie graduated from Natchez High School and entered the US Army. After completion of training as a combat engineer and jump school, he was stationed in Darmstadt,

Germany. He was selected to attend the army prep school at Fort Monmouth. His military contract was nearly up when he was retained to serve in Desert Shield and Desert Storm. Upon his return to the US, he enrolled in school at Co-Lin and then Delta State University. After graduation in 1994, he married Audrey Geneva Craven who resided with her parents in Marigold, MS and graduated at the same time. They moved to Louisburg, WV for Charles to attend the West Virginia School of Osteopathic Medicine. Audrey worked as a secretary and part-time Spanish teacher in a private Christian school. Charles Devon Leckie was born in 1997. Charles Edwin completed his course work in 1998 and moved to Tupelo, MS for his residency work. All requirements were met by July 2001 and he entered family practice with Dr. Charles Borum in Natchez, MS in August 2001. Geneva Colleen was born in 2001 in Tupelo and Scarlett Paige was born in 2002 in Natchez.

JAY BOCK LEHMANN & ELIZABETH DYER EUSTIS.

Jay, an LSU graduate, was born Jan. 5, 1943, the only child of Jonas Bernard (b. 1905, d. 1984) of Adams County, MS, and Naomi Lorriane (Bock) Lehman (b. 1927, d. 1998) of Port Gibson, MS. Jay married Elizabeth Dyer Eustis (b. Oct. 18, 1947, New Orleans) on Feb. 14, 1975. She was the second of four children born to Fenwick Eusits (b. 1912, d. 1988) and Anna Fort Pipes (b. 1914, d. 1985).

Jay worked as a food broker from 1962 to present and in spare time enjoys golf. Elizabeth is a retail gift shop buyer and manager and reared three children: Joni (Lehmann) Lefkowitz, Joshua Bock Lehman and stepchild Margaret Cupples.

Jay's father Jonas was the son of Jonas Bernard Lehmann, a jeweler, and Janet Mayer. Elizabeth descended from Stephen (b. Feb. 29, 1760, d. Nov. 29, 1815) and Katharine Minor (b. Aug. 4, 1770, d. Jul. 9, 1844) and Horatio Sprague Eustis (b. Dec. 25, 1811, d. Sep. 4, 1858) and Catherine Chotard (b. 1820, d. Feb. 12, 1877).

MARY GRACE LOWRY & WILLIAM CARLTON GREER SR.

In the summer of 1949, the Lowry family moved from Blytheville, AR to Natchez, MS. Earl Emmitt Lowry had been working in Natchez for a few months on a dragline for St. Catherine Gravel Co. When school was out for the summer, Earl came home to Arkansas to move the four of them to Natchez. The rest of the family is Lula Marie Riggins Lowry (Mother), the kids, Mary Grace Lowry and Robert Edward (Bob) and the dog, Sambo. Dad raised rabbits so on the back of the truck with all the furniture was the rabbits and cages.

Marie (b. Oct. 18, 1916 in Black Oak, AR, d. Mar. 28, 1988 in Natchez) and Earl (b. Jan. 22, 1915, Jackson, MS, d. Mar. 1, 1971 in Natchez) were members of the Tri-County CB Club and loved to help in a crisis when they could. They loved animals and had rabbits, chickens, dogs, horses, cats, and a couple of cockatiels.

On the way to Natchez, they stopped off and on to get gas and eat something. They would check the truck to make sure the rabbits were doing well for such a long trip. On one of the stops Dad left first and Mom followed. Mary Grace was riding with Mom and they thought Bob was with Daddy. Daddy thought Bob was riding with us. About two miles down the road they passed Daddy and discovered that Bob wasn't with him. They stopped on the side of the road and after a short discussion, they realized that Bob had been left at the last stop. They went back and sure enough, he was still there waiting for us to come back and get him. From then on everybody checked to see where everyone else was riding

before they got back on the road. After about eight hours on the road they finally made it to Natchez.

That fall when Bob and Mary Grace started school, Bob was in the 4th grade and Mary Grace was in the 5th. Mary Grace took dancing and was in the Girl Scouts. In high school she played the clarinet in the band and was a majorette for four years. Bob was in Boy Scouts and played the drums in the band.

Taken in 1943, adults are Earl Emmett Lowry and Lula Marie Riggins Lowry. The children are Mary Grace Lowry and Robert Edward Lowry.

That winter, they got a large collie dog named Jack. He had one blue eye and one brown eye. A short time later they got another collie and named her Jill. Daddy taught Jack to pull a sleigh made from a wooden apple crate. In the wintertime Jack would pull the sleigh with us riding on it. When needed, Jack would pull the sleigh with trash or things on it to help out.

After graduating high school, Mary Grace married William Carlton Greer Sr. and had three children. Bob went to college for two years before he married Belzora Ann Abernathy and had four children.

ROBERT D. MACKEL JR. & SELMA DENT.

Whenever the United States called its men for duty in its defense during various military conflicts, 10 men from the family of Robert D. Mackel Jr. and wife Selma Dent Mackel answered the calls, served well and were honorably discharged.

Staff Sergeant Robert D. Mackel III (b. Jan. 17, 1917, d. Dec. 26, 1986) served in New Guinea, Japan and Korea. Following his discharge he graduated from Atlanta School of Mortuary Science. He joined the partnership of Robert D. Mackel and Sons Funeral Home at the corner of Jefferson and Pine (now M.L. King) in Natchez, MS.

Derrec C. Harris

Louis T. Mackel (b. Nov. 2, 1925, d. Apr. 21, 1987) served the U.S. Army in Korea. He later graduated from Atlanta School of Mortuary Science and joined the family business.

Walter Mackel (Korea) and Alexander Washington Sr. (Italy)

Michael Mackel (b. Feb. 23, 1953), the son of Louis T. Mackel and Dorothea Mackel, served the U.S. Army in Greece. He now lives in Adams County and works for International Paper Mill.

Staff Sgt. Walter B. Mackel Sr. (b. Jul. 21, 1929) joined the Army and served in the Korean War. Following his discharge, he worked 36 years for the Natchez branch of International Paper Mill. After his retirement he now manages the family funeral home.

Sgt. Edward L. Mackel (b. Sep. 28, 1931, d. Apr. 12, 2000) served in the Army in the Korean War. He worked for the city of Chicago until his death.

First Lt. Alexander W. Washington Sr., the son-in-law of Mr. and Mrs. R.D. Mackel Jr., was a graduate of Officer Candidate School in Fort Monmouth, NJ and joined the Tuskegee Airmen in Italy during World War II. He had received a BS degree from Natchez College, however, following his overseas service he remained in service and attended Ohio State University where he received another BS degree and a master's degree in education. Upon retirement he taught in a number of colleges including Alcorn State.

His son Alexander Jr. (b. Dec. 24, 1946) and a grandson of R.D and Selma D. Mackel served in the U.S. Public Health Service as a physician in Staten Island, NY and New Orleans, LA in the early 70s.

Charles J. Harris Jr. (b. Sep. 8, 1946), the grandson-in-law of Mr. and Mrs. R.D. Mackel served honorably in the Army in Vietnam. He graduated from Grambling

Michael E. Mackel

Charles J. Harris Jr.

Alexander Washington Jr. (US Public Health Service)

Charles Dent (USA)

Louis Mackel (Korea)

Robert D. Mackel III (Korea) and Edward Mackel (Korea)

State University. He now owns and operates Charlie Harris Body Shop in Natchez.

His son Derrec C. Harris (b. Oct. 5, 1970), great-grandson of the Mackels served in the U.S. Army. He lives in Los Angeles and is a retail manager and entrepreneur.

Robert S. Cole

Robert S. Cole another great-grandson (b. Mar. 27, 1969) served in the U.S. Army in the Desert Storm conflict in Saudi Arabia. Following his discharge he graduated from Southern University in Baton Rouge, LA. He further studied at University of Illinois at Chicago. He now works as a pharmaceutical representative in Houston, TX. This is to show how one Natchez family proudly served their country.

Charles Fleetwood Dent (b. 1915 in Muskogee, OK) was the nephew of Selma Dent Mackel. Charles served in the U.S. Army during World War II His last contact with the family was in the early 1990s at which time he was living in Hollywood, FL.

CATHERINE TYLER JUNKIN-MAHAN (maiden name unknown) lived most of her 71 years in Natchez, but was born in Kentucky on Aug. 3, 1780. She migrated to Natchez around 1794, at a time when most Kentucky settlers traveled to Natchez on flat boats coming down the Ohio and Mississippi Rivers. The Spanish controlled the Natchez District when she arrived there, and in 1817 she witnessed Mississippi become the 20th state. She survived the 1811 Natchez earthquake, the 1840 tornado, and epidemics of yellow fever. During her lifetime the population grew from about 4,500 for the Natchez District to about 18,600 for Adams County.

In October 1794, Catherine married Thomas Tyler. He was a resident of Natchez, a merchant and a landowner, and was involved in many land transactions. Between 1788-89, Thomas took the oath of allegiance to Spain. When he met his untimely death in February 1805, Catherine, age 25, was left a widow with three young children.

Catherine and Thomas Tyler's three children are named in Mississippi Court Records, 1808-16.

1) Sally Tyler married Joseph Boon on Feb. 3, 1814 in Adams County.

2) Mary "Polly" Tyler married John Bathos on Jan. 30, 1812 in Adams County.

3) Margaret Tyler (b. ca. 1804) md. Samuel McCammant/McClammant on Feb. 24, 1821 in Adams County. He was born about 1779 and died Sep. 10, 1828. They had one known child, Mary

McCammant. Margaret married her second husband, Richard F. Smith on Jan. 20, 1834. Richard's will was recorded in Concordia Parish, LA on Nov. 30, 1842. Margaret's will, probated in Adams County in March 1856, states, *I give and bequeath to my grandchildren Richard James, and James Smith, and William and Mary Clair Phillips the plantation on which I now reside named Selma.* In December 1828, Margaret stated she was the only living heir of Thomas Tyler when she filed a statement with the Adams County Chancery Court (Box 48).

On Apr. 7, 1806, Catherine Tyler married her second husband, William Junkin. Two children were born to this union:

1) Eliza Jane Junkin (b. 1809, d. Jul. 25, 1865 in Natchez) md. Thomas Paine on Apr. 21, 1825. (See Eliza Jane Junkins and Thomas Paine.)

2) Joseph R. Junkin (d. before 1851).

After four years of marriage, Catherine was widowed a second time, when William Junkin died (before Nov. 17, 1810). Then on Jul. 5, 1813, Catherine married her third husband, Arthur Mahon. Arthur was born in Ireland in 1772. This marriage lasted eight years, as Arthur died on Nov. 9, 1821.

According to the Adams County Sexton Records, Catherine died of old age on Aug. 10, 1851; she was 71 years of age. When her estate was probated on Oct. 11, 1851, two heirs were named: Eliza J. (Junkin) Paine and Margaret (Tyler) Smith. Catherine was buried in the Old Catholic Section of the Natchez City Cemetery next to her third husband, Arthur Mahon. *Submitted by Ginga Hathaway.*

LEVIN ROTHROCK MARSHALL was born Oct. 10, 1800 in Alexandria, VA. He was the son of Henry and Eve Rothrock who were married in Baltimore, MD in 1798, but later moved to Virginia. In 1817 he moved to Woodville, MS to become cashier of the United States Bank of Woodville. In 1825 he led a group to welcome the Marquis de Lafayette to Natchez. In 1826 he married Maria Chotard. They had five children, only one of whom, George Matthews Marshall, survived to maturity.

In 1831 he was appointed cashier of the Bank of the United States in Natchez. In 1832 he purchased Richmond Plantation and greatly expanded the early dwelling that had been erected there in the 18th century. After the untimely death of his wife in 1833, he married Sarah Elliott Ross. They had six children. He was one of several businessmen to establish the Commercial Bank of Natchez and served as its first president. Another group of financiers of whom Marshall was a member formed the Natchez Steam Packet Company in 1838 to provide planters with a means of transporting their cotton directly to the European markets. He also owned the fashionable Mansion House Hotel, plus numerous cotton and sugar plantations in Mississippi, Louisiana and Arkansas.

At the time of the Texas War for Independence, Marshall loaned Sam Houston money to fight the war and in turn was given a large tract of land near what later became Marshall, TX. Because of the chicanery of some Texas business associates, he later lost most of this investment.

He was opposed to secession and remained a neutralist during the Civil War.

His expanding business interests drew him more and more to New York City, where he owned a home on Madison Avenue and at Pelham in the Bronx. He died in Westchester County, NY on Jul. 24, 1870. His descendants still live at Richmond and at Lansdowne in Natchez. *Submitted by Devereux Marshall Slatter.*

NATHAN GREEN MARTIN FAMILY. Nathan (b. Jul. 21, 1821 in Winchester, TN), the son of John T. Martin and Rachel Burns, was a young man when his parents moved across the state line to Jackson County, AL. He carried the mail on horse back across the Appalachian Mountains, as did his oldest brother. He was initiated and passed in Utica Lodge No. 98 of the Masons. He served as a Junior Deacon from 1885-86. He was in good standing when he died May 6, 1886. He and some others were cutting small trees for fencing and while throwing one up on the wagon suffered an internal injury and died shortly afterwards. He came to Raymond, MS with an older brother, Robert, about 1841 or 42. Robert went on to Texas where he married and had a large family, he returned years later and lived with a niece until his death.

Nathan married Nancy Jane Robison Feb. 9, 1843. They only had one child to live to maturity, Mary Elizabeth "Molly" (b. Jun. 10, 1849 near Utica) md. Henry Lawrence McNair on Oct. 1, 1867 in a double wedding with his sister, Louisa. They lived near Raymond.

Nathan then married as his second wife Laura Jane Boyd Thornton, the widow of Carleton Thornton. Laura was born Jul. 27, 1848 to Juliann Boren and Archibald Boyd and died on Christmas Day of 1924. She and Nathan had four children: Jessie Bell (b. Oct. 11, 1874) md. Dick Wright; John Wade (b. Aug. 9, 1877) md. Fannie Cordelia Stevens (b. Nov. 13, 1902 in Claiborne County); Nathan Wesley (b. Nov. 8, 1879) md. Mary Jane Eley; William Thomas (b. Jan. 13, 1882) md. Minnie Greer. All four children were born in the house that Carleton Thornton left his widow and child, Carley, now called the Keith House in Utica.

l-r: Francis Marion (sitting), Willie, Fannie (holding Lola), Edna, John (holding Effie Mae), John Everett, Ernest Noel, made in Nashville, AR, 1921

John Wade and Fannie had a total of 10 children; the first five were born in Claiborne County and the other five were born in Howard County, AR. John and his brother Will moved their families to Howard County before May 29, 1915 to farm and work in timber. John and Fannie had Lewis Howard (b. Jan. 27, 1905) md. Lula Hudson near Hope, AR; Ernest Noel (b. Aug. 25, 1907) md. Allie Mae Curtis; Francis Marion (b. Jul. 24, 1909) md. Nellie Marie Scott; Willie Lee (b. May 16, 1911) md. Alma Cagle; John Everett (b. Aug. 9, 1913) he was killed May 9, 1945 during WWII in Germany, while serving in the US Army; Edna Fay (b. Apr. 13, 1916) md. Denmon D. Westmoreland; Effie Mae (b. Nov. 30, 1918) md. Waldon Henry Hines; Lola Hazel (b. Nov. 4, 1920) md. Jesse Harold Martin of Terre Haute, IN; Harvey Lee (b. Sep. 9, 1922) served as a Marine during WWII, married Alma Frances Johnson; Lela Irene (b. Oct. 14, 1925) md. Burl Weaver, after his death from an auto accident she married Albert Kuykendall. John Wade moved his family back to Hinds County in 1925.

Francis Marion Martin married Nellie Marie

Scott, the daughter of Norval Scott and Lenora Dixon Scott. Nellie was born Mar. 19, 1913 and died Mar. 14, 1985 of a massive heart attack near Ferriday, LA. She saw Marion, as he was called, in Utica one Saturday while there with her parents buying groceries. He was six-foot tall, dark hair and eyes and weighed about 180 pounds, very handsome. She commented to either a friend or one of her sisters, there stands my husband. Of course, no one took her seriously but on Mar. 11, 1933 they married in Raymond. He loved to dance and she had two left feet, but she would sit and watch him dance with everyone else, especially the waltz, as he was a wonderful dancer. They had a family of five children, the oldest being this compiler, Carolyn Elane, followed by another daughter Bobbye Jean, then three boys: Robert, Michael and Terry.

Marion was unable to serve in WWII because of a leg injury he sustained when he was a young boy. He was a mechanic and heavy equipment operator. In 1942 he took a job that required him to move to Indianola, MS, where he lived in a boarding house, while building runways for student pilots training for the war. Of course going home as often as possible. When this job was completed, in late 1942, he took a job with the Mississippi Highway Department moving his family first to Belzonia and then in April 1943 to Rolling Fork. What a wonderful little town this was for us growing up. We grew to know everyone and could wander all over town without a worry to our parents, as all adults acted as surrogate parents. If we did something we were not supposed to, someone would call our mother and she knew about it before we got home and then were we even more in trouble!

We visited our cousins in Utica often and in summer stayed several weeks, roaming the pastures and woods. We knew where every plum thicket and blackberry patch was located, seldom going to the house for lunch. What a wonderful way to grow up. This was our Mayberry, USA.

RAY ELDRED MASON & CARLA PAUL.
Carla Ruth (b. Dec. 25, 1944 in Ferriday, LA) is the daughter of Marvyn Trisler and Carl Paul of Concordia Parish, LA. Marvyn is the daughter of Ruth Dale and Sam Trisler. Carla married Jun. 26, 1976 in Monterey, LA, to Ray Eldred Mason (b. Dec. 5 1932 in Monticello, MS).

Carla Paul and Ray Mason

William Dale, of Edinburgh, Scotland, was in the Natchez, MS/Concordia Parish area in the early 1800s. Prior to the Civil War, he owned two steamboats and three plantations, living at New Era, LA, which he named after striking a tree with his sword and exclaiming that a "new era" had begun for his family. After the war, all he had left was his best plantation, Dale Ridge, continuously occupied until recent years and maintained by the Dale family.

William's son, Robert Morris Dale, is buried in the family cemetery there underneath a marker proclaiming him a "citizen of Scotland." Robert's

daughter, Ruth Dale, became Carla's grandmother and namesake. Carla's grandfather, Samuel Albert Trisler, was descended from Henry Clay Trisler, who traveled the Natchez Trace to this area as a lone 12-year-old, was the father of James Scott Trisler and the grandfather of Samuel Albert.

Carla's father was descended from Lucien Talen (b. 1653 in France), who became part of LaSalle's Expedition in 1683-84. Lucien's son Robert, born on board ship, became LaSalle's godchild. Settling in Texas, LaSalle founded a fort. Indians massacred all the members of the fort except for Robert and his sisters, who were taken by these Indians until rescued by a Spanish expedition and returned to France via Spain. Robert later returned to Texas looking for word of the original explorers.

Robert's grandmother, Jeanne Talon, married Louis LaPrairie of Bohemia. Their son, Louis (b. 1733), had daughter Anne LaPrairie (b. 1772 in Rapides Parish, LA). Anne married Jacob Paul III, of Rapides Parish, a descendant of Jacob Paul I, a North Carolina resident in 1710. Jacob I had four sons who fought in the Revolutionary War, but in 1776 his son Jacob II moved with grandson, Jacob III, to Natchez, MS, where they were given a British land grant on South Creek. Their son, Jacob IV, who fought in the Battle of New Orleans, married Delores Belgrade, and they were the parents of Daniel Paul. Daniel's son Lahare moved to the Catahoula Parish area, birthplace of Carla's grandfather, Joseph Paul, who married Hilie Warwick, daughter of Martha McClure and Hiriam Mendenhall Warwick.

Ray Mason, according to family history, is descended from General Robert E. Lee through his grandmother, Annie Mason. Also, Ray is a distant cousin of the robber and murderer, Samuel Mason, a Natchez Trace highwayman during the early 1800s, who was eventually betrayed and whose severed head was brought to Jefferson County, MS, for bounty by his outlaw co-horts, Big Harp and Little Harp under assumed names, but who were immediately recognized and hanged on the spot.

JOHN MCCALEB & MARIA COLLINS.
John (b. Mar. 12, 1777 in Pendleton District, SC), the fourth of 10 children born to Captain William and Ann MacKey McCaleb. He married Maria "Polly" Collins on Jul. 22, 1805 in the home of her parents William and Jeanette "Jane" Pipes Collins at Pine Ridge, MS. She was born circa 1791, died after Mar. 16 1832, when she is known to have deeded property; burial place unknown. He died Jul. 18 1823 and was buried in the Peachland Plantation Cemetery.

Educated as an engineer in South Carolina, John was about 22 when he came with his parents to Claiborne County, MS. He was one of four men appointed in 1803 to purchase land for a courthouse, jail, stock pillory and whipping post.

He became a leading planter, increasing his land every few years in Claiborne, Jefferson and Adams counties of Mississippi. In 1806 he acquired 365 acres in Claiborne County that adjoined land of his brother Samuel. In 1806 he obtained 650 acres on Bayou Pierre, in Claiborne County that he named Elmwood; in 1808 he bought a large tract of land in Jefferson County. He raised cotton, mules and had many slaves; each property was operated as a unit with so many slaves per hundred acres.

The property he acquired in 1808 in the Pine Ridge Community of Adams County he named Peachland. He built a two-story clapboard house in a park like setting with several ells, wide upper and lower galleries across the front. This house was home to five generations of his descendants

before it was dismantled in the 1960s. The grounds have changed little around the modern house now there, however, the burial ground is no longer identifiable.

John and Maria had eight children; the four oldest were baptized Oct. 11, 1812 at the Salem Presbyterian Church, later called Pine Ridge, and became active members. Their children were:

1) Indiana (b. 1806, d. before 1857) md. William Bougham in 1824; they had two children, Anne and Indiana.

2) David William (b. 1808, d. 1839) md. Anne Matilda Dunbar in 1828. They had two children, James Dunbar and Elizabeth Bisland.

3) Francis (b. 1810, d. before 1851) md. Louisa C. Harrison in 1830. They had one child, Henrietta.

4) James Franklin (b. 1812, d. 1878) md. 1st, Sophia Moore (b. 1814, d. 1845) had nine children, seven survived Sophia; md. 2nd, Martha Jane Bisland in 1846 and they had seven children. (See her biography.)

5) Elizabeth Jane (b. 1813 d. 1823).

6) Henrietta (b. 1816, d. 1848) md. George Rogers Clark Girault in 1833. They had seven children: John, James, Anna, Elizabeth, Charles, Matthew and Farrar.

7) Mary (b. 1818, d. 1849) md. Charles Hannah Rochester in 1834; they had seven children. (See her biography.)

8) John Jr. (b. 1823, d. 1856) md. Indiana Booth in 1845. They had five children: John, Sarah, James Franklin, Mary and Anna.

In 1832 Maria and second husband, William Miskell, deeded Peachland to Maria's son James and sold her other land. *Submitted by Ella McCaleb Young.*

JAMES FRANKLIN MCCALEB & MARTHA JANE BISLAND.
Martha Jane (b. Mar. 8, 1822, d. May 30, 1900) was the oldest child of eight born to James and Mary King Bisland. On Sep. 16, 1846 she married James Franklin McCaleb (b. 1812, d. 1878), son of John and Maria Collins McCaleb, whose wife Sophia Moore had died in 1845.

She went to live at Peachland Plantation and became the stepmother to seven children, ages 2 to 15. They were Mary Elizabeth (b. 1831, d. 1922) md. James Dunbar McCaleb in 1852; William Collins (b. 1833) md. in 1870 to Martha Harris (d. 1875), md. 2nd, Elizabeth Buckner; James Jr. (b. 1836, d. 1862 in the Battle of Bowling Green); John Moore (b. 1837, d. 1912) md. Catherine H. McCaleb in 1860; Helen Amanda (b. 1839, d. 1917) md. Prosper King Whitney in 1860; Caroline Roach (b. 1840, d. 1860) md. Putnam Darden in 1858; Thomas (b. 1841, d. 1842); Lawson (b&d. 1843); and Jonathan (b. 1844, d. 1918) md. Mary Martin McCaleb in 1874, she died in 1904 and he married 2nd, Mrs. Eliza J. Ketteringham. Three of these children married a McCaleb first cousin.

The high regard shown Martha Jane is indicated by her stepdaughter Helen naming a daughter, Martha Bisland Whitney.

Martha Jane and James Franklin had seven children:

1) Bisland (b. 1847, d. 1904) md. Grace Blankenship in 1885, they had three children: Alexander, Louise and Otis. Grace died and he married 2nd Olivia Dunbar Archer in 1899, no issue. Olivia drew family trees for both the Archer and Dunbar families, a great genealogical source for future generations.

2) Louisa Witherspoon (b. 1849, d. 1883) md. Thomas Dicks in 1876; they had two children, William and Louis.

3) Anna Henrietta (b. 1852, d. 1938) md. William Sidney Briscoe in 1872; they had four children: Pierce, Lillian, Sidney and Leon.

4) Susan Bradford (b. 1854, d. 1934) md. Joseph Hutton in 1881; they had four children: Henry, Lillian, James and Joseph.

5) Elizabeth Chamberlin (b. 1856, d. 1947) md. James Archer in 1884; no issue. He was a brother to Olivia, second wife of Elizabeth's brother Bisland.

6) Douglas Bisland (b. 1857, d. 1918) md. Louisa Weltha Robson in 1881, they had five children: Sidney, Caroline, Edgar, Jefferson and Belle.

7) Samuel Lambdin (b. 1859, d. after 1900) was single.

In 1812, James and his three older siblings were baptized at the Salem Presbyterian Church, later called Pine Ridge, where for 24 years he was the only elder. In 1835, Martha was received into the Pine Ridge Church.

Her will, left in the hands of her oldest stepson, Dr. William McCaleb, left her property in equal amount to her children and the children of her late husband. She desired that the Peachland property be kept in the family and hoped her sons, Bisland and Samuel, would be allowed the option to purchase the interest of the other heirs. Martha, James and Sophia are all buried in Pine Ridge Church Cemetery.

MRS. MCCALEB - THE LADY WITH PEARLS.

One of the heirlooms that has been passed down to the descendants of the McCaleb family for many generations is this small miniature of a well dressed lady with pearls. Unfortunately, her identity has been lost with certainty, but it seems likely that she may have been an ancestress from Natchez. In the 1820s and early 1830s the McCaleb Family of Adams County, MS, often summered at the Graham Springs Hotel in Harrodsburg, KY. It was during one of these summers that Miss Mary McCaleb (b. 1818, d. 1849) met and was wooed by Charles Hannah Rochester (b. 1817, d. 1894). They were married at Mary's family plantation in the Pine Ridge Community of Adams County, MS in 1834. Mary was the daughter of John McCaleb (b. 1777, d. 1823) of Peachland Plantation in Adams County, and his wife, Maria Collins. After John's death, Maria, also known as Mary and Polly, remarried to William A. Miskell in 1826. She died in the early 1830s in Kentucky according to family tradition. Is the lady in the picture Maria Collins, or is she her daughter, Mary McCaleb? It may never be known for sure.

The picture has been passed down through the Rochester Family descendants of the McCalebs with other heirlooms. Among the children of Charles and Mary (McCaleb) Rochester of

Lady with pearls

"Mount Airy" in Danville, KY was a daughter, Sarah Lewis Rochester (b. 1845, d. 1901), known as "Lulie." She became the wife of the Reverend Dr. Howard Lansing Burrows (b. 1843, d. 1919) formerly of Richmond, VA, in 1867. Dr. and Mrs. Burrows lived in Lexington, MO; Bordentown, NJ; Lexington, KY; Augusta, GA and Nashville, Tennessee where he served as pastor of Baptist churches in those places. Living with them much of her life was Lulie's maiden sister, Mary McCaleb Rochester (b. 1840, d. 1928), known as "Mamie," who died in the home of her niece, Mary Adelaide

Burrows (b. 1875, d. 1949), the only daughter of Dr. and Mrs. Lansing Burrows. Known as "Madelle," Miss Burrows married George Crawford Mays (b. 1870, d. 1922) of Augusta, GA in 1900. Mr. and Mrs. Mays lived in Montezuma and Thomasville, GA before settling in Albany, GA in 1912, where he was president of the Georgia Cotton Co. Their daughter, Mary Crawford Mays (b. 1906, d. 1993) md. Green Floyd Alford Jr. (b. 1903, d. 1986) of Sylvester, GA in 1929. They made their permanent home in Albany, Georgia although Mr. Alford owned and operated seasonal resorts and hotels in Florida, New Jersey, Michigan and New Hampshire. Their daughter, Mary Mays Alford Faulk is the present owner of the picture of the lady, who is only identified as being related to the Rochesters.

It seems fitting that the picture has passed down from one generation to the other, through possibly six generations of Mary's. The name carries on through Mrs. Faulk's two granddaughters, Mary Katherine Faulk and Mary Simpson Montgomery, known as "Molly." *Submitted by Mary Alford Faulk.*

SIDNEY BRISCOE MCCALEB & ANNE MATILDA FARRAR.

Anne Matilda (b. May 8, 1887 Greenwood Lodge, Wilkinson County, MS, d. Feb. 3, 1983 Houston, TX) was the daughter of Ella Cornelia "Hallie" Ford (b. Aug. 2, 1854 Wilkinson County, d. Sep. 11, 1919) and Thornton "Tone" Hardy Farrar (b. Sep. 24, 1843, Adams County, MS, d. Mar. 4, 1917). Hallie and Tone married Feb. 9, 1879 in Wilkinson County.

Anne married Sep. 10, 1914, Wilkinson County to Sidney Briscoe McCaleb (b. Jul. 9, 1882, Greenwood Plantation, Adams County, d. Aug. 6, 1967, Adams County). Sidney was the son of Douglas Bisland McCaleb (b. Nov. 12, 1857, Peachland Plantation, Adams County) who married Feb. 22, 1881 in Adams County to Louisa Weltha Robson (b. Oct. 9, 1853, Adams County), daughter of Caroline Boyd and John Robson Jr. Louisa died Dec. 13, 1907, Adams County and Douglas died Jan. 26, 1918, Ensley, AL, near Birmingham.

Anne walked to grammar school in Wilkinson County, then for a short time attended Edwin McGehee College, Woodville, until she became ill and had to withdraw from school. For three years, Sidney attended school in the Session Room of Pine Ridge Presbyterian Church, Adams County. For two six-month terms, he went to school at Travelers Rest, Adams County, home of Louisa and Louis Lambdin Winston. Then, he rode horseback for about eight miles to study with other students at Rose Hill Plantation, Adams County. Finally, from 1900-01 he attended Mississippi A&M College, Starkville, MS.

From 1914 Sidney and Anne were members of the Kingston United Methodist Church, where he was Sunday School Superintendent, a Steward, and a frequent delegate to quarterly and annual conferences. She was one of the founding members of the Descendants of the Jersey Setters, Adams County.

From 1901-03, Sidney worked as a grocery store clerk for Will O'Kelly in Ashwood, LA. All of his other jobs were in Adams County, where for some time he was an overseer on Sligo Plantation. From 1910-20, he was a tick inspector for eradicating the Texas fever tick. From 1921-35, he was deputy tax assessor. During the early 1930s, he and Anne both worked for the WPA (Works Progess Administration). From 1933-35, he drove a school bus for the Kingston Consolidated Schools. From 1937-54 he operated a country grocery store at Kingston, in addition to farming and raising cattle.

Anne and Sidney had five children: Mary

Louise Mcaleb, Anna Belle McCaleb, Josephine Thorn McCaleb, Sidney Briscoe McCaleb Jr. and Ella McCaleb.

Mary Louise McCaleb was born Oct. 30, 1918. (See separate biography on Mary Louise McCaleb/Roy Howard Tarver.)

Anna Belle McCaleb (b. Jun. 8, 1920, Wilkinson County).

Sidney McCaleb and Anne Matilda Farrar, 1914

Sidney Briscoe McCaleb Jr. was born Jun. 2, 1922. (See separate biography on Rose Silletti/Sidney Briscoe McCaleb Jr.)

Josephine Thorn McCaleb, born Nov. 10, 1923, Adams County.

Ella McCaleb was born Jun. 7, 1928, Smithland Plantation.

SIDNEY BRISCOE MCCALEB JR. & ROSE SILLETTI.

Sidney Briscoe McCaleb Jr., son of Anne Matilda McCaleb and Sidney Briscoe McCaleb Sr., was born Jun, 2, 1922 in Wilkinson, Wilkinson County, MS, and married in Tucson, AZ, on May 1, 1944 to Rose Silletti (b. May 12, 1921 in Torito, Italy, and grew up in Jersey City, NJ), the daughter of Rose La Forgia and Paul Silletti. Sidney grew up on Smithland Plantation, Adams County, MS, and graduated from Wilkinson County Agricultural High School at Woodville, MS. While he attended school there, he helped to plant the live oak trees that surround the Court House Square in Woodville. In 1940 he served in Camp Fl1 Civilian Conservation Corps in Meadville, MS. After joining the U.S. Army Air Corps on Jul. 1, 1940, Sidney served until November 1945, in various Southern states and in Arizona as an aviation mechanic.

For more than 50 years Sidney and Rose lived in the area of Los Angeles, CA, where he was a carpenter and contractor. Later he became a realtor there. They were members of the Sepulveda United Methodist Church. He was a Master Mason of Masonic Lodge 378. He also belonged to the American Legion, "The Forty &

Sidney and Rose McCaleb

Eight," the Carpenter's Union, the Sierra Club, the National Parks Trust, the World Wildlife Federation, the National Wildlife Federation, the Rails to Trail Conservancy, the Audubon Society, the Arbor Day Foundation, and the National Parks Conservation Association.

In 1998, Sidney and Rose decided to move back to Mississippi. As they were traveling from California, Rose died on Oct. 25, 1998 at Van Horn, TX. Later, Sidney and his sons scattered her ashes in the Pacific Ocean. Arriving alone in Adams County, MS, Sidney built himself a three-bedroom steel home on Smithland Plantation, Adams County. He attends Kingston United Methodist Church, where he teaches an adult Sunday School Class. He is president of the Natchez Scottish Heritage Society, and is a member of the Descendants of the Jersey Settlers of Adams

County, MS, for which organization he has served on the Cemetery Committee for several years.

Sidney is a descendant of several early settlers of the Natchez District: Richard Swayze, Caleb King, William McCaleb, Alexander Farrar, George Dougharty, William Collins, Windsor Pipes, John Bisland, Moses King, Peter Rucker, Morris Custard, John Robson Sr., Eliza Sojourner, Joseph Thomas, and both Alexander Boyd and his sister Mary Boyd.

Rose and Sidney had two sons, Douglas "Doug" William McCaleb and Bruce Paul McCaleb.

Douglas "Doug" William McCaleb was born May 16, 1949 in Burbank, CA. (See separate biography, Douglas "Doug" William McCaleb.)

Bruce Paul McCaleb was born Oct. 17, 1952 in Van Nuys, CA. Submitted by Polly Scott.

DOUGLAS "DOUG" WILLIAM MCCALEB was

born May 16, 1949 in Burbank, CA, the older son of Rose Silletti and Sidney Briscoe McCaleb Jr. Rose and Sidney had a second son, Bruce Paul McCaleb (b. Oct. 17, 1952 in Van Nuys, CA). Rose (b. May 12, 1921 in Torito, Italy), the daughter of Rose La Forgia and Paul Silletti, grew up in Jersey City, NJ. Sidney (b. Jun. 2, 1922 in Wilkinson, Wilkinson County, MS) md. Rose in Tucson, AZ, on May 1, 1944. Sidney grew up on Smithland Plantation, Adams County, MS, and graduated from Wilkinson County Agricultural High School, Woodville, MS.

Graduating in 1971 from the University of California, Berkeley, CA, Doug entered the U.S. Coast Guard, where he served as a personnel officer and flag lieutenant in New Orleans prior to doing graduate work in international law and diplomacy at The Johns Hopkins University, Washington, DC. From 1977-84 Doug served as a foreign affairs officer in the U.S. Department of Commerce, specializing in international ocean policy.

In 1987 he received the master of divinity degree from the General Theological Seminary in New York City, NY. He began his pastoral work in 1987 at St. John's Episcopal Church in McLean, VA, as associate rector. In 1993 he became assistant minister at St. John's Episcopal Church, Lafayette Square, Washington, DC, where he served through October 1994.

Doug became interim rector of Christ Episcopal Church, Winchester, VA, in January 1995 and was installed as rector on Oct. 8, 1997. In the diocese, he served on the Commission on Liturgy and Church Music from 1988-92 and on the Standing Committee from 1997-2000. He is currently the provincial representative for the General Theological Seminary (since 1993) and serves on the Commission on Ministry (1989-92 and 1995-present). He founded the Downtown Cluster of Congregations and serves on the following boards: the Grafton School, Berryville, VA; American Red Cross, Frederick County, VA; and the Northwestern Virginia Parish Nurse Coalition.

Douglas William McCaleb

Many of Doug's paternal ancestors were early settlers of the Natchez District of the Mississippi Territory: Richard Swayze, Caleb King, William McCaleb, Alexander Farrar, George Dougharty, William Collins, Windsor Pipes, John Bisland, Moses King, Peter Rucker, Morris Custard, John Robson Sr., Eliza Sojourner, Joseph Thomas, and both Alexander Boyd and his sister Mary Boyd.

DAVIE LOU MARCANTEL & JOHN AUBREY MCGEE, D.D.S.

Davie Lou (b. Nov. 27, 1936 in Iowa, LA) is the daughter of the late Hazel Martha and David Hampton Marcantel. John Aubrey McGee (b. Nov. 30, 1934 in Copiah County, MS) is the son of the late Carrie Beatrice and John Aubrey McGee. Davie Lou and John married Sept. 21, 1959 in New Orleans, LA. John received a doctorate in dental surgery from Loyola University in New Orleans in 1960. Davie Lou graduated from Louisiana State University in May 1959, receiving the BS degree in nursing. Dr. John McGee served in the U.S. Navy from 1960-62 at Camp Pendleton, CA. Upon discharge he established a dental practice in Natchez, MS in September 1962. John and Davie Lou have three children: Carrie Martha, Tara G., and John Aubrey III "Jay".

John Aubrey McGee Family

Carrie Martha (b. Jun. 7, 1961 in Laguna Beach, CA) md. Mark Gregory Iles May 23, 1989. She received a doctorate in dental surgery from Louisiana State University in May 1993. She is the first dental student to maintain a 4.0 grade point average for four years of dental school. Carrie practices dentistry in Natchez, MS. She and Greg have two children, Madeline Marcantel (b. Oct. 21, 1993) and Mark Gregory (b. Dec. 6, 1996).

Tara G. (b. Mar. 18, 1965 in Natchez, MS) md. Jeffrey Brent Walker May 26, 1990. She graduated magna cum laude from the University of Mississippi School of Accountancy in May 1987. Tara and Jeff live in Houston, TX and have two children, Caroline Haley (b. Aug. 31, 1993) and Carrie Lou (b. Jun. 9, 1995).

John Aubrey McGee III "Jay," (b. May 23, 1969) attended the University of Mississippi, and graduated from the University of Southern Mississippi in 1993 from the College of Engineering. He resides in Dallas, TX.

Dr. John McGee retired from dentistry after 40 years, leaving his practice to his daughter Dr. Carrie Iles.

LEICESTER MCGEHEE & BETTY SHIELDS

shared ancestors in Peter and Sarah Rucker, who settled in Adams County in 1775, descending separately from their two daughters, Catherine and Susanna.

Catherine married John Turnbull, land speculator and trader, and they settled in West Feliciana Parish, LA. The descendants of their daughter, Susan (sister of son Daniel who built Rosedown) drifted into neighboring Wilkinson County, MS where Judge Edward McGehee of Bowling Green was established as a planter. It was Edward's great-grandson, Harry Percy McGehee, who married Susan Towles LeSassier, descendant of the Turnbulls. Their son, Fielding Merwin McGehee (b. in Pinkneyville, MS on Sept. 27, 1900), moved to Natchez where he became manager of farm properties for Britton and Koontz bank. On Dec. 20, 1923 he married Clara "Lallie" York Reber,

daughter of Annie Vernon and Judge Thomas Reber (manager of a Natchez steamboat line), and they lived on plantations which he managed in Adams and Wilkinson counties. Their three children, who were all born and attended public schools in Natchez, were: Fielding Merwin Jr. (b. Nov. 17, 1924), Leicester Reber (b. Mar. 11, 1926) and Ann Vernon (b. Nov. 23, 1929). In 1935 Fielding and Lallie bought property in Adams County near the Natchez Trace where they built a home and farmed until Fielding was disabled by a stroke in 1943. Leicester had by then graduated from Natchez High School and took over management of the property.

Susana Rucker married John Bisland of Pine Ridge in Adams County. Their great-granddaughter, Sarah Stelle Bisland, married her second cousin, physician, Dr. Joseph Dunbar Shields. Their son Ralph Bisland Shields (b. Sept. 25, 1900 at the family home, Mt. Repose), was a student at Jefferson Military College and VMI before graduating from Mississippi State College in 1922 with a degree in civil engineering. He was employed by the state of Mississippi building roads.

On Jul. 22, 1925, Ralph married Irene McMillan Newell (b. Feb. 4, 1904 near Newellton, LA), where her father, Ross Wade Newell had farming interests. He then began farming in Concordia Parish on land previously part of the Bisland estate. Their three children, all born in Adams County and educated in public schools in Vidalia were: Irene (b. Apr. 27, 1926), Ralph (b. Mar. 30, 1928) and Elizabeth "Betty" Wade (b. May 9, 1930).

Betty attended LSU, graduating in secretarial science in 1951 and then worked for a year as a secretary in Vidalia. Following their marriage on Jul. 19, 1952 at Trinity Episcopal Church in Natchez, she and Leicester moved into a small brick home built for them on the McGehee homestead. When Leicester's father died Mar. 7, 1953, he assumed full management of the family lands.

McGehee Family, front l-r: Bruce, Betty, Leicester, Kathleen. Back: Ross and Thomas

Over the next 33 years he increased the family holdings and engaged in a variety of farm related activities including cattle production. He was vitally interested in forest improvement and conservation practices until his death on Sept. 26, 1985. A fulltime homemaker, Betty fulfilled her life's objective, as mother to their four children: Thomas Leicester (b. Oct. 24, 1954), Ross Dunbar (b. Oct. 27, 1955), Bruce Shields (b. Aug. 16, 1957), and Kathleen Kell (b. Oct. 16, 1959).

ALBERT HAROLD MCINTOSH & FLORENCE MAXINE TARVER.

Florence Maxine Tarver (b. Aug. 23, 1932, Kingston, MS) was the youngest of nine children born to Frances "Fannie" Elizabeth Thornton and Isaac "Ike" Ham Tarver.

Ike Tarver (b. Oct. 20, 1887 in Lincoln County, MS) came to Adams County, MS, in the early 1930s to help build a railroad and to do logging for the Homochitto Lumber Co. The son of "Renia"

Burt and Jennings Cicero Tarver, Ike married on Mar. 28, 1910 Fannie Thornton, daughter of Frances Elizabeth "Bettie" Gatlin and Wiley Perley Thornton of Amite County, MS. Ike died Sep. 25, 1963 McComb, MS, and Fannie died Jul. 19, 1981. Both are buried at Ramah Baptist Church Cemetery, Franklin County, MS. As a blacksmith, Ike moved from area to area to make a living. Besides working for the Homochitto Lumber Co. in Natchez, he worked at Firo Machine Shop and for the Diamond Box Co.

On Jul. 25, 1953 in Natchez, Florence Tarver married Albert Harold McIntosh (b. Nov. 25, 1927, Crystal Springs, MS), son of Sally Bell and James Dampier McIntosh, Copiah County, MS. After service in the U.S. Army, Harold worked at International Paper Co., Natchez, retiring on disability.

Florence's siblings were Velma Bernice Tarver, George Harvey Tarver, Vince Edward Tarver, twins, Wilda Mae and Hilda Rae Tarver, Corine Tarver, Lloyd Tarver, and Roy Howard Tarver.

Florence Maxine Tarver

Growing up on Liberty Road in Adams County, Florence attended Kingston Consolidated School until the fifth grade, the Natchez Institute, then Natchez High School, where she graduated in 1950. While she was in school, she played basketball for five years, was involved in other types of sports, and was in the Pep Squad. Her first job was as a clerk with Abrams Annex on the corner of Franklin and Union Steets in Natchez. Other jobs were with Sam Abrams Co., Cole's, Commercial Credit Corp., Wal-Mart, and Reynolds-Whittington in Vidalia, LA.

From the marriage of Florence and Harold, four children were born:

1) Randall Eric McIntosh (b. Sep. 6, 1956, in Hazlehurst, MS) md. Susan Marlowe Collier. They have four children: Paul Wayne Collier, Jonathan Wade Collier, Stephanie Nicole McIntosh and Isaac Marlowe McIntosh.

2) Nancy Elizabeth McIntosh (b. Dec. 26, 1957 in Hazlehurst, MS) md. Anthony Best of Pascagoula, MS and from this marriage were born three children: Anthony Lee Best III, Jessica Elizabeth Best, and Jacob Robert Best.

3) Alan Brian McIntosh (b. Oct. 19, 1959 in Natchez) md. Ann Kaiser Aug. 19, 1995 in Natchez. They have one son, Kaiser Lane McIntosh.

4) Gary Lane McIntosh (b. Aug. 5, 1964 in Natchez) md. Kendra Jill Clayton Guy on Apr. 25, 1998 in Natchez. Kendra (b. Dec. 15, 1970, Natchez) is the daughter of Sandy and Larry Clayton, Clayton, LA. Gary and Kendra are the parents of Kelsey Brena Guy (b. Jul. 30, 1989) and Lindsay Breanna Guy (b. Mar. 9, 1992).

Florence and Harold divorced in 1975, and in 1982 she married Francis Roy Bankston, who died Aug. 10, 1983 in Natchez.

WILLIAM JAMES MCKINLEY & FRANCES BETO.

About 1913 William James McKinley, came to Natchez, MS from Jones County. He and two brothers-in-law were overseeing the plantation Bellemont with the intentions of buying the land. Three of his children attended school at Bellemont. Poor health (malaria) forced him to move back to Jones County where Avery Huff was born Nov. 8, 1920.

He graduated from Jones County in 1939, stayed in Jones County helping on the family farm and was also a carpenter. He enlisted when war broke out and received an honorable discharge as staff sergeant in the 306th Medical Battalion in January 1946. He entered Northern Illinois College of Optometry in Chicago, IL, graduating in 1949.

He brought his new bride Frances Beto McKinley, a native of Dell Rapids, SD, who was a graduate nurse from St. Lukes Hospital School of Nursing in Chicago.

They chose Natchez in 1948 for Avery to practice Optometry because of the good school systems; churches; industries: Johns Mannville, International Paper Co., Tire and Rubber Co., Box Factory, Diamond National, The Port; recreational facilities and activities; a new toll bridge connecting Mississippi and Louisiana; three hospitals plus a very helpful Chamber of Commerce. He opened his office 411 Main Street in 1949. She found work at Natchez General Hospital as an operating room supervisor.

Their first son, William Blair (b. Dec. 24, 1950), md. Elise Dawes, daughter of Harry and Leona Dawes, in 1953. They have two daughters, Chestney and Anna George. Blair's family lives in Starksville.

Second son, Paul Avery (b. Apr. 10, 1953), md. Tanya Brewer, daughter of Charlene and the late James Brewer, in 1976. They have three daughters: Lori Anne McKinley Mardis, Kristie McKinley Parker and Kara McKinley. Lori has a daughter, Berkeley Mardis. Paul's family lives on Berkeley.

Third son, Peter Francis (b. Sep. 28, 1954) md. Martha West of Hazelhurst, the daughter of James and Bessie West, in 1980. They have one daughter Elizabeth Frances and two sons, James Hunter and Peter Beto. Peter's family lives in Hazelhurst.

Avery and Frances were very active in the community and church affairs at Trinity, having taught Sunday school served on vestry and altar guilds. He was a past president of Jaycee's, Lion's Club and past District Governor of Lions Club. He was the originator of the Mississippi Lions Eye Bank which is known world wide.

Berkeley Plantation was purchased, 61 South, to keep the boys busy and off the streets. They could hunt, fish and entertain their friends out in the fresh air. They raised registered Angus cattle, quarter horses, soy beans and hay until they went off to Mississippi State. The work was too much. So all the live stock was sold and the land maintained for hunting. In May and June of 1985 *North and South* was filmed on the land.

Avery passed away in February 1996, while attending a mid-winter conference in Vicksburg. He got his wish, to die with his "boots on." Frances has continued practicing her nursing profession. After the Natchez General Hospital closed, she went to Jefferson Davis Memorial (now the Regional) and worked there until she retired in 1988. She taught at Delta Career College for several years and now is employed with Intensive Home Healthcare since 1991. Frances still works one day a week and is active in civic and church affairs. *Submitted by Francis McKinley.*

VIC MCLEAN & JOYCE THELMA RAGGIO.

My mother was Beatrice "B" Thelma Parsons Raggio

J.R. and Eunice Parsons somewhere in Arkansas in late 1920s or early 1930s

(b. Dec. 5, 1913 in Summit, MS), daughter of John Russell "J.R." and Eunice Lofton Parsons. J.R worked as a car inspector for the Natchez and Southern Railroad. In 1927, they bought property on Morgantown Road, that later was named Parsons Road. When J.R. died in 1942 the family moved to Ouachita Street and ran Burns Grocery on St. Catherine Street, until they moved back to Morgantown. In about 1946 they started Parsons Grocery which was operated by my mother, grandmother Eunice and her sister Louise Burns until the late 1960s. This past summer the old store building was torn down. My mother B was an only child.

My father was James Joseph "J.J." Raggio (b. Jun. 25, 1907, in Lafayette, LA), son of Stefano and Mary Elizabeth Grier Raggio. Their ancestor had wandered up and down the Bayou Teche with Evangeline. Dad was working for the Corp of Engineers when he met my mother. In later years he was a jailer and deputy sheriff under Sheriff Hebert, and as a

(Grandmother) Eunice Parsons, (Mother) Beatrice Raggio and (daughter) Joyce McLean

eighth grader, I lived at the old county jail on State Street. The upstairs was the family quarters. I enjoy telling people I lived at the jail to watch their reaction. Dad had the Hurricane Fence Co in 1955-59. I had a brother, Joseph Russell "Joe" who was two years younger. He was an attorney in Baton Rouge, LA until his death in 1999.

I attended school from the first grade to graduation at Washington School. I am still living in the house I was born in on Morgantown Road, and have been for the biggest part of my life. I have also lived in Frankfort, Germany, Texas, Georgia and South Louisiana.

I have two daughters: Gay (b. Dec. 21, 1966 in Morgan City, LA) md. Lonnie Bielefeld and they have a son Randy. My other daughter, Renee (b. Jan. 20, 1969 in Franklin, LA) is married to Dale Henderson and they have a son Dustin.

I married Vic McLean whose parents were George and Virginia Druetta McLean, whose family has a lot of history in this area. Vic was the record officer for the Natchez Police Dept. until he retired in 1983 because of a stroke. He passed away in 1987. I have seen a lot of changes on Morgantown Road; there were four or five houses between home and Hwy. 61. Now look how it has grown. I remember when they paved it, they put paper over the concrete until it dried, and my mom and other mothers would take turns walking us to the school bus and meeting us in the afternoon, until the paper was removed.

We still attend Lovely Lane Church, where my parents were some of the charter members.

JOAN M. MCLEMORE. Joan Crawford Meadows was born Aug. 24, 1929, in Bivens, TX. Her parents were James Leon Meadows Jr. and Dell Crawford. The Meadows family moved to Natchez in 1939, when Joan's father was employed by Armstrong Tire and Rubber Co. Joan and her brother James attended the Natchez Public Schools. She graduated in 1947. Joan attended Mississippi State College for Women. On May 6, 1950, she married Kenneth Lyons McLemore of Kirby, Franklin County, MS. Kenneth McLemore, a farmer, was born in Kirby on Mar. 5, 1926. His parents were Ephraim M. McLemore and Lura Cameron Lyons. A son, Ken Malcolm McLemore was born on Mar. 12, 1951.

Joan M. McLemore received the master of library science and BS from the University of Southern Mississippi. She served as library trustee in Franklin County from 1962-76. In 1976, she was employed as the librarian in the Franklin County Public Library, Meadville until 1990 when she was employed as Library Director for the Natchez Campus, Copiah-Lincoln Community College.

McLemore has been very active in the professional library world. She served as executive director of National Library Week one year for the Mississippi Library Association and has presented many programs for the Mississippi Library Association at their state conferences. She is also active in The Delta Kappa Gamma Society International, a professional educators organization. She has been an International Speaker and was also chosen to attend the Golden Gift Leadership Seminar at the University of Texas in Austin.

Joan McLemore

McLemore's maternal grandparents were Samuel Cook Crawford and Rachel Victoria Seal, natives of Copiah and Lincoln counties. Her maternal great-grandparents were William Martin Crawford and Melissa Graves of Copiah County, and Mark Anthony Seal and Mary Elizabeth Furr of the Little Bahala Community of Lincoln County. Great-great-grandparents were Anthony Seal and Winnie Jones of Pearl River County and George Crawford and Nancy Martin of Lawrence County. Great-great-great-grandparents were Christian Furr and Catherine Pierce from North Carolina. They settled in what is now Lincoln County.

James Meadows Jr. and Dell Crawford were married in Natchez on Jan. 16, 1927. He was a native of the Oklahoma Territory. He lived from Jan. 13, 1900 to October 1992. Dell Crawford was born in the Little Bahala Community, was reared in Sicily Island, LA where her parents moved when she was very young. James III was born in December 1927 and died June 1981. He is buried in the VA Cemetery, Houston, TX.

Joan McLemore moved to Natchez following the death of her husband in 1997. She is very active in heritage organizations, church activities, and historical groups. She is very much in demand as a public speaker.

Ken M. McLemore married Peggy Jean Arnold on Aug. 4, 1972. They have three children:

Bethany Jo (b. Aug. 29, 1979), Meredith Lacy (b. Jan. 3, 1981) and Samuel Arnold (b. Nov. 7, 1983). Bethany has a degree from MUW in broadcast journalism. The two younger children are students at Mississippi State University at this writing. Ken works at Grand Gulf Nuclear Plant. Peggy teaches at Chamberlain Hunt Academy. They make their home in Port Gibson.

JOHN THOMPSON MCMURRAN & MARY LOUISA TURNER. Mary Louisa Turner (b. Jan. 7, 1814) was the daughter of Eliza Baker and Edward Turner. On Jan. 5, 1831, Mary Louisa Turner married John Thompson McMurran and they settled at Holly Hedges in downtown Natchez. Born Apr. 19, 1801 outside McConnellsburg, PA in Franklin County near Chambersburg, PA, he was the son of Francis McMurran (b. ca. 1770, d. ca. 1825) and Martha Thompson (b. ca. 1775, d. Sep. 5, 1843). Their other children were Martha A. McMurran (b. Dec. 6, 1798; d. Sept. 27, 1880) md. Henry Hoke (b. Jan. 1, 1794) on Aug. 30, 1842; William McMurran (b. Mar. 6, 1806) md. Zusebia Harrison on Nov. 26, 1834); Jane McMurran (b. ca. 1808); Francis McMurran (b. ca. 1810); Marshall McMurran (b. ca. 1812); and Rebecca McMurran (b. ca. 1815) md. John B. Hoke on Jun. 22, 1837.

John T. McMurran moved from Pennsylvania to Chillicothe, OH to read law with his uncle, John Thompson. There he met John Quitman. In 1821 McMurran arrived in Mississippi, working first as a tutor for the children of Gerard C. Brandon. He then began to practice law in Natchez with John Quitman and William Griffith. Griffith had married a daughter of Edward Turner, and Quitman had married Turner's niece.

After Griffith's death in 1827, McMurran joined Quitman as partner in the firm. In 1832 McMurran became Secretary of the Bar in Natchez, and in 1835 he was elected to the state house of representatives but resigned at the end of the session. He became a co-partner with James Carson Jr. In 1842 McMurran was elected to the vestry of Trinity Episcopal Church, where he served almost continually until his death. At various times McMurran assumed whole or partial ownership of cotton plantations at Riverside in Wilkinson County, MS and Killarney and Moro in Louisiana, among others.

The children of Mary Louisa and John T. McMurran were Mary Elizabeth McMurran (b. Oct. 16, 1831, d. Jul. 31, 1833); John Thompson McMurran Jr. (b. Oct. 1, 1833; and Mary Elizabeth McMurran (b. Dec. 28, 1835, d. Mar. 31, 1864). McMurran bought land east of Natchez in 1841 to begin construction of his Melrose estate. The family moved in around 1848 amid a kinship network centered on the Quitmans at Monmouth, and Mrs. McMurran devoted her time to her family duties and to the flower gardens at Melrose. In 1854 the family made a grand tour of Europe.

McMurran was a unionist but sent his son to fight for the Confederacy. After the Civil War, the McMurrans sold Melrose to Elizabeth and George Malin Davis. They moved with their surviving grandson Fazee Conner across the bayou to Woodlands, where Mrs. McMurran's mother, Eliza Turner lived. John Thompson McMurran died in New Orleans Dec. 30, 1866 following the burning of the steamship *Fashion* near Baton Rouge on Dec. 26. Mary Louisa Turner McMurran died at Woodlands May 11, 1891.

JOHN THOMPSON MCMURRAN JR. & ALICE LATIMER AUSTEN. On Dec. 18, 1836, John T. McMurran Jr. (b. Oct. 1, 1833, Natchez) and his sister Mary Eliza were baptized at Trinity Episcopal Church where their father served on the vestry for nearly 20 years. The children lived at Holly

Hedges in downtown Natchez, then at Melrose. John McMurran Jr. attended Princeton, where he met Alice Latimer "Alie" Austen (d. 1899, Hopeville, GA), from Baltimore County, MD. They married at Filston, her family home in Maryland on Sep. 17, 1856 with his sister Mary Eliza and her husband Farar Conner attending. He then brought Alie south to Natchez and Melrose. They later continued on to Wilkinson County, where John managed his father's Riverside Plantation on the Mississippi/Louisiana line. John McMurran Jr. greatly preferred a planter's life to his father's legal profession. It was a great shock for his wife, a self-proclaimed farmer's daughter, to find herself "mistress of plantation" surrounded by "150 souls in some measure responsible for and dependent upon."

The children of John Thompson McMurran Jr. and Alice Latimer Austen were Mary Louisa McMurran (b. 1857, d. Jul. 14, 1858 of whooping cough at Melrose); Caroline "Carrie" McMurran (b. ca. Jan. 3, 1859 at Melrose) md. Frank Loring Dodds in Maryland on Aug. 24, 1880; Alice "Alie" McMurran ("b. Jul. 31, 1861); and an unnamed infant (b. May 22, 1868, d. of heart defect May 26, 1868). Alie McMurran came in to Melrose from the plantation for the birth of each child. In January 1859 she gave birth to her daughter Carrie at Melrose just six days after the birth of her sister-in-law's child in an adjoining bedroom. Carrie was a chubby, dark-haired child; and her sister Alie was fair. In 1901, Carrie's daughter Polly Dodds became the first May Queen on record at Oldfields, a school developed on the Austen family home near Baltimore.

In May 1861, John McMurran Jr. enlisted in the Confederate Army and left Natchez for Pensacola, taking his personal servant Bill Taylor to cook and wash for him. He received a medical discharge due to a hearing loss in November 1861. In 1862 they returned to Wilkinson County, where they rented a house five miles back from the river next to Riverside Plantation, where they could hear the sound of shelling at Fort Hudson and the Red River.

In 1863 he and his wife returned to Glencoe, MD. In 1864-65, probably through his father's family connections, McMurran was living in Washington, DC, working as a clerk recording the wounded and dead from the state of Pennsylvania and hoping for a swift Union victory to bring an end to the war. He was devastated by his father's death at the end of 1866. He and his wife lived apart for many years, and at the time of his mother's death in 1891 he was recorded as a resident of New York City. The date and location of his death are unknown.

METCALFES OF ADAMS COUNTY, MISSISSIPPI. Metcalf was a notable name in England as early as 1390 and established itself at Nappa Hall in Wensleydale in the early 1400s. Sir James Metcalf fought in the Battle of Agincourt and for his services was knighted. He became Lord of the Manor of the magnificent and vast estate of Nappa Hall, the battlemented fortress that he built about 1416.

From this nobleman and his descendants the name sprang into prominence and the surname is common in North Yorkshire today.

Sir James Metcalf had five sons. One, styled Bryan of Beare Parke, had four sons, two of whom were to become persons of special interest to genealogists centuries later. Each of these two brothers became the progenitor of a long line of Metcalfs, all cousins, of course, and they came together by a remarkable coincidence in the state of Mississippi at the time of our Civil War. Leonard, whose line came to this country when Michael Metcalf, a Puritan, and an owner of a cloth factory in Norwich, England, emigrated with his wife and nine children in 1637 and settled in Dedham, MA, and Richard, whose line first appeared on this continent when a John Metcalfe, said to have graduated from Cambridge and received a grant of land in 1716 in the colony of Virginia.

Metcalfe holdings in Adams County, MS, in the 1800s, include Montrose Plantation, Bourbon and York Plantations, Fair Oaks, and Ravenna. "Cousins" from each line, at different times, owned Cherokee.

A direct descendant of Michael Metcalf (b. 1587, d. 1664), the Dornix Weaver, and Sarah Ellwyn (b. 1593, d. 1644), Dr. Asa Baldwin Metcalfe was born on the road, as his parents moved from Vermont to Connecticut in 1800.

His parents Thomas Metcalf (b. 1764, d. 1827) and Sybil Chapin (b. 1768, d. 1869) then migrated to Chardon, Geauga County, OH and both are buried there. Asa was fourth in a family of 12 children.

Asa graduated from medical college in Philadelphia, PA, married Barbara Allen Harris (b. 1802, d. 1891), settled in Geauga County, OH and had two children, Ellen Josephine Metcalfe (b. ca. 1827, d. 1922) and George Edward Metcalfe (b. 1829, d. 1903).

From Ohio, Asa Baldwin Metcalfe brought his family to Adams County, MS about 1830 and settled in the Kingston Community. He practiced medicine in Natchez and New Orleans between 1830-50.

Asa and Barbara had another son and daughter, born in Kingston, MS, Henry Bascom Metcalfe (b. 1831, d. 1853) and Emma Zuleika Metcalfe (b. 1833, d. 1875).

Children of Dr. Asa Baldwin Metcalfe and Barbara Allen Harris Metcalfe:

1) Ellen Josephine Metcalfe married Judge M. John McHenry and migrated to California, where she died and is buried.

2) George Edward Metcalfe married Nancy Adeline Enlow (b. 1838, d. 1882) on Jun. 24, 1854 and they had six children: Jefferson Davis Metcalfe (b. 1858, d. 1934); George W. Metcalfe (b. 1873, d. 1955); Emma Metcalfe; Mollie Eliza Metcalfe; Orrin Metcalfe (b. ca. 1875); and Asa Baldwin Metcalfe (b. 1860, d. 1926).

George E. and Nancy Metcalfe lived, died and are buried in the Silver Creek Community in Wilkinson County, MS.

George E. Metcalfe fought in the War with Mexico, and was a member of the Natchez Southrons, Co B, 10th Mississippi Regiment during the Civil War.

Asa B. Metcalfe, son of George E. and Nancy A. Metcalfe and namesake of his grandfather, Dr. Asa Baldwin Metcalfe, married Francis Lucinda Keller (b. 1866, d. 1904) and they had nine children. Henry McNair Metcalfe, the second son of Asa B. and Francis L. Metcalfe, married Georgia L. Beattie Jan. 23, 1916, and they had six children. The youngest, Elgie G. Metcalfe (Waller), is the mother of this writer and editor. James B. "Jimmy" McManus, son of writer, was born here in Natchez and he and his wife, Rhonda (Ellis), live and work here.

Helen Gousset, standing, and Betty G. Lewis

3) Henry Bascom Metcalfe never married and was drowned in the Mississippi River at the age of 22.

4) Emma Zuleika Metcalfe married Dr. Will-iam Gilbert Hay, and they migrated to San Francisco, CA, where she died and is buried.

Dr. Metcalfe went to California in 1849 to, it was said, establish his two sons a business and, while there, was stricken with cholera and died a year later. He is buried in Sacramento, CA.

Barbara Allen Metcalfe, widow of Dr. Metcalfe, migrated to California a short time after he died and lived the remainder of her life there. She died in 1891 and is buried in Berkeley, Almeda, CA.

Many of Dr. Asa Baldwin Metcalfe's descendants still reside in Adams and Wilkinson counties in Mississippi.

I am told, the "e" was added to Metcalf when Dr. Asa Baldwin Metcalfe and his brother, Oren Metcalfe, migrated to Mississippi.

Thus, we have 17 generations of Metcalfs/ Metcalfes, from 1390 England to present-day Natchez. *Written by Betty G. Lewis and edited by Helen B. Gousset, great-great-great- granddaughters of Dr. Asa Baldwin Metcalfe and Barbara Allen Harris Metcalfe.*

DAVE MILLER & JERUSHA BARNES. Dave (Pleasant Davidson) Miller (b. Nov. 27, 1876 in Pea Ridge, AR, d. May 27, 1957 in Natchez, MS) was the son of William Henderson Miller and Nancy Lavinia Patterson. Dave's forebears were from Warren and Rutherford Counties in Tennessee. Dave Miller married Jerusha (Eliza Jerusha Aglentine) Barnes Feb. 10, 1898 in Seligman, MO. Jerusha (b. Aug. 30, 1881 in Seligman, d. Nov. 13, 1961 in Tipton, OK) was the daughter of Tom (Thomas Jubilee) Barnes and Ziporah Caroline Baker. Early Barnes family history began in Connecticut in the 1600s and the Baker family began in Virginia.

Jerusha and Dave Miller had three children while living in Barry County MO: (1) Electa (b. Aug. 18, 1902) md. Mark Deason July 10, 1921. They lived out their lives in Natchez. (2) Ruth Miller (b. July 2, 1904) md. Chase A. Gough Aug. 30, 1924 in Tipton, OK). He died in Tipton May 3, 1981 and Ruth died Oct. 23, 1995 in Oklahoma City. (3) Coyne (Coyne Connell) Miller Sr. (b. Jun. 25, 1907 in Barry County, MO, d. Oct. 3, 1986 in Natchez).

Coyne and his father, Dave, came to Natchez in the fall of 1924 and opened a market for northwest Arkansas apples. Dave's brothers owned orchards in Benton County, AR, and along with other growers, supplied Coyne and Dave with excellent apples. They supplied many of the apples sold in the Natchez area for several years. Coyne would deliver to the surrounding counties in Mississippi (and into Louisiana) while Dave operated a retail fruit store on Franklin Street. The store was called Miller's Apple House and Dave was known as "Apple Miller."

Coyne married Florence Kuehn on July 1, 1928 in Natchez. She is a daughter of Charles August Kuehn and Annie Elizabeth Annis (See Charles August Kuehn history). Coyne and Florence bought a service station on Homochitto Street in 1929. Coyne and Byron Webb (a cousin from Missouri) formed a partnership in 1933 and purchased a gas and oil distributorship from Walton Hootsell Sr. The partnership prospered for years and Miller and Webb became involved in ranching and real estate in later years.

Coyne and Florence had three children born in Natchez: Connell (Coyne Connell) Miller Jr. (b. Jun. 20, 1929); Mary Jean Miller (b. Feb. 23, 1931); and Ruth Allene Miller (b&d. Jan. 20, 1937).

Connell Miller Jr. married Mary Lou McKeel Aug. 28, 1954 in Allen, OK. Connell and Mary Lou attended Oklahoma A&M, graduating in 1956 with degrees in veterinary medicine and home economics, respectively. They then moved to Natchez where Connell established the Natchez Veterinary Clinic in which he practiced for 26 years. They are the parents of five children, all born in Natchez: Lacie Elizabeth (b. Oct. 16, 1958) md. Joe Gorder Jul. 10, 1982 and had Casey and Allison; Cheryl Leigh (b. Aug. 3, 1960) earned her degree in computer science at Ole Miss in 1982 and lives in Houston, TX; Melinda Lou (b. Feb. 16, 1963, d. May 11, 1963); James Davidson "David" and his twin Coyne Connell III "Connell" (b. Feb. 28, 1965). David married Kim Albritton and they have Logan and Lauren. Connell III married Brandae Ratcliff and they have Cade.

CLARA ANN MONTGOMERY & AUSTIN WILLIAMS SMITH. Clara Ann (b. May 10, 1845 in Fayette, Jefferson County, MS) was the ninth of 12 children born to Prosper King Montgomery and Maria Lanier Darden. Five of her brothers served in the Confederate Army, four came home. Her brother, Jefferson Darden Montgomery, was killed Jun. 20, 1862, near Charleston, SC.

Clara Ann married Austin Williams Smith of Adams County May 14, 1867. Austin served in the late war with the 4th Louisiana Battalion and was the Color Bearer. Clara and Austin married at the Montgomery home in Fayette.

The bride's aunt, Susan Sillers Darden, described Clara's dress in her diary. "Clara's dress was crape barege, white, trimmed with white ribbon running down each width. Rosett and bead at the end of each strip. There was seven rows in front and six in the back of the same trimming; the sleeves made tight, coat sleeve with two puffs at the top. White ribbon round the neck tied in a bow, white sash fastened in front. White rose in her hair. They were married with a ring."

The couple resided at Austin's Plantation home, Saragossa, about five miles south of Natchez. To this union were born four children. Anna Clotilde (b. Jul. 10, 1870); Willie Madison (b. Jun. 8, 1872; and twins, Davidson Routh and William Haslett (b. Dec. 16, 1880). William Haslett died at birth and was buried in the family vault at Saragossa.

There were many hard times ahead for Austin and Clara. By December 1867, it was said that Austin "has given up all, is broken entirely." However, they were able to continue, pay their taxes, keep some of their plantation land and were not immediately touched by the scourges of yellow fever and typhoid fever. The family did not escape tragedy though. Austin's brother, Haller Routh, died Jan. 5, 1867 while cleaning his rifle at Saragossa, William Madison died violently Nov. 9, 1871 in a gin accident in Vidalia, and John Davidson died Jan. 10, 1883.

Austin's mother, Anna Elizabeth Williams Smith, lived at Saragossa with Clara and Austin until her death Oct. 4, 1889. Her brother-in-law, Dr. Stratton, recorded in his diary "she had just completed her 69th year. She was unselfish and affectionate to the last degree. Her gentle spirit passed away from the worn out body without a pang or struggle."

Clara Ann died Jul. 30, 1897, "after an illness of only 20 hours. Her sudden removal was caused by some form of heart trouble" according to Dr. Stratton. Dr. Neel conducted her service at the Presbyterian Church, Jul. 31, 1897. Clara was buried in the vault with her mother-in-law and father-in-law in Routh Cemetery. A large number of friends attended the service. Her husband, Austin, died Apr. 15, 1911 and was buried with Clara and his parents in the vault.

Many years after Clara died, someone asked Caroline (Mammy) Burke to tell them about Clara. Mammy said, *Miz Clara was one blessed saint. Submitted by Diane Stovall Little.*

EDITH WYATT MOORE (b. 1884 in Tunnel Hill, GA, d. 1973) md. Frank Moore (b. 1883, d. 1930) from Villanow, GA, around 1903. Two daughters were born in Tunnel Hill, Camilla (b. 1906, d. 1985) and Virgina (b. 1910, d. 1990). The family settled in Natchez around 1915. Frank worked as an engineer for the Y-M-V and Mississippi Southern Railroads until his death in 1930.

Edith reared the daughters and after receiving degrees in history and journalism from LSU and Mississippi College, began researching the histories of many crumbling structures in this area. Her efforts resulted in the formation of the Historical Society and preservation of the beautiful homes that attract tourists to this region. Edith also traveled to many cit-

Edith Wyatt Moore at Connelly's Tavern, 1932

ies across America lecturing on Natchez's outstanding features and spent quite sometime in Washington, DC, lobbying Congress to make the Natchez trace a national parkway.

She served in the WAC from 1943-45, returned to Natchez, set up the library at the "new" Catholic school, wrote many articles for newspapers and national magazines, had a book published in 1965, *Natchez Under The Hill* (reprinted three times), and spent her last 20 years guiding thousands of tourists through Connelly's Tavern which was one of her Natchez Garden Club's early resto-projects.

Camilla Emerick (2nd on stairs) and Edith Wyatt Moore lower left

In death she left her two daughters, Camilla and Earl Emerick, an ICRR engineer; Virginia and Dr. Fred Geisenberger; two grandsons, Evan Emerick, a serviceman for Sears, his wife Judy Daniels and three great-granddaughters; and Wilfred Geisenberger, a prominent attorney.

LEOPOLD MORITZ & SOPHIA MARS. Leopold (b. 1808, d. 1879) and Sophia (b. 1820, d. 1902) had children: Celeste Moritz (b. 1845, d. 1890) md. David Arents, Leon Moritz (b. 1851, d. 1935) md. Dorothea Katherine Miller (b. 1850, d. 1899), Bernard Moritz (b. 1854, d. 1924), Charles Moritz (b. 1862), and David Moritz.

Leon and Dorothea had eight children:

A) Bernard Eugene Moritz (b. 1875, d. 1933) md. Rosa Gwin Swazye (b. 1881, d. 1985) and had children:

1) Bernard Eugene Moritz Jr. (b. 1903, d. 1958) md. first Evelyn Elizabeth Farr and had Leona Moritz; md. second Lillian Foster and had Mary Lou Moritz.

2) James Benton Moritz (b. 1906, d. 1959) md. Frances Mildred Moore and had Frances Moore who md. Kent Wilson.

3) Edith Elizabeth Moritz (b. 1910, d. 1985) md. Samuel Bentley Burns (b. 1908, d. 1969) and had Edith Rose Burns.

4) Joseph Samuel Moritz (b. 1919) md. Jane Stewart Enochs (b. 1922) and had Bernard Eugene Moritz III (b. 1941) and Joseph Samuel Moritz Jr. (b. 1945). Bernard Eugene md. Jeanelle Lowe and had:

a) Jennine Lowe Moritz who md. Scott Sherrill and had William Stewart Sherrill (b. 1998) and twins Anna Foster Sherrill and Maura "Molly" Sherrill (b. 2000).

b) Eugene Stewart Moritz (b. 1968) who md. Maura Kathleen O'Shea and had Claire Sidney Moritz (b. 1999).

B) Clarence Edward Moritz (b. 1876, d. 1932) md. Betty Polkinghorn and had Clare Moritz and Hartman Moritz who md. Mary Ethlyn.

C) Leo E. Moritz (b. 1880, d. 1945) md. Bertha Taylor (b. 1883, d. 1957). They had three children:

1) Leo E. Moritz Jr. (b&d. 1903)

2) Arthur Leon Moritz (b. 1904, d. 1985) md. Leonore Anna Koerber (b. 1906, d. 1992) and had Leonore Marie Moritz (b. 1931) who md. Paul Vincent O'Malley (b. 1930). They had four children:

a) Marilyn Denise O'Malley (b. 1953) md. first Danny Richardson, second Charles Michael Fields, third Carl Sandidge (b. 1950). They had two children:

i) Anna Denise O'Malley (b. 1971) who md. Christopher Michael Whalen (b. 1971) and had Riley Erin Whalen (b. 1994) and Christopher Paul Whalen (b. 1996).

ii) Carl Vincent O'Malley (b. 1976).

b) Paula Lynne O'Malley (b. 1954, d. 1990) md. William Felton Cameron (b. 1947, d. 1999) and had Christopher Albert Cameron (b. 1981) and Justin Stewart Cameron (b. 1985).

c) Arthur Austin O'Malley (b. 1956, d. 1983).

d) Kevin Albert O'Malley (b. 1960).

3) Rosalie Moritz (b. 1906).

D) Eva M. Moritz (b. 1882) md. S Sampson Levy

E) Beulah Moritz (b. 1884, d. 1890)

F) Harold Miller Moritz

G) Pearl Moritz

H) Estelle B. Moritz md. Walter H. May

Current Natchez residents are Mrs. Bernard Eugene Moritz Jr. (Lillian), Joe Sam and Jane Moritz, and Paul and Leonore O'Malley.

GEORGE WEST MOSS & MARGARET ABNEY. George West Moss was born on May 26, 1913 to Margaret Purnell Handy and Philip Ball Moss in Selma, AL and died Jul. 24, 2002 in Natchez, MS. George had four siblings: Marjorie, Ruth, Helen and Philip. He took a BS in biology (1935) and BS in physical education (1937), both from the University of Alabama. After serving as an instructor in the Army Air Corps in Madison, MS, he joined the OSS (Office of Strategic Service), which became the CIA following WWII.

Margaret Lola Abney Moss was born to Marietta Alexander and James William Abney on Nov. 3, 1921 in Montrose, MS. She is the sister of Alice Gammage and James Abney. After completing studies at East Central Junior College she

went on to earn a BA in Music from Mississippi State College for Women in 1942. Margaret then took a job at Madison High School where she taught music and there met George. George and Margaret were married on Jul. 15, 1943 in Montrose.

After the war George and Margaret moved to Birmingham, where George attended medical school at UAB and completed his residency

George W. Moss and Margaret A. Moss

at Birmingham's Hill-Burton Hospital. They moved to Natchez in 1951 and George established a medical practice with Swink Hicks and Alan Reed. George was a sole practitioner from 1963-91, completing 40 years of practice.

Texada, first brick house in Natchez, ca. 1795.

George was passionately committed to his practice of family medicine. He was an outstanding athlete from his youth onward, excelling at tennis, swimming, football, baseball, and basketball; he helped found the Natchez YMCA. An avid outdoorsman, George was also a hunter and fisherman. In his later years he enjoyed golfing, scuba diving, card and board games, as well as piloting airplanes. George was an Elder at First Presbyterian Church, a Rotarian, and an enthusiastic supporter of historic preservation.

Margaret was a deacon at the First Presbyterian Church and served as president of Women of the Church. She was music director for the historic Natchez Pageant for 18 years and a pianist for numerous Natchez Little Theatre productions. She was president of the Natchez Junior Auxiliary. She was twice president of the Natchez Garden Club and twice president of the Historic Natchez Foundation. In 1963 Margaret and George bought and restored Texada, at 222 South Wall Street, where Margaret resides and which she shows on the Fall and Spring Pilgrimage Tours. Margaret, with business partners, Mimi Miller and Neil Varnell, has restored three other historic houses in Natchez.

George and Margaret's four children are Lelia Alice Moss Mahood (b. 1944 in Jackson, MS) of Dallas, TX who was married to the late Stephen Carroll Mahood (d. 1998) and has two daughters, Katherine Waldrop and Margaret Struthers; George West Moss, Jr. (b. 1946 in Newton, MS) of Brownsville, TN who is married to Amy Floyd Moss and has three children: George III, Philip, and Emily Carpenter; James Abney Moss (b. 1949 in Birmingham, AL) of Jackson, MS who is married to Durden Pillow Moss and has three children: Mary Ann, Helen and Jim; and Helen Moss Smith (b. 1952 in Natchez) of Lafayette, LA who is married to Randall Lamar Smith and has four children: Hannah, Marietta, Randall Jr. and Andrew.

SOME INFO FROM 1880 CENSUS MCCLEAN COUNTY, IL & FLOYD COUNTY, IN PROBATE RECORDS & PHILSON CLUB VOL. 53, 1979, LOUISVILLE, JEFFERSON COUNTY, KY.

Clement Nance Jr. married Martha Chamberlain.

Jane Nance (b. Jan. 28, 1822, Floyd County, IN, d. Jan. 1, 1892, in Chicago) md. Andrew Jackson Snider; children: Albert W. Snider (d. ca. 1887-90 in Chicago).

George Goodwin married Lillian Green and lived in St. Louis, MO; children: Pearl Alice, Nona, Ann (called Pat) and __. Lillian married second Henry Meyer.

Pearl Alice Goodwin (b. Sep. or Jun. 11, 1881, d. Aug. 5, 1955, Cook County, IL) md. first, Andrew Curtis Snider (b. Jun. 3, 1870, d. Jul. 16, 1922); children: Curtis (stillborn) and Claude Henry. Pearl married second Jack Hollie and third Edmund Rheine.

Thomas Baxter (b. 1626 in England?).

Thomas Baxter.

John Baxter married Martha Close.

John Baxter married Lidia Belle Reed.

Daniel Reed Baxter married Bethia Crosby.

June Baxter (b. 1805, Madison County) md. Elizabeth Lennox (b. Chetauqua County); children, Walter and George, English Secretary for Styvesten.

Walter Baxter (b. 1829 in Chetauqua County, NY. d. between 1860-66) md. Delilah Rue Fairbanks on Jul. 20, 1851; children, Elizabeth and __.

Casper Snider an original settler of York County, PA and probably born in 1725; sons, Anthony and Jacob. Casper is a Swiss name.

Anthony Snider has sons, Anthony, Jacob and John

Anthony Snider (b. 1780 in York County, PA, d. l843) md. Elizabeth Brookhart May 9, 1803 in Jefferson County, KY. Elizabeth is the daughter of Philip from York County, PA, who is the son of Michael Brugart from Rotterdam and Barbara.

Andrew Jackson Snider (b. Oct. 20, 1817, Louisville, Jefferson County, KY, d. 1898, El Paso, Woodford County, IL) md. Jane Nance on Nov. 18, 1841; children, Albert W. Snider, __)

Albert W. Snider (b. 1846 in Floyd County, IN, d. 1876/80 in Livingston County, IL??) md. Elizabeth Baxter on Sep. 21, 1868; child, Andrew Curtis-shown in census living with his grandmother Delilah Rue Baxter (see Walter Baxter above). Both parents died before Andrew was 11 years old.

Andrew Curtis Snider (b. Jun. 3, 1869 in Pontiac, Livingston County, IL, d. Jul. 16, 1922, Chicago) md. Pearl Alice Goodwin; children, Curtis (stillborn) and Claude Henry.

Claude Henry Snider (b. Nov. 30, 1903 in Chicago, d. Jan. 15, 1956, in Des Plaines, Cook County, IL) md. first Margaret Fleming Persell in Chicago; child Neville Curtis adopted by George Marshall and called Neville Buck Marshall. Married second Edna M. Hoeft; children: Suzanne,

Alisan, Curtis Claude. Claude graduated N.W. Military Academy in Wisconsin, was surveyor for NW Railroad, Art Director for the National Dairy Assn. and associate art director for Rand McNally.

Neville Curtis Snider known as Neville Buck Marshall (b. Dec. 10, 1924, d. Dec. 26, 1990), child of Claude Henry Snider and Margaret Fleming Persell, married first Margaret Jeannette Burkley, married second Emily Stubbs Kelley, married third Jennie Lou Bryan (children: Margaret Katherine, Marion Jeannette, Charlotte Agnes Anne Elizabeth, Malquin Morgan, Neville Buck II and Joan Fleming).

Children of Claude Henry Snider and Edna: Suzanne C. Snider (b. 1931, d. September 1994), 708-577-9024, 1998 Stillwater, Arlington Heights, IL 60004.

Alisan Snider Srinivasan (b. 1942 (Sandhya, Leela, Nina, Neil) 914-454-3874; 15 Mark Vincent Dr., Poughkeepsie, NY 12603

Curtis Claude Snider (b. 1943 (Geoffry Curtis) 815-459-0557; 475 Edgebrook Dr., Crystal Lake, IL 60014

Children of Neville Buck Marshall (b. Dec. 10, 1924, d. Dec. 26, 1990) and Margaret Jeannette Burkley (b. Feb. 18, 1928).

Margaret Katherine "Kathy" Marshall (b. Oct. 12, 1950) md. Monroe Jackson Moody Jr.; children: Monroe Jackson "Jack" III (b. Feb. 15, 1968, d. Mar. 1, 2002, in Houston, TX, buried at Laurel Hill in Adams County, MS) md. Cara Winter, son Monroe Jackson IV Apr. 26, 2001; Merrick Rowan Dashiell (b. Feb. 6, 1972) md. Jackie Passbach Jan. 13, 2001, 1054 Lower Woodville Rd., Natchez, MS, 39120 (601-445-9760).

Marion Jeannette Marshall (b. Apr. 1, 1952) md. first Godfrey Forrester, married second John Darius Tassistro, married third Mike Holloway, married fourth Mark Drennen; children: Angelique "Angie" Devereux Tassistro (b. May 12, 1974), Rodney Darius Tassistro (b. Feb. 21, 1976), Adrienne Marshall Drennen (b. Feb. 7, 1985), lives in St. Francisville, LA.

Charlotte Elizabeth Agnes Anne Marshall (b. Jul. 13, 1953) md. first Elliot Brumfield, married second Alan Edmonds; children: Charlotte Aaron Brumfield (b. Sep. 6, 1974) md. first Casey Smith, son Walker (b. Aug. 21, 1996), married second, Jason Hennington, daughter Pressley, son Braden Starnes, Chesney Dawn Brumfield (b. Jun. 2, 1976) md. Jeremiah Wheeler, daughter Miah Brailey (b. Apr. 26, 2002), Elliot Buck Brumfield (b. Oct. 5, 1978), Rachel Megan Edmonds (b. May 7, 1981) md. Wesley Givens, son, Marshall (b. Feb. 10, 2001), 219 Clifton Ave., Natchez, MS 39120 (601-445-4889).

Malquin Morgan Marshall (b. Aug. 29, 1954) md. first Salvo Piazza, married second Peter Pevonka; children: Emily Johanna Piazza (b. Jan. 17, 1976), Jessica Conchetta Magdalena Piazza (b. May 17, 1977), 5824 S.E. 185th Ave., Micanopy, FL 32667 (904-466-0465).

Neville Buck Marshall II (b. Sep. 12, 1957) md. Beth Anderson; children, Charlotte Kay (b. Dec. 24, 1988) and Morgan Keene (b. Sep. 22, 1991), living in Flagstaff, AZ.

Child of Neville Buck Marshall (b. Dec. 10, 1924, d. Dec. 26, 1990) and Jennie Lou Bryan.

Joan Fleming (b. Sep. 6, 1976) md. Samuel Gatlin on Dec. 22, 2001). *Submitted by Joan Marshall Gatlin.*

ROBERT A. NEAL & NANCY DILLON. Robert Neal (b. Sep. 29, 1937 in Alva, MS) and Nancy Dillon (b. Apr. 5, 1938 in Memphis, TN) were married on Aug. 2, 1957 in Senatobia, MS. Both having graduated from Senatobia City High School, Robert attended Northwest Junior College, Senatobia, and Nancy attended the University of Tampa in Tampa, FL. Robert worked at

Senatobia's Royal Crown Bottling Co., of which his father was part owner. Robert worked as a route salesman, and Nancy worked in the office of the Superintendent of Education in Tate County, MS.

On Jan. 1, 1961 Robert and Nancy moved to Natchez, MS, and from C.J. Hinson they purchased the Royal Crown Bottling Co., located on the corner of Homochitto Street and John R. Junkin Drive, Natchez. Robert managed the plant, as well as being route driver. Nancy worked in the office and also as checker. Bottling operation was done at night after the routes had been finished for the day.

The Neals moved into their newly constructed home at 13 Shadow Lane, Natchez, on Feb. 7, 1961. Both Robert and Nancy soon became active members of nearby Parkway Baptist Church, where Robert was ordained as a deacon on Oct. 15, 1972.

Although the bottling operation continued for almost a year at the local plant in Natchez, the product was eventually bottled in Vicksburg and trucked to the Natchez plant. In 1965, the business was sold to Bill E. Sledge of Vicksburg, and on Nov. 5, 1965 Robert began working at Natchez Coca-Cola Co. as an extra route salesman. Within three months he was promoted to route supervisor. Thereafter, he became service manager, sales manager, and operations manager, retiring on Mar. 31, 1997.

In March 1966 Nancy began her employment with the Natchez-Adams School District at the Institute Building on Commerce Street. Spending her entire career in the business department, she was payroll clerk, administrative assistant, assistant business manager, business manager, and purchasing agent, retiring on Jun. 30, 1997.

Lisa Anne Neal, daughter of Robert and Nancy, was born Jan. 22, 1968 in Natchez. After attending Trinity Episcopal Day School and Montebello Elementary School, she graduated from South Natchez High in 1986. Lisa attended Copiah-Lincoln Community College in Natchez and North Louisiana University in Monroe LA. On Jun. 20, 1998 Lisa married Peter Christopher Hollingsworth of Memphis, TN, at Parkway Baptist Church, Natchez. The Hollingsworths reside in Southaven, MS. Lisa is a loan officer with GMAC, and Peter works at Memphis Coca-Cola. Their son, Dillon Christopher Hollingsworth, was born Sep. 4, 1999, in Memphis, TN.

RONALD E. "RONNIE" NETTLES & ROSE-MARY JONES. Ronald was born Apr. 25, 1961, in Natchez, MS. His mother is Mary Hadskey Nettles (b. Apr. 9, 1939, in Delhi, LA). His mother is a retired school teacher who taught in Natchez and Franklin County. His father is Ronald Edward Nettles (b. Nov. 21, 1934, in Natchez, MS). Ronnie's father was a self-employed paint con-

Ronnie and Rosie Nettles with children, Jordan and Brandon

tractor and cattle farmer in Jefferson and Franklin counties.

Ronnie was married to Rosemarie Jones "Rosie" Nettles on Nov. 28, 1988 in Natchez, MS, at St. Mary's Cathedral. Rosie's mother is Rita Eidt Jones Tebbetts. She is a homemaker who was born on Aug. 8, 1939. Rita is now married to Harvey Tebbetts, and they live in Natchez. Rosie's father was Walter "Wally" Eugene Jones (b. Sep. 9, 1930, d. Dec. 6, 1987), who owned and operated auto parts stores in Natchez and Vidalia, LA.

Ronnie has one brother, Jerry Wayne Nettles, and one sister, Lydia Elane Nettles Parker.

Rosie's brothers are Charles Hunter Jones, Vaughn Richard Jones, Walter Eugene Jones, and James Francis Jones. Her sisters are Valerie Ann Jones Heifler and Margaret Elaine Jones.

Ronnie grew up in the McNair Community in Jefferson County and attended Thomas Jefferson and Trinity Episcopal schools in Natchez. He graduated from Trinity Episcopal High School in 1979. Rosie was reared in Natchez and attended Cathedral School until her graduation in 1983.

Ronnie attended the University of Southern Mississippi in Hattiesburg and graduated with a BS degree in political science in 1983, and a master of education degree in counseling and personnel services in 1986. He graduated from the University of Mississippi with a doctor of philosophy degree in educational leadership in 1994. Rosie attended the University of Southern Mississippi and graduated with a BS in business administration degree in marketing in 1987 and a master of education degree in counseling and personnel services in 1990.

Ronnie serves as Dean of the Natchez Campus of Copiah-Lincoln Community College. He previously worked on the Wesson Campus of Co-Lin and at the University of Southern Mississippi. Rosie is the elementary counselor at Cathedral School. She worked previously at the University of Southern Mississippi, William Carey College, and Mississippi State University.

Ronnie and Rosie have two children, daughter Jordan Elaine Nettles (b. Oct. 10, 1993, in Hattiesburg, MS) and son Brandon Edward Nettles (b. Jul. 4, 1995, in Brookhaven, MS); both attend Cathedral School in Natchez.

Rosie and Ronnie are involved in the local community. Ronnie serves on American Red Cross Board and previously served on the Chamber of Commerce Board. Rosie is a member of Junior Auxiliary of Natchez. Ronnie and Rosie are active members of St. Mary's Basilica.

NEWMAN-WHITAKER-DOWNING. The patriarch of the Newman family settled in Adams County, MS, Territory in 1788, was Isaac Newman, the son of Henry Newman died in Somerset County, MD in 1774. Before Henry's death, Isaac moved to southwestern Pennsylvania. In 1788, due to Indian uprisings in the area, he sent his family to the Mississippi Territory.

Benjamin Newman and Ezekiel arrived in Natchez, January to July of 1788, with the family. Isaac and his family were in the 1792 Spanish Census.

Isaac Newman bought land on Cole's Creek that Charles King acquired in a Spanish Grant. Benjamin, Ezekiel and Simeon also settled here.

Isaac Newman died between 1805-07 in Adams County but his will has been lost. He married Nancy Robinson in Somerset County, MD ca. 1758, and they had the following known children:

Henry Newman (b. 1759, d. 1835) settled in Shelby County, KY.

Rachel Newman (b. 1761, d. 1826) md. George Selser Sep. 25, 1776 in Pennsylvania. They established Selsertown in Jefferson County by 1790 and had 13 children.

Benjamin Newman (b. 1763, d. 1819) md. Elizabeth McKinley and they settled on Cole's Creek. He died in Jefferson County They had seven children.

Ezekiel Newman (b. 1767, d. 1830) md. Elizabeth Harrison in Shelby County, KY in 1797, after her death he married Clarinda and had 13 children.

Reuben Newman (b. 1770, d. 1827) md. Sarah Rabb from Pennsylvania. They lived first on Cole's Creek and then Warren County, MS. They had nine children.

Simeon Newman (b. 1775, d. 1826) md. Margaret Harrison in Shelby County, KY in 1797. Simeon and Reuben inherited their father's land and in 1807, Simeon sold his half to Reuben. Simeon lived in Warren County for a while where his second marriage took place to Sarah Reese (Clark) Cook in 1823. He died in Jefferson County, MS and had nine children.

Ann Newman (b. Mar. 26, 1779, in Pennsylvania, d. Jul. 16, 1855, in Raymond, Hinds County, MS) became the second wife of Daniel Whitaker in Natchez on Jun. 6, 1795. His first wife was Elizabeth Gibson and they had three children. After Daniel's death in 1809, Ann married Thomas Downing in 1811. Her Whitaker children were Isaac, Daniel Jr., Elizabeth, Aaron, Hiram Robinson, and Sidney who died before 1820. These Whitakers all moved to Warren County, MS.

Ann and Thomas Downing left Adams County in 1818, moving to Marion County, MS and then to Raymond by 1829, where both died. Their children were:

Thomas Downing Jr. (b. May 17, 1812, in Adams County) md. Elizabeth Crane in 1833 and lived at Reeves Chapel. Thomas Jr. had 11 children and died Nov. 19, 1882.

Gerard Brandon Downing (b. Aug. 25, 1815, in Washington, Adams County) md. Hannah R. Belcher in 1847 and they had seven children. G.B. served in

Ann Newman Whitaker Downing around 1850.

the Civil War and died in 1870 in Raymond.

James Monroe (b. 1816, d. 1826).

Reuben Newman Downing (b. Dec. 20, 1820, in Marion County, d. 1853 in Bolton, Hinds County) md. Elizabeth Bolton in 1848 and had one daughter. He served in the Mexican War.

HALLER NUTT & JULIA WILLIAMS. In 1861, wealthy cotton planter Haller Nutt, son of Rush and Eliza Ker Nutt, and his wife Julia, daughter of Austin and Caroline Routh Williams, were building Longwood, an octagonal house unlike any Natchez had seen before. But the mansion was never finished. Some six months before completion, the War Between the States broke out and the workmen laid down their tools and paintbrushes, never to return.

In 1864, Haller Nutt died. The diagnosis was pneumonia, but legend insists that he died of a broken heart over his dream house. Julia and the children lived on in the basement doing only a minimum to maintain the great hulk looming over them. She died in 1897 and was buried beside her husband in the Longwood family cemetery.

Ten of their 11 children rest there with them. They are Fannie Smith Nutt (b. May 5, 1846, d. Aug. 21, 1848); Julia Williams Nutt (b. Apr. 3, 1857, d. Apr. 24, 1932); Lily Nutt Ward (b. Jun. 4, 1861, d. Jul. 12, 1930); Carrie Routh Nutt Forsyth

Longwood

(b. 1841/42, d. Jan. 3, 1867); Mary Ella Nutt (b. 1843/44, d. Aug. 19, 1901); Haller Nutt Jr. (b. Nov. ?, 1848, d. Dec. 10, 1899); John Ker Nutt (b. Feb. ?, 1850, d. Sep. 29, 1921); Austin Nutt (b. 1852, d. Jan. 7, 1860); Calvin Routh Nutt (b. Aug. ?, 1859, d. Apr. 28, 1909); and Rushworth Nutt (b. Mar. 26, 1863, d. Mar. 29, 1863). Their son, Sargeant Prentiss Knut, Lieutenant (JG) USNRF (b. May 1, 1855, d. Jan. 3, 1939) is buried in Section 6, Grave No. 9401 in Arlington Cemetery.

Grandchildren owned Longwood until 1968 and today, still unfinished, it is maintained by the Pilgrimage Garden Club. The average visitor will ask, "Why not finish it now?" "No," comes the answer, "leave it as a monument to the heart-rending break of the War Between the States. Let it mark the end of an era."

WILLIAM THOMAS AND ALICE LAFAYE O'BRIEN. William Thomas O'Brien Jr. (b. Jun. 24, 1916 in New Orleans) was the son of William Thomas and Wilhelmina Muhs O'Brien. William was reared in Bay St. Louis, MS and attended St. Stanislaus School. In 1941, he was graduated from Loyola University in New Orleans with the doctor of dental surgery degree. He enlisted in the U.S. Navy in 1941 and was stationed in Texas and California. From 1944 to 1945, he served as commanding officer of the naval base dental clinic on the Philippine island of Samar. William returned to New Orleans in 1945 and was discharged from the Navy with the rank of lieutenant commander. His grandfather, John O'Brien, served in the Fourth Louisiana Regiment of the Confederate Army and was captured at the Battle of Port Hudson, LA in 1863.

On Oct. 17, 1941, William married Alice Louise Lafaye in New Orleans. Alice (b. Jul. 28, 1919 in New Orleans), the daughter of Rayel Walter and Catherine Ring Lafaye, was reared in New Orleans and attended Sophie Wright High School. In 1940, she graduated from Loyola University with a bachelor's degree in music. Artistic talent was a prominent feature of the Lafaye family. Alice's aunt, Lucille Lafaye, was active as a performer in the New Orleans French Opera House; and her cousin, Julian Lafaye, who changed his name to John Carroll, was a successful screen actor.

In February 1946, William and Alice settled in Natchez, MS for its many quality opportunities. William started his dental practice on Main Street and the family made their home on Park Place. In 1956, the O'Briens purchased the home at 310 North Commerce Street that accommodated both William's dental practice and their large family. The O'Brien children warmly remember growing up surrounded by much love and happiness in this Victorian home. William retired in his 50th year as a dentist in 1991, and he and Alice have remained in Natchez since that time.

William and Alice's children are: Lynne Catherine (b. Nov. 4, 1943 in Galveston, TX) md. Robert L. Henry; Barbara Jeanne (b. May 5, 1945

60th wedding anniversary of William and Alice Thomas O'Brien. L-R: James, Lynne, Kathleen, William, Alice, Barbara, William III and David

in New Orleans) md. Wilba R. Brock; Kathleen Alice Letaw (b. Apr. 25, 1948 in Natchez); William Thomas III (b. Aug. 31, 1951 in Natchez); David Rayel (b. Jun. 29, 1954 in Natchez); and James Stewart (b. Jun. 27, 1957 in Natchez).

William and Alice are communicants of St. Mary Basilica, where Alice was assistant organist, and have participated in the Natchez community through the Natchez Garden Club, Kiwanis Club, Knights of Columbus, and American Legion. Alice also served as music faculty member of the Natchez Campus of Copiah-Lincoln Junior College, and taught piano to children and adults. Their children were educated in the Natchez Cathedral and public schools, and engaged in various activities that included scouting and the Natchez Pilgrimage Confederate Pageant. The O'Briens have 17 grandchildren and four great-grandchildren, and are in their 57th year of fondly calling Natchez their home.

ELIZABETH OVERAKER & GABRIEL TICHENOR. Elizabeth was born in the Mississippi Territory in 1782 and is the oldest daughter of George Overaker and his wife Margaret. On Apr. 10, 1805 Elizabeth married Gabriel Tichenor in Adams County, Mississippi Territory. From this marriage there was one child. The 1820 census for Natchez, Adams County, MS for the family of Gabriel Tichenor listed one white female of under 10 years of age. The 1830 census for the city of Natchez for the family of Gabriel Tichenor listed one female child of 5 and under 10 years of age.

In 1809 the Bank of Mississippi was chartered in Natchez. The bank had the exclusive right to do business in Mississippi for 36 years. Cowles Mead was one of the founding stockholders. Gabriel Tichenor was the cashier of the bank under Stephen Duncan, president. Many personal accounting records and correspondence of Gabriel Tichenor as cashier of the bank are on file with the Mississippi Department of Archives and History.

On Dec. 14, 1820 Gabriel Tichenor was appointed by J.C. Calhoun, Secretary of War, as agent to pay Revolutionary War Pensions in Mississippi. Gabriel Tichenor was one of the executors of the estate of Lewis Evans who died in Natchez in December 1823. Lewis Evans was the brother of Margaret, wife of George Overaker.

In about 1832-33 Gabriel Tichenor and his wife Elizabeth, Margaret Overaker and Maria Overaker moved to Cincinnati, OH. Most likely they went up the Mississippi and Ohio rivers by steamboat. The 1850 census for Hamilton County, OH, Fulton Township listed the family of Gabriel Tichenor to include his wife Elizabeth, Margaret Overaker and Maria Overaker. The census recorded Gabriel Tichenor to be a farmer, the value of real estate as $15,000, the place of his birth as New Jersey and Mississippi as the birth place for the other family members. The will of Gabriel Tichenor, probated Feb. 7, 1855 in Hamilton County, OH in the

city of Cincinnati, bequeathed to his nephew, Henry C. Freeman, his lot of land in Newark, NJ being a part of the family property called the Cove.

Gabriel Tichenor was a trustee of Lane Theological Seminary in Cincinnati during the time Lyman Beecher (father of Harriet Beecher Stowe, author of *Uncle Tom's Cabin*) was president. The seminary has no portrait painting of Gabriel Tichenor, although there are paintings of some other trustees of the seminary of his time. The family lived in the wealthy neighborhood of Walnut Hill in Cincinnati. Gabriel Tichenor died on Feb. 2, 1855 and Elizabeth died on Jun. 1, 1860. Gabriel Tichenor, Elizabeth Tichenor, Maria Overaker and Margaret Overaker were buried at Walnut Hill Cemetery and re-interred at Spring Grove Cemetery in 1878 in the Lane Cemetery plot. The daughter of Gabriel and Elizabeth Tichenor died at a very young age in Cincinnati. A notation in the old cemetery records Lane Seminary had in Walnut Hill states a debt of $1.75 to G. Tichenor for "interment of child." The records show this having been paid by cash. *Prepared by David P. Rakestraw.*

GEORGE OVERAKER & MARGARET EVANS. George Overaker was born in 1760. The country of birth is not known but is believed to be Germany. His father, Georg Overaker and his mother, Marget, were from Germany.

George Overaker lived in Winchester, Frederick County, VA and in the late 18th century moved to the Mississippi Territory. In about 1782 George Overaker married Margaret Evans, the sister of Lewis Evans, a prominent landowner and political figure in Natchez. George and Margaret had two children, Elizabeth and Maria L. Overaker. Elizabeth married Gabriel Tichenor on Apr. 11, 1810. Maria married Ortasmus L. Nash on May 12, 1830. Both marriages were in Adams County, MS. There is no record of what became of the marriage of Maria. She never changed her name. The will of Peterfield Jefferson dated Oct. 24, 1850 and filed on Sep. 8, 1852 in Hinds County, MS identified O.L Nash as a witness to the will. It could be Ortasmus L. Nash and O.L. Nash is one and the same person.

The earliest record of George Overaker settling in Natchez is the purchase of Lot No. 4 in Square No. 2 with house thereon on Feb. 27, 1796. His earliest date in Natchez as listed in *The Natchez Court Records* is August 1790. The record shows George in Natchez many times between 1790 and 1797. In 1798 he took the Oath of Allegiance to the United States in the Natchez District before Lewis Evans.

George Overaker returned to Winchester, VA for a brief time. It is recorded in the Deed Book for Frederick County, VA that in February 1800 George Overaker of the Town of Natchez, Adams County, MS Territory bought for the sum of $100 from Thomas Lindsey of the same place the personal estate in Winchester, VA Thomas Lindsey inherited from his father. One of the three witnesses to the deed was John Overaker now of Natchez, MS. In August 1801 George Overaker sold to Richard Bowen for the sum of $2,000 the real and personal property purchased from Thomas Lindsey. One of the four witnesses to this deed was Daniel Overaker of Winchester, VA.

On Jan. 10, 1802 a Cherokee Indian Agency

passport was issued by J. Meigs, Agent for the War Department, Tennessee, Southwest Point, for George Overacre, Esqr. with his family of seven white persons and 14 blacks to pass down the River Tennessee on his way to Natchez in the Mississippi Territory, with two large boats with their loading and furniture. Thus, on or about April 1802 George Overaker and family with Isaac Overaker and family left Winchester, VA for Natchez, Adams County and Mississippi Territory. It is believed that John Overaker and his wife Nancy were members of this boat party.

In Natchez George Overaker became a merchant and owner of White Horse Tavern. It is known that he was an Innkeeper at least by October 1799 since a deed indenture dated Oct. 16, 1799 recorded in Adams County, MS refers to George Overaker as an Innkeeper. He became prosperous and in March 1805 purchased property called Hope Farm from his brother-in-law, Lewis Evans. The family later owned a home called Hawthorn. George Overaker died on Jun. 6, 1820 and he is buried in the Old Catholic section of the Natchez City Cemetery. At the time of his death Hope Farm contained 221.74 acres and George Overaker owned other property in the city of Natchez. His wife, Margaret Overaker, was appointed sole executrix of his will. The legatees in the will of George Overaker, dated Aug. 17, 1816, are his wife, Margaret; brother, Isaac; niece of his wife, Elizabeth Patton; and his two daughters, Elizabeth Tichenor and Maria Overaker. Lewis Evans was named trustee for George's daughters. Isaac Overaker died two years before the death of George.

George Overaker's land was inherited by his wife, Margaret, and in trust for his two daughters, Elizabeth Tichenor and Maria Overaker. There was a free man of color who called himself George Overaker living on the George Overaker estate. In August 1826 Margaret Overaker sold this 4.7 acres for $600 to him. The family members also sold the remaining property they had inherited.

After the death of George Overaker, his wife Margaret built a home in the city of Natchez. In November 1832 Margaret Overaker sold this home to Thomas McDannold. This home is presently the Presbyterian Manse (Deed Book T, p 507). Margaret Overaker, Maria Overaker and Elizabeth Tichenor were members of the First Presbyterian Church in Natchez at least upon the arrival of Rev. George Potts in May 1823. Gabriel Tichenor became a member in 1832.

In Natchez the wives of Winthrop Sargent, William Dunbar, George Overaker and Elizabeth Tichenor founded the Female Charitable Society in 1816. Hope Farm, Hawthorn and the Presbyterian Manse are on the National Register of Historic Places.

In about 1832/33 Margaret Overaker and her daughters, Maria Overaker and Elizabeth Tichenor, and Gabriel Tichenor moved to Cincinnati, OH. Margaret died in October 1859 at the age of 89. Maria died in April 1864 at the age of 69. Elizabeth died in June 1860 at the age of 78, and Gabriel Tichenor died in February 1855 at the age of 72. *Prepared by David P. Rakestraw.*

ISAAC OVERAKER & REBECCA THORN. Isaac married Rebecca Thorn on Nov. 30, 1790 by minister Alexander Balmain in the city of Winchester, Frederick County, VA. In 1798 Isaac lived in Middletown, VA which is a small town south of Winchester but still in Frederick County. A daughter named Mary was born in 1796 in Frederick County. Two sons and two daughters were born in Natchez, Adams County, Mississippi Territory.

Land indentures in Frederick County, VA show the surname Overaker and Overacre spelled in various places in the same document. In July 1798

Isaac Overaker bought property from Peter Senseny. Another deed transaction in 1798 is for the purchase of lot No. 158 in the city of Winchester by Isaac Overaker from his father, George Overacre, with the stipulation that George Overacre and his wife could live in the house for the rest of their lives.

In January 1802 Isaac Overaker, his wife Rebecca and daughter Mary, traveled with two large boats with their loadings on the River Tennessee and the Mississippi River on their way to Natchez in the Mississippi Territory. Brothers of Isaac and their wives were members of this boat party.

In Natchez, MS Mary Overaker married James Trueman Magruder Jr. on Thursday, Jan. 29, 1818 by Rev. John Menefee at the home of Isaac's brother, George Overaker. That same year Isaac died intestate in Adams County, MS and James T. Magruder Jr. was appointed administrator for his estate on Jul. 18, 1818. There is no record of the work profession of Isaac Overaker in the city of Natchez. Isaac and his family lived in a home on Lot No. 4 in Square No. 14 in the plan of the city of Natchez. This property was sold to John Richards by deed trust in July 1817. George Overaker was the original owner of this lot acquired by Spanish Grant.

The two sons of Isaac and Rebecca Overaker marched away to Baton Rouge in the War of 1812 but returned home and are listed in the 1816 Adams County, MS census for the family of Isaac Overaker. It is believed that the 1820 Adams County census for James T. Magruder include in his household Rebecca Overaker and her two daughters, Pomona and Rebecca. In Natchez Pomona married Levi W. Taylor on May 15, 1823 and Rebecca married William B. Winston on May 18, 1823.

James Trueman Magruder Jr. operated a general merchandise store known as James Trueman Magruder Jr. and Co. in Natchez, MS during the period of about 1821-25. Of his marriage to Mary Overaker one child was born, Elizabeth Howard Magruder. Elizabeth was called Betty. On Jun. 21, 1838 in Clinton, MS she married Peterfield Jefferson, a lineal descendant of Field Jefferson an uncle of Thomas Jefferson.

After the death of James Trueman Magruder Jr. his widow Mary Overaker Magruder married Gen. Cowles Mead on Dec. 17, 1835. She was his third wife named Mary. There is no record of children from this marriage. They made their home at Greenwood.

While acting governor of the Mississippi territory Cowles Mead in January 1807 captured Aaron Burr when there was a warrant for his arrest after President Jefferson proclaimed Burr's conspiracy to separate the union a treasonous act. It is said Aaron Burr's sword hung on the wall of Greenwood until Mary Mead with her own hands buckled it upon Captain John W. Welborn, commanding officer of the Mississippi College Rifles. During the War Between the States Mary Mead and family left Greenwood for the safety of Alabama. When she returned home after the war Greenwood was destroyed with only tall chimneys standing.

Cowles Mead was born in Bedford, VA on Oct. 18, 1776 and died at Greenwood on May 17, 1844. Mary Overaker Magruder Mead, her daughter, Elizabeth Howard Magruder Jefferson and Peterfield Jefferson are buried in the Clinton, MS cemetery located next to Mississippi College in Clinton. *Prepared by David P. Rakestraw.*

JOHN OVERAKER of Winchester, VA migrated to the Mississippi Territory in the late 18th century. He is a brother of George Overaker and Isaac Overaker and the three brothers lived in the Natchez, MS area. What is known about John is that he was in Natchez and a witness to a will of J. Vauchere on Sep. 7, 1797. He was back in Winchester, VA and was one of three witnesses to a deed transaction dated Feb. 20, 1800 between his brother, George Overaker, of Natchez, and Thomas Lindsay, also of Natchez. John Overaker and George Overaker were subscribers to a memorial to Congress of the United States of America by Citizens of the Territory of Mississippi on Dec. 6, 1800.

No official record has been found of the marriage of John Overaker to Nancy. One daughter named Ann has been identified from this marriage. Ann married Henry Rider in Claiborne County, MS on Jan. 27, 1836.

Nancy Overaker, a widow, became the third wife of William Hazlip in Adams County, MS on Mar. 26, 1814. No children are recorded from this marriage. Nancy died Jun. 6, 1826.

BEVERLY BLUNT PARHAM & ALICE HARDY HERBERT HAYNES both grew up in New Orleans and were married there in Trinity Episcopal Church on May 3, 1883. Jefferson Davis was an honored guest at the wedding and his daughter, Winnie, served as a bridesmaid.

Beverly (b. Aug. 10, 1853 at Pecan Grove, Carroll Parish, LA) was the son of John Greenway Parham Jr. and Mary Eliza Blunt whose parents came to Warren County, MS from Virginia in the early 1800s. Alice (b. Jan. 11, 1861 in New Orleans), daughter of Captain Andrew Ferguson Haynes, Crescent Regiment, CSA, and Elizabeth Parkerson Dameron. The Haynes were from Warren County, MS and the Damerons from Norfolk, VA.

Alice and Beverly met when he was employed as an accountant for Jacob U. Payne, who was a prominent New Orleans cotton factor, and Alice's step-grandfather. A few years after their marriage they bought Arcola Plantation on Lake St. John, near L'Argent, LA, and over the years Beverly became a successful planter in Concordia Parish. Alice, a classically trained pianist who had studied both in New Orleans and in Europe, soon found herself overseeing a large house and a growing family. While Beverly was busy managing the plantation and participating as a member of the Levee Board, Alice saw to it that their lively home was filled with books, music, and religious instruction, as well as with many visiting friends and family members from New Orleans.

In all, Alice and Beverly had 13 children, 12 of whom reached maturity. They were Alice, Greenway, Andree, Archer, Mary, Fenner, Fred, Charlotte, Betty, Myrtis, Jocelyn and Beverly Jr. When Alice and Beverly moved to Natchez in 1912 after most of their children were away at school, they joined Jefferson Street Methodist Church.

Alice resumed her musical studies, this time with Mr. Ferris Bradley, and frequently played for her church and for the Natchez Music Club. Of their children, Andree, Fenner, Fred, Jocelyn and Beverly made their homes in Natchez in adulthood.

Greenway married Laverne Bisland of Cannonsburg, MS and they had one child, John Greenway Jr. Archer married Rosario Maga of the Philippine Islands and they had five children: Archer Jr., Beverly, John, Conrad and Alice. Mary and her husband, Norman Register, had two daughters, Mary Norman and Alice. Fenner married Isabel Lawrence of Natchez and had one son, Fenner Jr. Fred and his wife, Eliza McCabe of Natchez, had one son, Fred Jr. Betty married Thomas Grantham of Wilson, NC. Their daughter was Jean. Jocelyn married first Everard Green Baker III and had Beverly Alice; second, she married William A. Barlow. Beverly Jr. and his wife,

Carrie Braun of Gloster, MS had three daughters: Carolyn, Gail and Beverly. Most of these 15 grandchildren were born in time to brighten Beverly and Alice's last days. Beverly Sr. died in Natchez on Jul. 24, 1928 and Alice died, also in Natchez, on Apr. 30, 1931.

THOMAS PAINE & ELIZA JANE JUNKIN. Thomas Paine (b. about 1809) md. Eliza Jane Junkin in Natchez on Apr. 21, 1828. Eliza Jane was born about 1809 to William and Catherine Junkin. (See Catherine Tyler Junkins Mahan.) On Sep. 17, 1828, five months after their marriage, Thomas and Eliza Jane purchased Lot #3 in Square 13 in the city of Natchez for $500.

Of the six children born to Thomas and Eliza Jane, five were born in Natchez; their fourth child, Harriet, was born in Louisiana. All six children married in Natchez.

When Thomas Paine died on May 17, 1842, at the age of 33, his youngest son was not yet 2 years old. After his death, Eliza Jane took her five youngest children and went to live with her mother. They are in her household in the 1850 Adams County Census.

Eliza Jane died at the age of 55 on Jul. 25, 1865; she was buried in Plot 1, Old Catholic Section of Natchez City Cemetery. Her will, written on Jul. 24, 1865 in Vicksburg, was probated in Warren County in 1874. She bequeaths her Natchez home (fronting Pine Street and Rankin Street) to her son, Thomas Alet. B. Paine. To her daughter, Margaret Carkeet, she bequeaths a lot fronting Rankin Street.

The children of Thomas and Eliza Jane:

1) Catherine Paine (b. about 1832) md. Stephen C. Black on Dec. 27, 1848. Their son, William Black was born in Iowa about 1852. In 1860 the Adams County Census shows William Black, age 8, living with his grandmother, Eliza Jane Paine.

2) William W. Paine (b. about 1834) md. Susan Gray on Jan. 28, 1855. This marriage produced three children: John (b. 1857), Robert (b. 1859) and Edward (b. 1861).

3) Harriet "Hattie" Paine (b. Apr. 3, 1836) md. John David Miles on Nov. 23, 1852. John was a dentist. Their six children were: John Joseph (b. Oct. 9, 1853, Natchez); Mary Madora (b. May 15, 1856, Vicksburg); Charlotte (Apr. 19, 1858, Vicksburg); Benjamin Chamber (b. Oct. 29, 1859, Vicksburg); Frederick Baum (b. Nov. 4, 1860, Vicksburg); and Eliza Jane (b. Feb. 19, 1863, Natchez).

4) Margaret Paine (b. about 1838) md. William H. Carkeet (Karkeet) on Sep. 4, 1855. William (b. about 1834 in England) was a plasterer. During the Civil War he served as a private in Regiment 1, Mississippi Light Artillery, Co. H. Margaret died on May 5, 1866 and is buried in Natchez City Cemetery. They had five children: Margaret, John (b. about 1856), William (b. about 1858), Floyd (b. February 1860), and Rose Elizabeth (b. Oct. 26, 1861). Rose Elizabeth married Charles T. Alexander. (See Rose Elizabeth Carkeet and Charles T Alexander.)

5) Charlotte Paine (b. 1840) md. Andrew T. Gunning on Apr. 15, 1856. Andrew owned a retail dry goods store. He was born in Ohio in 1835 and died in Natchez on Apr. 29, 1877. Their daughter, also named Charlotte, was born on Feb. 23, 1857. Before their daughter was two months old, Charlotte (the mother) died on Apr. 17, 1857, and was buried in the old Catholic section of Natchez City Cemetery. Charlotte (the daughter) married her first husband, James H. Beresford, in Natchez in 1880. James was born about 1856 and died in 1888. He served as a corporal in Company L, Wood's Regiment of the Confederate Cavalry. They had four children: Rose G. (b.

1882), Ellen (b. 1884), James H. Jr. (b. 1886), and Sue (b. 1888). Charlotte's second marriage was to the Rev. John Owen Pierce in 1896; they had one child, Clara Owen. On Feb. 23, 1942, Charlotte Pierce died in Columbus, OH.

6) Thomas Aylette Buckner Paine (b. Mar. 6, 1841) md. Sarah Jane Higgins on Jul. 21, 1861. (See Sarah Jane Higgins and Thomas Aylette Buckner Paine.)

Sources: Official Records and written family history, recorded by Hattie Kline Monsell before 1948. Submitted by Ginga Hathaway and Marilyn Baland Gibson.

SARAH JANE HIGGINS AND THOMAS AYLETTE BUCKNER PAINE.

Thomas Aylette Buckner Paine was born in Natchez on Mar. 5 or 6, 1841. He was the son of Thomas and Eliza Jane (Junkins) Paine. Thomas married Sarah Jane Higgins, the daughter of John and Mary (Harson) Higgins, on Jul. 21, 1861. Sarah Jane was born in Natchez on Oct. 5, 1843. (See Eliza Jane Junkins and Thomas Paine and also Mary M. Harson and John Hodgkins Higgins.)

On Mar. 5, 1861, Thomas A.B. Paine enlisted in the Confederate Army at Natchez, as a private in Company B/new Company G, Blackburn's 12th Regiment, Mississippi; his name is on the roll of the *Natchez Fencibles.* Five months after his enlistment, he was injured in the battle of Manassas. Due to the disability resulting from his injury, Thomas was discharged on Dec. 6, 1861.

After the war, Thomas worked as a plasterer and a farmer. Sarah Jane was an excellent seamstress and often sewed in order to earn extra money. During the yellow fever epidemic of 1905 she went to Lake Providence, LA to help nurse patients. In 1870 Sarah's mother, Mary Higgins (now Mary Conner), and Richard Higgins, a

Sarah Jane Higgins Paine (b. Oct. 5, 1843, d. Apr. 23, 1908)

brother-in-law, were living in Thomas' household. Then about 1876, Thomas moved his family to Warren County, MS, where he remained for the rest of his life.

Thomas and Sarah Jane had three children:

1) Hattie Rosena Paine (b. Nov. 29, 1867 in Natchez) md. William Aloysius Hyland on Mar. 12, 1885.

2) Mary Elizabeth Paine (b. Aug. 14, 1870) married (1st) Franklin Pierce Findorf in 1892, and (2nd) Maurice Marcus in 1902.

3) Thomas Richard Paine (b. Apr. 2, 1881) md. Deborah Franklin Godwin on Jun. 28, 1904.

On Jul. 17, 1895, at the age of 54, Thomas A.B. Paine died. Sarah Jane died on Apr. 23, 1908, at the age of 65. They are both buried in Porter's Chapel Cemetery, Vicksburg, MS.

Sources: Official Records Submitted by Ginga Hathaway and Marilyn Baland Gibson.

JOAN BALFOUR PAYNE & JOHN B. DICKS.

One of Mississippi's most successful author/illustrators of children's books was born in Natchez, but has deep ancestral roots in both Adams and Jefferson counties.

Joan Balfour Payne (b. Dec. 2, 1923) was just a baby when her parents, Earl Payne and Josephine Balfour, moved to Minneapolis where her father managed several hotels.

The family lived in one of the hotels, and Joan

attended Northrop Collegiate School for Girls though the 8th grade. She then convinced her parents to take her out of school and provide a tutor so that she could concentrate on the fields of study which interested her most, art and languages.

She studied art under Gustav Krollman at the Minne-

Joan Balfour Payne

apolis Institute of Art. As a child her mother would write stories to amuse her daughter, and Joan began to create illustrations to accompany those stories. Then in 1941 Joan and her family moved back to Mississippi to The Cedars at Church Hill, a property her father had purchased in 1938.

In 1942 Joan and her mother collaborated on their first book, *The Little Green Island;* Joan was 18 years old. They subsequently co-authored four other books, two of which were honor books in the *New York Herald Tribune* Spring Book Festival.

In August 1952, Joan married John B. Dicks of Natchez. The Dicks family home was Glenburnie. The couple eventually moved to Sewanee, TN, where Dr. Dicks taught physics at the University of the South. They had four children: Ian, Merrill, Agnes and Josephine.

While at Sewanee Joan wrote and illustrated seven more children's books and did illustrations for other books as well. In addition to drawing, painting, sculpting and carving, when the chairman of the Fine Arts Department at the University of the South died, Joan was asked to teach his classes; quite an accomplishment for someone with only eight years of formal education.

Joan's mother, Josephine Balfour, was descended from William Suggs Balfour and Catherine Hunt.

William Balfour (b. 1827 in Madison County, MS) was the son of Dr. William L. Balfour, a prominent Mississippi planter.

Catherine Hunt (b. 1829 in Jefferson County) was the daughter of David Hunt, one of the wealthiest and most prominent men of that period in Mississippi history.

Their family home, Homewood, built in 1860, was considered one of Natchez's finest antebellum homes. It remained in the family until 1907 when it was purchased by Mr. and Mrs. William Kaiser. The mansion, located on Pine Ridge road, was destroyed by fire in 1940.

Joan's father, Earl Payne, was a descendant of Col. James Gilliam Wood, who migrated with his second wife, Martha Young and family, from Maryland in 1812 to Jefferson County where he purchased property at Church Hill (formerly known as the Maryland Settlement).

A planter and an astute businessman, Col. Wood was able to amass considerable wealth which enabled him to provide each of his children with a home and 400-600 acres of land, all near his own home, Auburn Hall.

When his daughter, Jane Caroline, married James Payne from Virginia in 1828, he built Oak Grove for them. That home, along with The Cedars, Lagonia and Woodland, are still standing today.

In addition, in 1828 Col. Wood donated the land for the site of the present day Christ Church, the oldest Episcopal Church in the state of Mississippi, and the Wood family have been active members of the congregation over the years.

Joan Balfour Payne died Jan. 6, 1973 and John B. Dicks died Sep. 11, 1990.

JAMES FRANKLIN PAYNE & MATHILDE ORMAND LEWIS.

Mathilde (Fr. pronunciation) was born Jan. 15, 1871, the daughter of Belle Stanford Newton and Ben Sims Lewis. She was reared in Louisiana but attended the Natchez Female College, graduating in 1889. Always fearful of the fevers of the low country near the river at Troy and Belle Ella Plantations at Waterproof and St. Joseph, LA, her family sent her to Church Hill to the home of her cousin, Wade Harrison, a Everton. There she married James Franklin Payne at Christ Episcopal Church in 1895. He was the great-grandson of James Wood of Auburn Hall, one of the founders of the Maryland Settlement.

At school Mathilde's best friends were the Montgomery twins, Irene and Inez, granddaughters of Civil War Governor, Charles Clark. Later, Irene became the mother of lifelong Natchez-resident, Mary Henderson Lambdin. Inez became a teacher and never married.

After Mathilde's untimely death, at age 26 on Nov. 28, 1897, her only child, Belle Wade Payne, spent summers at Church Hill, but was the ward of Inez during school terms. Inez and Belle Wade lived on Locust Plantation in Greenville, MS with Mary Adelia Clark Montgomery, Governor Clark's daughter and Inez's mother. At that tender age, Inez taught

Mathilde Ormande Lewis Payne

Belle Wade to call members of her family grandma, uncle, aunt, and cousin, before she was old enough to realize it was affectionate courtesy.

After graduating from MSCW at Columbus in 1916, Belle Wade Payne married John H. Bowen in Greenville in 1917 during World War I.

Her ancestor, Col. Aaron Lewis, and his ancestor, William Bowen, were commissioned in the same Revolutionary War Company in Washington County, VA in 1777. After many generations, the progeny of the two officers were married in Mississippi. Four children were born to them: Inez Montgomery Bowen (b. 1920, d. 1922); John H. Bowen "Buddy" received the Distinguished Flying Cross in the Navy in World War II; Belle Wade Bowen (b. 1924); Allen Campbell Bowen (a.k.a. Dinky) (b. 1926) admitted to the Georgia Tech Football Hall of Fame.

Commencement exercises of the Natchez Female College.

Inez Montgomery (b. 1872) was for many years a resident of Natchez and lived in Indianola with Wade Bowen Frame and J. Stewart Frame when she died in 1956. She was a greatly respected and beloved teacher and a much loved grandmother to the Bowen children.

PEALE FAMILY.

The Peale family name in Natchez had its beginnings in the mid-1830s when

Elijah Peale, a native of Franklin County, PA, came as a tutor to the children of the Rev. Mr. Benjamin Chase, pastor of Carmel Presbyterian Church, Kingston neighborhood. In 1838 he married Mary Nettles Henderson, youngest daughter of Scotsman John Henderson and his wife Selah Mitchell. She was also a sister to Thomas Henderson, builder of Magnolia Hall. Elijah Peale and Thomas Henderson became business partners as Cotton Factors in New Orleans. Elijah Peale moved his family from Natchez to New Orleans in 1847 and remained there until his death in 1874. His six children were all born in Natchez except one.

In 1862, Elijah's third child, Alexander Henderson Peale (b. 1842, d. 1912) enlisted at Washington, MS in the Breckenridge Guards. He was wounded at Chickamauga but recovered to fight in the Battle of Atlanta, was captured by the Yankees in 1864 and sent as an officer to Johnson's Island Prison in Lake Erie near Sandusky, OH. Upon return to Natchez he was married at Magnolia Hall to Emily Trask Welch, a great-granddaughter of Judge Samuel Brooks, the first Mayor of Natchez.

Emily Welch Peale was also a descendant of *Mayflower* passengers and other prominent New Englanders. To this union were born seven children, only three of whom opted to make their life-long homes in Natchez. All of the early Peales were communicants of the First Presbyterian Church until they married spouses of other denominations.

The eldest son of Alex and Emily Peale, Alexander Henderson Peale Jr. (b. 1869, d. 1909) md. Susan S. Metcalfe and had two children. Alex Peale organized and directed the choir at Trinity Episcopal Church.

Their third son, Eugene Welch Peale (b. 1873, d. 1935) md. Cornelia "Nina" Rogers. There were five children familiarly known as Eugene, Alex, Bobbie, Billy, and Little Nina who was married to Shelton "Doc" Cunningham. They were communicants in the Trinity Episcopal Church. Their home was at 35 Homochitto Street.

The fourth and youngest son of Alex and Emily Peale was Augustus "Gus" Welch Peale, Sr. (b. 1876, d. 1945), born at Frogmore, LA. He married in 1906, Katie Lou Seab of Franklin County, MS. Gus Peale was a dairyman and made his home on a small farm on Shields Lane, now Highway 61 By-pass. His family were members of the First Baptist Church. Children: Augustus Jr. Seab, Paul, and Effie Mae, married to Harmon Johnson. Paul, a WWII veteran, was a captain with the 20th Armored Division when they liberated the Jews from the Concentration Camp at Dachau, Germany.

Of the 18 grandchildren of Alex and Emily Peale only Paul in his late 80s and Effie Mae in her early 90s remain alive and active in their respective communities as of this publication.

Few by the surname of Peale remain today in Natchez. The many descendants of Elijah Peale are now scattered across America. Those that do remain in Natchez are the offshoots of the Eugene Welch and Nina Rogers Peale branch.

JOSEPH PERKINS FAMILY. Joseph in February of 1788 received from the Spanish government of West Florida a grant of 177 arpents of land situated on the waters of St. Catherine Creek, five miles north by east of the city of Natchez. The exact year he moved his family to the Natchez District is undetermined, but he arrived before 1784 as he is shown on that census. There are indications they arrived about 1792 and probably from the Pendleton District of South Carolina.

Joseph and wife Sarah had a family of nine children: Elizabeth (b. ca. 1772) md. John Elmore,

Ezekiel (b. ca. 1773) md. Elizabeth, daughter of Christian Harman; Priscilla "Sylla" (b. ca. 1775) md. Francis Henderson; Caleb (b. 1780), according to his application to the Spanish government for a grant of land, and married Sarah Adams; Charles (b. May 22, 1783) md. Elizabeth, daughter of Joseph and Mary Gibson Harrison; Joel (b. ca. 1785, d. unmarried in 1819); Sarah (b. ca. 1787) md. James Cocks/Cox; Mary (b. ca. 1790) md. William P. Thomas; Isaac (b. ca. 1790) md. Edna, daughter of John and Edna Gibson Bullin.

Caleb and Sarah Adams married about 1800. They lived in Adams County on 240 acres of land until Caleb's death in 1814. They had a family of two girls, the oldest and youngest, and four boys. They were Maria (b. ca. 1800) md. James Hooter; Joel (b. ca. 1804) md. Elizabeth, daughter of Daniel Heath; Charles (b. ca. 1806) md. Theresa Tison on Nov. 17, 1825 in Terrebonne Parish, LA; Caleb (b. Dec. 8, 1808) md. Cyrinthia Ann Whitaker, daughter of Isaac and Elizabeth Bullin Whitaker; Elihue (b. ca. 1810) md. Amanda, daughter of Amos Griffing; Ruth (b. after 1810 and before 1814) md. Lewis Bolls, both died in 1854 victims of cholera. Sarah married Jul. 30, 1815 Joseph Harrison as his third wife. They had one child Thomas Harrison who died in Jefferson County in June 1832. In 1822 Sarah had moved to Jefferson County northwest of Fayette, where she reared and educated her children. After all had left home she married her third husband, David Gibson, on Mar. 14, 1839.

Caleb (Jr.) was well educated and one wonders in what academy or college he received his schooling. Like his father and grandfather he choose as a vocation, the life of a planter. Caleb married the only child of Isaac and Elizabeth Bullin Whitaker, Cyrinthia Ann, on May 7, 1830 in Jefferson County. In 1835 they purchased "Cane Hill"

Francis M. and Sara Belzora (Perkins) Stevens

plantation in Claiborne County, where they reared their children. They were John W. (b. Sep. 28, 1831, d. young); W.M.W. (b. Jul. 31, 1833, d. as an infant); Theodore Monroe (b. Aug. 22, 1834) md. Emeline Douglass Davenport; Adeline Elizabeth (b. Jul. 27, 1836) md. David Shelby Davenport; David V. (b. Aug. 10, 1839, d. young); Demetrius (b. Oct. 22, 1841) md. Ophelia Harlan; Sara Belzora (b. Jan. 20, 1844) md. Francis Marion Stevens; Cordelia W. (b. Jan. 27, 1846) md. William Wallace Stevens, the brother of her sister's husband; Cyrinthia Jeanette (b. Jan. 19, 1848) md. Lumpkin Griffin; Caleb Elijah (b. Feb. 24, 1850) md. first, Mary Foster and second, Matilda Tatum; Clara (b. Apr. 10, 1852) md. first, Samuel Harris and second, Charles Harrell; Irene (b. Dec. 3, 1854, d. at age 2).

These families moved from Adams into Claiborne, Jefferson and Hinds counties and later into other states. Most had large families and were prosperous farmers. *Submitted by Carolyn Cole*

CARLOTTA METCALFE & HOUSTON SIDNEY BROWN. Carlotta (b. Oct. 26, 1908, in Adams County, MS) was the second of two children born to her parents, Eugene and Sarah Bernard Metcalfe. Her mother was one of eight children born to Amelia Buchanan who was half Indian and half African. Her father was the son of a 12-year-old slave girl and one of the master's sons. She

died at her residence on Dec. 23, 1998.

Carlotta attended public schools in Jackson and Natchez. In Jackson, she graduated from 9th grade at Smith-Robertson School. One of her classmates at Smith-Robertson was Richard Wright, who later became a well-known author. She enjoyed talking about him. She graduated from high school in Natchez at Brumfield High in 1927.

Ella S. Comer Reedy, great-grandmother of Eugenia Perry

Also in 1927, after graduation, she married Houston Sidney Brown and to this union five children were born: Eugenia "Jean," Alberta "Bert," Sarah, Helen and Houston Jr.

She was a talented seamstress who could create her own styles, and she never needed a pattern as a guide. Carlotta also did beautiful knitting and crocheting. During the 1940s she helped Vivian New sew ball gowns and hoop skirts that were worn by persons in the Pilgrimage pageants. After she retired, she participated in the Senior Citizens program and received a certificate for volunteer work done in that program.

Ruth Reedy Brown, grandmother of Eugenia Perry

Carlotta Metcalfe Brown, mother of Eugenia Perry

Carlotta was preceded in death by her husband Houston (Boise) Sidney Brown; parents, Eugene and Sarah Bernard Metcalfe; brother, Robert Metcalfe; grandson, Robert L. Nicholson Jr.

Children of Houston and Carlotta Brown. Siblings l-r: Helen B. Nicholson, Eugenia B. Perry, Houston S. Brown Sr., Alberta B. Ranson, Sarah B. Jamison

Survivors include four daughters: Eugenia B. Perry and Alberta (Francis Sr.) Ransom of Natchez, MS; Sarah (George) Jamison of Jackson, MS; and Helen B. Nicholson of Hattiesburg, MS; one son, Houston (Carolyn) Sidney Brown Jr.; 11 grandchildren: Sheri Brown of Bellevue, WA; Francis Ransom Jr. of Natchez, MS; Herman Sidney Ransom of Olathe, KS; Dexter Ransom of Fort Hood, TX; Cassandra Hubbard and Robelyn McNair of Lawrenceville, GA; Rhonda Williams of Woodbury, MN; Nicole Omi and Averall Brown of Rancho Cordova, CA; George W. Jamison of Jackson, MS; and Angela Johnson of Atlanta, GA; 16 great-grandchildren and other relatives.

Houston S. Brown Sr., father of Eugenia Perry

JOHANN PETERS & CATHERIN MARIE FRANK

were the parents of the Peters sisters, who married John Henry Stier, father of Julia Stier (See biography John Henry Stier & the Peters Sisters). Julia was the wife of Louis Armand "L.A." Benoist Sr. Issue of Johann and Catherin were M a r y Peters; Caroline Juliane Dorothea Henriette Peters (b. Jan. 7, 1823, d. 1903); Charles Peters (b. ca. 1828, d. May 1840).

The family attended the Lutheran Church at Oldenburg/Holstein. Family history is that Johann and his children sailed from Oldenburg, Hamburg or Bremer, Germany, settling first in Evansville, IN, ca. 1828, and then resettling in Natchez. Records show that the Natchez tornado of May 1840 took the lives of Johann, who lost both legs, and his son, Charles. The family home was also destroyed. Thereafter, tradition is that Johann's wife, the children's stepmother, remarried and moved to Iowa. *Prepared by Paul H. Benoist and Virginia Gerace Benoist.*

CHRISTINE & VALAN PIKE

are descended from Dr. Charles West, first practicing physician in the Natchez District who arrived here in 1785. He and his brother, Cato, acting territorial governor from 1802-05, from Farquier County, VA, were sons of William West Jr. and Mary Elzey West, and grandsons of William West Sr. and Mary Hychew West all of Loudon County, VA. They received Spanish Land Grants to tracts on the north branch of Cole's Creek just off the Natchez Trace in what is now Jefferson County (formerly Pickering), two miles south of Old Greenville and 16 miles north of Washington. Ed Mardis is the current owner of much of this property, which abuts Springfield Plantation.

Charles returned to Farquier County, VA to marry Sarah Withers in 1786. In 1791 he returned with his family. Their three children were: Charles Cato, Thomas W. and Mary. After Charles' death in 1795, Sarah "Sally" married William Lemon.

Cousins married cousins and every generation spawned more Catos and Marthas. To Cato and his first wife, Nancy Anna Winn (sister of Major General Richard Winn) of Winnsboro, SC, were born six children: William (md. Sarah Kirkland), Thomas Eliza (md. a McCoy), Anna (md. Joseph Winn), her twin Susan (md. Thomas W. West), and Cato Charles (md. Jennet Scott Chinn). To Cato and his 2nd wife, Martha Wills Green, of Springfield Plantation in Jefferson County, were born: Richard Claiborne West, John Smith West, Benjamin Franklin West (md. Pauline Wing), Martha Elizabeth (md. 1st James Montgomery and 2nd Robert Malloy), Mary Louise (1st wife of Edward Turner, 2nd wife was Eliza Baker), and Charles Cato West (md. Charlotte Neely). His 3rd

wife, Martha Harper, was pregnant at the time of the writing of his will (witnessed by Adam Cloud) in 1818. She secondly married William L. Davis and thirdly Robert Webb. To them was born Dr. Gerald Bertram Webb who married the granddaughter of Jefferson Davis, Varina Howell Hayes.

Thomas W. West married his cousin, Susan West (daughter of Cato). She presumably died soon after because he next married Mary Jane Ingles Chinn of Woodville. Mary Jane was the sister of Judge Thomas Withers Chinn of Cypress Hall Plantation in St. Francisville. Their sister Agatha, was the 2nd wife of George Poindexter, senator and governor of Mississippi. Another sister, Margaret became the 2nd wife of Gen. Robert McCausland of Springfield Plantation in Laurel Hill, LA.

Their father, Chichester Chinn, was a Kentucky senator, whose mother Janet Scott, was a cousin of Sir Walter Scott. Chichester, educated in Edinburgh, Scotland by his maiden aunts, initially accepted an ensign's commission they had secured for him in the British navy and served in the war between France and England. But after he was captured and paroled, he resigned his commission and came to America, for which he was disinherited. Chichester's wife and mother of the aforementioned Mary Jane was Susan "Sukey" Withers, whose sister Sarah, was the wife of Charles West.

Martha Octavia West was born to Thomas W. and Mary Jane West abt. 1816. After her father's death in 1833, Martha Octavia married Lewis Davis, son of Major Robert Davis and Mary Nicholson of Valhalla Plantation in Feliciana. Major Davis was also the brother of Martha Davis, the first wife of General McCausland, who later married Dr. Richard Roach. Two of Lewis' brothers, Hugh and Robert, were married to Lucinda and Mary Ellen, sisters of Jefferson Davis.

Martha Octavia, her planter husband, and their two surviving sons, Robert Thomas Davis and Hugh Howard Davis, lived in Carroll and then Holmes County when Lewis died abt. l847. Following his death, they returned to Feliciana and in 1850 she married planter and Cumberland Presbyterian minister, Rev. Robert Malloy.

Valan and Christine Pike

Rev. Malloy had previously been married to Martha Elizabeth West, the daughter of Cato. This Martha had previously been married to James Jefferson Montgomery, son of Alexander and Lydia Swayze Montgomery, before his death in 1835 and hers in 1845.

She left a son for whom Robert was guardian, Franklin Alexander Montgomery (b. 1830, d. 1903), who became a colonel in the CSA, attorney in Rosedale, and husband of Charlotte Clark. Also at least two daughters were born to Martha and Robert, Francis and Jane Malloy, who in 1856 married James Harper.

Ella Octavia was born to Robert and Martha Octavia Malloy in 1852, on their plantation outside Zachary, LA. Following the war, by which time her father declared he "had been rendered insolvent by the emancipation proclamation" Ella lived with her widowed half-sister, Jane, in Crystal Springs. In 1872 she married CSA veteran and Methodist minister Rev. Henry Pollard Bowen of Union Church in Jefferson County, MS. Three sons were born to them: Henry, Robert and

James, while he was serving as circuit pastor variously in the Pearlington, MS district and later in Seguine, TX. There he died in 1878.

Ella returned to Crystal Springs to collect her widow's pension of $557.65 then moved to Cotula, TX where she built a house in town and became acquainted with the future writer O. Henry (W.S. Porter) who had moved to that dry climate for his health. She also met cattleman, Rufus Pike, from Booneville, MS who, in 1870, was ranching in Gonzales, TX. She and Rufus married in 1884 and had two children in Cotulla, "Little Rufus" who died in 1886 at age 6 months, and daughter Mayme. There they suffered the four plagues of the Brush Country: rattlesnakes, smallpox, outlaws, and Indian raids. By 1890 they had moved to San Antonio where Hugh and Alfred were born to them and Rufus worked as a carpenter.

In 1904 the family moved to Galveston where her sons owned and operated "Bowen Brothers," a corner store of "staple and fancy groceries, fish and oysters." There Rufus died in 1916 and Ella in 1927. Their son Alfred, an operations controller for the Association of American Railroads, married Viola Alice Jones, a telephone operator from Chicago. They moved to Forest Lawn, IL, where Wesley was born in 1923. A barber, he married Betty Moline, daughter of Axel (of Tistleskog, Sweden) and Ina Mae Tibbs Moline. Wesley and Betty had three sons: Phillip, Steven, and Brent. Steven, an economist, married Candace Johnsen-Rod when they were in graduate school at Florida Atlantic University in Boca Raton, FL. Christine was born to them in 1982 and Valan in 1988. They live with their mother and step-father, Candace and Peter Bundgard at Belle Rose on the Natchez Trace.

JOHN SANGUINETTI & DORIS COUILLARD.

The great-great-grandchildren of John and Doris are ninth generation descendants of Joseph Quegles who came to Natchez in the late 1700s. He was born in Pollanza on the island of Mallorca (Majorca), Spain in 1775.

Joseph Quegles, the son of Bartolomeu and Rosa Capo Quegles, was married in 1808 in New Orleans to Louise Melanie Adam, daughter of Luis Adam (Adan) and Luisa Debeon, natives of France.

Maria Melania Francisca Catarina Quegles was married in 1830 to Louis Emile Gustav Profilet, jeweler and silversmith, and born in France in 1801.

Dr. Louis Emile Profilet, educated at Yale, was married in 1867 to Eliza Feltus Sims, a descendant of Curtis Clay and Elizabeth Lohra of Philadelphia.

Mary Lacoste Profilet was married in 1890 to James Gilbert Couillard, a descendant of Guillame Couillard and Guillette Hebert of Quebec, Canada.

Doris Louise Couillard was married in 1919 to John Henry Sanguinetti a purser on the steamboat *Betsy Ann*.

The nine children of John and Doris Couillard Sanguinetti are Ann Elizabeth "Betsy" Yowell, Slater, MO; Mary Profilet Whitam, Natchez, deceased; Abbie Elsie Arnold, Natchez; Doris Imelda "Dottie" Arceneaux, Jacksonville, FL; John Henry Sanguinetti Jr., Natchez; Kathleen Louise "Tootie" Officer, Slater, MO, deceased; Joseph Lacoste Sanguinetti, Natchez; Ellen Frances Trosclair, Natchez; James Whitson Sanguinetti, Covington, LA.

According to local records, Joseph Quegles lived in Natchez in 1798. In 1818 he served as a trustee for the Roman Catholic Society of Christians in the city of Natchez and its vicinity. He was a successful merchant, planter and acquired 24 properties in Natchez between 1813 and 1825.

Louis Emile Gustav Profilet settled in Natchez

during the 1820s. He was a successful merchant, blacksmith and accomplished silversmith whose pieces are considered among the finest examples of Natchez silver. Louis Emile served three terms as a parish trustee between 1829-33.

Dr. Louis Emile Profilet graduated from Yale in 1857 and served as a surgeon with the Confederacy and toward the latter part of the war was in charge of a hospital for paroled and exchanged prisoners. He later became health officer for Adams County.

Louis Emile Jeanne Baptist Profilet Silversmith

Mary Profilet Couillard was widowed at 33 and the mother of seven children. She was an accomplished pianist and supported her family teaching piano and playing for the silent movies and musical programs at the Baker Grand Theater.

Doris Couillard Sanguinetti was a housewife, mother and managed the gift department of Tom L. Ketchings Co. for many years.

Joseph Quegles' interest in church, family, business and community has been handed down for generations. Through the years there have been professionals in medicine, law, military, religious life, business, industry, educators, government, and dedicated, hard working blue collar workers.

Eliza Feltus Sims

Significant houses in Natchez related to the Quegles, Profilet and Couillard history are the Profilet House at 508 Washington Street; Van Court House, 510 Washington Street; Botto House, 600 Washington Street; Liberty Hall, 117 South Martin Luther King Street; and the McClure House, 403 North Union Street. In New Orleans, the Louis Adam House located at 722 Toulouse Street in the French Quarter now belongs in the Historic New Orleans collection.

JOHN ANTHONY QUITMAN & ELIZA TURNER.
John Anthony (b. 1799, d. Jul. 19, 1858) was the son of Rev. Frederick Henry Quitman and Anna Elizabeth Hueck of Rhinebeck, NY. His father was a native of Prussia, and his mother daughter of the governor on the Dutch island of Curacoa in the West Indies. John moved to Chillicothe, OH to read law, then to Natchez in 1821 where he formed law partnerships first with William Griffith, then with John T. McMurran. He organized the Natchez Fencibles Militia group in 1824, was elected to the state House of Representatives in 1832, and in 1835 he led volunteers to fight in the Texas Revolution then, in 1846, to the Mexican War where he served as governor of Mexico City. Quitman was elected governor of Mississippi, then to Congress. Quitman also owned cotton plantations at Springfield in Adams County, in Coahoma County, and in Warren County, plus extensive lands in eastern Texas and a sugar cane plantation on Bayou Grand Caillou in Terrebonne Parish, LA.

On Dec. 20, 1824, Eliza Turner married John Anthony Quitman. She was the daughter of Sa-

rah Baker and Henry Turner at Woodlands. In 1826 the Quitmans made their home at nearby Monmouth. Their children were Louisa T. (b. Jan. 28, 1826, d. 1884); John Anthony (b. Jul. 24, 1828, d. May 1833); F. Henry (b. Sep. 7, 1830); Edward Turner (b. April 1832, d. May 1833); Sarah Elizabeth (b. Mar. 14, 1834, d. May 1846); J. Antonia (b. Dec. 18, 1835, d. May 23, 1916); Mary Geraldine (b. December 1837, d. April 1845); Annie Rosalie (b. Jul. 5, 1841, d. Dec. 28, 1914); Eliza Theodosia (b. May 30, 1842, d. Jul. 8, 1867); and Fredericka (b. May 30, 1844, d. Aug. 25, 1911).

On Dec. 2, 1852, Louisa married the rector of Trinity Episcopal Church, Rev. John S. Chadbourne (b. in Maine ca. 1818, d. of yellow fever Sep. 27, 1853). They had a daughter, Eva Saub Chadbourne (b. Dec. 31, 1853, d. 1919). On Jan. 18, 1859, Louisa then married Joseph Lovell (b. Jun. 11, 1824) who adopted Eva. They had a daughter, Alice Quitman Lovell (b. Nov. 28, 1863, d. Nov. 17, 1920).

On Apr. 20, 1854, Henry married Mary "Molly" Gardner of Alabama. On Jun. 29, 1858, Antonia married Lt. William Storrow Lovell, brother to Joseph. Their children were John Quitman Lovell; William Strorrow Lovell Jr.; Antonia Quitman Lovell Nauts (b. Apr. 15, 1853, d. Apr. 25, 1898); Rose Duncan Lovell (b. Oct. 17, 1866, d. Jan. 29, 1939); and Joseph Mansfield Lovell (b. Dec. 28, 1870, d. Sep. 22, 1897). In June l861, Rosalie married William P. "Pat" Duncan (b. Sep. 28, 1830, d. Jul. 2, 1862). Theodosia married Stephen Routh Jr. Fredericka first married Francis E. Ogden (b. Feb. 12, 1835, d. Oct. 25, 1867). On Jan. 1, 1903, she married Austin Williams Smith (b. 1843, d. Apr. 14, 1911). John Anthony Quitman died on Jul. l9, 1858 and Eliza Turner Quitman died on Aug. 22, 1859.

RATCLIFF-BUNDGARD.
The first known ancestor in the Bundgard family to live in Mississippi was James Ratcliff. Born in South Carolina about 1775, he migrated westward to Williamson County, TN, then south to Mississippi. According to an old family letter, James and his brothers: Peter, Samuel, Henry and Benjamin, arrived in Natchez in the early 1800s, having come down the Mississippi River on flatboats, and settled in Amite County.

James and his first wife (name uncertain, Ann Caroline Davis according to some sources) had several children: Samuel N. (b. 1801), Wm. R. (b. 1803), Isaac B. (b. 1805), Edward L. (b. 1807), Allen D. (b. 1809). James married a second time to Ada Davis in 1812 in Amite County. Children of this union were Matilda Caroline (b. 1818), Jackson N. (b. 1814), Lois Ann (b. 1816), Nathaniel (b. 1817), Rufus King Sr. (b. 1819), James R. (b. 1820), Joseph S. (b. 1822) and Mary H. (b. 1824). James became a member of Galilee Baptist Church in Amite County in 1825. Around 1830, James sold his land in Amite County (a 758-acre parcel just north of present day Gloster) and moved to Yazoo County, where he married a third time, to Nancy O'Neal. James died in 1836 in Yazoo County; his gravesite has not been located, nor have the graves of his first two wives.

The second child of James' first marriage, William Richard Ratcliff Sr., is the next ancestor in the lineage. William, born in Tennessee, moved to Mississippi as a toddler. He married Abigail Rice, who had come from Canada as a young child, reportedly being the only survivor in her family, the rest having succumbed to yellow fever while en route southward. According to family legend, she was reared by and lived with a family named Richards until she married William in l825 in Amite County. William and Abigail moved to Yazoo County around 1830 and owned land there.

He left Mississippi and went to Tyler County, TX, in 1839, when his son, William Jr. (b. 1832) was about 7 years old. This move was apparently related to the financial crisis and the failure of numerous banks and financial institutions in Mississippi in the mid and late 1830s, the result of which being that William lost all his property, which was auctioned off at a sheriff's sale in the Spring of 1839.

In 1853 in Tyler County, TX, William Jr. married Lucy Blanche Collier (b. 1834 in Georgia). One of William Jr. and Lucy's children, Blanche Katherine (b. 1864), married Charles Columbus Hicks (b. 1861, Georgia) in Tyler County, TX. After moving to Lufkin, TX, their son, Charles Lewis Hicks, married Nancy Ella Bean in 1915. Their daughter, Marguerite Hicks

William R. Ratcliff (1834-1915) and Lucy B. (Collier) Ratcliff (1834-53), gg-grandparents of Peter A. Bundgard

(b. 1919), moved to Sacramento, CA, in the late 1940s where she married Phillip Bundgard in 1949. Their second child, Peter, was born in Turlock, CA. Peter graduated from the University of Kansas School of Medicine in 1982. After serving as a medical missionary in Zaire, Africa, in the late l980s, and practicing medicine in western Kansas, he and his wife moved to the Natchez area in 1996. Dr. Bundgard works as an ER physician in several area hospitals following a brief employment at a family practice clinic in Natchez. Peter and his wife Candace live at Belle Rose, part of the original Brandon plantation, near the southern terminus of the Natchez Trace Parkway. Candace, a historian, is of Scandinavian heritage, being descended on her father's side from windjammer sea captain Karl Anton Johnsen-Rod, and on her mother's side from Lady Inger of Castle Austraat on Trondheimsfjord in Sor Trondelag, Norway.

STANFORD RAYNE JR. & HELEN DAVID BRANDON SMITH.
Helen David, a premature baby, was born in Greenwood, MS, the first to use their incubator, but she was reared in Natchez, MS in the home of her grandfather, Gerard Brandon, (b. Nov. 5, 1861, d. Jun. 21, 1956), the patriarch of the family, a remarkable, highly intelligent, empathetic, Victorian gentleman.

A graduate of Ole Miss, Gerard was superintendent of the Natchez Schools at the age of 21, but he developed an eye infection so severe from reading during a bout with measles that maggots were used to treat it; and his mother read to him his law books. He practiced law until in his 90s. He married Daisy Patterson (b. 1867, d. Jun. 21, 1947) on Dec. 20, 1893 at First Presbyterian Church; educated his five unmarried sisters at Sophie Newcomb; took care of his mother and mother-in-law until their deaths; fathered and educated four children and parented four grandchildren.

Helen's mother, Ethel Monette Brandon (b. Dec. 3, 1894, d. Jan. 6, 1948), whose ancestry included the first native born governor of Mississippi, Gerard Chittoque Brandon (b. Sep. 21, 1788, d. Mar. 28, 1850); Col. Charles Broadwater (b. 1719, d. 1806), a member of General Assembly and a delegate to Continental Congress; John Wesley Monette, noted physician, writer and historian; Thomas Newman (Revolutionary); Caleb

Massey (Revolutionary) married in Trinity Church to David Lawson (Lemmon) Smith (b. 1891, d. Mar. 7, 1965), an optometrist, born in Donaldsonville, LA (Ancestry: Col. Charles Broadwater; Ester Ball, aunt of George Washington; Chichester Chinn, cousin to Sir Walter Scott; Sgt. Enoch Keene Withers [Revolution] and Judge Thomas Withers Chinn, U.S. Minister to the two Sicilies.)

Helen's siblings are Margaret Gerard Smith (Jan. 10, 1918) md. on Nov. 5, 1938 Marion Theodore Wesley (b. Aug. 7, 1911, d. Mar. 5, 2001); Mary Jane Smith (b. Dec. 14, 1921, d. Jan. 13, 1990) md. Oliver McDonald Hornsby (b. Nov. 3, 1911, d. Mar. 31, 1985); David Gerard Brandon Smith (b. Feb. 3, 1924, d. May 17, 1974) md. Thelma Stackpole of Washington. All attended Natchez public schools.

Helen resigned nurses training to marry Stanford Rayne Jr. "Buddy" on Dec. 2, 1943. An engineer, he served as captain during WWII, and worked for Mobil Corporation in several managerial capacities. He adopted Helen's son of a previous marriage, Alan Christopher Damian Arenas, renaming him Alan Christopher Rayne, (Jan 3, 1942). In 1952 they adopted Robert Theodore "Tad" Rayne. Alan married Molly Baxter in Beaumont, Texas and had three sons: Alan Christopher, Eric Joseph and Matthew Kurt, all married and they live in Colorado. "Tad" Robert married Kathleen Kelly in Pennsylvania and they live in Christiansburg, VA. "Kathy" had a son and daughter by a previous marriage whom "Tad" adopted. (Sean married and is a policeman in Christiansburg, VA with a daughter by each of his two previous marriages; and Kelly is a lawyer in Memphis, TN). Sara Rose Rayne (b. Aug. 4, 1979) is a graduate student in psychology in Virginia Tech. Helen has 10 great-grandchildren.

Active in the Episcopal Church, they also participate in many social and service organizations. A choir member and Altar Guild leader, Helen, also, is a member of the art guild, musical art league, two historical societies, the DAR (past regent) and Progressive Study Club (president). Both are inaugural members of Habitat for Humanity. "Buddy" is a Lay Eucharistic minister and lay reader. He enjoys golf and is a member of Beau Pre' Country Club. *Submitted by Helen D. Rayne.*

THOMAS REBER & ANNIE VERNON.

Thomas (b. March 1843 at Sandusky, OH), son of George and Amanda Boalt Reber. Of German descent George Reber was a prominent Ohio attorney serving in the State Legislature. Amanda died in 1847 leaving Thomas and a daughter, Clara, who were reared in their father's home after his marriage in 1849 to Mrs. Nancy Stiles Kilborne.

In 1861 Thomas enrolled in Ovid Agricultural College in New York. In 1862 he enlisted in the Union Army as private in Co. K, 88th Ohio Volunteer Infantry at Columbus, OH; later he transferred to 196th, was promoted to first lieutenant, then to brigade quartermaster and stationed for a time at Fort Federal Hill near Baltimore. He was honorably discharged in June 1865.

Judge Thomas Reber

Associated with a Cincinnati firm after the war, Thomas was sent to Cuba where he remained several years before migrating to Louisiana/Mississippi where he began a prolific career in civic affairs and business during the South's reconstruction.

In Louisiana he was appointed circuit judge of Concordia and Tensas parishes, holding court in Vidalia, thus the title "Judge" by which he was known thereafter. He served a term as tax collector of Concordia Parish and served on the Concordia Parish Police Jury being elected president Dec. 16, 1872.

Judge Reber at the landing

In Vidalia, Thomas Reber met Miss Annie Vernon, daughter of the late William Rousseau Cox Vernon and Rowena Crane Vernon. They married Dec. 30, 1872 and lived in Vidalia where Reber was active in the progressive developments of the parish.

The first railroad in Concordia Parish, a "narrow gauge" two or three miles long extending from the river to Lake Concordia and used for transporting freight and cotton, was built by Reber and H.M. Gastrell. In 1881 Reber was one of the incorporators of the Natchez, Red River and Texas Railroad which built a "narrow gauge" road from Vidalia to Black River.

In the early 1880s, the Reber family moved to Natchez where he was traffic manager of J.N. Carpenter's Natchez and Vicksburg Packet Co. for 20 years; also, superintendent of Captain R.F. Learned's packets, *Betsy Ann* and *Little Rufus*. Granted a master's license, he became known as "Captain" rather than "Judge."

In other business interests Reber and Isaac Lowenburg in partnership purchased property in North Natchez subdividing into 79 lots known as Rebertown or Woodlawn Addition.

Reber built the first street railway in Natchez, a horse-car system which ran from The River landing to Broadway, up Main and out St. Catherine 2.5 miles to a park and casino, an auditorium seating 2,000. Reber installed the first electric plant in Natchez to furnish light for "Thomas Reber's Forks-in-the-Road Casino."

In 1890 Mrs. Reber was purchaser of lots in Williamsburg Addition where a permanent home was built for the family at 829 Main and Orange Ave.

Reber played a leading role in organizing the Natchez Mardi Gras in 1898 and reigned as King in 1905.

Judge Reber's book *Proud Old Natchez* was written as a souvenir of President William H. Taft's visit to Natchez on Oct. 29, 1909; it describes lavish preparation and pageantry connected with that event in which he had a major role.

Annie Vernon Reber died Jan. 16, 1910. Eight children and a despondent husband survived. Thomas Reber followed her in death Apr. 29, 1912. Their graves in Natchez City Cemetery are marked with a marble obelisk inscribed, *Erected 1916 to the memory of Thomas Reber as a tribute of love and gratitude by his friends of Natchez, MS. Submitted by L.R. McGehee.*

SIDNEY JOSEPH REEDY & ELLA JOHN COMER.

Ella John Comer was born in Ferriday, LA in October 1862, the daughter of John Comer and Caroline Cochran. John Comer, an emigrant from Ireland, was a merchant and municipal judge in Ferriday. Caroline Cochran was born in Natchez, the daughter of an Irishman and a woman who was half African and half Choctaw. Caroline worked as a barmaid at the Natchez Inn, an establishment that John frequented on weekends. Caroline and John could not marry because of laws against mixed race marriages; however, John took Caroline to live at his home in Ferriday in 1862 during her pregnancy with his child. Caroline and Ella John remained in Comer's household until the end of the Civil War in 1865. Comer continued to provide for his daughter financially, even paid for her to attend the Natchez Academy, until her marriage in 1879 to Sidney Joseph Reedy.

Sydney was the son of an Irish emigrant, Andrew Reedy, and a slave in the McPheeters household named Sarah. Andrew gambled away his farm in Tennessee in a poker game and became a riverboat town evangelist. Whenever he reached Natchez, Andrew stayed for awhile with Sarah, and ultimately, the couple had three children together: Isabella, Virginia and Sydney Joseph. Sydney, born in 1856, was named for Mr. Sydney Fineberg, a merchant who had accepted Andrew's money left on credit for Sarah and the children while he worked up and down the Mississippi River.

Following their marriage in 1879, Sydney and Ella produced nine children: Stella (b. 1880), Ruth (b. 1882), Isabella (b. 1884), Caroline (b. 1885), Houston (b. 1887), Ella John (b. 1889), Sarah (b. 1892), Walter (b. 1899) and Sydney Joseph Jr. (b. 1902). Sydney supported his family by working as a lumber grader at Leonard's Lumber Yard. As time passed, Sydney was able to buy two horses and a carriage and establish a "taxi" company. Eventually, there were about half a dozen carriages in the building located just across the street from the Reedy home at 610 Monroe St.

Ella was a lifelong member of Zion Chapel AME Church where she was involved in a multitude of ministries. Sydney, reared Catholic, did not practice his faith. Both Ella and Sydney received as much secondary education as was afforded African-Americans at that time. Sydney was widely known for his ability to quote long passages from Shakespeare's plays and sonnets.

Ella John Comer

Sydney and Ella's nine children produced 28 grandchildren spanning 53 years: Stella (Charles Vessels), five; Ruth (Levi Brown), 10; Isabella (Burleigh Webster, Bradford Nichols), three; Houston (Faye __), one; Ella (George Hayden), two; Sarah (Allen Travis II), three; Walter (Marie Patterson), one; Sydney Jr. (Hilda Lawson), three. Ella and Sydney lost three descendants in the Rhythm Club fire on Apr. 23, 1940: Meletta Carroll, John Logan and Ruth Brown.

Living descendants of Sydney and Ella are now found throughout the United States in Florida, Georgia, Alabama, Washington, California, Maryland, Virginia, Michigan, New York, New Jersey, Massachusetts, Indiana, Illinois, Iowa, Missouri, Kansas and Mississippi. Ella John Comer Reedy died on Dec. 26, 1938. Sydney Reedy Sr. died on Mar. 27, 1914.

SIDNEY JOSEPH REEDY JR. & HILDA LAWSON.

Sidney Joseph was the third son, ninth and last child of Sydney Joseph Reedy, Sr. and Ella John Comer Reedy. Born on Apr. 28, 1902, Sidney was his parents' only child born in the 20th century. Sydney Sr. (b. 1856, d. 1914) was a Natchez native, the son of an Irishman, Andrew Reedy, and an African-American slave named Sarah. Ella was born in Ferriday, LA in October 1862 to John Comer, an Irish emigrant and Caroline Cochran, a multi-racial woman of Irish, African and Choctaw ancestry. Sidney excelled in school, the building was just over the fence from his parents' side yard, so Sidney and his siblings ate hot lunches prepared by their mother and handed across the fence at the noon hour. Sidney was unable to finish school in Natchez because, when his father died on Mar. 27, 1914, his mother decided that he and his next older brother, Walter, needed a man to rear them. In August 1914, Sidney, supplied with a box lunch, boarded a train headed to Joplin, MO to live with his oldest brother, Houston.

In Joplin, Sidney finished grade school and ninth grade, the extent of schooling provided to African-Americans in Joplin at that time. Sidney then moved to St. Louis, MO where he lived with his father's cousin, Gertrude Barrett, and family. Sidney attended Sumner High School where he was made to repeat ninth grade because of the poor reputation of Joplin's educational system. Still, he graduated in seven semesters as salutatorian of his class. After working three jobs to earn money for college, Sidney matriculated at Lincoln University in Jefferson City, MO. Graduating at the head of his class, Sidney began working as principal and teacher at the high school for African-Americans in Poplar Bluff, MO.

Before returning to Lincoln University in 1928 as principal of the Lincoln University High School, Sidney also taught at Frederick Douglass High School in Columbia, MO. In 1928 Sidney was awarded a master of science degree in education from the University of Iowa, and in August 1939, he received a PhD in education from what is now the University of Northern Colorado. From 1940 until his retirement in 1972, Sidney taught at the college and graduate levels at Lincoln University. During those years Sidney served as director of the university's graduate programs and as advisor to graduate students in the field of education. He contributed articles to a number of education journals and served as associate editor of the *Midwest Journal*.

In 1923 Sidney converted to Catholicism and was baptized at St. Peter's Cathedral in Jefferson City on Mar. 23, 1923. In 1928 he became a member of the Kappa Alpha Psi fraternity, and in 1932 was co-founder of a chapter of that fraternity at Lincoln University. In 1939, after his mother's death, Sidney changed the "y" in his first name to an "i."

In 1940 Sidney met Dr. Hilda Lawson, an assistant professor at Lincoln from Washington, DC. Dr. Lawson received her PhD from the University of Illinois in January 1939, the first African-American woman to receive a doctorate there. Hilda was of Swedish, Scottish, English, African and Cherokee ancestry. On Sep. 6, 1941 the two were married at St. Augustine Catholic Church in Washington, DC. To this union were born three sons:

Sidney Reedy Jr.

Sidney Joseph III (b. 1942), Michael Patrick (b. 1947) and Dennis Lawson (b. 1951). To those sons were born three grandchildren: Christian Edward Reedy (b. 1970), Michelle Lynn Reedy Bradley (b. 1972) and Cara Kathleen Reedy (b. 1975).

HILDA CULIPHER REGISTER & THOMAS E. YOUNG SR.

Thomas E. Young Sr. in the uniform of the English army, WWI, 1914

Thomas Richards married Mary Ann Ellen Campbell (Richards) on Aug. 18, 1867 (Marriage Ref. #Y010224, London, England) and was the father of Mary Ann Richards, formerly Campbell (b. Aug. 16, 1871) (Birth Ref. #8002552, Middlesex, England).

Charles Frederick Young married Mary Ann Ellen Richards on Aug. 23, 1891 (Marriage Ref. #MX981577, London, England) and was the father of Thomas Edgar Young Sr. (b. Jan. 19, 1898) (Birth Ref. #BC184112, England).

Thomas Sr. served in WWI in 1914, and sustained a very severe head wound in combat which required the insertion of a silver plate in his skull. He carried that plate for the remainder of his life. He married Hilda Culipher Register on Sep. 14, 1921, and was the father of Thomas Edgar Young Jr. (b. Jun. 28, 1924) (Ref. Birth Certificate Adams County).

JOHN FITZ ROBERT & ADA DE BELIAL.

1) John Fitz Robert, Baron of Warwick, md. Ada, daughter of Hugh De Belial.

2) Robert Fitz John md. Isabel.

3) Robert Fitz Robert md. Margery De La Zaush.

4) Euphenice Robert md. Ralph Neville, 1st Lord Neville.

5) Ralph Neville, 2nd Lord Neville, md. Alice, daughter of Hugh De Audley.

6) John Neville, 3rd Lord Neville, md. Maud Percy, daughter of Lord Henry Percy.

7) Ralph Neville md. Joan De Beaufort, daughter of John of Gaent (she was a granddaughter of King Edward III).

8) Elinor Neville md. Henry, 10th Earl Percy (d. 1455), descendant of Llewellyn the Great of Wales and Edward I and Ferdinand III of Spain.

9) Thomas Percy md. Matilde Hubert.

10) Henry Percy (d. 1527) md. Catherine Spencer, a descendant of William the Conqueror.

11) Sir Thomas Percy (d. 1537) md. Eleanor Harbottle.

12) Joan/Johanna Percy md. Arthur Harris.

13) William Harris (d. 1556) md. Joan/Johanna Cooke.

14) Arthur Harris (d. 1597) md. Dorothy Waldgrove, descended from Edward I.

15) Sir William Harris (d. 1616) md. Alice Smith.

16) Capt. Thomas Harris (b. 1586, d. 1611) md. Adrian Osborne.

17) Mary Harris (b. 1625, d. 1703) md. Col. Thomas Ligon (d. 1677 in Henrico County, VA, Burgess 1655).

18) Johan Ligon (b. 1656, d. 1728) md. Robert Hancock (b. 1656, d. 1708) in 1672 of Henrico County, VA.

19) Johan Hancock md. April 15, 1700 to her first cousin Samuel Hancock (d. 1760) Henrico County, VA.

20) Samuel Hancock (b. 1702, d. 1760) md. Elizabeth Jameslin.

21) Phoebe Hancock (b. 1719) md. in 1735 to John Watkins (b. 1710, d. 1765) Cumberland County (now Powhatan County), VA.

22) Samuel Watkins (b. 1750, d. 1795) md. Elizabeth Goode (d. 1790), Powhatan County, VA.

22) Powhatan Wooldridge md. Elizabeth Watkins, daughter of John Watkins and Phoebe Hancock, Versailles, KY.

23) Philip Watkins (b. 1782, Woodford County, KY) md. Phoebe Wooldridge.

24) Catherine Wooldridge Watkins (b. Aug. 18, 1812, d. Sep. 29, 1893) md. Oct. 20, 1834 to Thomas Mountjoy Buck (b. Mar. 1, 1811, d. Mar. 9, 1894) Charlottesville, VA, gg-grandson of Marquis de la Calmes (b. 1705, d. 1751) of Williamsburg.

25) Samuel Henry Buck, named for Henry Clay because his uncle was Clay's stepfather (b. Oct. 9, 1841, d. Jan. 6, 1929) md. Oct. 11, 1870 Annie Fleming (b. Oct. 15, 1848, d. Oct. 12, 1912).

26) Marion Buck (b. Mar. 20, 1873, d. Jan. 21, 1962) Natchez, MS, md. Sep. 27, 1904 Ralph Gould Persell (b. Feb. 21, 1882, d. Oct. 2, 1950), Summit, MS. Children: Margaret Fleming, Anne Fleming and Ralph Montijoy.

27) Margaret Fleming Persell (b. Dec. 12, 1905, d. Feb. 9, 1993) md. first, Claude Snider; second, George Matthews Marshall III. Children: Neville Buck (Neville Curtis Snider) adopted by Marshall; Margaret Devereaux, George Matthews IV.

28) Neville Buck Marshall (b. Dec. 10, 1924, d. Dec. 26, 1990) md. first, Margaret Jeannette Burkley (b. Feb. 18, 1928); md. second, Emily Stubbs Kelley; md. third, Jennie Lou Bryan. Children: Margaret Katherine, Marion Jeannette, Charlotte Agnes, Anne Elizabeth, Malquin Morgan, Neville Buck II (all by MJB) and Joan Fleming (by JLB).

29) Margaret Katherine "Kathy" Marshall (b. Oct. 12, 1950) md. Monroe Jackson Moody Jr. Children: Monroe Jackson "Jack" III (b. Feb. 15, 1968, d. Mar. 1, 2002 in Houston, TX, buried at Laurel Hill in Adams County, MS) md. Cara Winter, son Monroe Jackson IV (b. Apr. 26, 2001); Merrick Rowan Dashiell (b. Feb. 6, 1972) md. Jackie Passbach Jan. 13, 2001. 1054 Lower Woodville Rd, Natchez, MS 39120 (601-445-9760).

29) Marion Jeannette Marshall (b. Apr. 1, 1952) md. first, Godfrey Forrester; md. second, John Darius Tassistro; md. third, Mike Holloway; md. fourth, Mark Drennen. Children: Angelique "Angie" Devereux Tassistro (b. May 12, 1974), Rodney Darius Tassistro (b. Feb. 21, 1976), Adrienne Marshall Drennen (b. Feb. 7, 1985). Lives in St. Francisville, LA.

29) Charlotte Elizabeth Agnes Anne Marshall (b. Jul. 13, 1953) md. first, Elliot Brumfield; md. second, Alan Edmonds. Children: Charlotte Aaron Brumfield (b. Sep. 6, 1974) md. first, Casey Smith, son, Walker (b. Aug. 21, 1996); md. second, Jason Hennington, daughter Pressley, son Braden Starnes); Chesney Dawn Brumfield (b. Jun. 2, 1976) md. Jeremiah Wheeler, daughter Miah Brailey (b. Apr. 26, 2002); Elliot Buck Brumfield (b. Oct. 5, 1978); Rachel Megan Edmonds (b. May 7, 1981) md. Wesley Givens, son, Marshall (b. Feb. 10, 2000). 219 Clifton Ave., Natchez, MS 39120 (601-445-4889)

29) Malquin Morgan Marshall (b. Aug. 29, 1954) md. first, Salvo Piazza; md. second, Peter Pevonka. Children: Emily Johanna Piazza (b. Jan. 17, 1976), Jessica Conchetta Magdalena Piazza (b. May 17, 1977). 5824 S.E. 185th Ave., Micanopy, FL 32667 (904-466-0465)

29) Neville Buck Marshall II (b. Sep. 12, 1957) md. Beth Anderson. Children Charlotte Kay (b. Dec. 24, 1988), Morgan Keene (b. Sep. 22, 1991), living in Flagstaff, AZ.

29) Joan Fleming (b. Sep. 6, 1976) md. Samuel Gatlin Dec. 22, 2001.

28) Margaret Devereaux "Devie" Marshall (b. May 11, 1926) md. first, Joseph Colson; md. second, McKenzie Nobles; md. third, William Slatter. P.O. Box 413, Natchez, MS 39120. Children:

29) Margaret Marshall Colson (b. Sep. 14, 1949) md. Larry Axelrod, child David.

29) Lisa Fleming Colson (b. Aug. 13, 1953) md. Burke Baker. Children: Anna, Andrew, Ashton.

28) George Matthews Marshall IV (b. Jan. 14, 1930) md. Mary Beecher Powell. P.O. Box 413, Natchez, MS 39120. Children:

29) George Matthews Marshall V (b. Mar. 2, 1961) md. first, Denise Roshto (now divorced) no children; married second, Kirsten, daughter Camille (b. 1999) and son George VI (b. January 2002)

29) Twins—Holly and Heather Marshall (b. Nov. 14, 1968).

JOHN ROBSON SR. & ANN WEATHERALL.

John (b. Mar. 18, 1793, in Durham, England), the son of John and Margery Robson, died May 21, 1856 in Adams County, MS. In March 1809, age 16, he left his father's at 60 Durham, England, and landed in North Carolina by way of St. Johns Newfoundland and Boston, MA. In the fall of 1809, he made application for citizenship in Hillsboro, NC.

He returned to England and married Ann Weatherell in July 1816, daughter of Margaret and John Weatherell, in Hughington Church, England. She was born Nov. 2, 1794 and died Feb. 18, 1860 aboard the steamer *General Quitman,* Vicksburg.

They went to America in 1816; ship repairs had to be made in Ireland. They landed in City Point, James River, VA; from there they staged to Fayetteville, NC. In 1818 he, after failing in business, surrendered all property to creditors, but stayed until 1821 to influence the selling of his business. He headed West with his wife in a four wheel carriage and two horses. Accompanying them were Margaret, Mary Ann, James McDonald and Elizabeth Palmer - no relationships known.

They had six children: Margaret P. (b. May 1817, d. Sep. 18, 1860) md. Henry J. Bass; Mary Ann (b. 1822, d. Apr. 28, 1834; John Jr. (b. Nov. 25, 1826, d. Feb. 24, 1870) first married Caroline Boyd and second, Anna Barlow; William (b. August 1828, d. Jun. 26, 1829); Emeline (b. 1830, d. Jan. 7, 1872 in Dallas, TX) md. Robert Tickell; Matilda W. (b. Aug. 29, 1832, d. Oct. 17, 1835).

He began a business in Adams County at the Old Court House on Apr. 2, 1822, with a capitol of 38 pounds, 800 pounds in debt and some debt with Pearce & Robson. They moved to Prospect Hill in January 1828 where he farmed. In December 1831, he was appointed Postmaster for Palestine, Adams County, MS, and held that position until 1839.

In 1832, because of poor health, he left the business of merchandizing. In 1845 he moved near Natchez to a house purchased from Holmes Iving and L.R. Marshall. On Feb. 7, 1854, the home burned, destroying personal property and furniture, but without personal injury.

In the 1850 Adams County census he was listed as a planter, worth $26,000. He died at Prospect Hill Plantation and is buried in the Natchez City Cemetery with Ann and all their children except Emeline.

His will, probated in Adams County court term of May 1858, named his three children: John Jr., Margaret and Emeline, sons-in-laws, Henry J. Bass and Robert Tickell. His wife received property on Commerce Street between Main and State Streets, and three slaves. His son and sons-in-law were to share and share alike in the Prospect Hill Plantation consisting of 950 acres, more or

Ann Weatherell Robson (b. Nov. 2, 1794, d. Feb. 18, 1860) and John Robson Sr. (b. Mar. 18, 1793, d. May 21, 1856)

less, the Bullet Bayou property containing 1500 acres; and property on Franklin Street between Wall and Pearl Streets. *Submitted by Ella McCaleb Young.*

JOHN ROBSON JR., son of John Sr. and Ann Weatherell Robson was born Nov. 25, 1826, in Adams County MS and died there, Feb. 24, 1879. He was a farmer. He married twice: first on Jul. 3, 1851 to Caroline Boyd, born Feb. 21, 1831 at Magnolia Hill Plantation, home of her parents, Alexander and Wealtha Thomas Boyd. She died Apr. 15, 1863 and was buried in the Boyd Cemetery on Magnolia Hill. Caroline was the second child and oldest daughter of 10 children. Her father's will states he gave her the south half of Pine Grove plantation, seven slaves and 21 head of cattle with an estimated value of eight thousand dollars.

Caroline Boyd Robson and John Robson Jr.

Caroline bore John seven children:

1) Margaret Anna (b. Apr. 19, 1852, at Prospect Hill Plantation, d. Oct. 12, 1860, at Greenwood Plantation.

2) Louisa Wealtha (b. Oct. 9, 1853, at Magnolia Hill) md. Douglas Bisland McCaleb on Feb. 22, 1881, at Stephania, home of her sister Virginia Robson Ireland; she died there Dec. 13, 1907. They are buried in the Pine Ridge Presbyterian Church Cemetery.

3) Baby girl Robson (b. Jun. 6, 1855, at Windy Hill Plantation and died the same day).

4) Mary Josephine (b. Jun. 28, 1856, at Windy Hill Plantation) md. William John Thorn at Magnolia Hill, Apr. 6, 1883, and died Jun. 20, 1942, Smithland Plantation; they are buried in the Jersey Settlers Cemetery.

5) John Alexander (b. Dec. 27, 1858, at Greenwood Plantation, d. Dec. 25, 1883, Concordia Parish, LA, buried in the Natchez City Cemetery) never married.

6) Virginia Fox (b. May 18, 1860, on Greenwood Plantation) md. John Dorsey Ireland on Jan. 15, 1879, at Magnolia Hill Plantation. She died Jun. 13, 1932, in Ensley, AL; both are buried in the Natchez City Cemetery.

7) William Albert (b. Feb. 7, 1862, Greenwood Plantation, d. Mar. 3, 1862).

John Robson Jr. taught his children Latin, Greek and Math, but he had a governess who taught other subjects. One governess was "Cousin Annie" and it is not known if she was truly related, or if that was a courtesy title. He married Anna B. Barlow (Cousin Annie) on Dec. 12, 1866, in her mother's home in Natchez, the service conducted by Rev. Joseph B. Stratton. Anna bore him one child, Henry Barlow Robson (b. Sep. 20, 1867, at Greenwood Plantation, d. Nov. 28, 1947). Henry married Lelia Miller Jan. 18, 1906, in the Washington Methodist Church. She was born Feb. 25, 1881 and died Apr. 30, 1973. They are buried in the Natchez City Cemetery.

A funeral notice pasted in the Robson Bible says John Jr. was buried from Trinity Episcopal Church; handwritten under Deaths says "buried in the Natchez Cemetery." There is a large marker in the Robson plot for Anna, but none for John Jr. *Submitted by Ella McCaleb Young, great-granddaughter.*

CHARLES HANNAH ROCHESTER & MARY McCALEB.

Mary (b. Jan. 2, 1818, at Peachland Plantation, in the Pine Ridge Community of Adams County, MS) was the seventh child of eight born to John and Maria Collins McCaleb. Surrounded by much family, in the same community lived her Collins grandparents, her mother's sister Elizabeth Chamberlin and husband Samuel; at the Hermitage, in Claiborne County, lived her parental grandmother, Ann McCaleb, widow of Captain William. Mary was five years old when her father died and his brother, Jonathan, and Mary's mother were made guardian of her and the other minor children. When she was 8 her mother married William A. Miskell.

Mary married Dec. 10, 1834 at Peachland, home of her brother James, to Charles Hannah Rochester (b. Jan. 20, 1817), son of John and Sallie Lewis Rochester, both native Virginians, then of Danville, KY where they went to live. She died Mar. 18, 1849 and was buried in the Rochester Cemetery.

Charles was a first cousin to Sophia Moore, first wife of Mary's brother James, who had gone to school at Centre College in Danville, as had Charles, who graduated in 1834. Sophia probably brought about the acquaintance of the two when Mary had enjoyed the season at Graham Springs, Harrodsburg, KY, where many Southern Belles from the South frequented in the summer to escape the heat. Mary was heir to a considerable inheritance from her father, her Collins grandparents and her mother's sister, Elizabeth Chamberlin. Charles endeavored to support her in the manner to which she was accustomed.

In 1836 Charles' mother deeded him a brick mansion called Mount Airy that had been built for his father by a noted Danville architect, Robert Russell Jr.

They were both reared in the Presbyterian faith and were involved in church affairs. Charles served as a Deacon and later an Elder. Her obituary said she was greatly loved and admired for her Christian life. She had been seriously ill for sometime before her death, but the nature of her illness was not revealed.

Mary and Charles had seven children:

1) Henrietta (b. 1835, d. 1922) md. Junius Caldwell; no issue.

2) Susan Lewis (b. ca. 1837) md. first, Franklin Owsley. Children: Margaret, Ophelia, Mattie, John and Florence. She married second, H.M. Burke, no issue.

3) Edwin Taylor (b. 1839, d. 1900) md. Emma Helm. Children: Edwin, Mattie Welsh, Lulie Burrows, Grace Gatewood, Willa W. and Henrietta.

4) Mary McCaleb (b. 1840, d. 1928) was called Mamie and remained single.

5) John McCaleb (b. 1843, d. 1889) md. Sallie Welsh in 1871. Children: Mary McCaleb, Bettie Welsh, Henrietta Caldwell, Lula Burrows, Mattie and John Welsh.

6) Sarah Lewis (b. 1845, d. 1901) md. Howard Lansing Burrows DD, Baptist minister. Children: Charles Lansing, John Rochester and Mary Adelaide.

7) Charles Hannah Jr. (b. ca. 1847) md. Margaret A. Carson in 1867. Child, Eddie M.

After Mary's death, Charles married Mary Letitia Caldwell by whom he had seven children: Annie Caldwell, William J., George Alfred, Junius C., Richmond, Percy and Lettie Lee.

He died in 1894 and Letitia died in 1902, both buried Woodlawn Cemetery, Independence, MO. *Submitted by Ella McCaleb Young and Erick Montgomery.*

ROGILLIO FAMILY.

Ysidero Policarpo Reguillo (b. Jan. 26, 1766), son of Joseph Reguillo and Mary Rufina Gonzoles in La Suza, District of Toledo, Spain (Baptism in Parish Church of Our Lady of the Assumption, town of Lezuza, Spain). He died Aug. 30, 1832 and is buried McQueen Cemetery, Jackson, LA (D.A.R. inventory, Clayton Library, Houston, TX).

The earliest mention of Policarpo was in the Favret Papers, Vol. 3, p. 126.

It lists him as a member of a regiment of Spanish soldiers stationed in the village of Natchez in 1789. (Equivalent of a non-commissioned officer.)

He married Margarita Thomas (b. Oct. 8, 1768), daughter of Elias and Catherine Smith of Virginia, in the village of Natchez on Aug. 22, 1793 (recorded St. Joseph Cathedral, Baton Rouge, LA). She died May 5, 1829 and is buried McQueen Cemetery, Jackson, LA.

Margaret and Policarpo Rogillio had 12 children, three born in the Natchez District: Joseph (b. Sep. 22, 1793) and twins, Antonio Santiago and Emanuel (b. Sep. 27, 1795).

There are records in Book C, page 25 Natchez records that Policarpo Rogillio, soldier in the Regiment of Louisiana, bought 95 arpants on St. Catherine's creek from William Vousdan for $80. Later he sold this land and petitioned the Spanish government to establish himself and family of three grown white persons on Buffalo Creek. He was granted 300 acres by Carondelet in New Orleans Mar. 28, 1794 bound by Buffalo and Piney Woods Creeks and on Apr. 25, 1798 this land was assigned to William Dunbar for $50. It was about this time that he obtained a Spanish land grant on Thompson Creek, near what is now Jackson, Feliciana Parish, LA. For many years maps showed a community of Rogillioville in this area. It was here that all the rest of the children were born. Joseph and Antonio went with their parents to Feliciana Parish, LA, but one of the twins, Emanuel Rogillio remained in the District of Natchez where he lived at what became Pine Ridge, Adams County, MS with Rachael Smith Foster and William Foster whom he called aunt and uncle.

He married in Claiborne County, MS, Eliza Tannehill (Teanehill), born Dec. 9, 1805, the daughter of Rachael Foster Tannehill and George Tannehill and granddaughter of James Foster of Foster's Mound, Pine Ridge, MS (brother to the above William Foster).

Emanuel had land granted to him on Apr. 20, 1820 from U.S. government and in 1834 he inherited property from Eliza's great uncle William Foster (called Poverty Hill). Emanuel acquired other acreage and sometime between 1834 and 1843 they built their home which they named "Mount Olive." On this land in Pine Ridge, MS and

Mount Olive, Pine Ridge, MS, built by Emanuel and Eliza Rogillio.

land in Concordia Parish, LA, he grew cotton.

Emanuel Rogillio died Dec. 3, 1862 and Eliza Rogillio on Aug. 10, 1880. Both are buried on part of their inherited land called the Gibson Cemetery. They had eight children all born at Pine Ridge, Adams County, MS:

1) Tennessee Rogillio (b. Jan. 29, 1824, d. Mar. 17, 1908) md. Jordon Gibson Sep. 17, 1839. Family records record these children: Laura Elizabeth, Eliza Ann, Emmanuel M. and a second marriage to Daniel Willis, Nov. 27, 1862

2) Thomas S. Rogillio (b. Aug. 16, 1826, d. Jan. 21, 1853), buried Gibson Cemetery.

3) Margaret E. Rogillio (b. Jul. 19, 1828, d. Feb. 25, 1908) md. John Henry Berry Nov. 8, 1845, Adams County. They had 13 children.

4) William J. Rogillio (b. Aug. 23, 1830, d. Feb. 19, 1839), buried Gibson Cemetery.

5) Serena Catherine Rogillio (b. Nov. 21, 1833, d. Jun. 21, 1852) md. John C. Barnett, Feb. 13, 1851 and had one son who died young.

6) Mary Adeline Rogillio (b. Aug. 31, 1836, d. Jul. 9, 1964) md. first, Martin L. Rogillio on Jun. 26, 1855 and lived on her father Emanuel's land in Concordia Parish, LA. They had two children who both died young. Her second marriage was to Abner Mardis, Feb. 28, 1867, Pine Ridge, MS, 1880 census; four boys Campbell, Charles, Edwin, A. Abner.

7) Elias Julian Rogillio (b. Mar. 31, 1841, d. Mar. 29, 1866).

8) Barbara Helen Rogillio (b. Jul. 20, 1846, d. Nov. 12, 1932) md. Melvin D. Gibson, Confederate veteran, Sep. 20, 1866, both buried at Pine Ridge Presbyterian Cemetery.

Barbara Helen inherited from her mother, Eliza, the home "Mt. Olive." The 1880 Pine Ridge census shows: Eliza Rogillio, Melvin Gibson and wife Barbara, their children Elias J. James, Lavinia, Rosanna, Susanna, Eva, Mollie and Helena.

On Apr. 20, 1820 Emanuel Rogillio received a grant from the U.S. Government for 237 and 53/100ths acres of land in Adams County and in 1834 Emanuel and his wife Eliza inherited property from Eliza's great-uncle, William Foster. Emanuel acquired other property around this property until it came to 2,000 acres on which he raised cotton. They built their home, Mount Olive (ca. 1840), facing Foster Mound Road. The house stands on an old Spanish Land grant of 180 acres. It was of cypress construction both inside and out. It had a hip roof and a columned gallery stretching across the front. The exterior of the house was white with green shutters and brown, possibly grained, doors. It had one and a half stories with two dormer windows upstairs and small, six over six windows with wooden panels under each elsewhere in the structure. The doors, complete with William IV locks and keys inside and out with three sets of double doors which lead from three rooms onto the gallery. The off-centered front door is opened to the hall which connects the gallery to

the back center room. Four rooms have centered fireplaces and brick chimneys. An enclosed stairway leads from the back center room to the second floor which has two small rooms on either side of one large room.

Mount Olive is architecturally significant because it documents the taste and life style of an American 1840 farmhouse. Emanuel and Eliza borrowed ideas for their home from Greenfield Plantation (Eliza's great-uncle Thomas Foster's home) and from Mistletoe (Eliza's Aunt Barbara Foster Bisland's home).

JOHN & MARY ESTELLE SANGUINETTI FAMILY.

John (better known as Sonny) and Mary Estelle Sanguinetti have lived most of their lives in Natchez and have ancestors that go back several generations in the Natchez area. They celebrated their 50th wedding anniversary in 2001 and have resided in Mary Estelle's family home on South Union Street for most of their married life.

Sonny's grandfather, John Sanguinetti, migrated from Italy and married Lizzie McInnery from Ireland in Natchez. His father married Doris Couillard, who was a fifth generation descendent of Joseph Quegles and Melanie Adam as outlined in another article in this book.

Mary Estelle's mother was Alyce Barland Whodine. She was the 8th child of John and Mattie Elizabeth Barland of Claiborne County, MS. Mattie died when Alyce was 5 years old. Her father was not able to take care of the younger children so Charles and Stella Whodine brought her to Natchez, gave her their name and reared her as their own, even though they never legally adopted her. Charles was a half-brother to Fred Henderson, who was married to Mr. Barland's sister, Martha. Charles Whodine was from Sweden and Stella Murta was from Canada. It is not known what brought them to Natchez but they were married here. Stella was a seamstress and Charles was a grocery salesman and later he owned and operated a broom factory, which was located near where the tire plant is now.

Alyce married Patrick Puderer, who came from New Orleans to work at the broom factory as a salesman and that is how they met. Pat and Alyce were married in February 1930 and moved to New Orleans, where Mary Estelle was born in November.

John and Mary Estelle Sanguinetti at their 50th wedding anniversary with their nine children: Johnny, Paul, Charlotte, Margaret, Kathleen, Pat, Mark, David and Andrew

In 1933 they moved back to Natchez when Charles Whodine died, just prior to the birth of their second daughter, Patricia Ann. In 1935, when Stella died they moved into the Whodine home on South Union Street. This was during the depression and in order to be able to keep the house, they rented rooms and apartments, keeping only two rooms for their family to live in. Through the years Pat worked at many different types of jobs and owned several businesses. He sold custom-made suits and shoes, operated a brokerage firm and had several eating establishments (J&J Bar, Pat's Luncheonette, Pat's Eats, Windmill Cafe, The Old South Cafe, ran a lottery and a cab company.) Alyce helped him in many of these endeavors and held several jobs as a bookkeeper. Alyce was a 5th generation descendent of William Barland, who was the first owner of the Elms. He received this property through a land grant from the Spanish government.

Sonny and Mary Estelle reared a family of nine children (six boys and three girls). They have been active members of St. Mary Catholic Church, and the children have all attended and graduated from Cathedral School. Mary Estelle was bookkeeper for the school for 16 years and after retiring from the Exxon Service Station business, Sonny has spent many hours of volunteer work for the school. They are proud to say that one of their sons, Pat, has returned to Natchez as principal of Cathedral School.

BOBBY SCOTT & PAULINE "POLLY" TARVER.
Polly (b. Feb. 26, 1940, Natchez, MS), the third child of Mary Louise McCaleb and Roy Howard. Polly's siblings are Betty Anne Tarver Britt, William John Tarver, George David Tarver, Daniel Howard Tarver, and Benjamin Edward Tarver. Polly married Bobby Scott, whom she met in junior college.

Polly Tarver and Bobby Clay Scott in Scottish attire

Her parents met in Kingston, MS, the community in which Mary Louise lived and was attending Kingston School where Roy was working for the Homochitto Lumber Co. Roy later worked in Natchez for the International Paper Co., Johns-Manville Co. and various oil companies. He died Jan. 4, 1985 and is buried in the Kingston Cemetery.

Polly grew up in Adams County, attending the city schools of the Natchez Separate School District, graduating from Natchez High in 1958. She worked in Natchez as a legal secretary for John Mulhearn Sr., Attorney-at-Law, and for the law firm of Laub, Adams, Forman, and Truly. In 1960 she graduated from Clarke Memorial Junior College in Newton, MS, and in 1962 from William Carey College, Hattiesburg, MS, with a BA in English. On Jan. 16, 1969 in Newton, MS, she married Bobby Clay Scott of Coldwater, MS, the son of Doris Rae Pryor and Clay Morrison Scott. Bobby was born in Tate County, MS, on May 28, 1939, grew up in the Greenleaf Community of Tate County, MS, attended the public schools of Tate County, and graduated from Coldwater High, Coldwater, MS, in 1958. He graduated from Clarke Memorial Junior College in Newton, MS, in 1961 and from William Carey College, Hattiesburg, MS, in 1963 with a BA in social studies.

Polly taught secondary English for 30 years in Forrest County, MS, first at Petal High, Petal, MS, and then at Forrest County Agricultural High School, Brooklyn, MS, where she was selected as Teacher of the Year in 1990. Bobby taught social studies 21 years, first at Petal Jr. High and then at Forrest County Agricultural High School. After that, he was technician for 8 and 1/2 years at Camp Shelby, MS, a military installation south of Hattiesburg. Bobby was a member of the Mississippi National Guard for 20 years. In 1978 he

was selected as the first Outstanding American History Teacher for the Mississippi Daughters of the American Revolution.

Retiring in 1992, Polly and Bobby moved to Smithland Plantation in the Kingston Community, Adams County, MS.

Polly and Bobby, who have no children, are members of Parkway Baptist Church, Natchez, where she is one of the editors of a history of Parkway. They are the organizers of the Natchez Scottish Heritage Society and are members of the Caledonian Society of Mississippi. She is a member of the Natchez Chapter DAR, the Governor George Harlan Chapter Colonial Dames XVII Century, the Alpha Alpha Chapter Delta Kappa Gamma, the Rose Craft Garden Club, First Families of Mississippi, the Mississippi Dames of the Magna Charta, and the Descendants of the Jersey Settlers of Adams County, MS.

MURRAY SEAB & FREDIE TERRAL.
Natchez in the 1950s was growing and many people were moving into the area. Murray Seab of Roxie was working at the California Oil Co. He had attended Co-Lin Junior College after being discharged from the Marines. Fredie Terral from Jena, LA, was teaching at Washington High School when they met and in September 1953 they were married.

From then until they moved back to Natchez in 1962, Murray worked for an engineering company out of Oklahoma City. After leaving the business he opened with his brother-in-law, he started Murray Seab Carpet and Tile, which he operated for over 30 years.

Fredie resumed her teaching career at Braden Elementary School and was named Star Teacher by the Mississippi Economic Council. Her next assignment was as elementary principal at McLaurin School (Montebello) for the next 19 years.

Their daughters, Sue and Kay, graduated from South Natchez High School, and both attended Northeast Louisiana University where they graduated in December 1975. Sue is now a CPA employed in Baton Rouge, and Kay (Mrs. Gerald Davey) is an accountant in Luling, LA.

Murray, the second son of Clyde and Sue O'Connor Seab, was born in Detroit, MI where Clyde was employed at the Continental Motor Co. It was here he met and married Sue O'Connor from Harrisville, MI. As the depression worsened, Clyde returned to the family farm in Roxie, MS, where Murray grew up.

Joseph Seippe and his wife Mary Ninaber, immigrants from Germany, settled in Franklin County in the 1840s and their name Anglicized to Seab. From this couple the large Seab family is descended. Their son Joseph Marion married Emma McMillan, daughter of Monroe McMillan and Martha Benton. In 1810, Sarah Foster, daughter of Thomas Foster and Sarah Smith, was married to Daniel McMillan in Natchez. They settled in Franklin County, where their son Monroe was born.

Fredie and Murray Seab, 1996

Fredie Terral, daughter of J.B. "Buddy" and Ethel Shaifer Terral, was born in Jena, LA, and received her degree from Louisiana College. During holidays and school breaks she stayed with her aunt, Gladys Shaifer, and worked at H.F. Byrne Department Store.

She is descended from a number of the early

settlers of Mississippi. Among these are Edward Young Terral Sr. and Artelissa Stephens of Jasper County; Nathan and Everette Smith from Franklin County; Jonathan Sermons and Raymond Roberts from Copiah County, John Cockerham and John Tarver from Amite County; and the Shaifer family from Claiborne County. Moving to Natchez she was returning to her roots.

Murray and Fredie both retired in 1990 at which time Murray became very active in politics and civic duties, serving for a number of years as president of Adams County Tax Payers Association. He never lost his love for growing things and was known for the beautiful roses that he grew. Fredie was involved in church activities, family research, and educational organization. She was an active member of the Natchez Chapter of DAR and Colonial Dames XVII Century. Murray and Fredie were both members of First Families of Mississippi. *Submitted by Fredie Seab.*

RICHARD DUNCKLEY SESSIONS & RUTH CRUTCHER.
Dr. Richard Dunckley Sessions was born Oct. 8, 1868 in Brookhaven, MS to Major Joseph Ferdinand Sessions and Susan Eliza Dunckley. He attended Jefferson Military Academy and upon graduation went to Tulane University, where he ob-

Dr. R.D. Sessions

tained his degree. He was a member of the first medical school class at Tulane required to go through three years of medical training. Following an internship at the old Natchez Charity Hospital and a surgical residency in New York, he established a practice at the Natchez Sanatorium.

Marrying Ruth Crutcher, they moved into a house on Clifton Heights with his widowed sister Ada Sessions Proby. Although they had six children only four grew to be adults. His children were Ferd, Proby, Richard and Lee.

The Sessions were active members of the First Presbyterian Church of Natchez. He was a member of the Masonic Lodge rising through the ranks to become a Shriner. In February of 1907 he served as King of the Natchez Mardi Gras.

Sessions was a surgeon sought for his medical expertise by many people from Memphis to St. Francisville. Because he was a talented artist, he often illustrated a procedure for patients by sketching what he intended to do.

He was one of the few doctors left in the area during WWI. Often he lamented his inability to help his many patients when l9l8 Flu Epidemic struck. In those days few effective medicines were available to combat the problem. During the course of the epidemic he spent long hours in his office and in his car making the rounds of house calls.

Sessions loved to hunt and fish. He was a member of several hunting clubs and during deer season that was where he could be found. A boat and motor were permanent fixtures in his garage. His collection of fishing rods and lures was extensive.

He always had a bird dog. Many were more pets than they were hunting dogs for his habit was to spoil them. Remembering the dog's names was not difficult because all of them were called "Pat."

He was a chess expert. A game was nearly always set up in his home. He often competed with people away from Natchez by mail. Once upon mailing a play, he discovered he had put himself into checkmate jeopardy. Sending a telegram to the postmaster in his opponent's town in north Mississippi asking that the postcard be intercepted, he mailed another to his opponent. To his surprise he received a return telegram from the postmaster confirming the card's intercept, but telling Sessions that he, the postmaster, was the chess opponent.

Sessions was one of the first people in Natchez to own an automobile. An early edition of the *Democrat* contains an item complaining that Dr. Sessions was racing up and down the streets at 10 miles an hour, scaring horses, and causing buggy accidents.

Dr. Sessions was my grandfather. I remember him as a loving grandfather who found it impossible to say no to a small granddaughter. *Submitted by Ruth C. Sessions.*

GLADYS SHAIFER was born Sep. 23, 1905 in Pollock, LA. She was the youngest of eight children born to T.W. Shaifer and Nannie Wagner. T.W. Shaifer died when Gladys was 2 years old and her mother was left to rear the children alone. At this time, Nannie moved to Natchez and opened a boarding house for the cotton mill workers.

Gladys found her first job as a clerk at Kress' and after a short time began working at H.F. Byrne Department Store. Her natural aptitude for salesmanship helped her learn the retail business, which combined with her sense of style and trends, led to her position as buyer for the ladies' ready-to-wear department for the store.

In a time when a young lady led a very sheltered life, Gladys was going on buying trips to New York City alone. This was quite an accomplishment, as she made this business trip for many years.

Gladys was considered a fashion consultant for many Natchez residents much of her life. She was active in First Baptist Church, civic clubs and worked in the annual Pilgrimage. She lovingly cared for her aging mother, and helped many of her nieces and nephews get their education or their start in life.

Gladys Shaifer

Her career at H.F. Byrne spanned 55 years. As Gladys grew older, she would work fewer days each week. On her 77th birthday, she announced she was retiring. She was not feeling well. Shortly afterwards she was diagnosed with cancer, a battle she faced as she had all of the challenges of her life, with determination, dignity, and courage. Gladys died Jun. 6, 1983 at the age of 77, leaving a legacy of love and caring to all who knew her.

DR. JOHN SHAW. In 1805 John Shaw wrote a letter to President Jefferson in which he expressed his admiration for the President's politics and introduced himself as "a native of North Carolina, descended from European parents." He had been in the Natchez District and active in politics as early as 1797 when he served on a Citizen's Committee whose duty it was to keep order until the Spanish struck their colors and pulled out of Natchez. Andrew Ellicott, surveyor general and government representative who was present for the occasion, noted Shaw as "an itinerant attorney of some education and abilities."

Shaw was a dedicated Republican who supported Jeffersonian policies completely, an avid member of the Mississippi Republican Society, along with friends such as Thomas M. Green, Cato West, Judge David Ker and Edward Turner. He was never shy about his stand and was constantly in one political battle or another. He and Judge Thomas Rodney had a disagreement about the qualification of territorial judges which led Judge Rodney to attack him as "a quondam pill maker from the frog ponds of North Carolina."

He was the first settler of Clifton, also named Hayes City, which he called Lowenburg. In addition, he was the first postmaster of Greenville in Jefferson County, MS, and a practicing physician there. In 1804-05, he served as a representative from Jefferson County to the Mississippi Territorial Legislature. He was one of the founding members of the Franklin Society in Greenville in Jefferson County in 1806. Also that year, he was commissioned by the governor as an attorney in that county.

During the 1807-11 era, he was involved in many activities, including editing for a time, the *Mississippi Messenger,* one of the first newspapers in the territory and printing the Acts of the Territorial Legislature. For several years, he served as a member of the Natchez Mechanical Society which was a city council of sorts, and in 1810 became its president, similar to a mayor of today. During this time his life was never dull. The attorney general of the Mississippi Territory, Seth Lewis, even brought suit against him and other prominent Republicans who were giving Governor Williams a very difficult time.

By 1815, he moved to Franklin County, MS where he continued as a doctor, lawyer, and postmaster. He and the Baptist minister, Bailey Chaney, were arch political rivals. Shaw wanted the Mississippi Territory divided into the two states of Alabama and Mississippi; Chaney did not.

Shaw ran successfully against Chaney for the legislature seat from Franklin County in 1817, and in July was a member of the State Constitutional Convention. Unfortunately, he died during the session on August 1 at the home of Anthony Campbell near Natchez. For the remainder of the convention all delegates wore black crepe armbands in his memory and honor. Judge Edward Turner said of him, "He was a man of wit and honor, an ardent politician, and a caustic writer, well educated and a respectable poet."

Partridge in *Debow's Review* in 1860 said of him, *His style was rough, rasping, and vigorous, and his power of ridicule and satire were of the highest order. He was also a poet of the Hudibrastic school, and was famous for epigrams and pasquinades. He belonged to the Jeffersonian party and, for the reason mentioned, was greatly dreaded by his adversaries. He lived at Natchez, and afterwards at Greenville, in Jefferson County, once a gay, refined and thriving village, but now entirely extinct. Dr. Shaw was for a longtime a member of the Territorial legislature, and was also a member of the convention which framed the first constitution of the state of Mississippi.*

Known descendants of John Shaw were Thomas Breckinridge Shaw, Elizabeth Shaw, Mary Shaw, and Saxton Shaw. The author descends through Elizabeth who married Robert Griffing Apr. 4, 1807, in Jefferson County, MS. *By Sue Burns Moore.*

DEVEREUX SHIELDS SR. FAMILY. Devereux Shields Sr. (b. Apr. 24, 1869, Laurel Hill Plantation, Adams County, MS) was the third son of Wilmer Shields USN and his second wife, Julia Devereux Ashton.

After his graduation from of the University of the South, Sewanee, TN, Devereux returned to Natchez. He was chosen captain of the Natchez Rifles and appointed lieutenant colonel in the National Guard.

At Elgin Plantation near Natchez, Nov. 4, 1897, Devereux married Julia Dunbar Jenkins, daughter of John Flavel Jenkins and Helen Louisa Winchester.

At this point in his life, if Devereux Sr. had been asked, "How is Julia?" he could only respond with, "Are you asking about my mother, my sister or my wife?" as all three were named Julia.

When Spain declared war on the United States Apr. 24, 1898, Devereux Sr. applied for and received a commission as lieutenant colonel in the Second Mississippi US Volunteer Regiment. He was stationed at Jacksonville under the command of General Fitzhugh Lee. He was mustered out at Columbia, TN when the Spanish-American War ended Dec. 10, 1898. While he was serving in this war, his first child, Devereux Shields Jr., was born in Natchez.

On Mar. 2, 1899, Congress asked for 35,000 volunteers to help in the suppression of the Filipino rebellion led by Emilio Aguinaldo. Devereux Sr. applied and received a commission of captain, 29th US Mississippi Volunteers on Jul. 5, 1899. His regiment sailed October 1899, arriving in the Philippines time for the battle of San Mateo. For the next six months,

Devereux Shields Sr. with children: Thomas Clifton, Margaret Graham and Devereux Jr. about 1908

Devereux served as governor of the island of Corregidor. In June 1900, he was detailed with his company to take charge of the island of Marinduque. He and his troop were ambushed. During the battle Devereux was twice wounded, once in the shoulder; the next shot entering the back of his neck and exiting through his cheek almost killed him. Those alive after the battle were held prisoner for four weeks before being rescued. After regaining his strength in a Manila hospital, he was invalided home, arriving Dec. 16, 1900. He was welcomed home with a parade through the streets of Natchez and an elaborate program at the Temple Opera House, during which he was presented with a beautiful sword by the citizens of Natchez in commemoration of his bravery. This was followed by a reception at the Institute Hall.

Devereux settled down to civilian and family life, working as an engineer in the Mississippi/Louisiana area. A second son, Thomas Clifton, was born Oct. 11, 1901, followed by a daughter, Margaret Graham on Nov. 11, 1903.

Then on his birthday April 24, 1908, tragedy struck. His beloved wife, Julia, was killed by the tornado which struck Lucerne Plantation in Louisiana. Julia had gone there to attend her younger sister, Louise (Jenkins) Winston, during the birth of Louise's first child. Julia's children, Thomas and Margaret, who had gone with her were unharmed. Devereux Sr. never recovered from the death of his wife. He died less than two years later on Feb. 16, 1910. *Submitted by Julia Ann Dunbar (Shields) Mills.*

DEVEREUX SHIELDS JR. FAMILY. Though Devereux lived all his adult life in Oklahoma, he never forgot Natchez, his beloved boyhood home or his many friends and family there. He often said that, as a boy, every fifth person he passed on the streets of Natchez was one of his cousins. He visited Natchez as often as possible.

Devereux Shields (b. Aug. 29, 1898, Natchez, MS), the eldest child of Devereux Shields Sr. and his wife, Julia Dunbar Jenkins, was christened in Trinity Episcopal Church. He was attending school in Natchez the day the 1908 tornado struck Louisiana and Mississippi, killing his mother. He was living with his Grandmother Shields when his father died two years later. Not long after his father's death, his brother, Thomas, went to live with his aunt and uncle, Louise (Jenkins) and Harrison Louis Winston at Lucerne Plantation in Concordia Parish, LA. His Grandmother Shields and his sister, Margaret, went to live with Agnes (Shields) and George Marshall II at Lansdowne. Devereux, age 14, was invited to come to Oklahoma City to live with his aunt and uncle, Julia (Shields) and George Pendleton Balfour. While living with their family, he formed a close bond with his cousins, Julie and Josephine Balfour, which lasted throughout their lives.

Devereux Shields Jr.
(b. 1898, d. 1970)

He attended Central High School, Oklahoma City and Oklahoma A&M College, Stillwater, OK. A week after Congress voted to enter WWI, Devereux enlisted in the U.S. Army, Apr. 6, 1917. He saw service on the front lines in France. He was appointed Supply Sergeant, Company F, 111th Ammunition Train Mar. 15, 1919. He was honorably discharged on Aug. 26, 1919 at Camp Bowie, TX.

Returning to Oklahoma City, he worked as foreman of the Smoked Meat Department at Wilson & Co. He married April 1925, Mable Cora Bridgess (b. Jan. 29, 1904, Sentinel, OK, d. Mar. 19, 1973, Oklahoma City), daughter of Francis (Campbell) and Albert Bridgess.

Mabel gave birth to a son, John Ashton Shields (b&d. May 12, 1928), and a daughter, Julia Ann Dunbar Shields (b. Feb. 21, 1936).

In 1944, Devereux began his own business, Shields IGA Grocery in Oklahoma City. In 1948, he sold that business and moved to Ada, OK where, in partnership with W.D. Clemmons, he opened an IGA Grocery on East Main. In 1951, Devereux and his family returned to Oklahoma City where he worked first in the grocery business then as manager of the Capitol Hill Veterinary Hospital. He was a member of the American Legion, the Masonic Lodge and a vestryman of St. David's Episcopal Church.

Devereux died 1970, Bethany, OK and is buried at Spring Creek Cemetery, Oklahoma City. He was survived by his brother Thomas Shields, California; his sister, Margaret Hendrix; niece, Julia Stone of Natchez; one uncle, Hyde R. Jenkins of Sibley, MS; his wife, Mabel; his daughter, Julia Mills; one grandson and two granddaughters.

Devereux was the first Shields male in his line in five generations to live long enough to see his grandchildren.

JOSEPH DUNBAR SHIELDS & SARAH STELLE BISLAND. Born Jul. 5, 1873 at Lagonia in Church Hill, MS, Joseph Dunbar Shields was a son of Dr. Bisland Shields and Laura Jane Payne. Dunbar's schooling began at Church Hill in a brick store across the road from "the Church." At age 12 he walked four miles to the Lynwood School for additional summer sessions, followed by 1889-92 at Chamberlain Hunt Academy at Port Gibson.

Inspired by his father, resident physician of Church Hill, and toilsome experiences of milking,

cultivating the family garden, and raising cotton, Dunbar determined to be a country doctor. He entered Tulane Medical School in the fall of 1893, later transferring to Memphis Hospital Medical College (now University of Tennessee), receiving a diploma in March 1895. Passing the Mississippi State Board of Health and receiving a medical license dated April 1895, Dunbar proceeded to Pine Ridge in Adams County to practice medicine.

He boarded at Mt. Repose with his cousin, Benjamin Williams, who later introduced him to Miss Sarah Stelle Bisland of New Orleans. Sarah was visiting relatives at nearby Edgewood. A brief courtship resulted in an engagement which was perpetuated through correspondence and culminated in marriage Apr. 20, 1899, at Trinity Church in New Orleans. Sarah and Dunbar made their home at Mt. Repose which became the center of the extended Shields/Bisland family life. Ralph Bisland Shields was born here Sep. 25, 1900, as was Caroline Louise Shields on Aug. 22, 1901.

About 1905 Dr. Shields moved his family to Church Hill where he assisted his aging father with his practice. The family lived at The Cedars, home of Sarah's widowed mother, Mrs. William Alexander Bisland. Joseph Dunbar Shields Jr. was born here Jun. 17, 1907. After the death of Dunbar's father in 1911, followed by the death of Sarah's mother, Dr. Shields resumed his practice at Pine Ridge. His personal memoir gives colorful details of experiences in 67 years of medical practice in Adams and Jefferson counties.

Dr. Shields was dedicated to the education of young people. He was Trustee of the Pine Ridge School in 1905, appointed to Adams County School Board 1916, serving as secretary until Jun. 1, 1954, when he was elected president. Physical infirmities caused his resignation Jan. 3, 1955, after 50 years of public service.

Elected to the State Legislature in 1932, he served one term as representative of Adams County. In 1933 he was elected to the Board of Trustees of Jefferson Military College at Washington, MS.

Joseph Dunbar Shields was baptized Aug. 17, 1874 at Christ Episcopal Church, Church Hill, where his predecessors held leadership roles. A confirmed member of the body, he was elected to the Vestry March 1907, continuing uninterrupted until October 1940, when elected senior warden, an office he held until his death.

Dr. Shields and his family were also associated with Pine Ridge Presbyterian Church where he was elected to the Board of Trustees Jun. 27, 1952, serving until his death Feb. 16, 1962, at his home, Mt. Repose. Funeral services were held at Pine Ridge Presbyterian Church and burial in Natchez City Cemetery beside Sarah

Dr. Joseph Dunbar Shields

and son, Ralph, who preceded him in death.

He believed *All things work together for good to them that love God, to them who are called according to His purpose.* Romans 8:28 *Submitted by L.R. McGehee.*

MARGARET GRAHAM SHIELDS was born Nov. 14, 1903, Natchez, MS, daughter of Julia Dunbar (Jenkins) and Devereux Shields Sr. She was an orphan by age 7, a circumstance that she felt deeply all her life. She grew up at Lansdowne

Plantation near Natchez with her cousin Agnes Marshall.

Margaret married William Alpheus "Bill" Hendrix on Dec. 30, 1920. She always said he was the love of her life. They moved to Alabama to live with his parents, Joseph Edward and Leila (Coxwell) Hendrix. Their only child, Julia Devereux Hendrix, was born Nov. 2, 1921. Margaret returned to Natchez after a disagreement, fully expecting Bill to follow and beg her to return. When he did not, they divorced. Both remarried, Margaret to Leslie Lewis Farr, Sep. 7, 1930, in Natchez.

1st LT Margaret Graham (Shields) Farr, 4th from left, at christening ceremony of USS Shields.

Following the attack on Pearl Harbor, Congress passed an act in May 1942, creating the Women's Army Auxiliary Corps (WAAC). Margaret enlisted in the WAACs Oct. 10, 1942.

First Lieutenant Margaret Graham (Shields) Farr became the first Army officer to sponsor a navel ship, Dec. 4, 1944, Puget Sound Naval Yard, Bremerton, WA, when she christened the USS *Shields*, a Fletcher class destroyer, named for her great-grandfather, Thomas Shields, a hero of the War of 1812. "After the Battle of New Orleans the British began a retreat to their ships and Purser Shields, with five boats and a gig manned by 53 men, set out to harass this move. During the expedition the Shields force captured 132 prisoners and destroyed eight craft."

Thomas Shields (b. ca. 1783, New Castle, DE, d. May 22, 1827, New Orleans) was the son of Ann (Bayard) and Thomas Shields Sr. He entered the U.S. Navy as a midshipman in 1804, served on the *Congress*, the *Constitution*, and the *Nautilus* and was appointed Purser of the Port of New Orleans Apr. 25, 1812. He married first, Mary Stiles, 1811, Baltimore, MD; married second, Ellen Blanchard Ker (b. Sep. 12, 1799, Fredericksburg, VA, d. Jan. 24, 1834, New Orleans, LA), daughter of Margaret (Benson) and Dr. David Corbin Ker. They were the parents of Lt Commander Wilmer Shields, USN, grandfather of Capt. Devereux Shields, USMV, Margaret's father.

Margaret's guests at the christening ceremony were her friend, Fay Francis Beal, with daughter, Bertine; Margaret's cousin, Mrs. Agnes (Marshall) Ward, Natchez; and Margaret's brother, Devereux Shields with daughter, Julia, Oklahoma City.

The WAAC, an Army support group, became the Women's Army Corp (WAC), a branch of the army, Jul. 3, 1943. The WAAC were given the option of re-enlisting or resigning. Margaret re-enlisted. She and Leslie Farr divorced Jun. 13, 1944. They had no children. Captain Farr was honorably discharged Nov. 17, 1945.

In 1949 Margaret remarried Bill Hendrix. They lived for a time in Mexico, then returned to Natchez. They remained happily married until his death Jan. 12, 1957.

In later years, Margaret served as a hostess at Longwood. She wrote a booklet, published in 1972, on its history. She died Oct. 18, 1982, at the home of her daughter, Julia Devereux "Judy" (Hendrix) Stone. She and Bill are buried in the Natchez City Cemetery. *Submitted by Peter Devereux Mills.*

WILMER SHIELDS FAMILY.

Most Shields descendants living in the Natchez area today can trace their ancestry to Archibald (b. 1739, Pennsylvania, d. 1794, Virginia) or Thomas (b. 1743, Pennsylvania, d. 1803, Abbeville, SC), sons of Martha __ and William Shields, Chester County, PA (b. ca. 1739, d. 1782). Archibald and Thomas married sisters, Rebecca and Ann Bayard, descendants of the Bayard family who came to New Amsterdam in 1647.

Archibald's son, William Bayard Shields, came to Natchez in 1803 and served as a District and Federal Judge. He married February 1807 Victoire Beniost, died April 1823. Wilmer Shields, grandson of Thomas, came in the 1850s.

Wilmer was the son of Purser Thomas Shields, USN, and his second wife, Ellen Blanchard Ker. Thomas and Ellen's children were Wilmer Shields (b. Jul. 2, 1817, New Orleans), named for his father's friend, James Wilmer, who died in the Great Lakes Battle, War of 1812; Emma Gordon married Hezekiah H. O'Callaghan; Julia Laurentia married Joseph Watkins Houston; Margaret Caroline married Henry Windle; and Thomas married Cora Hepp.

After Thomas died, Ellen married second, Levi Pierce, Jan. 19, 1833. When Ellen died Jan. 24, 1834, Dr. William Newton Mercer, who as a young naval surgeon had been befriended by Thomas Shields, was asked to serve as guardian of the Shields orphans and he and Wilmer became good friends.

Wilmer entered the Navy as a midshipman in October 1835; was promoted to master Mar. 23, 1847; then lieutenant on Sep. 14, 1848. At the request of his friend, Dr. Mercer, Wilmer resigned from the Navy Apr. 6, 1852, to manage Dr. Mercer's plantations. Wilmer moved his first wife, Agnes, daughter of Henry Vernon Somerville and Rebecca Tiernan, whom he had married Sep. 10, 1845 in Maryland to Dr. Mercer's plantation, Laurel Hill, near Natchez.

Wilmer Shields (b. 1817, d. 1879)

When Wilmer's sister, Emma, died in 1850, he was appointed guardian of her children, Charles Lee and Emma, who thereafter used the surname Shields. Charles died of wounds received in the Civil War. He had

Julia Devereux (Ashton) Shields (b. 1842, d. 1915), second wife of Wilmer Shields

no children and Emma became a nun. Agnes died Jan. 26, 1861, shortly after giving birth to a daughter, Agnes Somerville Shields who died Feb. 4, 1864.

On Jun. 1, 1865, Wilmer married second, Julia Devereux Ashton (b. 1842, Maysville, KY, d. 1915, Lansdowne), daughter of Mary (Devereux) and Richard Watts Ashton. Their seven children born

at Laurel Hill were William Newton Mercer (died age 3); Wilmer Jr., a Natchez attorney and judge, died without issue; Devereux married Julia Jenkins; Agnes married George Marshall II; James Ashton, a Panama Canal engineer, died without issue; Julia Devereux married George Pendleton Balfour, and Thomas Clifton, died without issue.

The family story is, Wilmer did not participate in the Civil War, saying he would not fight against the country he had sworn allegiance to upon entering the Navy or against his fellow officers. Neither would he fight against family and neighbors. Wilmer's brother, Capt. Thomas Shields, CSA, was killed in the battle before Atlanta. Three of his sons: Pintard, Theodore and Walter, were living with Wilmer in 1870.

Following Dr. Mercer's death in 1874, the Shields family moved to the Shields Town House, in Natchez. At that time only two other houses were near them, The Burn, the Walworth family home, and Bird Nest, home of Wilmer's second cousin, Joseph Dunbar Shields.

Wilmer died Jan. 1, 1879 of pneumonia while on a business trip to New Orleans, leaving his young widow to raise their six surviving children, ages 4 months to 12 years.

HERMAN BANKSTON SKATES & DOROTHY MARIE CURTIS.

Herman was born in Utica, MS on Nov. 2, 1922. His mother was Thelma Louise Bankston Skates and father was George Washington Skates Jr. (b. Dec. 24, 1897). His mother was going to Belhaven College in Jackson, MS, but his father talked her into quitting and marrying him. His mother's parents were very upset over this.

Herman had three brothers: George Washington Skates III, William Reed Skates and Barney Lee Skates. They are all deceased. His five sisters are Thelma Louise Skates Womack (b. May 14, 1924); Eleanor Martile Skates Womack; Martha Ruth Skates Hennington (b. Jan. 11, 1930); Jean Skates Warren (b. Jul. 23, 1931) and Ella Mae Skates Loftin (b. May 30, 1934).

When Herman was a year old, he became ill with diphtheria. His grandparents, Herman Jesse Bankston and Ella Mae Robbinette Bankston, took him so that he could stay quiet. After he was well, he wanted to continue to stay with his grandparents, which he did.

Herman grew up in Learned, MS, and graduated from Raymond High School.

In 1942 he was drafted into the Army and served with the 5th Army in Europe. He fought from Italy to Germany and received five Battle Stars. Herman did not get a furlough to come home in the three years he served. His hand was injured once when a bomb landed in front of their truck. Luckily it landed in a mud hole, throwing mud everywhere and putting the truck out of order. Herman could have received a Purple Heart, but he never reported his injury.

He married Dorothy Marie Curtis (b. Jan. 27, 1927) on Oct. 12, 1946 and they moved to Natchez, MS, where they have lived ever since. They have four children: Peggy Marie Skates June (b. Dec. 23, 1948); Ray Herman Skates (b. Oct. 3, 1950); Barry Lester Skates (b. Nov. 25, 1956); Charlotte Dorene Skates Bunch (b. Mar. 11, 1959).

He owned Stakes Body Shop until he retired in 1985. Herman and Dorothy live on 200 acres of land joining the Adams County Airport. They are active members of Covington Road Church of Christ.

ALBERT SMITH & HARRIETT WILLIAMS.

Harriett was born Oct. 22, 1917 in Wilkinson County, MS, the daughter of Sam and Malissa Williams. She was placed in foster care with a

white family, Mr. and Mrs. Jenkins, at the age of 7 years. Little, if any, recollection of her biological parents exists. The siblings of Harriett Smith are Andre LaRue Jackson (deceased), Laurena Williams Johnson (deceased), Emma Williams Burns (deceased), Georgia Williams Baldwin (deceased), Ellen Williams Woods (deceased), Lucy Williams Perry and Moses Williams.

Harriett grew up on Longview Plantation, located on Lower Woodville Road in southern Adams County and resided there until her death.

Mr. Winchester Jenkins and wife Clotilde (Smith) Jenkins, foster parents of Harriett Smith - 1924.

Mother often spoke of a childhood filled with fond memories. She frequently told of her lifelong desire for an education, her delight in her first car ride, and the fact that she had led a sheltered life, never being exposed to people of her race until young adulthood.

She was not fortunate enough to attend school; therefore, she did not receive a formal education. Mother's first job came at the tender age of 7 years. She helped with the household chores assigned to her by Mrs. Jenkins.

Mother married my dad, Albert Smith, when she was 27 years old. Dad was 30 years her senior. They were united in holy matrimony at Grove African Methodist Episcopal Church in Natchez. Four children resulted from this union: Edward James Conner-Natchez, Joyce Marie Smith Brown-Natchez, Barbara Jean Smith Winston-Natchez and Maxine Smith Lyles-Jackson, MS.

Harriet Smith Farmer received an award from President George H.W. Bush and wife Barbara in 1999

When mother reached adulthood, she became a member of Grove African Methodist Episcopal Church. She was an active member of the Knights and Ladies of White Star Lodge Number 4. In 1999, she was selected by Blue Cross and Blue Shield of Mississippi as a regional winner in the Love of Learning category. The program recognizes seniors 65 and over, whose accomplishments inspire others. Mother possessed a desire to become fluent in reading. At the age of 75, she began attending tutorial sessions at the Natchez Senior Citizen Center.

On May 18, 1999, Mother was honored as National Ageless Hero. For her love of learning the Blue Cross and Blue Shield Association selected her one of six winners from a field of 6,500 nominees. As part of the celebration, she traveled to Chicago to dine with former President and Mrs. George Bush. She joined Mrs. Bush at a reading and literacy event at the Harold Washington Library. Former President Bush presented Mother with the Ageless Hero Award during the luncheon. $5,000 was presented to the Natchez Retired and Senior Volunteer Program in her name. Quite an accomplishment - from orphan to dining with a President!

Harriett Williams Smith, orphan, former housekeeper, life-long learner, dedicated mother and friend, died Jul. 19, 2000. Information submitted by Barbara Smith Winston.

J. HARVEY SMITH & RUTH STARNES moved to Natchez from Jefferson County in 1967. Harvey (b. May 27, 1907 at Union Church), the son of Jesse Marion and Ellen Wilkinson Smith. His ancestors include William "Captain Billy" and Delilah Kees Smith who moved from Georgia to Fair River (Lincoln County, MS) in 1810. "Captain Billy" Smith served in the War of 1812, fighting Indians before taking part in the Battle of New Orleans.

Ellen Wilkinson's parents were Peter Calvin and Mary Farris Wilkinson. Peter's parents were Neil Ray and Huldah Trevillion Wilkinson. Neil's father, Peter Wilkinson, came to North Carolina from Scotland ca. 1793, and married Sarah "Sallie" McNair. They moved with their family to Union Church, MS in 1820.

Ruth Eugenia Starnes was born Nov. 15, 1916 at Dennis Crossroads in Jefferson County. She is the daughter of William Scott Starnes (b. Dec. 24, 1882 in Brandywine, MS) and Orlena Pearl Darsey (b. Aug. 13, 1894 in Franklin County). Scott's parents were Samuel Scott Starnes Jr. and Ruth Rebecca Stephens. After Samuel's death Ruth Rebecca operated a boarding house in a leased building on High Street in Natchez. Scott operated a streetcar. He

Back row l-r: Mary Pearl Starnes, Ruth Starnes, Pearl Darsey Starnes. Center: Eugenia Addie Darsey, William Scott Starnes. Front: Inos Lee Starnes, Exermenia Starnes

met Pearl Darsey while she was working with his sister, Mary, at the Salvo and Berdon Candy Co. Pearl wrapped candy for 25 cents a day. Pearl later worked at Kress before she and Scott were married Oct. 4, 1911, in Natchez. Their children were Mary Pearl (b. Jul. 3, 1914), Ruth Eugenia (b. Nov. 15, 1916), Gladys Exermenia (b. Nov. 29, 1918), and Inos Lee (b. Aug. 28, 1925).

Ruth Rebecca Starnes inherited the family plantation in Jefferson County and the entire family moved there about 1912.

Scott was the great-grandson of Moses and Nancy Graves Starnes, who came to the Natchez territory from Georgia in 1799. Moses' grandfather, Peter Starnes, fought in the Revolutionary War in South Carolina when he was 70 years old, serving for 706 days. He was a descendant of Charles Stearns, who came to Watertown, MA from England ca. 1630.

Pearl's parents were Henry Preston Darsey (b. Sep. 7, 1866 in Franklin County) and Addie Eugenia Bruce (b. Jul. 23, 1872). Henry had a furniture repair shop on the corner of Franklin and Pine Streets in Natchez about 1920. He also was the school photographer for the Jefferson, Franklin and Pike County schools.

Eugenia Addie Bruce was the ward of George and Amanda Armstrong. She lived with them on their Jefferson County plantation until she and Henry were married on Jun. 10, 1890.

Harvey and Ruth Smith were married Jan. 7, 1934 in Jefferson County. They owned a cattle farm at Dennis Crossroads, owned a "rolling store" before 1941, then ran it on the home place until 1957. Harvey's enterprises included logging and sawmill businesses. Ruth ran the store and home. After moving to Natchez, Harvey filed saws for mills in Roxie and Ruth worked in several clerical positions before retirement. Their children are Roy Harvey, Ruby Kathrine, Lucian Turney, and Margie Annette. *Submitted by Ruby Dickerson.*

STALLONE-DOLLAR. Marian Bernice Williams (b. Jun. 4, 1925 in Irene, LA) and Premo Joseph Stallone Jr. (b. Nov. 5, 1923 in Natchez) were married on Aug. 9, 1942 in Natchez. Both were educated in the Natchez public schools. The couple has three children: Cynthia, Adrian and Janet, born in Natchez

Marian is the daughter of Vernon Williams (b. Nov. 11, 1902 of Copiah County, MS, d. Dec. 1, 1985) and Genevieve Remondet (b. Sep. 5, 1903, d. Apr. 29, 1998), both died in Natchez.

Vernon is the son of Dexter Williams (b. Aug. 23, 1869) and Marettie Crausby (b. Jul. 10, 1866) who married Jan. 13, 1892 in Wesson. Bearing five children the couple moved to the Natchez area when Vernon was a child, and where he attended Natchez public schools and later worked as a carpenter.

Genevieve's parents were Henry Remondet (b. Jul. 27, 1869 of Woodville, d. Jan. 10, 1948 in Natchez) and Emma Guidici (b. Jul. 27, 1866 in Europe, d. 1924 in Natchez). Following the death of both parents in northern Mississippi in 1874, 8-year-old Emma was brought to Natchez and reared at St. Mary's Orphanage. After his parents died, 2-year-old Henry came to Natchez in 1871 and lived with a Lambert family. At six Henry moved to D'Evereaux Hall Orphanage. Learning his parents' identity while a young adult, Henry changed his name from William Henry to Henry Heirn. Emma and Henry received Catholic education in Natchez. They were wed at St. Mary's Cathedral in Natchez Apr. 30, 1887, and had 10 children.

Premo Jr. is the son of Premo Stallone Sr. (b. May 5, 1903 in Italy, d. May 23, 1955 in Natchez) and Columbia Verucchi (b. February 1901 in Italy, d. Jun. 25, 1997 in Natchez).

Columbia and Premo were married in Natchez in 1922 and had two children. Premo Sr. was the son of Edwardo Stallone and Mary Bignami, Italians immigrating to Mounds, LA in 1904 and Natchez in 1911. Columbia was born to Gisto Verucchi and Martha Gruppi, immigrants from Italy who joined other families coming to the United States as farmers in 1904 and arriving in Natchez 1911. Italian youngsters, Premo and Columbia, were educated in the Natchez public schools. As a young adult Premo Sr. was employed as a sheetmetal worker. He opened his own sheetmetal and plumbing shop around 1931, later adding electrical and air conditioning.

In 1942 Premo Jr. graduated from high school, married Marian, and was drafted into the army. He served three years during WWII, most of which was spent in the China-Burma-India Theatre of Operations. Returning home in 1946, Premo worked as an electrician for his dad until operating the business in 1955 as a result of his father's death and continued until his retirement in 1989.

Cynthia Stallone (b. Sep. 23, 1943) received her education at Natchez Cathedral Schools. She married Jewel Ray "Dick" Dollar (b. Sep. 19, 1940) on Thanksgiving Day, Nov. 23, 1961 at Assumption Church in Natchez. They have three children: Denise (b. Oct. 17, 1962) living in Washington;

Natalie (b. Nov. 21, 1963) md. Dan Becraft on Aug. 12, 2002 and lives in Oregon; Paige (b. Jul. 10, 1979) md. Barry Iseminger on Jun. 16, 2001 and lives in Alabama with Barry and daughter, Fisher (b. Jun. 11, 2002).

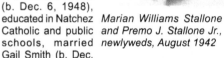

Marian Williams Stallone and Premo J. Stallone Jr., newlyweds, August 1942

Adrian Stallone (b. Dec. 6, 1948), educated in Natchez Catholic and public schools, married Gail Smith (b. Dec. 24, 1950) at Natchez St. Mary's Cathedral, Aug. 10, 1968. They have three children: Adrian Jr. (b. Mar. 31, 1973 of Baton Rouge; Amy (b. Jul. 10, 1975) md. to Don Smith Jan. 29, 2000, having a daughter, Colby (b. Jul. 31, 2000) and son Layne (b. Nov. 13, 2001) of Canton; and Premo, III (b. Jan. 25, 1977) of Hattiesburg.

Janet Stallone (b. Mar. 27, 1951) educated in Natchez Catholic and public schools, married Carney Jones in 1977, bearing a son, Stallone Jones (b. Jan. 7, 1978) of Texas. She later married Alpha "Butch" Cody (b. Oct. 1, 1947) on Jun. 14, 1980 in Natchez and has two sons: Yancy (b. Dec. 23, 1982) and Wacey (b. Nov. 19, 1986) both living in Texas.

JOHANN PHILLIP STIER & MARTHA ELIZABETH STETEFELD. Johann Phillip (b. Jul. 3, 1787, confirmed 1801, d. 1854 at Natchez) and Martha Elizabeth Stetefeld, daughter of Heinrich Stetefeld, tailormaster at Marburg, married on the 19th day after Trinity in 1813 at Marburg. They were the parents of John Henry Stier, who was the father of Julia Stier, wife of Louis Armand "L.A." Benoist Sr.

According to German records, Johann Phillip, a Lutheran butchermaster residing at Untergasse, was the son of Johann Stier and Anna Dor Stier. Phillip Stier's funeral was on Sunday, Jun. 4, 1854, at son Henry's home at the corner of Pearl and State streets in Natchez.

Martha Elizabeth Stetefeld, probably born at Marburg, died at Natchez in 1857 at age 92. In later life, Martha lived with daughters, Kate and Mary. A funeral notice in the family collection states that the funeral was on Jun. 27, 1857 at son Henry's home. Martha had a diploma for midwifing issued by the local

Martha Elizabeth Stetefeld

Medical Office of Dukedom of Hesse, Midwife Order, Jul. 10, 1830, and was granted permission by the Police Commission to practice midwifing at Marburg, Oct. 31, 1832 (Document certified at Marburg Dec. 17, 1839).

Children of Johann Phillip Stier and Martha Elizabeth Stetefeld were Heinrich (John Henry) (b. Mar. 27, 1816, d. May 8, 1874); Konrad (b. Nov. 19, 1818, d. Dec. 25, 1818); Johannes (b. Dec. 30, 1819); Bernhard (b. May 9, 1823); Katharina Margarethe (b. Apr. 19, 1827) (Aunt Kate S. Rietz at Rodney near Ghost Town); Marie Eleonore Johannette (b. Apr. 7, 1832) (Aunt Mary Stier Schwartz lived in Natchez, married John

George Schwartz (b. 1832, Nussdorf, d. 1873, Natchez). *Prepared by Paul H. Benoist and Virginia Gerace Benoist.*

JOHN HENRY STIER & THE PETERS SISTERS.

John Henry Stier

John Henry Stier, a merchant, married sisters. He first married Mary Peters on May 25, 1840, and after her death, married her sister, Caroline Peters, on Nov. 14, 1849. The Peters sisters were the daughters of Johann Peters of Oldenburg/Holstein and Cathrin Marie Frank. John Henry and Caroline Stier were the parents of Julia Stier, who married Louis Armand "L.A." Benoist Sr. at Natchez. John Henry was the son of Johann Phillip Stier (b. Jul. 3, 1787, confirmed 1801, d. 1854 at Natchez) and Martha Elizabeth Stetefeld, daughter of Heinrich Stetefeld, tailormaster at Marburg. Johann Phillip Stier and Martha Elizabeth Stetefeld married on the 19th day after Trinity in 1813 at Marburg.

John Henry Stier was born Mar. 27, 1816 in Marburg, Germany and died May 8, 1874. Caroline Peters is listed as Caroline Juliane Dorothea Peters, according to the records of Oldenburg/Holstein and as Caroline H. Peters in the Natchez record. She was born Sep. 13, 1823/1828 and died Feb. 8, 1903. John Henry Stier and Caroline H. Stier are buried at the Natchez City Cemetery in the Benoist Plot.

Tradition is that John Henry Stier arrived at New York in 1836 and traveled to Lexington, KY, where he worked as a cabinet maker for Knobe Piano Co. Records show that he then moved to Natchez, and in 1844, Henry Stier, late the subject of William II, Duke of Hesse, Cassel, became a citizen of the United States, according to minutes of the Circuit Court at Natchez.

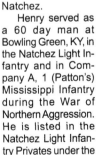

Mary Peters Stier

Henry served as a 60 day man at Bowling Green, KY, in the Natchez Light Infantry and in Company A, 1 (Patton's) Mississippi Infantry during the War of Northern Aggression. He is listed in the Natchez Light Infantry Privates under the command of Capt. Henry Latrop. Company Muster Roll shows him at Corinth, MS with one Mississippi rifle. He was an alderman and a member of the Protection Fire Company No. 3 and Concord Lodge No. 127 OOF, and German Benevolent Society. When he died, his funeral was at his residence at 615 Washington Street, Natchez, on May 9, 1874. Issue of John Henry Stier and Mary Peters were:

Caroline Peters Stier

1) John Peters Stier (b. Apr. 23, 1843, d. December 1889) md. Frances Stedman, Aurora, IN.

He is listed as a private under Capt. W.S. Lowell, Quitman Light Artillery (Independent Battery), enlisted Apr. 9, 1861.

2) Julius Augustus Stier (b. Dec. 15, 1845/1846/1848, d. Feb. 7, 1923) md. Frances Hamilton of St. Louis, MO.

3) Name unknown.

Issue of John Henry Stier and Caroline Peters were:

1) Mary, died in infancy.

2) Julia (b. Jul. 25, 1860, d. Dec. 12, 1951).

3) Virginia "Virgie" Lee (b. Dec. 29, 1863, d. Aug. 28, 1945).

4) Sonora "Nora" F. (b. 1852, d. 1922) md. Hazen S. Stedman (b. 1852, d. 1916).

6) William Henry Stier, died Sunday evening, Jul. 13, 1879, at age 12 of typhoid fever. He was the youngest son of the late John Henry Stier and Caroline Peters Stier. His funeral was held at the family residence at 615 Washington Street at Natchez on Jul. 14, 1879.

John Henry Stier's first home was at the corner of State and Pearl streets and then at 615 Washington Street in Natchez. The 615 Washington Street is known as the "Caroline Stier House." *Submitted by Paul H. Benoist and Virginia Gerace Benoist.*

JOHN BROWN STEVENS FAMILY.

John Brown (b. Jun. 30, 1783 in North Carolina, d. Oct. 10, 1842 near Vicksburg) came to the Mississippi Territory about 1810 according to his obituary. On Mar. 18, 1813 he married Mary L. (Roberts/Robinson) Cole the widow of James Cole. She was born Jan. 1, 1796 in Tennessee to James and Winnifred Roberts/Robinson. John and Mary are buried at Antioch Cemetery on Fisher Ferry Road in Vicksburg, MS. Their children were James Green (b. Feb. 3, 1814, d. Jul. 6, 1814); Mary (b. Oct. 14, 1815, d. Oct. 10, 1847) md. William H. Sparke Aug. 31, 1833 in Warren County, MS; Henry G. (b. Nov. 7, 1819) md. Adeline Harrison; Eli Thompson (b. Sep. 18, 1821) md. Susan Elizabeth Richards; John Brown Jr. (b. Jun. 2, 1824) md. Emily Foster; Levi Holmes (b. Apr. 15, 1827); Joel Ormand (b. Dec. 1, 1829) md. Elizabeth Stevens; William Barnabus (b. Jan. 2, 1833) md. Sultana Luckett; Benjamin Franklin (b. Jul. 29, 1837) md. Susan E. Baker.

Eli Thompson Stevens and his wife, Susan Elizabeth Richards, were married in Warren County on May 17, 1839. Their children were John Oscar (b. Oct. 31, 1838/9) md. Emmeline Hackler; Francis Marion (b. 1841) md. Sara Belzora Perkins; Mary Olivia (b. 1844); William Wallace (b. Apr. 11, 1845 near Port Gibson, d. Jan. 20, 1921 McAlester, OK) md. Cordelia Whitaker Perkins; Bruce (b. about 1847); Susan Richards (b. May 10, 1849) md. James Harvey Shannon; Eli T. Jr. (b. about 1854); Elizabeth (b. about 1855); Alice Gertrude (b. Jan. 10, 1858) md. Junius Greenway Parham and lived in Rolling Fork, MS; Robert Quitman (b. about 1859); Emma Goldsmith (b. about 1860); Andrew McCullen (b. Nov. 27, 1862).

William Wallace Stevens and Cordelia Whitaker Perkins (b. Jan. 27, 1846, d. Feb. 3, 1887), daughter of Cyrinthia Ann Whitaker and Caleb Perkins, married Sep. 10, 1862 Claiborne County, MS. They had a family of 13, the last two being twins. William W. (b. Jun. 26, 1864, d. Nov. 12, 1864); Clara Markey (b. Dec. 14, 1865) md. George Monroe Harrell; Sallie W. (b. Jun. 28, 1867) md. Mr. McIntyre and lived in Lawton, OK; Mary Jennie (b. Dec. 7, 1869) md. Walter DeCamp and had four children, then married C.W. Belcher and had four more children; Alice C. (b. Jul. 27, 1871) probably died before her father; George Bruce (b. Nov. 9, 1872); Jessie Bell (b. Jul. 15, 1875) md. Franklin Sylvester Johnson; Adeline

Bellzora (b. Feb. 3, 1876) md. Edward Alfred Scott and lived near Memphis, TN; Francis Marion (b. Apr. 17, 1880, d. 1909) died in Los Angeles while working for the railroad (he is the one who my father was named for); James Emmett (b. Feb. 15, 1881) md. Fannie Edna Sisson; Lawrence M. (b. Mar. 24, 1884) md. Mamie King; Dannie Adelia (b. Jan. 27, 1887) md. Albert Joseph Wrenn and her twin, Fannie Cordelia, married John Wade Martin. A little family rhyme went: *Fannie and Dannie were twins, one married a Martin, the other a Wrenn.*

John Brown Stevens

At the death of their mother, aunts and uncles reared the younger children. The twins were separated and did not know each other until after they married and had children. They started writing to each other, hoping some day to get together. Marion and Willie took their mother to Fitler, MS to see her twin Dannie, shortly after the 1927 flood. Where the roads were still muddy they cut small trees and put them across the road so the car would not get stuck in the thick gumbo mud. It was not an easy trip by any stretch of the imagination. After this reunion they continued to visit and remained close until the death of Fannie in 1941. Their children stayed in touch and even today some of the younger generation keeps in touch with their second cousins. *Submitted by Carolyn Cole*

WILLIAM EDWARD "BILL" STEWART & BETTY MARGARETTA DEWEES.

Bill (b. Dec. 9, 1924), son of Robert Percy Stewart Sr. of Natchez and Virginia Lowry Hodge of Natchez, married Betty Margaretta Dewees of Florence, Rankin, MS on Aug. 11, 1957. She was born Sep. 2, 1933, the only child of Harry Hayward Dewees, son of Margaretta Chipley and Timothy Bryan Dewees, and Euna Betty Compere, daughter of Cordella Montgomery and Arthur L. Compere.

Bill was a General Insurance agent in Natchez from 1948-87. He graduated Ole Miss in 1948 with a BA, the first business graduate to major in insurance. He was a veteran of World War II, serving as a pilot in the 9th Air Force, 387th Bomb Group, 558th Bomb Squadron.

Children of Bill and Betty Stewart are Betina Cooper (Paul), Suzanne and Ed Jr.

Robert Percy Stewart Sr. (b. Mar. 28, 1892, Natchez, d. Apr. 17, 1968, Natchez) was the son of William Percy Stewart and Katie Beatrice Schwartz. Percy married Virginia Hodge Feb. 12, 1918 in Natchez. She was born Nov. 2, 1895 to Edward Joseph "EJ" Hodge of Natchez and Grace Allen of Grand Lake, Chicot, AR. Children: Grace Allen Brister (Andy); Robert Percy Jr. (Betty Lou George); Bill; and Virginia Wilson (Robert N.).

William Percy (b. May 20, 1858, Natchez, d. Apr. 25, 1928, Natchez) was the son of Robert Hill Stewart and Caroline Heermans, daughter of William P. Heermans and Rachel Harder of Rensselaer County, NY. On Dec. 22, 1881 he married Katie Beatrice Schwartz (b. Oct. 31, 1858 in Natchez, d. Dec. 16, 1920), the daughter of John Conrad Schwartz, of Rhein Pfalz bei Landau, Bavaria and Catherine Eisenhart of Prussia. Children: Catherine Power (George), Percy Heermans, Margaret, and Robert Percy.

John Conrad came to Natchez with other members of the Schwartz family about 1840. He was a confectioner with his brother-in-law,

Frederic Crone before he established J C Schwartz Hardware located on Main Street where Darby's is now. He married Catherine Eisenhart Jul. 10, 1850 in Jefferson County, MS. Their children: Magadalen, Willie, John Edward (Annie Stewart), Katie, Dora, Mary Ellen, Estelle Carson (Thomas James) and Agnes Metcalfe (James).

At J.C. Schwartz's death, his son John Edward and son-in-law, W.P. Stewart, carried on the business as Schwartz and Stewart. R.P. Stewart ran the business until the 1930s.

Robert Hill (b. Mar. 4, 1824 in Natchez, d. Mar. 15, 1899) was the son of Robert Stewart and Susan Marschalk, daughter of Andrew Marschalk and Susan McDonald. He married Caroline Heermans Jul. 14, 1853, in Pittsford, NY. She was born Feb. 23, 1822, Nassau, Rensselaer, NY and died Jun. 23, 1892, Natchez. He had a furniture and cabinetmaker business in Natchez. Children: Robert Livingston, Mary Amelia, William Percy, and Walter Lee (Krissie Johnson).

Robert Stewart (b. Nov. 29, 1795 in Pennsylvania, d. Jun. 7, 1866 in Carroll Parish, LA) md. Susan Marschalk on May 14, 1818 in Natchez. She was born Oct. 24, 1802, Adams County, d. Oct. 1, 1878 in Natchez. He was a cabinetmaker and came to Natchez from Cincinnati after 1815. Children: Andrew, Samuel (Sarah Patterson), Sidney Ann, Robert Hill, Charles Andrew, Miller M. (Sarah Pitts Mardis), William Henry (Eliza Baker), Anna Maria, George Washington (Ann Gahan), Edwin Francis (Laura Williams), John Rollin (Annette Claiborne), Andrew Brown, Jane Eleanor Kellog (Amasa), Susan McDonald Mundinger (Chris). *Submitted by William E. Stewart.*

CATHERINE EUNICE "BIG MAMA" BROWN STONE.

When I was a just a little girl, Big Mama instilled in me a love of reading. On special occasions she always gave me books. I especially remember the "Honey Bunch" series. Honey Bunch was her pet name for me.

My little brother, Jimmy was always bringing home stray cats. Our parents wouldn't let him keep them but he knew he could count on Big Mama. She didn't keep them inside, but she fed and cared for them and Jimmy could go to play with them anytime to his heart's content.

Big Mama had a corner grocery store on the corner of Madison and Canal with her dwelling attached, right where the Salvation Army Thrift Store is now located. (The 1950-51 City Directory lists her grocery store at 200 Madison St.)

The candy display case had all kinds of mouthwatering goodies. One Halloween my sisters, brothers, cousins and I went Trick-or-Treating. We considered trick-or-treating at Big Mama's, but decided she couldn't afford to give her profits away. We learned the next day that she was very disappointed that we had not come.

When I was around 9 or 10, I "helped out" in her store. I loved being with her, but I'm not sure how much help I was; however I did climb up to reach items for customers up on high shelves.

Mr. Carl Hicks used to call on her. He brought paper items, dishes, medicinal things and insecticides, coal-oil lamps and just many things. Mr. Hicks told me he remembers her as really pleasant and nice to visit. "I never saw her get ruffled, even when kids came in and misbehaved. I remember that she was always interested in other people. Sometimes I had a time getting away from her," he added with a chuckle.

A new product became available at the store, Joy dishwashing detergent. One lady said she used it to wash her hair, that it was much cheaper than shampoo and worked just fine. I never paid attention to the condition of her hair.

Big Mama had an old space heater in the store,

right in front of the candy display case. One day as I was warming myself with the heat rising under my skirt, the side of my right knee touched the heater. Ouch! - Big Mama rubbed some butter on my leg, then told me to sit on the floor with my leg near the heater. She said the fire could "draw out the burn." I did it for a little while, but the

Catherine Eunice Brown Stone

pain seemed worse to me, so I slyly went to the cold drink case and plunged my hand into the icy water. Then I sat back on the floor near the fire and held a chilled soft-drink bottle I had retrieved against my injured leg. I never told her that I had disobeyed her. *Submitted by Rita Claire Eidt Jones Tebbetts.*

JACK BRYAN STUBBS & DOROTHY "DOTTY" LAWRENCE

were married Sep. 24, 1946 at the First Presbyterian Church in Baton Rouge, LA, by the Rev. James Gregory, a former pastor there who came from his pastorate in Virginia at Dotty's request to perform the ceremony.

Jack (b. Aug. 18, 1921 in Norfolk, VA) was the second son of Olin Leslie Stubbs and Louise Lesesne Thames, who were married Nov. 25, 1913 in Sumter, SC. Both parents were South Carolinians who were living in Norfolk where his father worked first for the railroad, then for a cotton seed oil company. Jack had an older brother Olin Lesesne (b. 1914, d. Jan. 3, 1981) and a younger sister Mary Louise Stubbs James (b. 1924, d. Feb. 1, 2002). He also had a foster sister, who was 6 weeks older than he, Dallas T. McGlynn, who lived next door to the Stubbs family from about age 3 and came to live with them at age 12 when both of her parents died within six months of each other.

His brother, whose widow, Margaret Wright Stubbs lives in Alexandria, VA, had one daughter, Jane Stubbs Dixson, of Arlington, VA, and his sister had a daughter, Sue James Smith, of Springfield, VA, and a son, Larry F. James of Raleigh, NC. His sister Dallas had two daughters, Peggy (now deceased) and Linda McGlynn Echenfels of San Antonio, TX.

Dotty (b. May 19, 1922 in Wilmington, DE) was the daughter of Samuel Eugene Lawrence and Odile Schaefer who were married Apr. 15, 1913 in Dallas, TX. Her older brother Samuel Eugene Lawrence Jr. (b. Sep. 30, 1914) md. Lillian Bollin of Columbia, SC on Jun. 7, 1948. They made their home in Columbia and he is presently in a Veterans Home there. They are the parents of three children: Lucy Lawrence Marriott, Samuel E. Lawrence III and John Bollin Lawrence. Dotty's older sister Marian Katherine Lawrence (b. Sep. 27, 1920 in Wilmington, DE) never married and died Apr. 18, 2001 after living most of her life in Baton Rouge, LA. She had been an employee of the state of Louisiana and LSU.

Jack and Dotty are the parents of three sons:
1) Olin Lawrence Stubbs (b. Sep. 28, 1948) md. May 1978 to Linda Smith (b. Jun. 6, 1950) of Clinton, LA. Olin is an LSU graduate and a Forester, now retired from the state of Louisiana Dept. of Forestry, while Linda is a social worker in a Veterans Home in Jackson, LA. They make their home in the country between Clinton and Greensburg, LA. They have two sons, Olin Luke Stubbs (b. May 22, 1980) who works for a contractor at a paper mill in St. Francisville, LA, and

Jack Willis Stubbs (b. Jan. 21, 1983) a sophomore at LSU.

2) Samuel Eugene Stubbs (b. Aug. 18, 1950 in Baton Rouge) md. May 31, 1986 in Houston to Melinda Martin (b. May 22, 1959). Sam is a graduate of the University of Texas in Austin and the University of Houston's Bates College of Law in Houston. He is a partner in a large Houston law firm. Melinda, also a graduate of the University of Texas, is a stay-at-home Mom. They have four children: two from Sam's previous marriage, Whitney Elizabeth (b. Jun. 18, 1982) now a junior at Pomona College in California, and Maxwell Lawrence (b. Dec. 6, 1983) now a freshman at Duke University. Their two younger sons are Charles (b. Dec. 29, 1987) who now attends Briarwood, a special school in Houston for children with disabilities (autism), and the youngest boy, Andrew Davidson (b. Sep, 5, 1989) a Boy Scout and a seventh grader at Houston's Kinkaid School.

3) Kenneth Wilson Stubbs (b. Apr. 16, 1953) md. Karen Culotta (b. Nov. 8, 1955 in Baton Rouge) on Jul. 2, 1977 in Baton Rouge. Kenneth is a physician in the practice of internal medicine in Natchez, MS. He is a Summa Cum Laude graduate of LSU and a graduate of the LSU School of Medicine in New Orleans. Karen is also a graduate of LSU with a major in fine arts. She, too, is a stay-at-home Mom. They have four children: Nathaniel Kenneth (b. Dec. 17, 1980 in Baton Rouge), a student at Baton Rouge Community College; Andrew James (b. Jun. 11, 1982 in Baton Rouge), a junior at the University of Mississippi in Oxford, MS; Joanna Lee (b. Aug. 8, 1984 in Baton Rouge), a high school senior at Cathedral School in Natchez; and Julian Lawrence (b. Mar. 14, 1991 in Natchez), a sixth grader at Cathedral School.

Jack worked for what is now Exxon for 39 years and 4 months before retiring in Baton Rouge on Sep. 30, 1982. He is a Phi Beta Kappa chemistry graduate of the University of North Carolina at Chapel Hill, NC in 1943, after which he began his career in Baton Rouge involving process control laboratory work, process engineering, large-scale computer programming and business systems design. Dotty is a fine arts graduate of LSU. She had attended in 1939-40 Belhaven College in Jackson, MS, before transferring to LSU.

Dotty and Jack lived in retirement in Baton Rouge, LA for 14 years before moving in 1996 to Natchez, MS. Having their doctor son there was a great incentive to move to Natchez, as was the fact that four of their 10 grandchildren lived there

Jack and Dotty Stubbs family; standing, from left: Olin and Linda Stubbs; Melinda, Charlie and Sam Stubbs; Maxwell Stubbs; Luke Stubbs and Kelly Cain; Karen and Kenneth Stubbs; Kathryn Thornton and Jack W. Stubbs; sitting on couch: Julian, Joanna, Dotty and Jack Stubbs; kneeling at right: Nathan Stubbs; kneeling in front: Andrew D. Stubbs; not pictured: Andrew J. Stubbs, son of Kenneth and Karen Stubbs, and Whitney E. Stubbs, daughter of Sam and Melinda Stubbs

and none lived in Baton Rouge. They love Natchez and are indeed thankful they made the move. They are very active members of the First Presbyterian Church, Jack having served earlier as an Elder on the Session and Dotty currently serving in that capacity. In 1999 they were chosen by the local newspaper, *The Natchez Democrat*, as two of the community's "Unsung Heroes" because of their many volunteer activities.

SUTTLE/JOHNSON/WOODS NATCHEZ AREA DESCENDANTS.

Richard Swayze was one of the Jersey Settlers who came to Adams County about 1773. He brought with him his daughter, Lydia and her husband, Job Cory, son of Elnathan Cory and Sarah Simpson. Martha Cory, daughter of Job and Lydia, married Thomas Reed. Their son William Reed (b. 1796) md. Jemima Stampley (b. 1800, d. 1840), daughter of John Stampley and Martha Curtis. Martha was the daughter of Phoebe Courtney Jones and Richard Curtis Sr. The Curtis and Stampley families were early settlers who came to the Natchez area from North Carolina on flatboats via the Holston, Tennessee, Ohio and Mississippi Rivers.

Britain and Makenna Morris, descendants of Richard Swayze

William and Jemima Stampley Reed had seven children. Martha Ann Reed (b. 1818, d. 1890) md. John Craig Holmes (b. 1817, d. 1897), son of Thomas Holmes and Margaret Craig of Virginia. After William's death, Jemima Stampley married Thomas Holmes, her daughter's father-in-law. Jemima is buried in Winston County in the Holmes Burying Ground.

John Craig Holmes was a landowner and part owner of Hashuqua Cotton Factory in Winston County and served the Confederacy in the Civil War. John Holmes and Martha Ann Reed had four children. Their daughter Margaret Reed Holmes married first, Henry Wesley Anderson and second, Epathus Burroughs Suttle. John and Martha Holmes are buried at Good Hope Baptist Church Cemetery in Winston County.

Margaret Reed Holmes Anderson Suttle and E.B. Suttle had five children: Martha Ann, Olena, William Woodward, Margaret Elizabeth and Birdie Ella.

Martha Ann Suttle married John William Johnson, a Winston County farmer and landowner. They had three daughters: Karon (b. 1895, d. 1986); Inis (b. 1898, d. 1957); and Birdie Lee (b. 1900, d. 1959). Karon married first, Leland B. Curtis Sr. and second, Knox McLeod Broom. Inis married Kenneth Myron Warner. Birdie Lee married John Forrest Woods Sr., a Noxapater merchant. The three Johnson daughters were educated at Blue Mountain College.

Birdie Lee Johnson and John Forrest Woods had three children.

1) John F. Woods Jr. (b. 1925) md. Mary Olive Eudy of Eupora. They reside in Greenwood, MS and have two sons, John and Michael. They enjoy their grandchildren, Daniel, Mark, Josh and Mary Aven.

2) Martha Elizabeth Woods (b. 1930, d. 1982) md. Harry Lee Green and had three children: Martha Ann, Harry Lee Jr. and Linda Kay. Martha had a beautiful soprano voice and sang in the choir at Bellevue Baptist Church, Memphis, TN.

3) Gloria Ann Woods (b. 1933) md. Melville E. Mitchell (b. 1928, d. 1990). They had three daughters, Cynthia Inis (b. 1957), Sandra Louise (b. 1957) and Melanie Claire (b. 1960).

Gloria is a retired medical technologist and resides in Clarksdale where she serves on the Vestry and Altar Guild at St. George's Episcopal Church.

Cynthia is a graduate of Indiana University and Harvard Law School and resides in Clarksdale. Sandra is a graduate of the University of the South and obtained her PhD from the University of New Mexico. She resides in Wyoming. The twins are marathon runners and enjoy skiing.

Melanie is a graduate of Delta State University. She married James Moody Morris at Monmouth Plantation, Natchez in 1990. They reside in Madison, MS and are the parents of Britain Robert (b. 1993) and Makenna Elizabeth Grace (b. 1996). *Submitted by Gloria Woods Mitchell.*

BENJAMIN EDWARD TARVER & GAIL ELAINE COOKSEY.

Gail Elaine Cooksey (b. Aug. 5, 1947 in Jackson, MS) is the daughter of Dorothy Mae Lee and Clyde Bernice Cooksey of Jackson. Clyde (b. Jul. 4, 1907) and Dorothy (b. Jul. 19, 1919) were both born in Newton County, MS. Their children: Thelma Clyde Cooksey, Daisey Lee Cooksey, James "Jimmy" Corbett Cooksey, Ottis Paul Cooksey, Pamela Kay Cooksey, and Gail Elaine Cooksey. Clyde died in February 1992 and Dorothy in January 1996.

Most of Clyde Cooksey's family moved to Goree, TX, after 1876, but his father, Isham Cooksey, did not like Texas and returned to Newton County, MS, to rear his family. His ancestors included Samuel Cooksey, a Confederate soldier who was captured in Vicksburg, MS, during the War Between the States, and was released on Jul. 7, 1863. Another ancestor of Clyde's was William Cooksey, who served with the Georgia Militia during the American Revolutionary War and died in Covington County, MS in 1828.

Gail first married David Thornton, and they had the following children, all born in Hinds County, MS:

1) Rhonda Gail Thornton (b. Sep. 5, 1967) md. Harold Yarbrough, and they have children Cody Lewis Yarbrough and David Brady Yarbrough.

2) Tanya Lynn Thornton (b. Jun. 14, 1971) md. Steve Rogers, and they have children, Payton Chandler Rogers and Neely Logan Rogers.

3) Jason David Thornton (b. Aug. 17, 1975).

Gail divorced David Thornton, and on Oct. 27, 1983 in Jackson, she married Benjamin Edward Tarver, who had been divorced from his first wife.

Ben and Gail Tarver, 1992

Benjamin Edward Tarver (b. Jul. 30, 1944 in Natchez, MS) is the son of Mary Louise McCaleb and Roy Howard Tarver. (See separate biography.)

Mary Louise and Roy were the parents of six children: Betty Anne Tarver, William John Tarver, Pauline "Polly" Tarver, George David Tarver, Daniel Howard Tarver, and Benjamin Edward Tarver.

Ben first married on Dec. 16, 1964 in Natchez to Jean Ruth Campbell (b. Nov. 3, 1945 in Vidalia, LA), the daughter of Maurine Ester Small and James Curtis Campbell. (See separate biography)

Ben and Jean were the parents of the following children:

1) Melissa "Missy" Ann Tarver (b. Aug. 5, 1965 in Vicksburg, MS). (See separate biography)

2) Benjamin "Benji" Edward Tarver II (b. May 25, 1971 in Natchez). (See separate biography).

3) James Isaac "Ike" Tarver (b. Oct. 2, 1969 in Natchez). (See separate biography).

4) Samuel Tarver (b. May 25, 1971, d. May 26, 1971 in Natchez).

Ben grew up on LaGrange and Liberty Roads in Adams County, MS. He attended the Natchez public schools, graduating in 1962 from Natchez-Adams County High School. He then attended Copiah-Lincoln Junior College in Wesson, MS. He became an automotive mechanic and is presently the owner of "Tarver Automotive, Ltd." in Pearl, MS, where he and Gail live.

DANIEL HOWARD TARVER & ALICE FAYE MAGEE.

Alice Faye Magee (b. Aug. 31, 1945 in Natchez, MS) is the daughter of Ethel Odie Burr (b. Dec. 14, 1919 in Franklin County, MS, d. Feb. 18, 1987) and Thomas Louis Magee (b. Oct. 17, 1914 in Franklin County). In 1941 the Magees moved to Natchez, where they worked in the Shell Plant during World War II. He then worked for Armstrong Tire & Rubber Co., Natchez, from which he retired at age 62. They were the parents of Tommie Eugene Magee, James Ronald Magee (d. Sep. 2, 1940 at 8 months), Jesse Lee Magee, Alice Faye Magee and Harold Louis Magee.

Dan, Alice and Paul Tarver

Growing up in Cranfield, MS, Alice graduated in 1963 from Natchez-Adams County High School. On Oct. 6, 1963 in Natchez, she married Daniel Howard Tarver (b. Jun. 26, 1943 in Adams County, MS), son of Mary Louise McCaleb and Roy Howard Tarver.

Mary Louise (b. Oct. 30, 1918 in Adams County, MS), the daughter of Anne Matilda Farrar and Sidney Briscoe McCaleb of Smithland Plantation, Kingston, Adams County. Roy (b. Aug. 10, 1911 in Smithdale, Amite County, MS, d. Jan. 4, 1985 in Natchez) was the son of Frances "Fannie" Elizabeth Thornton and Isaac "Ike" Ham Tarver of Lincoln County and Natchez. Roy worked for Armstrong Tire Plant, International Paper Co., Johns-Manville, and Wilson Box Factory, plus several oil field companies. Mary Louise and Roy had children: Betty Anne Tarver, William John Tarver, Pauline "Polly" Tarver, George David Tarver, Daniel Howard Tarver, and Benjamin Edward Tarver.

Growing up near and on Liberty Road, Dan graduated from Natchez-Adams County High School in 1961. After graduation, he worked as a mechanic for Natchez Equipment Co. Alice and Dan's son, Paul Howard Tarver, was born in Natchez Mar. 28, 1965. He married Pamela Sue Robbins Hoover in Lauderdale County, MS, on Mar. 6, 1999.

In 1969 Alice, Dan and Paul moved to Jackson, MS, where Dan worked as a mechanic for Blackwell Chevrolet, International Harvester Co., and then for himself as Tarver Repair, LTD. He was shop foreman for Richard's Auto Parts, then meat salesman for Boteler & Corey Meats, from which he recently retired. Alice worked for several insurance agents in Jackson before retiring in 1993 from Allstate Insurance Co. as senior account representative.

Dan and Alice were members of the Congregational Fellowship Church, Jackson, where Dan was a Deacon and Sunday School Superintendent. Alice was the pianist, Sunday School teacher, and for over 25 years a member of a Ladies Trio and also sang solos. An officer in the Insurance Women of Jackson, she is a member of the Natchez Chapter Daughters of the American Revolution.

Alice's ancestry goes back to Scotland, where the Magees had been McGregors. Dan is descended from several early settlers of the Natchez District, including names such as Swayze, King, McCaleb, Farrar, Dougharty; Collins, Pipes, Bisland, Rucker, Custard, Robson, Sojourner, Thomas, Ford and Boyd.

GEORGE DAVID TARVER & BETTY JEAN WALLEY. Betty Jean Walley (b. Sep. 5, 1946, in Bucatunna, MS) was the daughter of Ouida Nell Busby and Nollie Walley. Ouida (b. Dec. 15, 1924 in Lela, AL, d. Jun. 8, 1980 in Vicksburg, MS) was the daughter of Lottie Mae Dyess and Joseph Grady Busby of Waynesboro, MS. Ouida married on Dec. 14, 1940 in Clara, MS, to Nollie Walley (b. Nov. 16, 1914), the son of Mandy Elvira Smith and Jesse Walley of Waynesboro. Nollie died Jan. 20, 1983 in Natchez, MS. Nollie and Ouida were the parents of the following children: Betty Jean Walley, Charles Donald Walley, Joseph Jesse Walley, Brenda Ophelia Walley, Mary Jane Walley, James Edward Walley and Jerry Lynn Walley.

On Jun. 5, 1965 in Natchez, Betty Jean married George David Tarver (b. Apr. 24, 1941 in Natchez, the fourth child of Mary Louise McCaleb and Roy Howard Tarver. (See separate biography—Roy Howard Tarver & Mary Louise McCaleb)

George and Betty Jean Tarver with sons David, James and Johnny, 1985

George grew up on LaGrange and Liberty Roads in Adams County, attended the city schools of the Natchez School District and graduated from Natchez High School in 1959. After graduation, he joined the U.S. Marine Corps, serving in North Carolina and in Okinawa, where he specialized in automotive mechanics and heavy equipment. Presently, he is the co-owner of "Engine & Equipment Repair Co." and "George Tarver Operating." "Engine and Equipment Repair Co." is a mechanic shop that specializes in the repair of starters and alternators for trucks and heavy equipment. "George Tarver Operating" is a company that owns some oil wells, operates other oil wells, and rents and services motors for the oil wells.

Having attended schools in Adams County, Betty Jean is now a sergeant at Louisiana State Prison, Angola, LA. She has taught various Sunday School Classes at Cliff Temple Baptist Church, Kingston, as well as Vacation Bible School. George is a deacon of Cliff Temple, where he teaches a men's Sunday School Class. Betty Jean and George live at Smithland Plantation, Kingston Community, Adams County. They are the parents of three sons:

1) David Tarver (b. Dec. 3, 1966 in Natchez) md. first Rebecca Hope Morris on May 22, 1993 in Adams County. They are the parents of Matthew Jordan Tarver (b. Apr. 20, 1995 in Hattiesburg, MS) and Christian Luke Tarver (b. Sep. 30, 1997 in Natchez). David divorced Hope and married in Pensacola, FL, to Francine Lee.

2) James Richard Tarver (b. Oct. 29, 1969 in Natchez) md. first on Nov. 23, 1991 in Adams County to Elizabeth Lynn Flournoy (b. Jan. 16, 1973, in Mobile, AL). They are the parents of Kaitlynn Elizabeth Tarver (b. Aug. 29, 1992 in Natchez). James married secondly in Natchez to Jean Malone Karabellum (b. Dec. 6, 1977) and they are the parents of George Wesley Tarver (b. Apr. 24, 2001 in Natchez).

3) John Dlynn Tarver (b. Jan. 20, 1977 in Natchez). (See separate biography—John Dlynn Tarver & Ginger Ann White).

JOHN DLYNN TARVER & GINGER ANN WHITE. Ginger Ann (b. Jul. 8, 1972 in Blytheville, AR) is the daughter of Peggy Ann Verucchi and Danny Lynn White, who were married in Natchez, MS on Mar. 25, 1969. Peggy (b. Aug. 15, 1950 in Natchez) is the daughter of Annie Halford and Mike Verucchi of Natchez, who were married on Aug. 25, 1935 in Ferriday, LA. Danny White (b. Mar. 19, 1949 in Natchez, d. Mar. 17, 2002 in Natchez) was the son of Mildred Bradford (b. Mar. 30, 1926 at Walters, LA) and Floyd White (b. Apr. 15, 1925 at Meadville, MS) who were married Jul. 12, 1947 in Meadville, MS. Peggy and Danny White have two daughters, Tammy Lynn White (b. Nov. 8, 1970 in Blytheville, AR) and Ginger Ann Tarver.

On Apr. 15, 1989 in Natchez, Tammy married Kenny Brown of Natchez, and they have the following children: Kimberly Marie Brown (b. Aug. 15, 1988 at Natchez); Katherine Donna-Mae Brown (b. Nov. 5, 1989 at Natchez); Kenneth Daniel-Michael Brown (b. 5 Oct. 5, 1990 at Natchez); and Kyle Andrew Brown (b. Feb. 5, 1992, d. Oct. 30, 1992 at Natchez).

On Mar. 20, 1999 Ginger Ann White married at Adams County to John Dlynn Tarver (b. Jan. 20, 1977 in Natchez), the son of Betty Jean Walley and George David Tarver. Betty Jean (b. Sep. 5, 1946 in Bucatunna, MS) is the daughter of Ouida Nell Busby and Nollie Walley. Ouida (b. Dec. 15, 1924 in Lela, AL, d. Jun. 8, 1980 in Vicksburg, MS) md. Nollie Walley in Clara, MS, on Dec. 14, 1940. Nollie was born Nov. 16, 1914, d. Jan. 20, 1983 in Natchez.

George David Tarver (b. Apr. 24, 1941 in Natchez) md. in Natchez on Jun. 5, 1965 to Betty Jean Walley. George is the son of Mary Louise McCaleb and Roy Howard Tarver of Natchez. Mary Louise (b. Oct 30, 1918, Adams County, MS) md. Roy on Jul. 10, 1936 at Franklin County, MS. Roy (b. Aug. 10, 1911 in Amite County, MS, d. Jan. 4, 1985 in Natchez).

John Dlynn Tarver is descended from several very early settlers in the Natchez District: Richard Swayze, Caleb King, William McCaleb, Alexander Farrar, George Dougharty, William Collins, Windsor Pipes, John Bisland, Moses King, Peter Rucker, Morris Custard, John Robson Sr.,

Eliza Sojourner, Joseph Thomas, Dr. Henry Ki[?] White Ford, and both Alexander Boyd and his sister Mary Boyd.

Johnny and Ginger Tarver

After attending schools at the Natchez Christian Academy, Ginger worked in video stores in Natchez, as well as in Alexanderia, LA. She is currently the secretary and bookkeeper at Engine & Equipment Repair, a company co-owned by her husband, John Tarver, and his father George. John, who attended the Adams County Christian School in Natchez and the Natchez city schools, is also co-owner and service man for George Tarver Operating, which owns some oil wells, operates others, and rents oil well motors, which he services and keeps running.

ISAAC "IKE" HAM TARVER & FRANCES "FANNY" ELIZABETH THORNTON. "Fanny" was the daughter of Frances Elizabeth "Bettie" Gatlin and Wiley Perley Thornton. Bettie and Wiley had the following children: Audis H. Thornton, Benjamin Wiley Thornton, William Charlie Thornton, Francis "Fanny" Elizabeth Thornton, Alice Vertna "Dolly" Thornton, Lee Franklin Thornton, Bessie Marcilas Thornton, John Taylor Thornton, Prentiss Leroy Thornton, Dennie Idell Thornton, James Rhesa Thornton, Lillie Margarette Thornton, Len Burton Thornton, Marion Ratcliff Thornton, and Vera Mae Thornton. Fanny (b. Sep. 10, 1894 in Amite County, MS, d. Jul. 19, 1981 in Natchez, MS) md. Mar. 28, 1910 in Amite County to Isaac "Ike" Ham Tarver (b. Oct. 20, 1887 in Lincoln County and died Sep. 25, 1963 in Brookhaven, MS). Fanny and Ike had the following children: Roy Howard Tarver (b. Aug. 10, 1911); Loyd Tarver (b. Apr. 3, 1913) never married; Corene Tarver (b. Aug. 12, 1916); Hilda Rae Tarver (b. May 13, 1921); Wilda Mae Tarver (b. May 13, 1921); Vince Edward Tarver (b. Mar. 10, 1923); George Harvey Tarver (b. Feb. 2, 1927); Velma Bernice Tarver (b. Nov. 12, 1929); and Florence Maxine Tarver (b. Aug. 23, 1932).

"Ike" Ham Tarver came with his family to Adams County, MS, in the 1930s to log and to help build a railroad for the Homochito Lumber Co. Later, Ike, who also was a blacksmith, worked for Firo Machine Shop and the Diamond Box Company in Natchez. Ike Tarver was the son of Lorena "Rena" Burt and Jennings Cicero Tarver of Lincoln County, MS. "Rena" was born in 1855 and died in Franklin County on Sep. 30, 1927. "Rena" and Jennings Cicero had the following children: Mary Jane Tarver (b. ca. 1877); James Walter

Ike Tarver and Fanny Thornton, 1910

arver (b. Oct. 30, 1880); Loney Tarver (b. about May 13, 1883); Isaac "Ike" Ham Tarver (b. Oct. 20, 1887); and Jennings "Bud" Cicero Tarver (b. Nov. 18, 1888).

Jennings Cicero Tarver was the son of Celia Newman and Isaac Hamilton Tarver, who had the following children: Jennings Cicero Tarver (b. 1855); John Tarver (b. 1858); James "Jim" Tarver (b. ca. 1859); Mary Tarver (b. 1862); Frances Tarver (b. 1862); Liningus Tarver; Martha Ann Tarver (b. 1866); Adelizer Tarver (b. 1867); William R. Tarver; and Isaac Ishmael "Ish" Tarver (b. 1872).

Isaac Hamilton was the son of Rachel Bunch (b. ca. 1800 in Wilkinson County, d. between 1880 and 1900) and Dempsey Tarver (b. ca. 1800 in South Carolina, d. 1854 in Lincoln County). Rachel and Dempsey were married in Wilkinson County on Jun. 21 1821 and had the following children: John Tarver (b. 1825); Elizabeth Tarver (b. ca. 1829); Thomas Tarver, Sarah Tarver, Martha Tarver; Charles Wesley Tarver; Mark M. Tarver; William Tarver; Isaac Hamilton Tarver (b. ca. 1830 in Mississippi, d. Dec. 6, 1901 in Pineville, LA); Elvire Tarver (b. May 1, 1835); Mary Ann Tarver (b. 1838); and James J. Tarver (b. ca. 1838).

JAMES ISAAC "IKE" TARVER & MARIA ROSA RAMIREZ. Maria Rosa (b. Sep. 13, 1974 in Tampa, FL) is the adopted daughter of Rosalia Aviles and Victor Ramirez. Rosalia was born in Balzar, Ecuador, and Victor was born in Havana, Cuba. They were married Mar. 12, 1965 in New York.

Ike, Maria, Victoria and Grant Tarver

Maria grew up in New Port Richey, FL. She attended Elfers Elementary School in Elfers, FL, then St. Anthony School at St. Antonio, FL. In 1992, she graduated from Central Catholic High School, Clearwater, FL. In 1997, Maria graduated with a degree in liberal studies for professional education from Christian Brothers University, Memphis, TN, where she is working on her masters of education. Having taught five years at Shelby County School in Memphis and at Crump Elementary School, she is currently teaching first grade at Dogwood Elementary School in Germantown, TN.

On Aug. 6, 1988 at New Port Richey, FL, Maria married James Isaac "Ike" Tarver, son of Jean Ruth Campbell and Benjamin Edward Tarver. Jean (b. Nov. 3, 1945 in Vidalia, LA) md. Dec. 26, 1964 in Natchez, MS, to Ben, who was born Jul. 30, 1944 in Natchez. Jean was the daughter of Maurine Ester Small and James (Olin) Curtis Campbell. Maurine was the daughter of Elizabeth J. Lange and Albert Orange Small of Princeton, IL. James was the son of Cora Albritton of Georgia and Larkin Albert Campbell of Alabama.

Ben was the son of Mary Louise McCaleb and Roy Howard Tarver of Natchez. Mary Louise (b. Oct. 30, 1918 in Kingston, Adams County, MS) was the daughter of Anne Matilda Farrar and Sidney Briscoe McCaleb of Adams County, MS. Roy (b. Aug. 10, 1911 in Smithdale, Amite County, MS) was the son of Frances "Fanny" Elizabeth Thornton and Isaac "Ike" Ham Tarver of Adams County. Mary Louise and Roy were married Jul. 10, 1936 in Roxie, Franklin County, MS.

Jean and Ben had the following children: Melissa "Missy" Ann Tarver (b. Aug. 5, 1965 in Vicksburg, MS); Benjamin "Benji" Edward Tarver II (b. May 25, 1968 in Natchez); James Isaac "Ike" Tarver (b. Oct. 2, 1969 in Natchez); and Samuel Tarver (b. May 25, 1971, d. May 26, 1971 in Natchez). After divorcing Jean, Ben married Gail Cooksey on Oct. 27, 1983 in Jackson, MS.

Ike is descended from several early settlers of the Natchez District: Richard Swayze, Caleb King, William McCaleb, Alexander Farrar, George Dougharty, William Collins, Windsor Pipes, John Bisland, Moses King, Peter Rucker, Morris Custard, John Robson Sr., Eliza Sojourner, Joseph Thomas, Dr. Henry Kirk White Ford, and both Alexander Boyd and his sister Mary Boyd.

Graduating from Pearl High School, Pearl, MS, in 1988 and from the University of Southern Mississippi, Hattiesburg, MS, with a BS degree in construction engineering in 1995, Ike is currently a project manager at W.G. Yates Construction Co.

Maria and Ike are the parents of Victoria Maria Tarver (b. Mar. 21, 1999 in Memphis) and Grant Reed Tarver (b. Jul. 16, 2002 in Memphis).

ROY HOWARD TARVER & MARY LOUISE MCCALEB. Mary Louise (b. Oct. 30, 1918 at Smithland Plantation, Kingston, Adams County, MS), the daughter of Anne Matilda Farrar and Sidney Briscoe McCaleb Sr. of Smithland Plantation. After graduating from Natchez High School, Mary Louise married on Jul. 10, 1936 at Roxie, Franklin County, MS, to Roy Howard Tarver (b. Aug. 10, 1911 in Smithdale, Amite County, MS, d. Jan. 4, 1985), the son of Frances "Fannie" Elizabeth Thornton and Isaac "Ike" Ham Tarver. Mary Louise resides at Smithland.

Mary Louise and Roy met in Kingston, where she was attending Kingston School and he was working for the Homochitto Lumber Co. Roy also worked for the Armstrong Tire Plant, the International Paper Co., the Johns-Manville Co., and the Wilson Box Factory, in addition to several oil field companies. For about 12 years Mary Louise worked as a hostess at Elms Court during the Natchez Spring "Pilgrimage." She is a member of Cliff Temple Baptist Church, Kingston, where she teaches a Sunday school class for ladies.

Mary Louise is a descendant of several early settlers of the Natchez District: Richard Swayze, Caleb King, William McCaleb, Alexander Farrar, George Dougharty, William Collins, Windsor Pipes, John Bisland, Moses King, Peter Rucker, Morris Custard, John Robson Sr., Eliza Sojourner, Joseph Thomas, Dr. Henry Kirk White Ford, and both Alexander Boyd and his

Roy Tarver, 1935

sister Mary Boyd. Mary Louise and Roy had six children:

1) Betty Anne Tarver (b. Jul. 22, 1937, Smithland Plantation. (See separate biography on Betty Anne Tarver & Paul Britt).

2) William John "Will" Tarver (b. Aug. 16, 1938 in Adams County) never married. Earning a master's degree in chemistry from the University of Southern Mississippi, Hattiesburg, MS, Will taught chemistry for some years at Jones Junior College, Laurel, MS, and later worked at Mississippi State University, Starkville, MS. Retired, he lives near Pearl, MS.

3) Pauline "Polly" Tarver (b. Feb. 26, 1940 Natchez, MS). (See separate biography—Bobby Clay Scott & Pauline "Polly" Tarver).

4) George David

Mary Louise (McCaleb) Tarver, 1935

Tarver (b. Apr. 24, 1941 Natchez). (See separate biography—George David Tarver & Betty Jean Walley).

5) Daniel Howard Tarver (b. Jun. 26, 1943 Adams County). (See separate biography—Daniel Howard Tarver & Alice Faye Magee).

6) Benjamin Edward "Ben" Tarver (b. Jul. 30, 1944 Natchez). (See separate biography—Benjamin Edward Tarver & Gail Cooksey).

CHARLOTTE & WILLIAM "BILL" TAYLOR were a married couple associated with the John T. McMurran family as slaves. Bill Taylor was working as a gardener at McMurran's Riverside Plantation on the Mississippi/Louisiana line in 1856. Charlotte Taylor, a household servant at Melrose, gave birth to a baby girl in August 1857 with doctors concerned for her health because of her size. For six months in 1861, Bill Taylor accompanied the McMurrans' son, John T. McMurran Jr. into service with the Confederate Army as a personal valet.

CLIFFORD RANDOLPH "RANDY" TILLMAN & LEE ANN COMBS. Randy (b. Oct. 30, 1950) was the second of four children born to Clifford Tillman, M.D., and Sarah Ann Gardner of Rossville, GA. He married Lee Ann Combs on Aug. 15, 1970. Lee Ann was the first of two children born to Carl Wiley Combs and Virginia Lee Long Combs.

Randy Tillman worked as a physician (gastroenterologist), 1981-present. He enjoys boating, flying a helicopter, farming, motorcycles and belongs to the Rotary Club. Ann Tillman is an auto dealer/owner, Great Rivers Chev/Cad/GMC/Nissan.

Randy and Ann have six children: Catherine Elizabeth (b. Jul. 28, 1972), Clifford Randolph Jr. (b. Dec. 22, 1975), Margaret Ann (b. Jan. 18, 1979), Rebecca Claire (b. Nov. 2, 1983), Laura Madeline (b. Aug. 18, 1986) and Rachel Victoria (b. Aug. 18, 1986).

They lived 1983-95 in the Winchester House on Main Street and from 1995-present in Glen Auburn on Commerce Street. Ann is also active in historic preservation.

EDWARD TURNER & ELIZA BAKER. Edward Turner was born in Fairfax County, VA, the son of Lewis Ellzey Turner (b. 1754, d. Oct. 9, 1823) and Theodosia Payne (b. Jan. 22, 1751, d. 1828). Edward Turner moved to Kentucky in 1786, where he graduated from Transylvania College. He arrived in Natchez in 1801, and in 1802 was elected clerk of the territorial house of representatives.

He married first, Mary West (d. Feb. 18, 1811) on Sep. 5, 1802. Mary was the daughter of Cato West who was Secretary of the Mississippi Territory. Their children were Theodosia Lavinia Turner (b. 1805, d. Feb. 19, 1827) md. William Griffith (d. 1827) on May 12, 1823; Martha Ann Turner (b. 1807, d. Oct. 29, 1827); and Mary W. Turner (b. 1809, d. 1811). In 1805 Turner moved to

Jefferson County and in 1810 moved to Palmyra in Warren County. In 1811, the year Turner was elected to the territorial legislature from Warren County, his first wife died.

On Dec. 27, 1812, Edward Turner married Eliza Baker (b. Jan. 20, 1789), who was the sister of his brother Henry's wife. Born in New Jersey, Eliza Baker was the daughter of Mary Cassidy and Looe Baker (b. 1757, d. Dec. 4, 1827). Edward and Eliza Turner moved to Natchez in 1813. He practiced law, served as city magistrate and president of the board of selectmen, and represented Adams County in the territorial legislature. He prepared a digest of statute laws, served on the statehood convention, and was twice elected speaker of the house. He served as an Adams County delegate to the constitutional convention that created the state of Mississippi in 1817.

Edward Turner purchased Holly Hedges in 1818; the family also maintained a country home at Franklin Place. Turner served in the state legislature from 1818-22, then served on the state supreme court, elected chief justice in 1829. He became the state attorney general in 1830 and state chancellor in 1834, but lost a bid for governor in 1839. In 1843 he retired from the bench and served as a state senator from Jefferson and Franklin counties, 1844-48. At 6'2" tall with thick white hair, he was referred to as a "portly and commanding figure." The 1850 census records Turner as a farmer with $15,000 in real estate and 191 slaves. In 1853 he purchased Woodlands, the home of his deceased brother Henry.

The children of Elizabeth Baker and Edward Turner were: Mary Louisa Turner (b. Jan. 7, 1814, d. 1891); Edward Turner (b. November 1815, d. Aug. 24, 1823 at Woodlands); Elizabeth Frances Turner (b. Aug. 6, 1827 at Franklin Place, d. Jul. 17, 1828 at Franklin Place); and Elizabeth Frances Turner (b. Dec. 7, 1829, d. 1910) md. Lemuel P. Conner (b. 1827, d. 1891) on Jan. 6, 1848 at Franklin Place.

A long-time member of the Episcopal Church and 32nd degree Mason, Edward Turner died at age 81 on May 23, 1860. Eliza Baker Turner died on Jul. 17, 1878.

WILLIAM TURNER. The search for the ancestors and descendants of William Turner who came to Greene County, MS in 1810 has been in progress for 33 years. Although still incomplete, more family information has been obtained since the first printing of *The William Turner Family of Greene County, Mississippi* in 1993. An annual reunion is held each year at the Pine Level Baptist Church, Greene County, MS. The annual reunion has been very successful in renewing family ties and acquaintances, exchanging family information, and encouraging family members to return to Greene County and visit points of interest to the Turner Family. Because of the interest of family members, the family book is being updated to include the revisions and additions since it was first printed.

The earliest known origin of our Turner family is in Ireland in the 1700s. Our oldest known family member is William Turner who immigrated to the United States, arriving on Jan. 12, 1768, at Charleston, SC. On this date, the clerk boarded the *Snow James and Mary* from Larne, Ireland (north Ireland, Ulster), John Moore, Master, and administered the oath to "the poor Protestants...who had lately arrived in her..." Among those who took the oath were William and Margaret Turner and their three sons: Alexander, John and James. Soon after arrival, William petitioned for warrant of survey, ON THE BOUNTY, for 200 acres of land in South Carolina. Two of his sons, Alexander and John, also petitioned for 100 acres each. James was not old enough to

own land and therefore probably did not file a petition. On Apr. 29, 1768, the Governor signed a grant of land for William Turner in Berkely County, SC, for 200 acres. At the time of this grant, the Bounty Acts had expired and William was indentured for his land grant.

Since our Greene County Turner Family descended from John Turner, son of William and Margaret Turner, this is the only Turner line that has been researched. John Turner appeared on the 1790 South Carolina Census in the Orangeburg District (South Part) with his wife, three sons and three daughters. John Turner died and his will was probated in 1806 in Barnwell, SC. Named in his will with his wife Mary Ann are his children: Sarah Turner Williams, James Turner, Elizabeth Turner Patterson, William Turner, Verily Turner, Joseph Turner, John Turner, Savannah Turner, and Mary Turner.

In 1809, the family of John Turner began preparing for its journey to Geene County, MS. Why the family decided to leave Barnwell, SC is unknown. In early January 1810, the Executive Department of the state of Georgia issued a passport for safe travel through the Creek Nation of Indians (the western part of Georgia and most of Alabama). Included on this passport were William Turner, with his mother and five of her children and one Negro; John Williams with his wife and five children; John Taylor with his wife and child; and Benjamin Williams and his wife and five children.

The children of John and his wife Mary Ann __ Turner are accounted for as follows:

1) James Turner does not have a passport recorded in his name but he did come to Greene County by 1815 and lived next door to William Turner that year. James did not stay in Greene County long, but probably moved to Alabama or to some family member with whom he lived.

2) Sarah Turner married Benjamin Williams and they appear on the Georgia Passport with their five children and the rest of the family who came from South Carolina. They were early settlers in Greene County, but later moved to Alabama. Their descendants are the Williamses of Greene County.

3) Elizabeth Turner Patterson may not have been in Greene County. If so, she was probably the mother of Neal Patterson and was living with her son but, without her husband.

4) William Turner was on the Georgia Passport with his mother and five of her children. He married Mary Catherine Feebecker. Some family members believe she was from the coastal area while some believe she was a school teacher from New Orleans. A search of the records in Mobile, New Orleans, and Mississippi has not located a Feebecker. However, John Feebecker and his family were enumerated on the 1790 South Carolina Census in Orangeburg District (South Part) near our John Turner family. In early 1813, William Turner of the Mississippi Territory, returned to Barnwell, SC, and sold land to George Turner. The land he sold adjoined the Benjamin Williams (husband of Sarah Turner) and William Patterson (husband of Elizabeth Turner) tracts. Sarah Turner Williams and Elizabeth Turner Patterson had inherited land from their father, John Turner. It is quite possible that William Turner married Mary Catherine Feebecker when he returned to South Carolina for this land sale and she returned with him to the Mississippi Territory. Although we do not know the date of their marriage, the first child of William and Mary Catherine Feebecker was born in Mississippi on Oct. 13, 1814.

5) Mary Turner married Ruben Ard. Very little is known about this family. She is listed in the census in the household of her brother John Turner in 1860 in Greene County, MS.

6) Verily Turner married William Issac Taylor. He is the son of John T. Taylor who is listed on the Georgia Passport with William Turner and his mother.

7) Joseph Turner was on the Georgia Passport. Never married, he lived with his mother, Mary Ann "Mariah" and later with his brother, John Turner, in Alabama. He was a minor child on his father's will.

8) John "Jack" Turner Jr. married Gracy Lucretia __. He is also on the Georgia Passport. They lived in Greene County and later moved to Alabama. His descendants married back into the descendants of his brother, William Turner.

9) Savannah "Susannah" Turner married Edmond Merritt, son of Robert Merritt.

The John Turner family arrived in Greene County and settled in the area near the Chickasawhay River known as Turner Dead Lake. William J. Turner, son of William Turner and Mary Catherine Feebecker, came to the Pine Level Community tending cattle that were on free range. Here he met and married Margaret Brewer. They homesteaded what was later known as the Dean Turner old home place. This site was chosen because it had a good spring for a water source. Other family members moved to Alabama and some later returned to Green County, MS.

The descendants of William Turner of Ireland and his son John Turner, whose wife and children came to Greene County, MS, now number more than 1,100. Some are still in Greene County, but many are scattered all across the United States. This is the William Turner Family of Greene County, MS as we know it today. *Submitted by Margaret Turner Sowell, gg-granddaughter of William Turner of Greene County, MS.*

JOHN NEIL VARNELL was born Feb. 23, 1945, in Cleveland (Bradley County) TN, the son of Robert Wayne (b. Jun. 26, 1913, d. 2000) and Mary Ruth Dethero (b. Sep. 5, 1911, d. 1989) Varnell, both of whom were born and reared in Cleveland where they married on Jul. 22, 1940. Neil's sister, Katie May Varnell (b. Jul. 5, 1941) md. Carl M. Edstrom of Denver, CO where they now reside with their two children, Gretchen Edstrom Hays and Amy Ruth Edstrom Harney, two sons-in-law, and five grandchildren. Neil's older brother, Robert Wayne Varnell Jr. (b. Dec. 25, 1943, d. 1993) md. Judy Foster in Cleveland and had two children, Robert Wayne III and Margaret Varnell Birkitt.

Neil earned his BA in English and Sociology at Emory and Henry College in 1967 before working three years in Sarawak, Malaysia, with the Methodist Church. Upon his return to the states, he entered graduate school at the University of Southern Mississippi where he earned his MA and PhD in psychology in 1975. He came to Natchez in September 1975 to serve as the psychologist of the Southwest Mississippi Mental Health Center before setting up his private practice in clinical psychology in Natchez in 1978. He closed his practice in December 1995 and joined the University of Maryland in January 1996 to teach college psychology in Asia and Europe on American military bases.

He returned to Natchez in August 2000, and in 2001 he opened Bluff Top Bed and Breakfast in his home at 205 Clifton Avenue. In addition to his psychology practice and B&B, Neil has been active in the Historic Natchez Foundation, Natchez Community Concert Association, Natchez Opera Festival, Natchez Little Theater, Natchez Audubon Society, and the Natchez/Adams Mental Health Association.

He restored his own home on Clifton Avenue and, with his business partners, Margaret Moss and Mini Miller, three additional properties at 206 and 208 Washington Street and 205 Wensel Lane. He strongly supports the fine arts, the protection of the natural environment, and the preservation, interpretation, and presentation of Natchez and its history so that the citizens of Natchez and the world may enjoy and appreciate Natchez for years to come.

WILLIAM ROUSSEAU COX VERNON.
William (b. Jan. 14, 1805 at Leaksville, NC) was the second son of Dr. Tinsley Vernon and Ann Barrygrove Cox. He left his paternal home near Murfreesboro, TN in 1829 going to Washington, MS, where his grandfather, Dr. John Coates Cox of Rockingham County, NC, had migrated with his family in 1807.

Vernon was enticed by the economy thriving from cotton production in the South. At age 24 he decided to follow Cox relatives and go into business. In 1831 he operated the retail business of W.R.C. Vernon & Co., which apparently evolved into Vernon & Metcalf, Metcalf being a relative.

William Rousseau Cox Vernon

Providentially W.R.C. Vernon and Miss Rowena Crane converged upon Washington, about the same time in 1829. Rowena (b. Apr. 12, 1814, in Massachusetts) was the only child of Eli and Sarah Colton Crane. A graduate of Wesleyan Academy at Wilbraham, she came to Washington at age 16 to accept a teaching position at Elizabeth Female Academy where her aunt, Mrs. Caroline P. Thayer, was head mistress.

Given time for Vernon to establish himself in business, for Rowena to grow into womanhood, and time for courtship, they married Sep. 4, 1836. A son born in October 1838 died unnamed. Another son born in October 1839, died in November. Rowena's widowed mother joined this grieving couple and was part of the household until her death Sep. 2, 1851 in Vidalia, LA.

The depression caused by the Panic of 1837 and the failure of Natchez's four banks had a devastating effect on the economy. Vernon was forced out of business and found employment as a scribe or clerk writing for commission houses and serving as agent in forfeitures.

In this desperate situation, aggravated by Rowena's fragile health, Vernon arranged for Rowena and Mrs. Crane to join his parents in Tennessee, accepting their shelter and nurture for almost three years. The 43 letters written by Vernon to Rowena, dated April 1840 - January 1843, report the status of Natchez business, local events and family news.

In January 1843 Vernon was managing "Woodburne," family property on the river below Natchez, where he prepared quarters for Rowena and Mrs. Crane's return. They lived there until fall when their last move was made to Vidalia, LA. Over the next nine years Vernon filled successively stations of Deputy Clerk, Assessor, and Deputy Sheriff. In 1852 he was elected Sheriff of Concordia Parish, being thrice re-elected and died in office. Vernon Street, near his Front Street home, was so named in his honor.

Four children were born into the Vernon home: Virginia (b. 1849, died age 2), Sarah (b. 1852), Annie (b. 1853), and William Henry (b. 1855). See more about Annie in the Judge Thomas Reber biography. Other children have no surviving descendants.

On Feb. 27, 1859, Vernon was a passenger to New Orleans on *The Princess* when seven miles below Baton Rouge the steamer exploded. Vernon, suffering from severe burns, survived to be transported by the *"Natchez"* to his Front Street home in Vidalia where he died Mar. 6, 1859. Funeral services from the Methodist Church in Natchez were followed by interment at the Natchez City Cemetery where a large obelisk marks the graves of W.RC. and Rowena C. Vernon. *Submitted by Mrs. L.R. McGehee.*

ELIZA ADAMS JORDAN WARNOCK.
Eliza Ann Adams (b. Jun. 3, 1827 in Natchez, MS), daughter of Catherine Adams Warnock and David Warnock, was orphaned as a child when her parents died.[1] With her sister Marcy Leonard and brothers, Joseph Warren and Benjamin Franklin, she was reared in Natchez by William Adams,[2] her wealthy riverboat captain grandfather who owned a great deal of property in Natchez and Louisiana, or by her uncle, John Adams.[3] Since David Warnock left no will, John Adams divided his property among the four children.

In 1847, at about 19 years of age, Eliza married 45-year-old Levi Jordan in Natchez.[4] In 1850, Eliza Jordan is listed in the U.S. Census in Levi's household with an infant, Alice Jordan, age 5 months, and two males, Joseph Warnock, age 17, and Benjamin Warnock, age 13. By early 1853, Levi had died[5] leaving Eliza with a young child and her two brothers. A family diary gives this account: *Feb. 13, 1853: Cousin Levi Jordan died in Tensas parish, LA. Cousin Ann (his wife) and little child are in Natchez. They are sent for, but arrive too late. He is dead when they arrive. - Feb. 14, 1853: Uncle Ballence came up with Cousin Ann and her infant daughter, Alice. They brought Mr. Jordan's corpse up and buried him in the Warnock graveyard.*[6] Later that same year Eliza's brother, Joseph, died. *Cousin Ann's brother had an accident. Joseph Warnock, being intoxicated, fell from the Steamer, was taken up unconscious and carried to Washington Hotel in Vicksburg, where he was visited by friends. But consciousness never returned. He soon died. He is buried near his parents in Forest Grove Plantation.*[7]

The following year Eliza married Needham Burch Lanier who was born in Brunswick County, VA. They lived in the Vicksburg area and had seven children in addition to Alice, who was from Eliza's first marriage: Mary Katherine "Kate," Frank Burch, James Ballence "Jim," Laura Josephine, John Adams, Wood Edward and Sloan.

Meanwhile in 1852 Eliza Ann's sister, Mary Leonard Warnock, may have married the first of her three husbands. According to her great-granddaughter, *On Mar. 15, 1852 Mary married Joel E. Selman at the age of 19. Four months later Joel died...*[8] However, Joel's tombstone in the Warnock cemetery in Warren County, MS reads: *Joel consort of Mary L. Selman, d. Jul. 19, 1852 in the 33 year of his life.*[9] No marriage records have been found. The following

year Mary married William Vinton Hickey in Vicksburg, MS, who died 4-5 years later. In 1863, she married James Goodrum.[10]

Eliza Adams Jordan Warnock endured many hardships during her lifetime including numerous losses during the Civil War. Her hand-written memoirs of this time period are in the Special Manuscripts Collection of the Mississippi Archives. *Submitted by Sarah Herzog, ggg-granddaughter of Eliza Lanier.*

[1]Eliza Ann Warnock of the Old Natchez District, *Mississippi River Routes,* Vol. I, No. 1, Fall 1993, pp. 7-12.

[2]Eliza Ann Warnock of the Old Natchez District, *Mississippi River Routes,* Vol. I, No. 1, Fall 1993, pp. 7-12.

[3]Burroughs, Anna Sutton. Adams research.

[4]Mississippi Archives, Computer indexed marriage records, Adams County, MS 1808-1900. p. 138, ref. 6-856.

[5]Burroughs, Anna Sutton. Copied from Warnock cemetery tombstones.

[6]Sophia Ann Goodrum's diary, copied and sent to submitter by Anna Sutton Burroughs.

[7]Sophia Ann Goodrum's diary, copied and sent to submitter by Anna Sutton Burroughs.

[8]Saunders, Marnelle Hickey. Written transcript of family history written by great-graddaughter of Mary. L Warnock.

[9]Burroughs, Anna Sutton. Copied from Warnock cemetery tombstones.

[10]Saunders, Marnelle Hickey. Written transcript of family history written by great-granddaughter of Mary L. Warnock.

See WELCH LINE on next page

THEODORE V. WENSEL FAMILY.
T.V. Wensel died in 1902 and one of his sons, Francis Quegles Wensel, is not pictured in this photo of his remaining family, in-laws and friends. A very successful businessman, T.V. was a partner in the Rumble & Wensel Co., wholesalers and cotton factors. Upon the death of his parents, the Wilson family at Rosalie reared T.V. When he married Emma Kirksey in 1866, T.V. bought two small houses on Washington Street and combined them into what is now known as Holly Hedges.

Theodore V. Wensel family, ca. 1905/06, on steps of Holly Hedges. Back row, l-r: Emma Gene Wensel (Venn), George Kirksey Wensel, Jeanette Dicks (Bristow). 2nd row: Henry Carson, Annie Laura Wensel (Carson), George Schwartz, Emma Lee Smith (Schwartz), Sara Aldridge (Smith), David M. Dix Jr., Mary Lee Schwartz (Brennan), James Smith, David M. Dix Sr., Sallie Wensel (Dix), Leonora Koerber (Wensel), Theodore Vincent Wensel Jr. 3rd row: Emma Caroline Kirksey Wensel (Bonnie), William Barber Dicks, Jim Clinton (boy next to Bonnie), Anna Kirksey (Dicks), Mary Eliza Wensel (Huntington) holding Elise Huntington (Bell-Odom-Bristow). 4th row: Emma Wensel Dicks (Murdy), John Barber Dicks Jr., Mary Francis Smith (Richardson), Elizabeth M. Carson (Leake), Carolyn Wensel Carson (Nugent), Laura Sophie Dix (Junkin), Theodore Wensel Huntington.

WELCH LINE. Thomas Welch (b. May 9, 1822, d. Jun. 11, 1893) md. Julia Tyler (b. Sep. 16, 1823, d. Apr. 18, 1907). They were from Camden, ME; buried in Rodney, MS. Seafaring families (immigration papers for John Tyler with Danish wife - with flaming red hair - at New York public library). Children born in Maine: Maggie Floravene, Benjamin, and Stanley who was a lawyer/judge in Corpus Christi, ambassador to Mexico and assassinated during negotiations to settle dispute with Mexico - two families in Corpus Christi.

Maggie Floravene Welch (b. Feb. 18, 1857, d. Mar. 22, 1949) and Joseph Lorenzo Burkley (b. Mar. 11, 1857, d. May 10, 1912) were married in New Orleans. He died of intestinal cancer in New Orleans; both are buried in Rodney. Children: Stanley (born in New Orleans), Chess, Gladys, Theresa, Lorena, Maggie married Joseph Jacob and had Joseph, Peyton, Doris, Majorie (Joseph Jacob, 2009 Vinewood Blvd, Ann Arbor, MI 48104; Peyton Jacob, 2 Vianne Court, Orinda, CA 94563).

Chess had Arcola; Theresa had no decendants; Gladys married Maurice Wilson and had Bobby and Maurice; Lorena married Peter Shauff and had Jolly Prince (lots of children around Natchez and St. Joe, LA); Malquin Ducrest (one son Steve, two grandsons); Missue (had Gail now Gray); Marvin; Fred (Cutter)

Stanley Melton Burkley (b. Mar. 16, 1879, d. Oct. 30, 1949) md. Dec. 25, 1925 in Ocean Springs, MS, to Minneapolis Katherine Engbarth (b. Jun. 10, 1892, d. Aug. 29, 1970), both buried in Natchez City Cemetery. Children: Stanley Engbarth (b. Oct. 5, 1926, blond; twins-Joseph Emile (red head) and Margaret Jeannette (brunette) were born Feb. 18, 1928. *Submitted by Maggie Burkley.*

JASPER YOUNG WHITE & MARGARITE HILL ALEXANDER. Jasper (b. Apr. 12, 1917) was one of six children born to Jasper Young White and Nancy Young, both of Franklin, MS. He married Margarite (b. Apr. 8, 1916) on Dec. 26, 1936. Margarite was the third child of five born to Charles P. Alexander and Lou Hill Alexander.

Jasper Young was owner of a dry-cleaners, White-Way Cleaner, from 1962-82. He enjoyed playing golf and hunting.

Margarite spent her time at the cleaners and with sports. They had two children, Robert W. White (b. May 27, 1938) and Donald R. White (b. Dec. 2, 1940).

Jasper Young White

They lived in Roselawn Subdivision and attended Parkway Baptist Church. Schools attended were W.H. Braden Elementary and Natchez High School. *Submitted by Bob White.*

JESSE HEWLETT WHITE & LILLIAN MAY TABOR. Lillian (b. Mar. 1, 1916, Natchez, MS) was the daughter of Lillian Archer Hutton and Eugene Tabor who were married in Natchez, MS Aug. 2, 1906. Lillian Archer (b. Dec. 19, 1884, d. Mar. 6, 1951 in Natchez, MS) was the daughter of Susan Bradford McCaleb and Joseph Hutton, who were married Mar. 26, 1881. Eugene Tabor (b. Jun. 3, 1884, died Jun. 6, 1932) was the son of Mary Jane McCready (b. Oct. 20, 1862 in Adams County, d. 1928 in Natchez, MS) and William Edward Tabor (b. Jul. 1, 1857, in Jackson, LA, d. Feb. 14, 1923,

in Natchez, MS). They were married in Natchez, MS.

Lillian Archer and Eugene Tabor had two daughters and one son: Eugene Franklin Tabor (b. Aug. 23, 1911); Lillian May Tabor; and Sue Audrey Willard (b. Jun. 20, 1919 in Natchez). On Jun. 27, 1937, Sue Audrey married Louis Edgar Willard, they had one child: Louis Eugene Willard (b. Aug. 23, 1947 in Natchez).

Eugene Franklin did not marry and died 1936 in Natchez. On May 23, 1935, Lillian May Tabor married in Natchez to Jesse Hewlett White (b. Jul. 30, 1910, in McComb, MS), the son of Sarah Ann McManus and Jasper Young White. Sarah Ann (b. Jan. 24, 1879, in Meadville, MS) was the daughter of Saphronia Arnold and Stephen A. McManus. Saphronia (b. Nov. 11, 1857, in Feliciana Parish, LA, d. May 29, 1929 in Amite County, MS) md. Stephen A. McManus (b. Dec. 9, 1825, d. Aug. 8, 1910 in Amite County, MS) in Amite County, MS, on Feb. 6, 1876.

Lillian May Tabor White

Jasper Young White (b. May 26, 1889 in Meadville, MS) md. Mar. 16, 1907 to Sarah Ann McManus. Jasper was the son of Seburn White and Nancy Ann Young of Meadville, MS. Nancy Ann (b. May 1, 1837 in Franklin County, MS) md. Dec. 23, 1869 to Seburn. Seburn was born 1841 in Meadville, MS, where he also died.

Jesse Hewlett White

Jesse Hewlett White is descended from several very early settlers in the Amite and Franklin County areas of Mississippi: Winston White, Elisha Young, William Pate, and Charles McManus. His Pate line descends from the Haveringtons and Harlingtons of England to Colonel Joseph Ball, George Washington's grandfather.

Lillian May Tabor, a talented seamstress, was descended from several very early settlers in the Natchez district: John McCaleb, White Turpin, William Collins, John Bisland, Moses King, Peter Rucker, Turner Starke, and Windsor Pipes.

After attending schools in Natchez, Lillian and Hewlett married, worked, and lived in Natchez. World War II took this brave, young couple to Oak Ridge, TN to help with the war effort. Lillian managed an office with 22 women for Tennessee Eastman Corporation, and Hewlett worked as a steam fitter for X-10. Moving to Clinton, TN after the war's end, they opened Snow-White Cleaners. They had one child, Linda Sue White, in Knoxville, TN. Moving to Atlanta, GA, Hewlett managed six One-Hour Valet dry cleaning plants, 1955-61. They returned to Knoxville, TN, where they opened Norwood Cleaners. Their combined skills created a business that served an appreciative community.

Linda Sue White married James Marvin Rankin. They reside in Knoxville, TN with their two youngest children, James Kent Rankin and Marisa Anne Rankin. Their oldest daughter, Aveline Lissette Rankin Hayes and her husband, Brian Hayes, live in Atlanta, GA.

Hewlett was a mason, an avid golfer, enjoyed music and showing horses. He invented and patented several items, missing the patent on the aeronautical "Black Box" by 24 hours.

Among Lillian's favorite Mississippi memories were her endless hours at her Aunt Olivia's and cousin Louise's Peachland (John McCaleb's 1811 home at Pine Ridge) and her Gran's, Susan Bradford McCaleb Hutton's Oakland, (White Turpin's 1810 home) in the Washington area.

With an honest approach to life, this couple's core values of faith and generosity served their God, family, community, and nation with strength and integrity. *Submitted by Linda White Rankin.*

WILDS FAMILY. Richard Wilds (b. 1809, d. 1866), an engineer from Manchester, England, migrated to Natchez in 1834 and established its first iron foundry. Partial quote from book, *Old & New Natchez: Natchez in the 1830s: Richard Wilds built and ran a foundry near the ship landing; made his own engines; he was an expert (dear, noble Dick!); was the inventor of the first known cotton seed crusher.*

His son was Oliver N. Wilds (b. 1839, d. 1928). The following is from *Biographical & Historical Memoirs of Mississippi*, Vol. II, the Goodspeed Publishing Co., 1891, page 1035, quote excerpts: *One of the most efficient members of the Board of Supervisors of Adams County, and its present president is Capt. Oliver N. Wilds, who comes from one of the oldest families of the state. Born in Natchez in 1839 to Richard and Mary (Myers) Wilds. Oliver N. Wilds was reared in Natchez, attended the public schools and the Institute from which he graduated. He learned the trade of machinist and engineer, finishing his trade in Cincinnati. In 1861 he joined the Natchez Southerns under Capt. Richard Inge; was at the battle of Shiloh where he was badly wounded, and afterwards discharged, being unable to return to service. In June 1862, at St. Mary's Cathedral, he married Miss Barbara Regina Koerber, a native of Natchez. After The war, Capt. Wilds began planting in Adams County on a small scale. He rapidly extended his business until he became one of the most extensive planters in the county and Concordia Parish. In 1876 he was elected a member of the Board of Supervisors, later was made president and has been the presiding officer ever since.*

In the 1880s he became interested in the steamboat trade and built the *Stella Wilds* (named for his daughter), which became a well known and popular excursion boat. He later established a business with Capt. George Prince, with many boats servicing the Vicksburg to New Orleans trade (and tributary rivers), plus Natchez-Vidalia Ferry for many years before the bridge was built.

One son, Oliver K. Wilds (b. 1874, d. 1924), known as Capt. Ollie, piloted many of the Prince & Wilds boats until his early death. He lived at 900 Main St.

Another son, Richard S. Wilds (b. 1868, d. 1952) ran the plantations at Wildsville, LA. He was known as "Uncle Dick." Quote (partial) from *The Natchez Democrat*, Oct. 7, 1951: *Whatever became of Uncle Dick Wilds? This question, asked many times during the past decade from Natchez to New Orleans, finally sent a Democrat reporter to 'Uncle Dick's' home at Cottonwood Plantation near Wildsville. For Uncle Dick was a colorful state legislator during the fantastic period of Huey Long, was a close friend of Long and had a wide reputation as the jolliest law-maker in Baton Rouge. Uncle Dick, soon to be 83, was born in Natchez, the son of Oliver N. Wilds and Barbara Koerber Wilds. He received his schooling at the Catholic School, then known as 'The Brothers.' When young Dick was 22, he settled in Concordia Par-*

ish on his father's plantations to crop. He married Miss Mary Alice Beard whose parents were old settlers in the Black River section. For 32 years, he served on the Concordia Parish Police Jury. He became representative from Concordia Parish the same year that Huey Long became governor and served three terms under Long, Allen and Leche. Long and Uncle Dick were close personal friends. (End of quote: *Natchez Democrat*.)

Uncle Dick's youngest son, Oliver Newton Wilds Sr. (b. 1900, d. 1965) was born in Natchez, attended "The Brothers" school and Jefferson College in South Louisiana. Known as "Newtie," he worked with his uncle, Capt. Ollie Wilds, in the steamboat trade and later moved to St. Joseph, LA, where he owned a Ford Dealership and was town mayor for 20 years until his death.

O. Newton Wilds Sr's. son, Oliver Newton Wilds Jr. known as Newt, was born in Natchez and grew up in Natchez and Louisiana. With partner Robert E. Canon, he owned and operated a prominent and successful interior design business in Houston for 30 years. In 1975, with Mr. Canon, they purchased "The Briars" in Natchez on the bluff, which they operate today as The Briars Inn and Gardens. *Submitted by Newton Wilds.*

SUE AUDREY TABOR WILLARD

Sue Audrey Tabor Willard (1919-2000)

SUE AUDREY TABOR WILLARD was born Jun. 20, 1919, in Natchez, MS and died Dec. 12, 2000 in Natchez. She was the youngest of three children born to Eugene and Lillian Archer Tabor Hutton. Sue's older siblings were Eugene Jr. (b. 1911, d. 1936), single; and sister Lillian. Sue married Jun. 27, 1937, Louis Edgar Willard, son of Elmer and Willie Edna Stroud Willard. He was born Apr. 9, 1916 and died Mar. 13, 1988 in Natchez. Sue and Louis are buried in Natchez, MS. They were Presbyterian.

Sue and Louis had one son, Louis Eugene "Gene" who married first, Edith Nell O'Quin in 1968; divorced. He married second, Sharon Lynn Roberts Peak. Gene and Edith had two children: Hannah Suzanne Willard who married Christopher Painter and they have three children: Joseph, Jacob, and Seth.

Louis Edgar II (b. 1981, d. 2003) is buried Natchez, MS.

Gene has a BS in business administration from the University of Southern Mississippi and worked for the Concordia Parish School Board as sales tax collector. On retiring he and Sharon moved to Denham Springs, LA. *Submitted by Ella McCaleb Young and picture submitted by Linda White Rankin*

WALLACE ARTHUR WILLARD & MARY ROCHELLE FRANCIS.

Wallace was born Mar. 4, 1936 in Natchez, the son of Elmer and Willie Edna Stroud Willard. He was born the 13th child and 9th son and was named for his Uncle Arthur and the doctor who delivered him, Dr. Wallace Smith.

In 1909, Wallace's grandfather, Frank P. Willard (b. Mar. 6, 1861, d. Apr. 18, 1937), of West York, Clarke County, IL and with his wife Bertie Stuck Willard (b. Oct. 3, 1859, d. Oct. 2, 1927), three sons and daughter came to Louisiana. According to records in the Tensas Parish Courthouse, Grandpa Willard bought Shackelford Plantation west of Newellton in 1909. The plantation contained 1,550 acres and was bought for the sum

of $42,000 cash-in-hand. With Grandpa and Grandma Willard was Wallace's dad, Elmer (b. Jul. 8, 1890, d. Dec. 2, 1958); Edgar (b. Mar. 11, 1885, d. Dec. 15, 1957); Arthur (b. 1883, d. 1950); and Mabel (b. 1888, d. 1945).

Elmer married Willie Edna Stroud (b. 1893, d. 1973) on Feb. 4, 1914. Willie was the daughter of Laura Ella Hammock (b. 1862, d. 1939) and James Franklin Stroud (b. 1853, d. 1933). Her maternal grandmother was Ann Elizabeth Sinclair (b. 1835, d. ?) md. John Henry Hammock (b. 1834, d. 1916), both born in Northumberland County, VA.

In 1915 Willie and Elmer bought a farm in Adams County on Sandy Creek east of Natchez. On Sandy Creek the Willards farmed and started a dairy. In the 1930s the Homochitto Lumber Co. leased land from them and moved in a crew with their families and their houses! Elmer opened a store, grist mill and a gravel pit.

To Elmer and Willie were born the following children: Frank Elmer (b. Mar. 19, 1915, d. May 9, 2001); Louis Edgar (b. Apr. 9, 1916, d. Mar. 13, 1988); Herbert Martin (b. Jul. 28, 1918); James Robert (b. Feb. 9, 1920, d. Dec. 2, 1999); Henry Newlin (b. Nov. 26, 1921); Helen Eva (b. Jan. 7, 1923, d. Apr. 18, 1996); John Ray (b. Oct. 28, 1924, d. Mar. 3, 1991); Laura Barbara (b. Dec. 15, 1925); Mary Louise (b. Mar. 31, 1927); Mabel Lee (b. Aug. 20 1929, d. Jan. 18, 1982); Lloyd Benford (b. Dec. 6, 1932, d. Oct. 14, 1976); Willie Hugh (b. Dec. 6, 1932, d. Oct. 14, 1994); Wallace Arthur (b. Mar. 4, 1936); Charles Hewlett (b. Feb. 6, 1939, d. Jan. 7, 1992).

In World War II the Willards sent five sons: Louis, Bert, Bobby, Ray and Henry, to military service at the same time. Each night was spent listening to news broadcasts about the war on the radio. It was a miracle that all returned safely. The Korean Conflict took Lloyd and Billy to active duty and they returned safely.

Wallace spent his early childhood on Sandy Creek doing what country boys do, fishing, swimming in the creek, hunting, riding bikes, making slingshots and chinaberry pop guns, and playing with the neighbors. Wallace attended the Kingston school. He remembers that some of the food for school lunches was provided from the gardens of the parents and bought to the school in bushel baskets to be cooked in the school kitchen. In 6th grade he transferred to the Natchez Institute. In 7th grade he became a member of the Natchez High band under the direction of Frank Heard. Graduating from Natchez High in 1954 Wallace entered Copiah-Lincoln Junior College. He attended Mississippi State majoring in civil engineering. His father passed away in 1958 and he returned home to help take care of the farm, working part time at the family owned Natchez Gravel Co. and enrolling in the National Guard (1961-67).

On Nov. 23, 1962 he married Mary Rochelle Francis (b. Nov. 2, 1939) a 1961 graduate of

(seated): Bertie Stuck Willard, Frank P. Willard. Standing: Elmer, Arthur, Edgar, Mabel

MSCW with a degree in library science. Mary is the daughter of Robert Lee (b. 1901, d. 1971) and Effie Cole Francis (b. 1905, d. 1995) of Lee County, MS.

In 1963 Wallace worked at International Paper as a machinist. In 1974 he entered business in Natchez as W.A. Willard Builder. The business consists of remodeling, restoration, and new home construction.

Elmer and Willie Edna Willard family, 1st row l-r: Hewlett, Willie, Elmer, Wallace; 2nd row, Lloyd, Billy; 3rd row, Laura, Helen, Mary Louise, Mabel Lee. 4th row, Ray, Henry, Louis, Bert, Bobby, Frank.

Wallace and Mary have a daughter, Rochelle Cole Willard Bird (b. Oct. 23, 1969) who graduated from University of Alabama in 1991 with a degree in political science and a son Judson Andrew (b. Apr. 16, 1973) who graduated from University of Mississippi in 1995 with a degree in business administration.

Wallace and Mary are members of the Westminster Presbyterian Church where Wallace serves as Elder. They are interested in conservation education concerning our natural resources and Wallace serves as chairman of the Adams County Soil and Water Commission. Hobbies include traveling, camping, and working on genealogy projects.

CARLETTE GREER WILLIAMS FAMILY.

There were three children in our family. Lucie Maria was the oldest, being born Sep. 10, 1959 at the old General Hospital in Natchez. Carlette was the middle child (b. Aug. 25, 1961 at the old General Hospital) and the youngest child, William Carlton Jr. "Carl" was born almost 7-1/2 years after Carlette on Feb. 9, 1968 at Jefferson Davis Memorial Hospital which is now called Natchez Regional Hospital.

They were born to the parents of Mary Grace Lowry Greer (b. Nov. 12, 1938) and William Carlton Greer Sr. (b. Jan. 3, 1938).

Carlette loved animals. While growing up she would always be the one to bring home a new pet. There were pet dogs, cats, rabbits, a bird now and then, and even a pony. She got her love of animals from her grandfather, Earl Lowry, who brought his pet rabbits all the way from Arkansas when they came to Natchez. When she was 18 years old, she inherited a palomino stallion named Sonny who ended up being her favorite pet. He lived to be almost 30 years old.

Carlette and Maria started working for AT&T as long distance telephone operators in 1979. They worked there for about 10 years before the phone company closed the office in Natchez and relocated to Jackson.

During that time, Carlette increased the type of pets she owned. She had up to four or five horses at one time, rabbits, goats, pigeons, and chickens. Sometimes the neighbors' children would have show and tell at school. Carlette would take a rabbit or pony for the children to pet and

Cliff and Carlette Williams. Children l-r: Thomas, Robert and Marie - 2000

ask questions. She would take one or two ponies to children's birthday parties.

On Nov. 13, 1992, Carlette married James Clifton Williams. (Yes, this was a Friday.) Carlette and Cliff never had children of their own but they reared Cliff's three children from a previous marriage. Robert Lee and Eleice Marie were born in Texas and Thomas Martin was born in Natchez. Robert played the trumpet and French horn in band at school. Marie loved to play softball. Thomas was in the Student Council at school.

Cliff is the son of Amy Virginia (Willard) Williams and James Barkston Williams (b. Sep. 3, 1943, d. Dec. 15, 1990). He was born Nov. 29, 1962. When he was very young, doctors discovered that he had been born with a small hole in his heart. The doctors were going to operate but decided to let nature take its course and as he grew older the hole became smaller. He started doing electrical work in high school and it became his profession.

"Mary Had A Little Lamb"
Mary Grace has a little lamb
Its fleece is white as snow
She went to the studio one day,
and the lamb just had to go.
She climbed up in the willow chair
The lamb got up there too,
and this is the way they both look,
Now don't you think they're cute.

Carlette worked off and on while the children were growing up, but mostly she stayed home to take care of the children. She liked doing volunteer work at school and for fund raising groups. She liked researching her family history and is planning on publishing a book on her "Greer" family.

EULA ROUTH WURSTER (b. Sep. 11, 1923, Jonesville, LA), occupation insurance salesperson, md. Aug. 22, 1943, in Florida, Richard Charles Daggett (b. 1921, Medford, MA), son of Fred L. Daggett and Mildred Ethelind Jones, occupation businessman and planter. Eula died Oct. 30, 2001, Alexandria, LA and buried Nov. 2, 2001, Evangeline Cemetery, Wildsville, LA. Eula Routh had a BA from Boston University in business. She had attended Louisiana State University in Baton Rouge where she was a beauty in the yearbook, *the Gumbo,* and she was also the LSU Water Carnival Princess. She sold Metropolitan Life Insurance for 20 years. She retired and enjoyed being with her grandchildren and husband. She also played golf and sang in the choir at the Methodist church in Jonesville.

The following was written and read by her granddaughter, Sarah Louise Young, at the funeral of her grandmother, Eula Routh Wurster Daggett on Nov. 2, 2001 at the First Methodist Church, Jonesville, LA.

"Mammie: When I found out Mammie passed away, my first reaction was shock. Then the memories started flowing. Out of this sudden sadness I have looked back and realized this isn't something to be sad about, because Mammie lived a very, very fulfilling life. She was always celebrating whether it was a birthday, a special occasion, or just because everyone was in town. I hope I will be able to accomplish and live a life that's even half as wonderful as hers. You can look here today and realize how loved she was.

"The most important thing I have learned from Mammie is LIVE LIFE TO THE FULLEST. We had a little get together this past Sunday in Zachary, where she got to meet a lot of my fiancée's family. She looked great and was talking up a storm; by the time she left everyone there loved her.

"She always loved to meet new people and she was always interested in what was going on in her grandchildren's lives. I don't remember one tennis game or basketball game that Mammie or Grandpa didn't make. You could always count on them being there. It didn't matter what was going on elsewhere.

"She and Grandpa have been great role models for all of us. She never would let illness or discomfort bring her down. She took control of her life. She wouldn't let things take control of her.

"The main four things she has taught me is: How important my education is; family always comes first; how to be a strong person and stand up for what I believe; and to always enjoy life.

"We are so lucky to have had role models like Mammie and Grandpa. I can definitely say she has touched my life in so many POSITIVE ways and she still does. We all have a little of Mammie in us that will be passed down the line from generation to generation.

"So I think we are here today to reflect and celebrate her life, and the time we all got to spend with her, and I know she would want us to keep going."

Richard Charles grew up in Newton, MA. The summer of 1937, he entered Tabor Academy in Marion, MA. He graduated from Tabor in June 1941. In September 1941, he entered Colgate University, Hamilton, NY. After WWII was declared, Dec. 8, 1941, he volunteered for military service in the United States Air Force as an aviation cadet. He became a fighter pilot and served in the Asiatic-Pacific Theater as a Flying Tiger. He was a Captain in the United States Air Force. While in the war he was stationed at Harding Field in Baton Rouge. Before he went overseas, he met and fell in love with Eula Routh Wurster who was attending LSU.

When World War II was over, he returned to college, entering Boston University and later held the position of personnel manager in his father's candy manufacturing firm, Daggett Chocolate Co. in Cambridge, MA.

After the death of his father, Fred L. Daggett, in 1958, the business was sold to The New England Confectionery Co. and the building to Massachusetts Institute of Technology (MIT).

In October 1954, Richard and his family moved to Jonesville, LA where his wife, Eula Routh Wurster's family lived.

(A) Candy Mildred Louise Daggett (b. Nov. 17, 1947, Boston, MA), occupation-teacher, married in 1971 in Jonesville, LA, divorced 1990, John Davis Young (b. May 17, 1944, Ferriday, LA), son of Francis Leo Young and Ella Mae Davis. Candy has a BA in education from Louisiana Tech University.

1) Ella Ruth Young (b. Apr. 18, 1972, Natchez, MS), occupation-financial banker, md. November 1995 in Ferriday, LA, Roy G. Spinks Jr. (b. Sep. 24, 1970, Louisiana), son of Roy G. Spinks Sr. and Mary Oalmann, occupation-CPA. Ella Ruth is a graduate of Louisiana Tech University, in finance. Kappa Delta Sorority. Roy is a graduate of Louisiana Tech University in accounting. Kappa Alpha Order Fraternity. Children: Garrett Evan Spinks (b. Jun. 21, 1999, Birmingham, AL) and Gentry Elizabeth Spinks (b. Mar. 21, 2001, Birmingham, AL).

2) John Davis Young Jr. (b. Dec. 25, 1973, Natchez, MS), occupation-funeral director. Johnny graduated from Louisiana Tech University, May 2001 with a BS in business (computer information systems). He is the manager of Community Memorial Funeral Home in Winnsboro and is married to Brandi Nichols of Gainesville, TX and they have one daughter, Caroline Routh Young (b. May 12, 2003, Monroe, LA).

3) Sarah Louise Young (b. Jun. 30, 1975, Natchez, MS), occupation-banker, md. Dec. 29, 2001, in Natchez, MS, Clinton Robert Hanchey, son of Ben Hanchey and Linda, occupation-law. Sarah has written for the paper *Delta Style* in Monroe, LA. She is presently employed with Union Planters Bank in Baton Rouge, LA. She is a 1993 graduate of Huntington High School in Ferriday, LA and graduated from the University of Louisiana at Monroe, LA, December 2001. She married Clint Hanchey in December 2001 in Natchez, MS. He graduated from LSU Law School and they will make their home in Monroe, LA. They are expecting their first child in November 2003.

B) Linda Routh Daggett (b. Oct. 5, 1950, Boston, MA) md. May 22, 1976, in Jonesville, LA to Thomas John Barrett (b. Jun. 3, 1951, Illinois), son of Thomas John Barrett and Evelyn Santoro) occupation-doctor of psychology. Linda is a graduate of Louisiana State University with a BA in history. Thomas has doctorate from Georgetown University in psychology. Children: Lindsay Elizabeth Barrett (b. May 7, 1984) and Stephanie Routh Barrett (b. Jun. 28, 1986).

C) Fred Rodney Daggett (b. Feb. 22, 1953, Boston, MA) md. Feb. 4, 1978, in Jonesville, LA, Penny Lee Calhoun (b. June 1958, Rapid City, SD), daughter of Jesse Walter Calhoun and Bobbie Nell Bass, occupation counselor in education. Children: Fred Rodney Daggett Jr. (b. Apr. 22, 1984, Natchez, MS); Betsy Lee Daggett (b. May 4, 1992, Natchez, MS); Ginny Calhoun Daggett (b. Jul. 13, 1994, Natchez, MS). Ginny was the page to the Queen in the 2000 Natchez Spring Pilgrimage.

THOMAS EDGAR YOUNG SR. & HILDA CULIPHER REGISTER married at Natchez, MS, Adams County on Sep. 14, 1921. They had two children, Thomas Edgar Young Jr. (b. 1924) and Anabel Register Young (b. 1922). Thomas was born Jan. 21, 1898 at London, England and died Mar. 24, 1970 at Albuquerque, NM.

Samuel Postlethwaite

Hilda (b. Apr. 2, 1894, Natchez, MS) was the child of Mary Ann Gustine McDonald (b. Aug. 18, 1866, Natchez, MS, d. Jan. 16, 1954, Natchez, MS) and Aaron Culipher Register (b. Jul. 31, 1868 at Tensas, LA, d. March 1930, Natchez, MS) who married on May 8, 1891.

Mary Ann Gustine McDonald was the child of Mary Ann Gustine Bledsoe (b. Jan. 31, 1847 at Natchez, MS, d. Sep. 13, 1924 at Natchez, MS) and Zimri McDonald (b. Sep. 10, 1831 at Marley's Mills, SC, d. May 11, 1881 at Washington, DC) who were married on Sep. 28, 1865.

Mary Ann Gustine Bledsoe was the child of Mary Ann Gustine Postlethwaite (b. Apr. 24, 1819 at Natchez, MS, d. Aug. 26, 1904, Natchez, MS) and Benjamin Sebastian Bledsoe (b. Nov. 20, 1807 at Campbellton, GA, d. Sep. 20, 1847) who were married on Feb. 13, 1838.

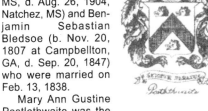

coat of arms

Mary Ann Gustine Postlethwaite was the child of Henry Postlethwaite (b. Oct. 28, 1778 at Carlisle, PA, d. Aug. 27, 1823, Natchez, MS) and Elizabeth Morgan (b. Sep. 9, 1787 at Carlisle, PA, d. Jul. 27, 1860, Natchez, MS) who were married on Jun. 10, 1804.

Henry Postlethwaite was the child of Samuel Postlethwaite (b. Jan. 8, 1738 at Lancaster, PA, d. Aug. 24, 1810, Carlisle, PA) and Matilda Rose who were married on Oct. 11, 1760.

THOMAS EDGAR YOUNG JR. was the second of two children born to Thomas E. Young Sr. and Hilda Culipher Register of Adams County, MS on Jun. 28, 1924 at the family home, King's Tavern. He was a descendant of the Bledsoes, Postlethwaits, Duncans and Registers on his maternal side.

Thomas' mother Hilda died at age 32 when Thomas was two years old. Earlier that same year Hilda's brother, John Aaron Register, had been killed when his Model A Ford malfunctioned and rolled backward down a hill.

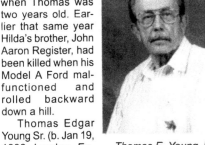

Thomas E. Young Jr.

Thomas Edgar Young Sr. (b. Jan 19, 1898, London, England) re-married and went to Arkansas, then to Albuquerque, NM where he died Mar. 24, 1970. Thomas and his sister were reared by their grandmother, Mary Ann

Pen and ink drawing of King's Tavern by Thomas Edgar Young Jr.

Gustine McDonald Register.

Thomas Jr. remembers his grandmother as being a very early riser, up at 3 or 4 o'clock every morning preparing for the walk over to Franklin Street (two blocks) with her market basket to meet the pushcarts and wagons of the street vendors to buy their fresh farm produce. Her income in those days, after the death of her husband, was largely from an annual bequest from wealthy relatives in France.

Thomas Jr. is at present a long-time member of the Natchez Church of God, McNeely Road. During his early years he attended Trinity Episcopal Church with his grandmother, aunt and sister. He recalls their weekly journey, usually on foot, from King's Tavern to the Natchez City Cemetery where his mother and her brother John are buried. They always took lunch and spent the day. He recalls being admonished by his grandmother many times, "Big boys don't cry."

Mary Ann Gustine McDonald and grandchildren: Thomas E. Young Jr. and Anabel Register Young

Thomas Jr. graduated Natchez High School and entered military service. He took infantry basic at Fort McClellan, AL; graduated Infantry School at Fort Benning, GA; and served in the European Theater during the Battle of the Bulge in WWII. After the military he joined the Mississippi National Guard.

On Dec. 22, 1949 he married Dorothy Dean Thomas, the second of five children born to Sam and Ivy Thomas. Thomas Jr. and Dorothy bought a home in Montebello Subdivision, Adams County, and later moved to the Pine Ridge area. Thomas worked 32 years at Armstrong Rubber Co., January 1955 to February 1987. Dorothy worked as a cashier, waitress and homemaker.

Thomas Jr. and Dorothy had four children: Michael Stephen Young (b. Sep. 22, 1950, d. Apr. 2, 1997); Kathleen Diane Young Harrison (b. Oct. 11, 1952); Thomas E. Young III (b. Dec. 30, 1953); and Robert Preston Young (b. May 22, 1960). Dorothy filed for divorce on Jun. 30, 1980.

Thomas Jr. kept a vegetable garden and enjoyed hunting, fishing and related activities such as swimming and camping. He was proficient at electrical work, self-taught air condition repair and installation and many of the manual trades, including art in several mediums – pen and ink drawings his favorite, most of which are copyrighted.

He traveled to many foreign countries: Germany, Jordan, Africa, Israel, England, Ireland, Scotland, Holland, India, Egypt, Mexico, Belgium, Italy, France, and Switzerland - some in the military, some with church groups, and some independently.

King's Tavern was put on tour shortly after the Natchez Garden Club organized the first Natchez Pilgrimage, and Thomas and his sister were both in the very early Tableau, as the pageant was originally called.

Many years having passed, Thomas believes it's now time to correct some of the ghost stories and eerie tales which abound about King's Tavern. They were all, he says, fabrications of fertile female imaginations, resulting perhaps from the times his grandmother would invite neighbors and friends to discuss strange tales and happenings from everywhere.

Having been reared there, he can, he says, with firsthand knowledge assert that there was no Matilda ghost, there were no creaking steps (unless they were being used), and there were no skeletons found in the basement. The dagger was supposedly found in the mortar of a fireplace (before his time), but his

Hilda Culipher Register Young

grandmother told him more than once that a male friend, enamored of her, made it and gave it to her.

Index

Brannick 55
Brassfield 64
Braun 95
Brayman 59
Brazil 34
Breckinridge 73
Breithaupt 68
Breland 44, 70
Brennan 115
Brewer 88, 114
Brewster 71
Bridges 79
Bridgess 106
Brinegar 56, 57
Briscoe 85
Brister 81, 109
Bristow 33, 115
British West Florida 8
Britt 24, 55, 104, 113
Britton 58
Britton and Koontz Bank 12
Broadwater 99, 100
Brock 94
Brook 45
Brookhart 92
Brooklyn, NY 12
Brooks 16, 73, 76, 97
Broom 111
Brothers of Sacred Heart 41
Browder 72, 74
Brown 11, 16, 35, 57, 65, 69, 76, 77, 79, 84, 97, 98, 100, 107, 110, 112
Brownell 38
Bruce 108
Brugart 92
Brumfield 45, 62, 63, 92, 101
Bryan 56, 81, 92, 101
Bryant 46, 81
Buchanan 97
Bucholtz 80
Buck 101
Buckholts 80
Buckholtz 80
Buckingham 53
Buckles 80
Buckley 37, 51
Buckner 61, 85
Buie 22
Builders 40
Bull 23
Bullen 34, 54, 66
Bullin 97
Bunch 40, 107, 113
Bundgard 5, 23, 98, 99
Bunyan 48
Burke 26, 41, 90, 102
Burkes 59
Burkley 45, 62, 92, 101, 116
Burnes 67

Burnham 62
Burns 16, 19, 41, 55, 56, 59, 60, 84, 88, 91, 105, 107
Burr 39, 95, 111
Burroughs 44, 115
Burrows 86, 102, 103
Burruss 39
Burt 88, 112
Busby 112
Bush 107, 108
Butchart 60
Butler 78
Buttross 4, 56, 57
Byers 16
Byrd 46
Byrne 16, 41
Byrnes 77

C

Cable 63
Cagle 84
Cahokia, IL 8
Cain 110
Caldwell 102, 103
Calhoun 16, 59, 71, 94, 118
Callon 13, 17, 40
Callon Petroleum 13
Calvit 62, 80
Cameron 40, 91
Cammack 59
Campbell 16, 23, 35, 40, 61, 65, 101, 105, 106, 111, 113
Candler 31
Cannon 63, 69
Cannonsburg 40
Canon 117
Capo 98
Carkeet 45, 56, 95
Carlisle, PA 11
Carlton 68, 69
Carmichael 77
Carnahan 71
Carolinas 8
Carpenter 23, 38, 92, 100
Carr 67
Carradine 73
Carriage House Restaurant 23
Carrol 22
Carroll 46, 74, 93, 100
Carson 89, 103, 110, 115
Carter 64, 65, 79, 81, 82
Cartwright 55
Cash 40
Cassidy 114
Cathedral High School 26, 41
Cathedral School 19
Catter 70
Causey 58, 80
Cauthen 33, 62
Cavalier 8

Cavin 62
Cawsey 58
Central School 33
Chadbourne 38, 99
Chamberlain 92
Chamberlin 53, 102
Chambers 54
Chambliss 64
Chancel Guild 38
Chandler 71
Chapin 90
Chapman 22
Charlemagne 23
Charleston 11
Chase 72, 73, 97
Chatman 46
Chattahoochee River 9
Chattanooga, TN 31
Chennault 67
Cherokee 12, 17
Cherokee Indians 8
Chester 75
Chicago 11, 31
Chickasaw Indians 8
China Grove Plantation 12
Chinn 98, 100
Chipley 109
Chisolm 34
Choctaw 11, 12, 17
Choctaw Indians 8
Chotard 58, 83, 84
Chouset 60
Christ Church 38
Christ Church of Church Hill 38
Christmas Tour of Homes 24
Church Steering Group 40
Ciaravino 81
Civil Rights Movement 14
Claesson 74
Claiborne 9, 10, 71, 80, 110
Claiborne County 24
Clark 56, 61, 75, 79, 93, 96, 98
Clarkston 31
Clay 101
Clayton 88
Clements 81
Clemmons 106
Cleveland, OH 38
Clifton 11, 13
Clifton Heights 13
Clinton 115
Close 92
Cloud 34, 38, 98
Co-Lin 32, 33
Coca-Cola Bottling Works 31
Coca-Cola Enterprises 31
Cochram 35
Cochran 41, 59, 82, 100, 101
Cockerham 104

Cocks 97
Cody 108
Coker 34
Cola Coca Co. 31
Cole 5, 47, 78, 84, 97, 109, 117
Coleman 80, 82
Collier 88, 99
Colligan 47
Collins 55, 61, 65, 75, 76, 85, 86, 87, 102, 112, 113, 116
Colson 102
Colton 115
Columbia 10
Combs 113
Comer 97, 100, 101
Commercial Bank 36
Commercial Bank and Banker's House 11
Committee on Church Extension 40
Compere 109
Concord 12, 17
Concord House 9
Concordia Parish 10, 24
Connelly 38
Conner 16, 23, 51, 55, 58, 71, 89, 96, 107, 114
Cook 36, 54, 57, 71, 77, 93
Cooke 78, 101
Cooksey 111, 113
Cooley 22
Cooper 22, 109
Coover 81
Copiah-Lincoln 32, 33
Copiah-Lincoln Community College 29, 32, 33
Copiah-Lincoln Junior College 32
Cory 35, 111
Costa 23
Cottage Gardens 11, 13
Cotton 16
Couillard 41, 98, 99, 103
Council Chambers 15
Covington 34
Cox 75, 97, 115
Coxwell 106
Cracker 46
Craddock 71
Craig 19, 53, 57, 58, 111
Crane 56, 77, 93, 100, 115
Crausby 108
Craven 83
Crawford 70, 89
Crews 62
Crocker 46
Crone 110
Crosby 92
Crothers 63
Crow 70, 71

The Men's Club: Men gather at the Elks Club on Franklin Street sometime in the early 1930's. The building is now the Guest House bed and breakfast.

Cathedral Boy Scouts Troop Three. Back row (L-R): Joseph Zuccaro, Carl Hicks, Robert Perry, Dave Whitlock, August Fore, Edward Lambert, Morris Raphael, John Hicks, Barnett Serio. Front row (L-R): Rene Damare, Edmund Burke, Joseph Snyder, Frank Perrault, Scoutmaster R. L. McLean, Thomas Thompson, Charles Cochran, Henry Hunter, George Snyder, William Garrity. (Information from Morris Raphael's "My Natchez Years", used with permission

Mt. Airy Plantation

A Gala Reunion–the 1935 graduates from Cathedral and St. Joseph Schools joined to celebrate their 25th anniversary at the Bellemont Restaurant in Natchez during the year 1960 (several were missing). Spouses came along to enjoy the festivities. Standing (L-R): Edmund Burke, Hubert Blair, Morris Raphael, Mrs. Edmund (Bobbie) Burke, Fred Berret, Mrs. Fred (Mary Louise Passback) Berret, Mrs. William (Catherine Goetz) Gill, Mrs. Curtis (Amelia Boschieri) Reed, William Gill, Mrs. Fate (Kate Sayers) Evans, Mrs. Carl (Marjorie Evans) Hicks, Carl Hicks and Fate Evans. Seated, (L-R): Mrs. Hubert (Margaret Kincke Blair, Mrs. Conway (Noreen Burns) Aubic, Ms. Mildred Garrity, Ms. Elsie Burns and Mrs. Morris (Helen) Raphael.

Printed in the USA
CPSIA information can be obtained
at www.ICGtesting.com
JSHW060055150824
68134JS00032B/2736

9 781681 625256